UContent

UContent

The Information Professional's Guide to User-Generated Content

Nicholas G. Tomaiuolo

Information Today, Inc.
Medford, New Jersey

Contents

Acknowledgments

I wish to thank the following individuals who all played roles at some point in making this book a reality. First, the three people who during my career gave me opportunities at pivotal times: Victor Triolo, professor emeritus of information and library science at Southern Connecticut State University, who was my mentor and became my friend; Barbara J. Frey, who offered me my first professional position in a library; and Barbara Quint, without whose encouragement my words would have no voice. Thanks also to Gary Koropatkin, software and hardware technologist extraordinaire, who kept all my devices and apps running without interruption; Kristin Tomaiuolo for her sense of balance behind the camera; Ben Tomaiuolo for his input on the text; and Michael D. Calia for his consultation on the project.

I also thank Phoebe Ayers, Dreanna Belden, Walt Crawford, Meredith Farkas, Janet Flewelling, Rich Hanley, Ran Hock, Chuck Jones, Sean Robinson, Kate Sheehan, and all the other information professionals who generously responded to my questions and requests. A special thanks to Steff Deschenes, award-winning author of *The Ice Cream Theory*, for her fresh perspectives on self-publishing. And a very appreciative shout-out to Professor Péter Jacsó. I have learned a great deal from Péter's many years of database analysis, candor, insight, and wisdom.

I'd like to remember and posthumously thank the creator of Project Gutenberg Michael Stearns Hart, my dear friend, for launching the first ebook library on the Web, and jump starting my user-generated content experiences.

Finally, I wish to convey my gratitude to the publishing professionals at Information Today, Inc., who take raw files and create polished manuscripts: Thomas Hogan Sr., John B. Bryans, Heide Dengler, Kara Jalkowski, Danielle Nicotra, Amy Reeve, and Brandi Scardilli.

"Wikipedians," folks from around the world who share the goal of writing the most comprehensive encyclopedia (in all languages!) that they can. It is a nonprofit project that depends not just on reader donations to stay running, but also on the goodwill and time of the thousands of editors who make up the community of the site and who feel responsible for it.

Wikipedians, by sharing what they know in a structured manner as well as what others know (adding scholarly references is a core task of writing the encyclopedia), have helped create an online culture of sharing and participation that is foundational for today's web and, indeed, today's experience of finding information. The services and sites profiled in *UContent* all depend on a community of participation: Without people pitching in and contributing, repository sites like Flickr and SlideShare wouldn't exist, collaborative works like Wikipedia would quickly become unusable, and social networks like Facebook would wither.

For librarians who want a shortcut guide to what it means to be a participant in these and many more community sites, *UContent* provides a quick introduction to the practical ins and outs of participating, as well as how libraries are using these services and projects. Understanding the web and the many resources it offers our patrons (many of them created by their peers) is certainly a core job of the information professional, and *UContent* helps provide an orientation in a confusing, buzzword-y space. All libraries are situated within communities of participation in real life—within schools, research labs, or cities—and the internet is no different. The question is: Where will you participate?

—Phoebe Ayers,
librarian, University of California,
and Davis trustee, Wikimedia Foundation

Preface

The ubiquity of user-generated content (dubbed *UContent* in this book) on the read/write web in which we work and play is the overarching topic of this book. Wherever we travel on the internet, it seems we can set up an account, set our preferences, and personalize our experience. Barbara Quint, my editor, had a long list of sites, resources, and angles she wanted me to cover, and writing this book has been an exciting and challenging opportunity. While I gathered information, researched topics, and interacted with the websites and services I discuss throughout the book, I had the chance to run into some old friends and to make some new ones. It didn't seem to matter whether they were the altruists giving away books at Project Gutenberg, the "biblio-paparazzi" over at Flickr, the map mashup mentors at YouTube, or the dozens of librarians sorting through innumerable issues in the blogosphere. I learned something from each interchange, from each file uploaded and downloaded, and in (almost) each link I pursued.

It's quite a turn of events to perceive the web as the repository for content its users are creating. When I first used the web, the content was in place. Companies, associations, governments, professional organizations, or librarians placed it there for people to use. Now, however, much of the content is dynamically created by us web users. While we create that content, we learn more about ourselves, each other, and how we can inform one another on so many topics almost effortlessly. The resources are in place; all we have to do is swoop down and use them.

What I have attempted to do with most of these chapters—with most of these manifestations of UContent—is to experiment with them and experience them. I added links to Wikipedia and added presentations to SlideShare, SlideBoom, and authorSTREAM. I mashed up some data to create some maps, dabbled in citizen journalism, and joined groups (and started one) at Flickr; I even self-published a book at CreateSpace. At each service, whether Yahoo! Pipes, Google Custom Search, Delicious, LibraryThing, or Facebook, contributors must learn specific tasks to use the resource and, having learned those tasks, can gain a better understanding of how others have used the resource. We can then imagine more ways to exploit the resource and try to implement them. Throughout the book you will find that I have laced the chapters with industry news and helpful links, and, ever mindful of the social networking mechanism of crowdsourcing, I've called upon experts for answers and elucidation.

If you are already familiar with UContent in its many varied forms, I hope this book will complement your knowledge. If you are expert in contributing to these forms of UContent, I hope my experiences resonate with you. If you are new to UContent, I hope this book serves as a genial welcome and a dose of encouragement. Please also use this book's companion webpages, which begin with a table of contents page at web.ccsu.edu/library/tomaiuolon/UContent/toc.htm, to access links to the articles, websites, and examples of UContent discussed in this book.

The Evolution of UContent

User-generated content (UContent) drives more than half the websites listed in the top 10 most popular internet destinations. A glance at website traffic statistics from the California-based internet information service Alexa (www.alexa.com) shows Facebook in second place, YouTube in fourth, Wikipedia in fifth, Myspace in sixth, Blogger in seventh, eBay in ninth, and craigslist in tenth. Outside the top 10, we find blog host WordPress in the 20th position and Flickr in the 21st.[1] If that list is valid, recent projections by eMarketer, a firm that aggregates, filters, and analyzes digital marketing data from 4,000 sources, shouldn't surprise us. In April 2008, eMarketer projected that there would be 102 million UContent creators in 2011 (that's nearly half of all web users in the U.S.); it also projected that 139 million people would consume UContent (that's 66 percent of all web users in the U.S.). Tables 1.1, 1.2, and 1.3 illustrate the prodigious creation and consumption of UContent.

To summarize the main points of eMarketer's research, blogs are consumed more than any other content; social networking is the second most popular UContent, video viewers are third, and wiki content is the least frequently consumed type of UContent.

Appropriately subtitled "The Impacts of High-Speed Connections Extend Beyond Access to Information to Active Participation in the Online Commons," a report by John Horrigan for the Pew Internet & American Life Project issued findings that reinforce those of the eMarketer surveys. Horrigan writes, "The Pew Internet Project reported in a 2006 survey that 44 percent of home broadband users had done at least one of the following: having one's own blog or webpage, working on group blogs or webpages, remixing digital content and re-posting it online, or sharing something online created by the user (i.e., artwork, photos, stories, or videos)."[2]

Horrigan concludes that early broadband access to the web was adopted by only a "modest fraction of leading edge users," but recent expanded access via broadband (nearly half of all people in the U.S. had broadband connections in 2007) opened the doors to the internet to a much larger group of users. Broadband users are far more likely to generate UContent than dial-up

Table 1.1   Creators of UContent, U.S., 2007–2012 (in millions and percentage of internet users)

Year	Millions of internet users	By percentage of total internet users
2007	77.1	41.0
2008	83.0	42.8
2009	89.2	44.6
2010	95.7	46.4
2011	102.1	48.2
2012	108.5	50.0

Note: This table covers individuals who create any of the following online at least once per month: video, audio, photos, personal blogs, personal websites, online bulletin board postings, customer reviews, or personal profiles in social networks or virtual worlds.
[Source: eMarketer, "May 2008: User-Generated Content, Fad or For Real?," Interactive Advertising Bureau, May 2008, accessed August 3, 2011, www.iab.net/insights_research/947883/1675/287430?preview =1&psid=1&ph=bb5f]

users are. These new broadband users have a different vision for the internet, and consequently UContent "has shaped broad expectations about the primary purpose and uses of cyberspace."[3]

Other research demonstrates with statistics that increasing participation in UContent is worldwide:

- "Over half the U.K.'s population (53 percent) are now creating and actively sharing content online, heralding a wave of openness that utilizes blogs, video, audio, forums, reviews and comment."[4]

- "Chinese netizens have published 1.13 billion items of user generated content (UGC) in 2009, more than tripling the amount in

Table 1.2 Consumers of UContent by content type, U.S., 2008–2013 (as a percentage of all internet users)

	2008	2009	2010	2011	2012	2013
User-generated video	36.0	39.8	42.5	44.8	47.2	49.2
Social networking	41.2	44.2	46.9	49.1	50.5	51.8
Blogs	54.0	58.0	61.0	64.0	67.0	69.0
Wikis	33.9	36.6	39.0	41.0	42.6	43.9
UContent consumers	60.0	62.0	64.0	66.0	68.0	70.0

[Source: "User-Generated Content Draws Fans," eMarketer, February 3, 2009, accessed August 3, 2011, www.emarketer.com/Article.aspx?R=1006895]

2008, according to Daqi.com, a social media aggregation and marketing company in China. The UGC included forum posts, blogs, videos, and other media. In addition, statistics show that 73 percent of China's netizens use instant messengers, such as MSN and 222 million netizens access video sharing websites, and 181 million are bloggers."[5]

• Japan has 6.2 million bloggers and 25.4 million blog readers.[6]

An interesting footnote: One research article discovered that UContent follows the "90-9-1 Participation Inequality Rule." By analyzing the traffic at 11 websites that publish UContent, Ochoa and Duval proved that 90 percent of UContent users do not contribute, 9 percent contribute intermittently, and 1 percent contribute significantly to the sites.[7]

UContent: A Brief History

UContent, also called *peer production, user-created content,* and *consumer-generated media,* has been variably defined as "content created and published by the end users online,"[8] "various kinds of media content, publicly available, that are produced by end users,"[9] "a website where either the entire content or large portions of it are contributed by the site users,"[10] "a realm where people are not only consuming content, but also participating in creating content,"[11] and "content made publicly available over the internet

Table 1.3 Consumers of UContent by content type, U.S., 2008–2013 (in millions of UContent consumers)

	2008	2009	2010	2011	2012	2013
User-generated video	69.4	79.2	87.3	94.4	102.0	108.0
Social networking	79.5	88.1	96.2	103.6	109.1	114.6
Blogs	104.1	115.5	125.2	135.0	144.7	152.6
Wikis	65.4	73.0	80.1	86.4	92.1	97.1
UContent consumers	115.7	123.5	131.4	139.2	146.9	154.8

[Source: "User-Generated Content Draws Fans," eMarketer, February 3, 2009, accessed August 3, 2011, www.emarketer.com/Article.aspx?R=1006895]

which reflects a certain amount of creative effort, and is created outside of professional routines and practices."[12] These definitions are all approximately equal. My personal favorite, because it focuses on the fact that the content creator is not remunerated, is "the production of content by the general public rather than by paid professionals and experts in the field."[13]

Search the web for information on the origins of UContent and you'll discover a number of educators, students, bloggers, and businesspeople agreeing that UContent's history goes back about 32,000 years to paleolithic cave paintings. A trifle more recently, we can track the roots of "talk radio," another form of UContent, to 1930, when disc jockey John J. Anthony asked his listeners to phone the station and then repeated their comments for his radio audience.[14]

In tracing the history of UContent on the internet, let's acknowledge that Professor Michael Hart, founder of Project Gutenberg, deserves the distinction of entering text online for no other reason than to make it available for other users. He did this in 1971, when he was but a college freshman, by manually keying the Declaration of Independence into a TeleType RSS33. The RSS33's output was then fed into the Xerox Sigma V mainframe computer residing in the Materials Research Lab at the University of Illinois.[15] Thus he became the first producer of UContent on the internet. After Hart entered the Declaration, the production uploaded to Project Gutenberg was relatively scant for about 2 decades (Project Gutenberg now offers 30,000 titles at www.gutenberg.org, and more than 100,000 through its partners and affiliates). Between 1971 and 1979, Hart entered one book per year; he spent 1980–1990 working on the Bible and the works of Shakespeare.

Content on the web, however, is obviously not dependent on any one person. Although Hart's initial contribution was seminal, many critical events have occurred since. When reconstructing UContent's evolution, it's useful to consider these events separately and as part of the whole UContent phenomenon. It may also be interesting to reflect on where you were—professionally or educationally—when they occurred.

Although not directly related to the internet, but nevertheless of importance, in 1972 the Federal Communications Commission mandated that all cable television providers offer a public access television channel.[16] This event is clearly indicative of the movement toward the democratization of information, a hallmark of Web 2.0 and UContent. According to the Hobbes' Internet Timeline, the next notable event in UContent was the establishment of Usenet in 1979.[17] Created at Duke University by Tom Truscott and Jim Ellis, two graduate students who sought a means to send emails and files organized by categories, Usenet was born when they connected with computers at the University of North Carolina through their friend Steve Bellovin. Usenet eventually became an international conferencing network; the topical categories became known as Usenet Newsgroups. Hundreds of forums emerged (e.g., The Quilting Beehive, lt.autos.subaru, eLearning Technology and Development, and Club Britney Spears) that allowed end users to post questions and discuss topics of mutual interest. The Usenet Newsgroups' messages were searchable through Deja News, acquired by Google in February 2001 with a name change to Google Groups.[18]

Electronic bulletin boards gave individuals another place to be creative. On September 19, 1982, Scott Fahlman, a research scientist, formally wrote this message to his colleagues on the Carnegie Mellon computer science bulletin board service:

> I propose the following sequence for joke markers:
>   :-)
> Read it sideways. Actually, it is probably more economical to mark things that are *not* jokes, given current trends. For this, use:
>   :-(

And by hitting Enter, he became the "inventor" of the ASCII-based emoticon known as the *smiley*. Fahlman says the idea occurred to him after reading "lengthy diatribes" from people on the message board who failed to get the joke or the sarcasm in a particular post—which is probably what "given current trends" refers to in his now-famous missive.[19]

Computer scientists continued to flex their creative muscles in the 1980s. In 1984, Apple announced the Macintosh, and the number of individual computer users increased dramatically. In 1989, Tim Berners-Lee was working as

Vander Wal may have coined *folksonomy*, but Clay Shirky, in a 2005 blog posting called "Ontology Is Overrated," advanced the case for tagging by stating, "A library catalog, for example, assumes that for any new book, its logical place already exists within the system, even before the book was published. That strategy of designing categories to cover possible cases in advance is what I'm primarily concerned with, because it is both widely used and badly overrated in terms of its value in the digital world." But Shirky wasn't singling out library classification systems. He also found the Yahoo! Directory's classifications unnecessarily restrictive. The reason neither of these work well, he contended, is that the users know nothing about the classification systems—they simply know what they are looking for. Shirky continued, "One of the biggest problems with categorizing things in advance is that it forces the categorizers to take on two jobs that have historically been quite hard: mind reading and fortune telling. It forces categorizers to guess what their users are thinking, and to make predictions about the future."[32]

There is some debate over whether website designer Darcy DiNucci (in a 1999 journal article)[33] or tech book publishing magnate Tim O'Reilly (at a 2005 conference) coined the term *Web 2.0*. (The concept is usually associated with O'Reilly because his company has sponsored several Web 2.0 conferences.) Several Web 2.0 characteristics, as described by O'Reilly, touch directly on UContent phenomena. Specifically, Web 2.0 is a platform for many UContent services. Among the distinctions between Web 1.0 and Web 2.0 are transitions from content management systems to wikis, from taxonomies to folksonomies, and from publishing to participation.[34]

Citizen journalism, another hue on UContent's palette, has become increasingly popular. The middle years of the past decade brought us at least two prominent citizen journalism sites. The Global Voices website (www.globalvoicesonline.org), a product of ideas discussed at an international bloggers' meeting held at Harvard, was founded in 2004. Global Voices put international citizen journalism on the map. It screens thousands of blogs worldwide to "help all voices, everywhere, to be heard."[35] In 2006, CNN added its UContent section iReport to its website. The iReport section invites readers to submit reports, images, and video. And in 2009, the *New York Times* website launched two "local" editions staffed by citizen journalists. The locals are blogs that cover Fort Greene and Clinton Hill in Brooklyn, New York, and Maplewood, Millburn, and South Orange in New Jersey.

Other developments demonstrate individuals' increasing involvement with UContent: Google's 2008 launch of Knol (knol.google.com), where users can easily contribute articles on a wide range of topics, and the Library of Congress's 3,000-image photostream at Flickr, the photo sharing site (www.flickr.com/photos/library_of_congress). See Figure 1.1 for a timeline of many of these events.

Researchers Boyd and Ellison have stated that social networks have three distinct characteristics: 1) They allow individuals to post personal profiles, 2) they also allow users to establish lists of connections or groups with whom they share some common interest, and 3) they allow users to view the lists of connections that others have posted on the network.[36] These authors traced social networking sites back to the 1997 launch of SixDegrees.com, a site based on the "six degrees of separation" concept (an unproven theory that asserts that if a person is one step away from each person they know and two steps away from each person who is known by one of the people they know, then everyone is, at most, six steps away from any other person on Earth). Appearing on the scene in 1999, LiveJournal allowed users to select which other site members could follow their journals. But the explosion in social networking sites coincided with the millennium. Friendster, LinkedIn, Myspace, Flickr, YouTube, Xanga, and Facebook all appeared between 2000 and 2006. These popular networking sites have attracted massive numbers of users. Facebook alone claimed 500 million users in 2011; the LinkedIn blog reported hitting 100 million members in March 2011.[37,38] And people watch 2.5 million YouTube videos each day.[39]

Chatroulette, the newest UContent craze, puts users with webcams in touch with other users with webcams—at random! Once you're connected, you may be chatting on your webcam with someone across town or across the globe. National Public Radio's Omar Gallaga checked it out in March 2010 and provided a link to chatroulette.com. He blogged, "[I] should warn you before clicking the link for the site that you will see some *very* inappropriate things in the course of using it and you should keep kids far, far, *far* away from it. Personally, I found it to be disturbing, entertaining and strangely addictive once you get over the initial nervousness of chatting and if you have a strong stomach."[40]

Point/Counterpoint

Anything as popular and widespread as UContent, a phenomenon that seems to favor the average computer user over the experts, is bound to generate contrasting opinions. Is content contributed by end users of any value? Can it be trusted? Has it infringed on anyone's intellectual property? Who owns it? Does it have an impact on business? What are its legal implications? Numerous articles, presentations, and even a few books have been authored that attempt to answer these questions.[41]

On December 13, 2006, *Time* magazine proclaimed that its Person of the Year was You. In a short essay that took exception to Thomas Carlyle's belief that "the history of the world is but the biography of great men," writer Lev

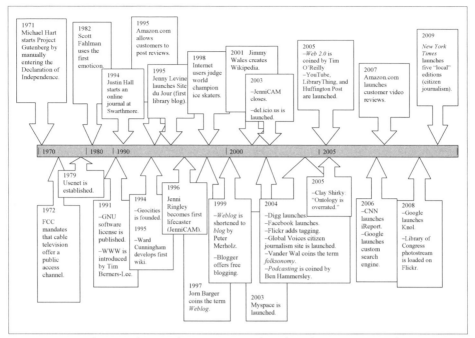

Figure 1.1   This timeline outlines events related to the internet and UContent.

Grossman observed that the year 2006 was a story of "the many wresting power from the few."[42] He was talking about communication, collaboration, and participation on a global scale—about the "new web." The article managed to mention most of the big UContent entities—Facebook, Wikipedia, Myspace, YouTube, Second Life—as it celebrated everything from blogging and podcasting to video uploading and mashups. The Person of the Year was anyone involved in creating user-generated content.

Just 3 days earlier, *New York Times* music critic Jon Pareles offered a different take on UContent, which he called "a tsunami of self-expression," while asking "why keep your creativity, or lack of it, to yourself when you can invite the world to see?" He cynically submitted, "Now that web entrepreneurs have recognized the potential for profit, it's also a sweet deal: amateurs, and some calculating professionals, supply the raw material free." Then he added a backhanded compliment: "It's often inept, but every so often it's inspired, or at least worth a mouse click." As for the theory that a democratic web permits everyone's voice to be heard and face to be seen, he remarked, "The promise of all the self-expression online is that genius will reach the public with fewer obstacles, bypassing the entrenched media. The reality is that genius has a bigger junk pile to climb out of than ever, one that requires just as much hustle and ingenuity as the old distribution system."[43]

Grossman and Pareles aren't the only two word-slingers in this debate. Commenting on *Time*'s tribute, political satirist Greg Gutfeld vented, "You may be chatting globally, but you're alienating yourself locally. The web does not connect people—it ramps up a mob mentality masquerading as community."[44] Also caught up in the fray, prolific author Nicholas Carr, known for his articles in the *Harvard Business Review* ("IT Doesn't Matter") and *Atlantic Monthly* ("Is Google Making Us Stupid?"), whipped up a blog post riposting Kevin Kelley's *Wired* article in which the web was venerated as "spookily godlike." Carr refers to several examples of bad writing in Wikipedia and importunes, "it seems fair to ask exactly when the intelligence in 'collective intelligence' will begin to manifest itself."

Reading these two assessments side by side is interesting and entertaining. On one hand we have Kelley, in sheer wide-eyed wonderment, musing:

> Everything media experts knew about audiences—and they knew a lot—confirmed the focus group belief that audiences would never get off their butts and start making their own entertainment. Everyone knew writing and reading were dead; music was too much trouble to make when you could sit back and listen; video production was simply out of reach of amateurs. Blogs and other participant media would never happen, or if they happened they would not draw an audience, or if they drew an audience they would not matter. What a shock, then, to witness the near-instantaneous rise of 50 million blogs, with a new one appearing every two seconds. There—another new blog! One more person doing what AOL and ABC—and almost everyone else—expected only AOL and ABC to be doing. These user-created channels make no sense economically. Where are the time, energy, and resources coming from? The audience.[45]

Carr, on the other hand, soberly asserts, "I'm all for blogs and blogging. (I'm writing this, ain't I?) But I'm not blind to the limitations and the flaws of the blogosphere—its superficiality, its emphasis on opinion over reporting, its echolalia, its tendency to reinforce rather than challenge ideological extremism and segregation."[46]

The champion of expert over amateur, by his own proclamation, is Andrew Keen. In *The Cult of the Amateur: How Blogs, Myspace, YouTube, and the Rest of Today's User-Generated Media Are Destroying Our Economy, Our Culture, and Our Values*, we find a number of tenable arguments against allowing ourselves to be part of Web 2.0's "seduction" (from Chapter 1, "The Great Seduction"). For example:

> Before the Web 2.0, our collective intellectual history has been one driven by the careful aggregation of truth—through professionally edited books and reference materials, newspapers, and radio and television. But as all information becomes digitized and democratized, and is made universally and permanently available, the media of record becomes an internet on which misinformation never goes away. As a result our collected information becomes infected by mistakes and fraud.[47]

That assertion, taken alone, is reasonable, and many reviewers agree with Keen's essential premise. They ultimately, however, find his unabated zeal and strident tone disagreeable. Prolific freelance journalist Toby Lichtig summarizes this general consensus: "Many of Keen's gripes in *The Cult of the Amateur* are reasonable; but, like his target, they dissolve in a miasma of polemical generalization and frenzied verbiage."[48] If we're looking for internal inconsistencies in Keen's thesis, we need look no further than Wikipedia co-founder Larry Sanger's comments in *New Scientist*. Sanger noted that Keen asserted amateur encyclopedias would put reference book publishers out of business:

> So how does Keen propose we solve our Web 2.0 woes? The first "solution" he refers to is a new website I have started called the Citizendium (www.citizendium.org), or the Citizens' Compendium, which I like to describe as Wikipedia with editors and real names. But how can Citizendium be a solution to the problems Keen raises if it has experts working without pay and the result is free? If it succeeds, won't it too contribute to the decline of reference book publishing?[49]

Carol Tenopir, professor of information sciences at the University of Tennessee, was willing to look at Keen's book through a librarian's lens:

> Enthusiasts tout the democratizing effect of Web 2.0. Keen warns, however, that when users and participants buy into the ideal that anyone can contribute information, we lose the accuracy that comes from reliance on experts. Indeed, expert authors and creators (and librarians) have valuable training, knowledge and experience.[50]

UContent detractors often argue that many individuals who create content simply aren't that talented. Blogger Mark "Rizzn" Hopkins of Mashable.com (168th most popular website in the U.S. with 28,000 incoming links) opined,

"There are only a finite amount of folks with talent, and while the technologies enable them to be found easier, in no way should we think there is value lurking in the average internet user."[51] Writing in *Adweek*, Mark Wnek complained that enthusiasm for technology and the love of immediate publication have led to poor writing.[52] In a "Debate Room" column of Businessweek.com, poet and fiction writer Sarah Davis suggested that Wikipedia, with its 9 million articles, and YouTube, where viewers watch 100,000,000 videos a day, are "flirtations with excess." She continued, "Gen Y members were told as kids they were special—and the user generated content trend feeds into that sentiment, which is blessedly false." Freelance pundit David Kiley, expressing an opposing viewpoint, said that the high use Davis referred to attests to a remarkable level of user engagement.[53]

Several endorsements for UContent emanate from the peer-reviewed literature. Guosong Shao, a professor in the Department of Communication at Pittsburg State University (Kansas), found that we use UContent for 1) *participating* in user-to-user social interaction (which enhances social connection), 2) *consuming* information and entertainment (creators have dramatically reduced entertainment content to light, bright, and digestible "snack food"), and 3) *producing* for self-actualization (self-expression is achieved through online behaviors such as blogging).[54] Ochoa and Duval stated that the most complete database of compact disc album and track information was CDDB and noted that it was not created by recording companies but by combining the submissions of anonymous end users who entered their personal cataloging.[55] If you've heard of Gracenote, you know about CDDB. Gracenote is the service launched in iTunes when you upload a CD to your library: It identifies the tracks. That brings us to another criticism.

Business Discovers UContent

As mentioned in the preceding paragraph, CDDB was originally created by end users adding track information to the database. Later, all that information was sold; the service called Gracenote now owns the information that end users contributed. Gracenote certainly is not the only case of profiting from material submitted by users. Technology writer N'Gai Croal, who observed that 10 hours of video is uploaded to YouTube every minute (the equivalent of 57,000 full-length films per week), wrote, "Whether they're creating content for sites such as YouTube and Wikipedia, viewer-submitted news services such as CNN's iReport or videogames such as Spore and LittleBigPlanet, today's most valuable employees will most likely never set foot inside the building—or collect a paycheck." But then he asked, "Is it really a sweatshop if none of the workers is complaining?"[56]

The latter fragment not only illustrates Nike's desire to own whatever UContent is deposited on its sites, but in a classic case of having one's cake and eating it too, the company also disclaims any liability associated with what a user contributes to its website. And this brings us to another major issue of UContent.

Legal Ramifications of UContent

Attorneys Robert P. Latham, Carl C. Butzer, and Jeremy T. Brown specialize in intellectual property law at the firm of Jackson Walker in Dallas, Texas. Their 2008 article in *Intellectual Property & Technology Law Journal* provides lessons for sponsors of webpages containing UContent; the most important intellectual property issue is copyright infringement. Businesses or individuals hosting UContent should be aware that there are three types of copyright infringement: *direct infringement, contributory infringement,* and *vicarious infringement:*

> UGC [i.e., UContent] service providers could face liability for copyright infringement under any of the three theories of copyright liability. For example, a service provider might be liable for direct infringement for violating the copyright holder's distribution rights by displaying certain UGC and distributing it across the internet. A service provider could be liable for contributory infringement if it knows that UGC is infringing another's copyright and facilitates the distribution, display, etc., of the infringing material. Finally, a service provider that profits from the infringing content may by vicariously liable if it has the means to monitor and detect infringing activity, yet allows the activity to occur because this allows the service provider to generate increased profits.[62]

Latham, Butzer, and Brown go on to say that the Digital Millennium Copyright Act (DMCA) of 1998 creates four limitations on liability for copyright infringement by internet service providers. Of these "safe harbors," UContent service providers will probably invoke the protection of the DMCA under section 512(c), which affords immunity from liability for copyright infringement "by reason of the storage at the direction of a user of material that resides on a system or network controlled or operated by or for the service provider." The service provider must also meet the following eligibility requirements:

- The service provider must not have "actual knowledge" of infringing activity.

- In the absence of "actual knowledge," the service provider must not be aware of facts or circumstances from which infringing activity is apparent.

- Upon obtaining actual knowledge or awareness, the service provider must act expeditiously to remove or disable access to the infringing material.

- The service provider cannot receive a "financial benefit directly attributable to the infringing activity," when the service has the "right and ability to control" such activity.

- Upon proper notification of claimed infringement, the service provider must respond expeditiously to remove or disable access to the infringing materials.

- The service provider must have designated an agent to receive DMCA notices and provided the requisite contact information on its website and to the [U.S.] Copyright Office.[63]

Example of a Case of Copyright Infringement

In the case *Viacom v. YouTube*, decided by the Manhattan federal judge Louis Stanton in 2010, Viacom alleged "massive intentional copyright infringement." YouTube countered that it promptly takes down infringing materials when notified by rightsholders. Viacom also alleged that YouTube facilitates infringement by allowing users to make hidden videos available to others through features such as Embed and Share. Viacom claimed to have identified on YouTube 63,000 unauthorized clips taken from 3,000 of Viacom's films and TV shows.[64] "Judge Stanton concluded that it was against the DMCA's purpose to hold YouTube legally liable for every video uploaded on the website—some 20 hours of video every minute—even if they might have had a general idea that the site was being used to violate copyright laws."[65] As of mid-2011, Viacom's appeal had not yet been heard, but a great deal was at stake regarding the issue of copyright.

A Google AdSense help page further illustrates the concern over copyright infringement and other possible points of law. Google AdSense warns participants to monitor the pages on which their ads appear. Google recommends that advertisers perform a human evaluation of each page before an ad is placed. Advertisers should beware of UContent, making sure they do not put an ad on a page that violates someone's copyright, sells term papers, promotes violence or racism, or other inappropriate activities.[66]

Example of a Case of Defamation

The Communications Decency Act also provides immunity for service providers (under certain circumstances). Section 230 of Title 47 of the U.S. Code at part C states, "No provider or user of an interactive computer service shall be treated as the publisher or speaker of any information provided by another information content provider." On April 3, 2008, in the case of *Fair Housing Council of San Fernando Valley v. Roommates.com*, the court found that Roommates.com was not immune because it had developed a question-naire that solicited information about sexual orientation and other room-mate preferences.[67] In doing so, it had *invited* and *collected* end-user content that was deemed discriminatory.

Contributing UContent has implications for one's privacy and publicity rights and, potentially, the rights of others whom the UContent may touch upon. One case involves a billboard advertisement produced by Virgin Mobile that included a young woman's image Virgin Mobile had downloaded from Flickr. The photograph had originally been uploaded to Flickr by a member of the young woman's church. The person who uploaded it gave it a Creative Commons license by which others could use the image for commer-cial purposes with attribution to the creator (that's quite a generous license). In the case of *Chang v. Virgin Mobile* (2007), the attorney for the woman in the picture argued that the woman had never authorized the uploading of the photo and that when a photograph is the subject of privacy, a stakeholder may be someone in addition to the photographer. Virgin Mobile essentially prevailed because the case was dismissed for "lack of jurisdiction."[68] This case demonstrates that the person uploading content (in this case, an image file) and granting a license may not have permission to do so from everyone who has an interest in the content.

After this brief introduction to UContent's history, its pros and cons, and the legal issues it raises, we can now explore the different outlets in detail while having some fun creating content!

Endnotes

1. "Top Sites in the United States," Alexa, accessed August 3, 2011, www.alexa.com/topsites/countries/US.

2. John Horrigan, "Broadband: What's All the Fuss About?" Pew Internet & American Life, October 18, 2007, accessed August 3, 2011, www.pewinternet.org/Reports/2007/Broadband-Whats-All-the-Fuss-About.aspx?r=1.

3. Ibid.

4. Graham Jones, "New Age of Openness: U.K. Shares More Than Ever Before," EPN Newswire, October 15, 2009, Factiva, accessed March 3, 2011.

5. "China's Netizens Publishing More Original Content," Xinhua Electronics News, December 14, 2009, Factiva, accessed March 3, 2011.

6. Organisation for Economic Co-operation and Development, "Measuring User-Created Content: Implications for the ICT Access and Use by Households and Individuals Survey," January 28, 2008, accessed August 3, 2011, www.oecd.org/dataoecd/44/58/40003289.pdf.

7. Xavier Ochoa and Erik Duval, "Quantitative Analysis of User Generated Content on the Web," Web Science Direct, April 2008, accessed October 25, 2011, journal.webscience.org/34/2/Quantitative_Analysis_of_UGC.pdf.

8. Annemarie Hunter, "User Generated Content," SEO Glossary, accessed February 10, 2011, www.seoglossary.com/article/746.

9. "User-Generated Content," Wikipedia, accessed August 3, 2011, en.wikipedia.org/wiki/User-generated_content.

10. "Internet Advertising Glossary," AdWords University, accessed August 3, 2011, www.adwordsuniversity.co.uk/index.php?q=21.

11. Patrick Phillips, "Blog, Web Terminology You'll Be Using," We Want Media, accessed August 3, 2011, journalism.nyu.edu/publishing/archives/wewant media/node/207.

12. "Participative Web and User-Created Content: Web 2.0, Wikis and Social Networking," Organisation for Economic Cooperation and Development, October 2007, accessed October 25, 2011, www.oecd.org/document/40/0,3746, en_2649_34223_39428648_1_1_1_1,00.html.

13. "User-Generated Content," PCMAG.com Encyclopedia, accessed August 3, 2011, www.pcmag.com/encyclopedia_term/0,2542,t=user-generated+content&i= 56171,00.asp.

14. "Timeline of Call-in Format in Radio & Television," C-SPAN.org, accessed August 3, 2011, legacy.c-span.org/C-SPAN25/timeline_a.asp.

15. Michael Hart, email message to author, February 14, 2010.

16. Douglas Kellner, "Public Access Television," Museum of Broadcast Communications, accessed March 1, 2011, www.museum.tv/eotvsection.php? entrycode=publicaccess.

17. Robert Hobbes Zakon, "Hobbes' Internet Timeline," accessed August 3, 2011, www.zakon.org/robert/internet/timeline.

18. For a detailed treatment of the history of Usenet, see "Netizens: An Anthology" at www.columbia.edu/~rh120 or "Giganews' Usenet History" at www.giganews.com/usenet-history/index.html. Also, this timeline may be of interest: www.google.com/googlegroups/archive_announce_20.html.

19. Tony Long, "Sept. 19, 1982: Can't You Take a Joke?" Wired, September 19, 2008, accessed August 3, 2011, www.wired.com/science/discoveries/news/2008/09/dayintech_0919.

20. "Sir Timothy Berners-Lee OM, KBE, FRS, FREng, FRSA, Longer Bio," World Wide Web Consortium, accessed August 3, 2011, www.w3.org/People/Berners-Lee/Longer.html.

21. "Marc Andreesen," Internet Pioneers, accessed August 3, 2011, www.ibiblio.org/pioneers/andreesen.html.

22. Krishna Ankar and Susan A. Bouchard, Enterprise Web 2.0 Fundamentals (Indianapolis: Cisco Press, 2009), 35.

23. J. R. Raphael, "A Decade of Internet Superstars: Where Are They Now?" PC World, October 8, 2008, accessed August 3, 2011, www.pcworld.com/article/176647/jennifer_ringley_jennicam.html.

24. Editors of the Huffington Post, The Huffington Post Complete Guide to Blogging (New York: Simon & Schuster, 2008), 16.

25. "The History of Blogger," WebHostingReport.com, accessed August 3, 2011, www.webhostingreport.com/learn/blogger.html.

26. "User-Generated Content Draws Fans," eMarketer, February 3, 2009, accessed August 3, 2011, www.emarketer.com/Article.aspx?R=1006895.

27. "Wiki Wiki Web FAQ," Cunningham & Cunningham, Inc., last edited September 12, 2010, accessed August 3, 2010, c2.com/cgi/wiki?WikiWikiWebFaq.

28. Ward Cunningham, "Correspondence on the Etymology of Wiki," Cunningham & Cunningham, Inc., November 2003, accessed August 3, 2011, c2.com/doc/etymology.html.

29. "About History," Creative Commons, accessed August 3, 2011, creativecommons.org/about/history.

30. "Folksonomy Coinage and Definition," Vanderwal.net, February 2, 2007, accessed August 3, 2011, www.vanderwal.net/folksonomy.html.

31. Thomas Vander Wal, "Tagging in Your Web World," SlideShare, January 23, 2007, accessed August 3, 2011, www.slideshare.net/vanderwal/tagging-in-your-web-world.

32. Clay Shirky, "Ontology Is Overrated: Categories, Links, and Tags," Clay Shirky's Writings About the Internet, accessed August 3, 2011, www.shirky.com/writings/ontology_overrated.html.

33. Darcy DiNucci, "Fragmented Future," Print Magazine, April 1999, accessed October 25, 2011, darcyd.com/fragmented_future.pdf.

34. Tim O'Reilly, "What Is Web 2.0?" O'Reilly, September 30, 2005, accessed August 3, 2011, oreilly.com/web2/archive/what-is-web-20.html.

35. "About," Global Voices, updated November 11, 2010, accessed August 3, 2011, globalvoicesonline.org/about.

36. Danah M. Boyd and Nicole B. Ellison, "Social Network Sites: Definition, History, and Scholarship," *Journal of Computer-Mediated Communication* 13, 2007, accessed August 3, 2011, jcmc.indiana.edu/vol13/issue1/boyd.ellison.html.

37. "Facebook Statistics, Stats & Facts for 2011," Digital Buzz Blog, accessed August 3, 2011, www.digitalbuzzblog.com/facebook-statistics-stats-facts-2011.

38. Jeff Weiner, "100 Million Members and Counting," LinkedIn Blog, March 22, 2011, accessed August 3, 2011, blog.linkedin.com/2011/03/22/linkedin-100-million.

39. "Infographic: YouTube Statistics, Facts, and Figures," Digital Buzz Blog, May 19, 2010, accessed August 3, 2011, www.digitalbuzzblog.com/infographic-youtube-statistics-facts-figures.

40. Omar Gallaga, "Chatroulette: Risky, Revolting, Revealing, and Revolutionary?" All Tech Considered, National Public Radio (March 1, 2010), accessed August 3, 2011, www.npr.org/blogs/alltechconsidered/2010/03/chatroulette_risky_revolting_r.html.

41. See for example: John I. Todor, *Get With It! The Hands-On Guide to Using Web 2.0 in Your Business* (Los Angeles: Silverado Press, 2008); Sankar Krishna and Susan A. Bouchard, *Enterprise Web 2.0 Fundamentals* (Indianapolis: Cisco Systems, 2009).

42. Lev Grossman, "Time's Person of the Year: You," *Time* magazine, December 13, 2006, accessed August 3, 2011, www.time.com/time/magazine/article/0,9171,1569514,00.html.

43. Jon Pareles, "2006, Brought to You by You," *New York Times*, December 10, 2006, accessed August 3, 2011, www.nytimes.com/2006/12/10/arts/music/10pare.html.

44. Greg Gutfeld, "Mad About 'You,'" *American Spectator* 40 (February 2007): 39.

45. Kevin Kelley, "We Are the Web," *Wired* 13, no. 8, August 2005, accessed August 3, 2011, www.wired.com/wired/archive/13.08/tech.html.

46. Nicholas Carr, "The Amorality of Web 2.0," Rough Type, October 3, 2005, accessed August 3, 2011, www.roughtype.com/archives/2005/10/the_amorality_o.php.

47. Andrew Keen, *Cult of the Amateur* (New York: Doubleday, 2007), 65.

48. Toby Lichtig, "Intellectual Kleptomania," *New Statesman*, June 14, 2007, accessed August 3, 2011, www.newstatesman.com/books/2007/06/keen-culture-internet-amateur.

49. Larry Sanger, "Review: The Cult of the Amateur by Andrew Keen," *New Scientist*, no. 2612, July 14, 2007, accessed February 27, 2011, www.newscientist.com/article/mg19526121.700-review-the-cult-of-the-amateur-by-andrew-keen.html.

50. Carol Tenopir, "Web 2.0: Our Cultural Downfall?" *Library Journal* 132 (December 2007): 36.

51. Mark Hopkins, "The User-Generated Content Reality," Mashable, October 28, 2007, accessed August 3, 2011, mashable.com/2007/10/28/the-user-generated-content-reality.

52. Mark Wnek, "Bad Writing Syndrome Goes Viral," *Adweek* 49 (February 4, 2008): 20.

53. Sarah Davis and David Kiley, "The Debate Room: User-Generated Content Is Junk," Bloomberg Businessweek, January 25, 2008, accessed August 3, 2011, www.businessweek.com/debateroom/archives/2008/01/user-generated.html.

54. Shao Guosong, "Understanding the Appeal of User Generated Media: A Uses and Gratification Perspective," *Internet Research* 19 (2009): 11.

55. Ochoa and Duval, "Quantitative Analysis of User Generated Content on the Web," 1.

56. N'Gai Croal, "The Internet Is the New Sweatshop," *Newsweek*, July 7–14, 2008, accessed August 3, 2011, www.newsweek.com/id/143740.

57. Jeffrey R. Young, "Colleges Try Crowdsourcing Help Desks to Save Money," *Chronicle of Higher Education* 56 (November 6, 2009): A1, A16.

58. Jeff Howe, "The Rise of Crowdsourcing," *Wired* 14, no. 6, June 2006, accessed August 3, 2011, www.wired.com/wired/archive/14.06/crowds.html.

59. Dara Solomon, "The Pros and Cons of User-Generated Content," Junta42 Content Marketing Blog, November 25, 2009, accessed August 3, 2011, blog.junta42.com/content_marketing_blog/2009/11/pros-cons-user-generated-content.html.

60. "User Generated Content License," American Red Cross, accessed August 3, 2011, www.redcrossblood.org/user-generated-content-license.

61. "User generated content," Nike, accessed August 3, 2011, store.nike.com/emeastore/plugins/help/html/UserGeneratedContent_en.html.

62. Robert P. Latham, Carl C. Butzer, and Jeremy T. Brown, "Legal Implications of User Generated Content: YouTube, MySpace, Facebook," *Intellectual Property & Technology Law Journal* 20 (May 2008): 2.

63. Ibid., 3.

64. Greg Sandoval, "Courtroom Rumble for YouTube, Viacom?" CBS News, January 7, 2010, accessed August 3, 2011, cbsnews.com/stories/2010/01/07/tech/cnettech news/main6070063.shtml.

65. Rob Arcamona, "What the Viacom vs. YouTube Verdict Means for Copyright Law," MediaShift, July 2, 2010, accessed August 3, 2011, www.pbs.org/mediashift/2010/07/what-the-viacom-vs-youtube-verdict-means-for-copyright-law183.html.

66. "Am I Responsible for User-Generated Content?" Google AdSense Help, accessed August 3, 2011, www.google.com/adsense/support/bin/answer.py?hl=en&answer=115995.

67. Martin Samson, "*Fair Housing Council of San Fernando Valley, et al. v. Roommates.com LLC,*" Internet Library of Law and Court Decisions, accessed August 3, 2011, www.internetlibrary.com/cases/lib_case484.cfm.

68. Evan Brown, "No Personal Jurisdiction Over Australian Defendant in Flickr Right of Publicity Case," Internet Cases, January 22, 2009, accessed August 3, 2011, blog.internetcases.com/2009/01/22/no-personal-jurisdiction-over-australian-defendant-in-flickr-right-of-publicity-case.

Project Gutenberg

In the early 1990s, when we were still experimenting with the original internet discovery utilities Gopher (a text-browsing application predating the graphical browser Mosaic) and search engine precursor Veronica (Very Easy Rodent-Oriented Netwide Index to Computer Archives), I recall a conversation with a colleague who said, "Nick, we're not going to need journals anymore—people are just going to publish their own papers on the internet." Having published my first article in the *Wilson Library Bulletin* (and proud of my accomplishment), I remember making some caustic rejoinder to the effect that nothing would *ever* replace formal print publications. When I wrote *The Web Library* (Information Today, Inc., 2004), a book that revealed many websites for finding ebooks and free journal articles, I found myself giving a few book talks at local universities. I recall professors asking me if I *really* thought people wanted to read books on a computer. But today you only need to look at the success of the Amazon Kindle, the iPod Touch, the iPad, and the Google Books Project to get your answer.

Printed books, journals, magazines, and newspapers may never go out of style, but their electronic equivalents continue increasing in popularity and use. But long before the ereader devices and long before Google Books, people were entering the text of books into the internet—and doing it manually! In Chapter 1, I made the claim that Michael Hart, sitting in the Materials Research Lab at the University of Illinois, was arguably the first person to add documentary content to the web just for the sake of wanting to share it.

For most librarians, an interest in books led to our decision to enter the field; we enjoy reading. When thinking about online books, the first site that comes to mind is, of course, Project Gutenberg (PG; www.gutenberg.org). Founded in 1971, it's not just another resource involving books built on UContent; it is the oldest resource on the internet engaged in accepting and distributing UContent. PG founder Michael Hart put his finger directly on a major UContent issue when he said, "Many people are concerned that the stuff they find on the 'net isn't very good. So let's make sure there's good stuff by creating it ourselves."

With the number and type of materials that Google continues to scan onto the web seeming incalculable, it may seem rather redundant to participate in PG. But participating in PG gives the donor the opportunity to choose the book and to become extremely familiar with it over time as he or she manually prepares it for the proofreaders. Contributing my time, energy, and two books to PG was not my first excursion into UContent, but it was the first time I was part of a team on a high-profile international project. Adding content to PG requires patience, good social skills (for interacting with your proofreader), and the ability to intuit what needs to be done to get your contribution online. Following is a journal of my experience.

Day 1

I began by exploring Project Gutenberg's history. The original PG is a repository of more than 30,000 works. Although PG occasionally accepts copyrighted works, it mainly deals with materials in the public domain. For books published in the U.S., any title copyrighted before 1923 is a candidate, but if you decide to become a contributor, choose a book you think you will enjoy. You'll be living with it close up and personal for some time when following the necessary steps.

The first step is to ask yourself, "What public domain material do I have access to that is not already available in PG?" Forget Shakespeare, Chaucer, Disraeli, Galsworthy, and Swift. Ditto for Zola, Moliere, Voltaire, and Hugo. PG doesn't need your Dostoyevsky, Chekov, or Gogol, nor does it lack Douglass, Hawthorne, or Conrad. Not surprisingly, I discovered it also doesn't want another copy of *Don Quixote* or an alternate version of the *Divine Comedy*.

You can enter your favorite deceased authors' names into the basic search, but, if you think there is a good chance that PG has already got your favorites covered, consider accessing PG's Online Book Catalog (www.gutenberg.org/catalog) and browsing to see what the project may lack that your library owns. If you recall reading something you thought was unique, something that perhaps no one else seems to have read, you can match your interests with the holdings. I had success using this strategy. My affinity for theater made me recall an interesting title I'd encountered in my library's special collections department: *The Treason and Death of Benedict Arnold: A Play for a Greek Theatre* (1910), by John Jay Chapman. The requisite search failed to turn up the title in PG's virtual holdings. I'm a guy who doesn't do well at slot machines and would never attempt to "count cards." Quickly discovering that I had an item Gutenberg might want was as close to "winner, winner, chicken dinner!" as I will ever get.

It's a good idea to make your first submission to PG something manageable (i.e., something short). The brevity of my selected work helped maintain my enthusiasm. Still, it's also a good idea to have a backup plan. My Plan B work was a government document at my library titled *Memorial Address on the Life and Character of Abraham Lincoln*, by George Bancroft. I put it aside in case I had time for an additional submission.

Total time to discover that *The Treason and Death of Benedict Arnold* was not held at PG: 30 minutes.

PG wants content, but it has policies. After you have preliminarily identified an item, the next step is to get "copyright clearance" (www.copy.pglaf.org). Here you determine whether the item is, indeed, in the public domain. This process took another half hour. I needed to create a username and password and then begin the submission of a "new copyright clearance request."

Be ready with the item in hand. You need to know basic bibliographic information in order to complete the clearance form. PG wants the author, title, and place and date of publication. Contributors, known as *producers* at PG, must also upload a scan of the title page and the verso. The preferred file types for scans are JPG, GIF, or PNG. (I discovered this only after I had saved my scans as PDFs, but the usually persnickety PG associates were willing to overlook this oversight.)

Having sent the bibliographic information and the required scans, producers may check the status of their potential ebook submissions by visiting www.copy.pglaf.org/status.php and logging in with their credentials. In the course of submitting *The Treason and Death of Benedict Arnold*, I was pleasantly surprised when I checked the link an hour later to find that my initial scans and information had cleared the first hurdle. A subsequent submission of the required information for an older title called *Some Passages in the Life and Death of John, Earl of Rochester* (1680) required much longer for acceptance—in fact, it took 4 weeks. This difference may have been because the title was printed in Great Britain and the U.S. public domain rule-of-thumb (works created before 1923) did not necessarily apply; the experience exemplifies, however, that it may take a while to get rolling.

Total time to scan title pages and versos for two items: about 10 minutes. Total time to request copyright clearance by entering the bibliographic information for two items and uploading scanned pages: 20 minutes.

Day 2

Having obtained copyright clearance, I now had to get the play into a format that PG could use and post. Skipping over the fine print, I thought that a high-quality PDF of the document would be perfect. So, using generic scanning hardware, I scanned the 75-page play, which took all of 30 minutes, and saved it as a PDF.

Next, I returned to PG's submission page (www.copy.pglaf.org/submit.php) and entered the basic bibliographic information; at the end of the page, a prompt appeared for uploading the actual submission. Uploading the PDF scan was simple (taking only a minute or two), but this is where the project became much trickier.

Everyone who contributes a book believes they've done a good job, but the submissions need to be proofread. Once PG has your file, you can expect an email from a *Whitewasher* (PG's term for proofreaders, and a nod to Mark Twain's Tom Sawyer). My email came from "Al," a PG volunteer in Canada, who introduced himself as the proofreader who would be working on my submission. His missive's tone was amiable but firm: "PDFs are an acceptable supplementary format, but it is mandatory that all submissions be uploaded as plain text (.txt files)." He referred to the site's Frequently Asked Questions (which I had neglected to read). Plain text is the "lowest common denominator" format, readable by all devices. Of course, materials submitted in Japanese or Chinese, for example, are exceptions.

The Whitewasher and I exchanged quite a few emails while I attempted to persuade him that PDFs were fine. "Everyone with a computer has free Adobe Reader software, right, Al?" During the exchange Al sent this *bon mot*: "There are now more than 3 billion cell phones in service, as compared to the over 1 billion computers; it will probably pay dividends to format for [the cell phones]." PG wasn't going to bend the rules, and frankly, its reasoning was valid. If one decides to participate in PG, one might as well accept the fact (sooner rather than later) that PG is prepared for any contingency and has many guidelines that its administrators are prepared to enforce.

Total time for my Day 2 interactions with PG (including checking, reading, and responding to emails): approximately 1.5 hours.

Day 3

It was time to investigate how to transform a PDF into a plain text file. Note that because Adobe Acrobat Professional cannot interpret graphic files, it can't resave a scan in PDF format as plain text. I was halfway through the seven stages of grief when Al the Whitewasher, who was really like a high school teacher waiting for a teachable moment, mentioned some options. The first daunting option was to manually render the play with a text-editing program, which, despite the excruciating agony it caused me, I attempted. Al, a true slave to duty, was, shall I say, somewhat underwhelmed by my production. A significant amount of reformatting needs to be done when one is adapting the hard copy of a published work to a plain text file. Here's just one example: Italics disappear, and italicized words need to be bracketed with underscores (e.g., _Tess_of_the _D'Urbervilles_). Unfortunately, there are innumerable italicized words in a play's script. In my zeal to submit the item, I had failed to properly render italics as I typed the text in.

Contacting the IT department on my campus was the second option. If you don't have access to an IT department, do you have a really "with-it" son or daughter or niece or nephew who is attending college? It's essentially the same thing. An associate at Central Connecticut State University's Instructional Design and Technology Resource Center took the PDF of the play (which I created on Day 2) and, using Acrobat Professional, converted it to a tagged image file format (TIFF) file and then imported the file to optical character recognition (OCR) software. The entire process required about an hour. Because the TIFF file was also a graphic file, I wondered why the OCR software managed to handle that format but not the PDF. The answer is that TIFF has an entirely different file structure, and that file structure is readable by OCR programs.

The IT department further converted the TIFF file into a Notepad (.txt) version of the play, ready for editing.

Time to manually (and erroneously) enter the text of the play: 4 hours. Time IT spent finding a fix and executing it: 1 hour. Total time for Day 3: 5 hours.

Day 4

Feeling rather confident that all I needed to do now was correct poorly converted characters, add a few underscores to set off italicized words, and look for instances of alphabetic characters dropped during scanning, I worked through the play.

Proofreading and editing your document requires concentration. You need to have both the plain text version and the scanned version on your computer's desktop because you have to compare the two versions line by line. Getting the text version of the play into a state I thought Al would accept took several more hours. I emailed it back to him the next day.

Total time committed on Day 4: 4 hours.

Day 5

Sigh. Choosing a play was probably not a wise way to begin my experiment as a PG producer. Although Al claimed no experience or acumen in dramaturgy, he was dissatisfied with the formatting of my submission. It became apparent that the play was going to require extensive editing. (To prove the point, see Figure 2.1 for a look at the "proofing interface" used by Al at PG.)

When people's communication is limited to email exchanges, which require a good deal of time to compose, instructions and comments are not always as clear as we might desire. Getting on the same page as my PG Whitewasher was proving difficult. I rarely leave projects unfinished, but I perceived that this particular effort would be unsuccessful.

Total time for emails, rumination, and self-reproach on Day 5: 1 hour.

Day 6

In 2004, while I was writing *The Web Library*, I interviewed Hart, founder and head of PG. I emailed him, and we discussed my current predicament. This exchange also gave me a chance to catch up on developments at PG. (As you can see in the interview that I did via email with him, which appears later in this chapter, he is not only informative but writes with considerable verve.)

Since I now had in hand this nice PDF of an interesting play, I asked whether there was "any way PG would simply use my play in its PDF format."

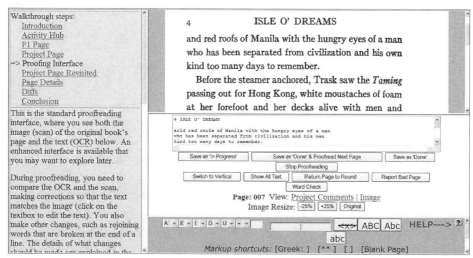

Figure 2.1   The Project Gutenberg proofing interface is used by the PG Whitewashers. [Courtesy of Project Gutenberg]

Hart replied that PG "does have a library that contains items that have only a PDF version, and you can send me the file for reposting to that site." He was talking about the PG Consortia Center (www.gutenberg.us). The Consortia Center is a portal that manages electronic books: It brings together 2 dozen ebook collections from beyond PG and, in so doing, permits a number of different formats, including PDF submissions.

I quickly forwarded *The Treason and Death of Benedict Arnold* to the Consortia Center. Only 1 day after sending this well-loved play to the Consortia Center, I received an email confirming my submission was available for readers to view at ebooks.gutenberg.us/AuthorsCommunity/ Treason_and_Death_ of_Benedict_Arnold.pdf.

My mission to contribute to PG was not yet realized, however. I wanted to get it right. I wanted to send a .txt file and have it posted on the original PG site. Remember my Plan B item called *Memorial Address on the Life and Character of Abraham Lincoln*? The item that my library owned was an original: The printing and publication date was 1866. I had already obtained copyright clearance for it, but the physical volume was so fragile, there was no way I could subject it to a scanner.

This was a perfect opportunity to put Google Book Search (books. google.com) to work. An advanced title search limited to "Full View Only" retrieved several digitized copies of the *Memorial Address*. I downloaded a PDF, which originated at the New York Public Library's collection, and then downloaded the accompanying plain text file. This procedure saved time and labor. It's a maneuver I recommend that you use; many books at PG bear "from the Google Print project" on their production notes. (Google Print was the original name for Google Book Search.)

Actually, I felt some qualms about using a Google Book Search digitized copy, even though PG was clearly willing to accept such texts. I checked with one of PG's legal advisors. He responded that the public domain status of the book gave me freedom to use it as I pleased; however, attributing the book to Google might be seen as using Google's trademark. So it was up to me. PG, as a noncommercial user of the product, falls into a category of user that Google's own service approves.

It was still necessary to go through the plain text file and compare it with the PDF. Although the converted file I used was relatively error free, some text required correction. For example, the names of several senators listed in the appendix of the *Memorial Address* ran together and needed to be separated. Also, the OCR software used in converting scanned PDFs into text files can convert an innocent word such as *our* into the meaningless *oue*. An experienced Whitewasher such as Al would frown on these glitches and send the text back to me.

While I am on the subject of Whitewashers, potential contributors will become acquainted with official PG Whitewashers only after uploading a contribution. At that point, a contributor will be assigned a Whitewasher. If you think you might want to contact a Whitewasher in the future for any reason, take note of the person who was assigned to you, because although a list of Whitewashers does exist, it is for PG internal messages only (see "How do PG volunteers communicate, keep in touch, or coordinate work?" at www.gutenberg.org/wiki/Gutenberg:Volunteers%27_FAQ at section 1.12 V.12).

Total time to prepare the file and email it to the Whitewasher: 7 hours.

Project Gutenberg's Version of the Steps Required for Contributing a Text

On its FAQ page, PG boils the process of adding an item down to four steps:

1. Borrow or buy an eligible book.
2. Send us a copy of the front and back of the title page, and wait for an OK.
3. Turn the book into electronic text.
4. Send it to us.

As my journal shows, climbing these four steps may involve breaking a sweat.

Day 7

I was happy when I read Al's email, which began, "This looks fairly good." He had attached an error report generated by a software program called Gutcheck. Gutcheck is a plain text proofreading computer program specifically tuned to report the problems that spell-checkers don't—errors such as mismatched quotes, misplaced punctuation, and unintended blank lines (Figure 2.2). It noted numerous "unbalanced quotation marks" and a few "duplicate punctuation marks" within my submission. Gutcheck refers to errors by line number, making correction easier. (Though Gutcheck is specifically built for aiding PG proofreaders, anyone may download the zip file without charge at pglaf.org/~jtinsley/gutcheck/gutcheck.zip.)

> *The gutcheck report* Japan, China, Australia , nay, the continent of Europe, holding an
> Line 3 column 25 - Spaced punctuation?
>
> , grateful for a dinner, endeavouring sadly to digest all he saw
> Line 6 - Begins with punctuation?
>
> and heard. But one was a Patterne; tbe other a Whitford. One had
> Line 7 - Query word tbe - not reporting duplicates
>
> genius; the other pottered after him to he a student. One was the
> Line 8 - Query he/be error?
>
> English gent1eman wherever he went; the other was a new kind of
> Line 9 - Query digit in gent1eman
>
> showing them an English seat on horseback: 1 must resign myself if
> Line 16 - Query standalone 1
>
> national song--if a congery of states be a nation-- and I must
> Line 18 - Spaced em-dash?
>
> Vernon away. He had serious thoughts of settling, means to
> Line 22 - No punctuation at para end?

Figure 2.2   Gutcheck goes beyond simple proofreading and queries the user to correct additional formatting problems. [Courtesy of Project Gutenberg]

Easy or not, corrections take time, but I finished them within an hour and sent the revised file to my Whitewasher. (Perhaps you're feeling like a ping-pong ball at this point, considering all the back and forth. I know I did. But as Blake wrote, "If the fool would persist in his folly, he would become wise.") It wasn't long before Al wrote back waving the lantern that was the light at the end of the tunnel, and when you get this kind of email from a perfectionist PG Whitewasher such as Al, it seems more like staring into the Bat Signal:

> Nick: If you're satisfied that the book has been *thoroughly* proof-read (and I do mean *thoroughly*—there's no skimping on this step), and the assorted Gutcheck items dealt with satisfactorily, I'd say to create a new copy of the file, and remove all those page splits from it. Watch out for places where the page following a split starts with a new paragraph, and leave a blank line between that paragraph and the one preceding it. At the Appendix, leave four blank lines before "Appendix" and two after it, to set it off as a section

title. Give the file a new version number, and send it back to me, and I'll re-run Gutcheck on it.

I looked the file over and sent it right back.
Total time dedicated to my project on Day 7: 1.5 hours.

Day 8

I checked my email with great anticipation and found a missive from Al asking, "Do you know how to handle zip files?" I replied in the affirmative, and he sent me a zipped folder with three files: the JPG image file of a portrait of Abraham Lincoln that was part of the original PDF, a text file with the Memorial Address that we had worked on together, and a big bonus—a beautifully formatted HTML file of the item. The image of Lincoln and the hypertext file were all Al's doing. He provided explicit instructions for uploading the content to PG and completing the PG form to indicate my responsibility for the item. I was off to www.copy.pglaf.org/submit.php (which I had visited on Day 2) to follow through with the submission. All things considered Day 8 was light duty.

Total time spent: just an hour.

Two days later, Al, whom I frequently suspected was out to thwart me at every turn, befriended me completely. But he was still a tough taskmaster and a terse correspondent: In his final email, he simply provided a link to the item (www.gutenberg.org/etext/26750) and thanked me (see Figure 2.3).

After all my kvetching about Al and my two successful submissions (one to the original PG and one to the PG Consortia), Hart wrote, "Just to give you an idea of how much Al does, he just posted 26 eBooks, mostly in French, from one of our volunteers in France, who does not understand our system of doing things and thus needs a certain, shall we say, level of hand holding. It was hard work, just like yours, and ended up being greatly appreciated on both sides."

I was pleased when I finally saw my contribution. After all, I'd run the gauntlet! But when it was over, I began to appreciate the exacting personalities at PG. It's people such as Al the Whitewasher, Michael Hart, and, in the final analysis, any fastidious pro with high standards and a book to contribute who make PG one of the highest-quality collections on the web.

On Reflection

My contributions to PG were definitely a memorable experience in UContent, but when contributing to PG, the user is not always in control of the content.

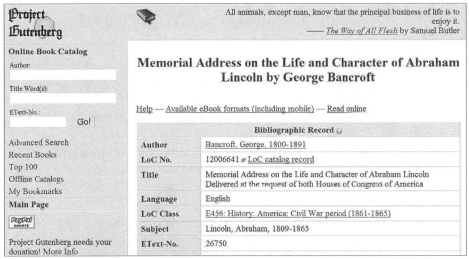

Figure 2.3   Pyrrhic victory? Nah! Seeing your contribution at Project
Gutenberg is very rewarding. [Courtesy of Project Gutenberg]

The user makes the selection, but by definition, the content is not authored by the user. We're simply polishing up old shoes and making them available for millions of people worldwide. PG's rigorous scrutiny means inspecting, reformatting, proofreading, double-checking, and, eventually, posting the content for access by the online community. In addition to the satisfaction of seeing your contribution in the holdings of PG, you get to read (and reread) a book that you may never have experienced so thoroughly. The procedure that PG requires necessitates that contributors become quite intimate with their contribution (you're able to read and reread it because you're working with it for hours and days), leading to a greater appreciation of whatever you submit. Life teaches us that anything worthwhile requires time, energy, and work. Preparing materials for PG is definitely worthwhile.

If you don't have the time to become a book producer, you could consider becoming a distributed proofreader (you can help by reading as little as one page per day—see www.pgdp.net/c). If you don't have the time or inclination for that, you might consider encouraging a friend to become involved with PG in some capacity.

Conversation With Michael Hart

Courtesy of Michael S. Hart

Michael Hart was one of the internet pioneers, sharing credit with Richard Stallman (at the Massachusetts Institute of Technology) for starting the open source movement in 1971. They began this work simultaneously but independent of each other.

Hart's choice for the first item to appear in PG was the Declaration of Independence. He began PG, the oldest site on the internet, at the University of Illinois.

He was also co-founder of the World eBook Fair, in which he begged and borrowed all the ebooks he could manage, many from John Guagliardo of the World Public Library and Brewster Kahle of the Internet Archive, both of whom had been his friends and fellow world changers for more than a decade. In 2008, they provided more than 1 million free ebooks, as well as 160,000 commercial ebooks at a discount.

Michael saw his greatest achievement—PG—as a place that has changed the world without ever making enough income to reach the average poverty line. Quoting from the great master Victor Hugo, he attributed his success to the fact that "There is no greater power on earth than an idea whose time has come."

He was incredibly generous with his time and attention, and we spent many hours talking and emailing.

Michael Hart passed away on September 6, 2011, at his home in Urbana, Illinois. He was 64.

Here are his responses to some questions I emailed him about PG.

Nick Tomaiuolo: *Michael, it has been 5 years since we last talked, and I note your enthusiasm and dedication to adding to one of the world's largest free online collections hasn't waned. Has anything changed at PG?*

Michael Hart: Several years ago, on October 15, 2003, as I recall, we had just passed the 10,000 ebook mark for the original PG teams, and those same kinds of teams were well past 30,000 at the end of the year 2008. In addition to ... the original PG site, we have www.gutenberg.org, with over 50 languages represented, and we also have www.gutenberg.cc with over 75,000 PDF ebooks in over 100 languages. So our grand total is now around 100,000. PG also co-sponsored the World eBook Fair (www.worldebookfair.com) from July 4 through August 4, 2008, which presented over a million free ebooks, plus 160,000 commercial ebooks at a discount. The grand total there was over 1,250,000 by August 4. And of course there's Project Gutenberg Australia at gutenberg.net.au, which has links to Australian history resources and has some different content because books there generally enter the public domain if the author died in 1954 or earlier. Project Gutenberg Europe (pge.rastko.net) has books in 59 languages, and there is also Gutenberg Canada (www.gutenberg.ca) where the collection reflects the fact that copyright generally lasts until 50 years after the end of the year of the author's death.

NT: *After a couple of tries I managed to contribute two items to PG. I did quite a bit of keyboarding, but not an entire text. Do people still key in the texts?*

MH: A lot of our volunteers still prefer to type them in; it's more fun and gives you a different "read" of one of your favorite books. I once did a 1,000-page book in a year, then I scanned and proofread the "prequel" in just 3 weeks, but the first one was sooo much more fun. It's a trade-off between what is fun [and] educational and [what is] mass production.

After all, the Gutenberg press was the very first example of mass production, and PG is the first example of what I have called *neo–mass production*, which I *hope* will start up what I have called the *neo–industrial revolution*. I found out while preparing texts for PG, scanners aren't always the solution. Of course, someday scanning and optical character recognition will be 99.99 percent accurate, or more. ...

NT: *After copyright has been cleared and a book has been uploaded, is there any chance that PG will reject it?*

MH: We haven't rejected anything in a long time, and even the one I am thinking of was eventually accepted.

NT: *I found creating an ebook for PG a satisfying experience. To your knowledge are there any systematic projects in place in which teams of people outside PG (for example, academic departments or students at library schools) are creating many ebooks and presenting them to PG?*

MH: We have Professor Mao in Taiwan, whose classes, in September 2008, moved ebooks in Chinese into the No. 3 slot for books in languages other than English, in PrePrints, and I have now moved on to Spanish as my next personal project since Spanish is the third-most-popular internet language but is just barely in our Top 10. As a result, my next major presentation is in Argentina to do some promotion of the Both Americas Project and also to do the honors in opening the Hart Library.

NT: *What "positions" constitute the PG community? I know you engage copyright attorneys, but do opportunities exist behind the scenes at PG for the run-of-the-mill bibliophile?*
MH: We don't have real "positions." However, Distributed Proofreaders is more position oriented; 50,000 volunteers proofreading a page a day is quite an accomplishment!

NT: *I encountered a proofreading innovation while I was working on my contribution, something called Gutcheck.*
MH: We collect up lots of errors and write programs to find them, which takes a load of work off human shoulders.

NT: *The vast majority of texts are available as "common denominator" ASCII text files. A random search for 20 books among the 28,000 at PG came up with eight that were available in PDF and 14 available in HTML as well. Do you maintain statistics of the composition of PG by file type (e.g., what percentage is also HTML or PDF)?*
MH: I think [that] if you redo that search in the "advanced search" menu, you will get many more PDF and HTM and HTML files. Actually there is at least one book, in French, that is not available as plain text, simply because the volunteer asked us not to do it without the accents. I'm pretty sure it is not the only one. Don't forget that most of the PDFs end up at the PG Consortia Center (www.gutenberg.cc). (And we also have plenty of French at PG of Canada.)

NT: *I noticed there is a small percentage of contemporary titles (not in the public domain) that are available at PG. What contemporary titles do you accept? Any memorable items?*
MH: Bruce Sterling's *Hacker Crackdown* comes to mind, as I spent three hard weeks getting it to look good on the screen.

NT: *Can individuals use PG to self-publish their novels or poetry if they haven't found a traditional publisher?*

MH: We try not to do much in the way of "vanity press" stuff, but we can always toss things we do not know how to do in the PrePrints section.

NT: *Have you any idea who your essential benefactors are, that is, who is actually contributing texts?*

MH: In any group of thousands, there is always at least one who totally stands out, some workaholic insomniac bibliophile or the like, and we always look so much better when we see one or two of those adding huge amounts to production. Most of them prefer to remain anonymous, and even I do big amounts of my work just as an anonymous volunteer.

NT: *Any words of advice or encouragement for potential contributors?*

MH: If you ever wanted to grab hold of Archimedes' famous lever and move the world, this is your chance! You could spend a week, or a month, or a year, or whatever length of time you wanted on a book a billion people might read in the future. ... Now that is leverage!

I see PG's use of the internet as the primitive, first steps. A sort of *Star Trek* communicator, transporter, and in the most important way, as a very primitive "replicator." You put a book in over here, and anywhere on the internet every person can have a copy, free of charge.

Today the personal computer becomes the personal library. The average computer today goes for under $500. For another $500 you can add your first few terabytes and hold enough books [in plain text .zip files] to make it into current lists of the 100 largest libraries *in the world*!

After all, there are 250 languages with more than a million speakers. If we cover only 40 percent of those, that's 100 languages. There are 25 million books in the public domain, not to mention newspapers, magazines, and so forth. If we do only 40 percent of those books, that's 10 million books. 100 languages ... 10 million books. ... If we just translate those 10 million books into those 100 languages, we have a 1-BILLION-BOOK LIBRARY! After all, people have never mentioned building a 1-billion-book library, but I see it as a foregone conclusion ... it's going to happen ... the only real question is when.

PG was designed to lift the world from the bottom upwards, rather than by the traditional trickle-down theory. Somehow those "trickle-down" projects rarely get to the masses but instead lift only the top portion of the pyramid to an even higher level, thus increasing the distance between the *haves* and the *have-nots*.

My own personal goal is to see that *1-billion-book library* being read on the average cell phone around the world when everyone, literally everyone who wants one, has a cell phone that reads, even one that reads out loud. That way *everyone can learn to read without any help from anyone else*! And every single one of those books could be owned for a lifetime by anyone with a petabyte of drive space. By 2020, petabyte drives will be affordable. Then where does the world of haves versus have-nots go? Eh?

chapter 3

Blogs

In a Web 2.0 world, where popular social phenomena such as tagging and user reviews are fluid and freeform, the blog may seem one of the tamest activities in UContent's repertory. Blogs have an immediately identifiable appearance, and though some of them may possess more bells and whistles than others, online journals organized in reverse chronological order are a comforting sight to web users continually traversing the flashy audio and video manifestations of web information. Blogs have been with us for quite a while. Justin Hall's online journal, Justin's Links From the Underground (www.links.net), launched in 1994, has the distinction of being the first blog. Blogs are a cornerstone of UContent that have stood the test of time while maturing and becoming more refined over the past decade. As one advertising bureau status report put it, "The advent of blogs was considered a tipping point for UGC [user-generated content; i.e., UContent]. It was the moment when UGC went from a small but significant component of the Internet experience to a predominant source of entertainment, information, and debate."[1]

A Rose by Any Other Name ...

In the enewsletter WordBiz Report, Debbie Weil published a list of 20 terse "definitions" for the words *blog* and *blogging*. Rather than representing comprehensive explications of those terms, however, her collection denotes various attributes of blogs. Blogs are "amateur journalism," "something to talk about at cocktail parties," and "your email to everyone." She goes on to mention that blogs are also "a way for a bunch of navel-gazers to communicate with each other" and "something to keep you occupied when you are unemployed." But ultimately she turns serious and proclaims that blogs are "a form of unedited, authentic self-expression," "an instant publishing tool," "a new form of knowledge management inside big companies," "a new way to communicate with customers," and "a way of writing with a distinctive voice and personality."[2] New York University professor Jay Rosen of PressThink (Rosen's blog, which concerns itself with how the web has changed journalism;

www.pressthink.org) has formulated arguably the most comprehensive yet brief description, defining a blog as "a personal web page, or online journal, updated easily by an author, that links outward to other material on the web, and presents original content—typically, links and commentary—in a rolling, day-by-day fashion, with the latest entries on top."[3]

Blogs as Social Software

Rosen's definition may approach a benchmark, but blogs have one more important characteristic. The ability to comment on a blogger's posts is a prominent social attribute and the feature that primarily distinguishes a blog from a personal webpage. Personal webpages and blogs may both be informational, but the former disseminates information unilaterally, whereas the latter encourages dialogue between author and readers. These dialogues can, over time, establish community. "Comments," writes Barnard College Library's emerging technologies and web services librarian Ellyssa Kroski, "epitomize the participatory spirit of Web 2.0, as they allow for a two-way conversation between the author and the audience."[4]

Although we all know one when we see it, a blog consists of elements that introduce the scope of UContent:

1. At the core of a blog are the *posts*. These are the articles that constitute the blog. The most recent post will be at the top, with previous posts following in reverse chronological order. In addition to text, posts may contain audio, video, images, and other graphics.

2. Even if a blog is great, if the initial page goes on forever, it may be too much of a good thing. *Archives* take over when the first page is "full." As the blogger continues to add posts, the previous posts are archived; blog posts are usually archived monthly, but the blogger may be able to adjust the timing. Most blog software offers extremely easy access to the archives.

3. Because the posts can move from the main URL to the archives, *permalinks* (i.e., permanent links) to each individual blog post facilitate quick access to specific posts.

4. Most blog software has a *search* feature or a search feature widget add-on. Regardless of where you are in someone's blog, use the search feature to find your keywords throughout the posts.

5. If you're one of the few information professionals who doesn't live to search, you'll be happy to know that most bloggers assign one or more

tags to each article that describe the content of the post. These tags may be listed on the side of the main content, in a drop-down menu, or in the *tag cloud*.

6. In addition to tags, the blogger may use *categories* to group posts by topic (if the blog software permits).

7. Most blogs have a *blogroll*. The blogroll is a list of sites that the blogger considers important and interesting. Links in the blogroll may point to anything—a PDF, a webpage, a search engine, other blogs, a photostream, and so forth.

8. Bloggers promote their blogs by offering *RSS feeds*. These feeds frequently show up somewhere on the blog as various colored symbols (sometimes orange, sometimes blue, but may be any color). Members of the blogger's audience can click the symbols and subscribe to the blog. Subscribing to an RSS feed ensures delivery of new blog posts to the subscriber's newsreader software.

9. Articles (i.e., posts) usually bear a *date* and *time stamp*.

10. The article's *author* is often indicated by "*Posted by*" or "*by*" information.

11. Through *trackbacks*, bloggers may be notified when other pages on the web link to their posts. Note, however, that trackbacks are not always automatic. For example, the free WordPress blog platform software will send automatic trackbacks to other WordPress blogs, but to send linking notification to a Movable Type blog, for example, the blogger must send a trackback manually.

12. A common Web 2.0 feature of blogs is *ratings* of posts (1 to 5 stars and other systems). This is another option that the blogger can control.

See Figure 3.1 for the components of a typical blog.

Blogs: A Big Slice of the UContent Pie

Statistics on blogging may conflict, but they are interesting nonetheless. In 2007, blog search engine Technorati claimed it tracked some 70 million blogs and estimated that 120,000 new blogs were created worldwide every day. ("That's about 1.4 blogs created every second," according to Technorati founder David Sifry.)[5] The 2008 State of the Blogosphere reported that 4.1 million people in the U.S. read blogs. (The more recent 2010 State of the

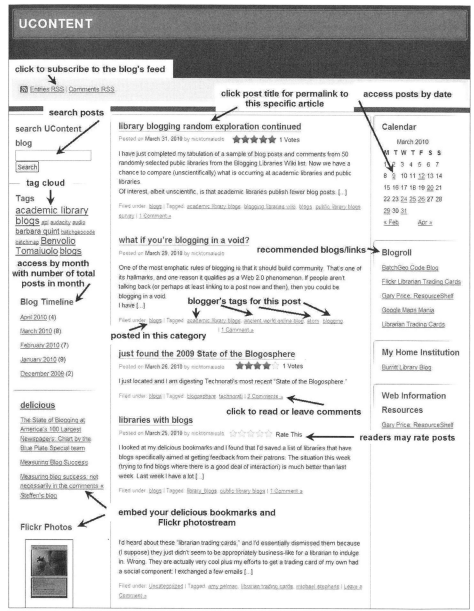

Figure 3.1   The arrows point to the components of a typical blog.

Blogosphere did not report the number of blog readers.)[6] By contrast, earlier in 2008, eMarketer claimed that the number of American blog consumers was 104 million.[7] The media agency Universal McCann claimed that 384 million people read blogs worldwide.[8] But even considering these staggering numbers,

Marshall Kirkpatrick of ReadWriteWeb reported that blogging seems to be slowing down. In 2008, he concluded, "There are on average 900,000 blog posts created every twenty-four hours. In last year's [2007 State of the Blogosphere] that number was 1.5 million. ... Just for context, 1.6 million people in the United States have defaulted on their mortgages last year. In 2005 there were 1.6 million people around the world who could speak Esperanto. 1.6 million people went to the Minnesota State Fair last year."[9]

But does a reduction in the number of posts really signal that blogging is "slowing down"? On the library and information science side, Walt Crawford (former president of the Library and Information Technology Association and one of the most cited authors in library literature) also noticed a diminution in posts but suggests that it isn't necessarily a bad thing. Crawford, who is also a veteran blogger, observed:

> (The) creation of liblogs [blogs written by librarians and information professionals who are associated with library work] and posting to liblogs peaked around 2006. ... We're seeing fewer new liblogs and existing bloggers are posting less often. I also have the sense that posts are getting longer—and we're seeing more comments per post. In other words, my sense is that liblogs are maturing. No longer the shiny new toy, they've become an established mechanism [that] works well for people with something to say. Those who still use them may use them less often, but to more effect.[10]

Crawford substantiates these impressions in his 2009 book *But Still They Blog*.

A Booming Blogosphere

Before examining blogs published by librarians and libraries, let's take a look at the range of blogs available. While everyone has favorites, there are several places where we can find lists of the "top blogs." Nikolai Nolan, a web interface developer, has been running the Bloggies (2011.bloggi.es) since he was a student at the University of Michigan in 2001. Every year Nolan asks members of the general public to nominate their favorite blogs. After the nominations are all in, he randomly contacts voters (a group that has numbered around 200 annually), who cast their ballots for best blogs in numerous categories (e.g., Best Asian Blog, Best American Blog, Best Food Blog, Best Humorous Blog, Best GLBT Blog). The winners in 2011 included Best Fashion Blog: Go Fug Yourself (www.gofugyourself.com), Best Entertainment Blog: We Come

From the Future (www.io9.com), and Best New Weblog: The Year of Blogging Dangerously (www.bloggingdangerously.com).

Kevin Aylward of the Wizbang blog ran his own Weblog Awards (www.weblogawards.org) from 2003 to 2008. After that the awards were canceled because, Aylward says, "resources required to handle the load of voting (nearly 1,000,000 votes in 2008) could not be adequately provisioned." Nevertheless, top blogs from the Weblog Awards have included The Dish in 2008 (www.andrewsullivan.theatlantic.com), PostSecret in 2007 (www.post secret.com), and Little Green Footballs in 2003 (www.littlegreenfootballs. com). Since 2008, *Time* magazine has published an annual list of the top 25 blogs. For 2009, the list included Talking Points Memo (www.talking pointsmemo.com), Huffington Post (www.huffingtonpost.com), BoingBoing (www.boingboing.net), and Lifehacker (www.lifehacker.com). For 2010, the list included Zen Habits (www.zenhabits.net) and BoingBoing for the second time. In 2011, the top three spots on the list were occupied by The Everywhereist (www.everywhereist.com), The Big Picture (www.boston.com/ bigpicture), and The Truth About Cars (www.thetruthaboutcars.com).[11]

You probably recognized many from these lists; some, such as The Dish and BoingBoing are written by professionals, while others, such as The Pioneer Woman, are written by nonprofessionals with a passion for blogging. On any day, check out Technorati's Top 100 list (www.technorati.com/blogs/ top100) if you want to see the blogs with the most "authority." (Technorati defines authority as a site's standing and influence in the blogosphere.) Academic, public, and school libraries began getting their own awards in 2010, when Salem Press began recognizing the profession's best blogs (see 2010's winners at salempress.com/Store/blogs/2010_blogs.htm and 2011's winners at salempress.com/Store/blogs/blog_home.htm).

On the basis of the number of comments bloggers had attracted, I visited several of these notable blogs to verify their popularity. Be forewarned: The readership of some heavy-hitting bloggers can be humbling. Take the well-regarded Huffington Post as an example. On April 26, 2011, Katla McGlynn's post titled "Bill Maher Bets Letterman a Week's Pay the Trump WILL Run for President" (www.huffingtonpost.com/2011/04/26/bill-maher-letterman-trump_n_853849.html) received more than 1,000 comments. The Pioneer Woman (www.thepioneerwoman.com), which recently won a Bloggie, can get up to 600 comments per post. Professional bloggers for major newspapers such as the *Chicago Tribune* and *New York Times* may receive zero to 60 responses per post, depending on the topic. But another *Time* magazine top-rated blog, DetentionSlip.org (www.detentionslip.org), which comments on education-related news stories and publishes between 20 and 50 posts per month, receives only one or two comments per day. The extremely useful How-To Geek blog (www.howtogeek.com) specializes in technology how-to articles that receive varying amounts of attention: A post about Tetris gets one comment, but blogger Matthew Guay's article "How to Create an iTunes Account Without a Credit Card" gets 11 responses. Guay's numbers are probably more typical of the interaction at "average" blogs.

I also used blogrolls in an attempt to learn more about blogger–audience interaction. That Blue Yak (www.thatblueyak.blogspot.com) does quite well, averaging 20 to 30 humorous posts, and 150 comments every month (a Yak post can get up to 20 comments per day). The 365 Days of Donna blog (www.365 daysofdonna.blogspot.com), with approximately 2 dozen posts per month, gets a few comments per week. A Google Blogs search (www.google.com/blogsearch) for *skull and bones* found M'Kayla's Korner (www.mkayla.wordpress.com), which received comments on each of its six posts for the month of May 2011 (with a single day high of 24 comments). A search on *asthma* found Hold Your Breath to Breathe (www.asthmadaytoday.word press.com); this randomly chosen blog had attracted 44 comments for its seven posts during May 2011.

My searching also made me aware that many individuals blog for a living or at least to supplement their main source of income. In his Launch Coach blog (www.thelaunchcoach.com), Dave Navarro, an internet marketing consultant and product launch specialist, warns that handing out blog content for free conditions readers to devalue the blogger and the valuable information in blogs.[12] Although I hadn't entertained the possibility that people should pay for blog content, Navarro's comments provide perspective on the whole UContent-for-free gestalt. As a general question for your consideration, can content be given away indefinitely?

Library and Librarian Blogs

Even as Paula Hane declared "Weblogs are a natural for librarians,"[13] another information professional, Laurel Clyde, was carefully attempting to assess whether information scientists were really enthusiastic about blogging. In 2004, Clyde published two articles demonstrating that her observations led to a much more skeptical view of blogs and librarians. In *Library Management*, she wrote, "An exhaustive search in October 2003 revealed only around 50 libraries with weblogs at a time when estimates of the total number of publicly available weblogs ranged from 1.5 million to 3.4 million."[14] And in the *Electronic Library*, she recounted remarks colleagues made concerning blogs, like "Weblogs—aren't they those online diary things?" and "Blogs are created by people with way too much time on their hands," as well as, ironically, "Weblogs may be useful for developing a sense of community in cyberspace, but what have they got to do with libraries?"[15]

Is the state of library and librarian blogging as bleak today as it was in 2004? Knowing the total number of librarian and information science blogs would provide an answer. But if you want to view a list of *all* libraries that blog or *all* librarians that blog, you will be as disappointed as I was to learn that these lists don't exist. I put out a distress call to various erudite associates, who explained that many lists are available, but none are comprehensive. The lists that people often consult show that there has definitely been appreciable growth in the "biblioblogosphere." (I was so interested in that ebullient term that I tracked down Karen Schneider, the Free Range Librarian at www.freerangelibrarian.com, and asked if she'd coined it. I was delighted when she replied, "Yes, indeed I did invent this term! I created it somewhat tongue-in-cheek, but it's turned out to be useful anyway, since it encompasses both library workers who write blogs [and] those who consume them.")[16] This healthy growth impressively illustrates information professionals' acceptance of blogs and the considerable interest that accompanies it. Following is a list of the sources I've scanned to become familiar with blogs by and for information professionals. There is overlap among all the lists, and some blogs that appear on one or more lists do not appear on others. Also, bear in mind that some blogs on these lists may no longer be updated:

- Blogging Libraries Wiki, "Public Libraries" (www.blogwithoutalibrary. net/links/index.php?title=Public_libraries), approximately 650 blogs included, and "Academic Libraries" (www.blogwithoutalibrary.net/ links/index.php?title=Academic_libraries), approximately 500 blogs included as of September 2011.

- Walt at Random, "Blogs in the Liblog Landscape (2007–2009)" (walt.lis host.org/blogs-in-the-liblog-landscape-2007-2009), approximately 500 blogs included as of September 2011.

- Information Wants to Be Free, "Favorite Blogs: List and Commentary" (meredith.wolfwater.com/wordpress/2007/09/30/favorite-blogs-list- and-commentary), approximately 180 blogs included

- Libdex, "Weblogs" (www.libdex.com/weblogs.html), approximately 310 blogs included

- Library Zen and LISZEN Wiki (www.libraryzen.com/wiki/index.php? title=LISZEN), approximately 800 blogs included

- LISWiki, "Weblogs" (liswiki.org/wiki/weblogs), approximately 950 blogs included

What Research Tells Us

Before delving further into the depth of interest in library and librarian blogs, I should share a few things I learned while reading the research of Michael Stephens, assistant professor in the Graduate School of Library and Information Science at Dominican University in Illinois. Stephens is a busy blogger and creator of TameTheWeb (www.tametheweb.com). His doctoral dissertation, "Modeling the Role of Blogging in Librarianship," provides many insights about librarians and blogging. In his research, he learned from survey respondents (n = 189) that librarians blog for different reasons, which include, in order of response frequency: 1) to share information or insight, 2) to participate in a conversation or community, 3) to archive information or experience, 4) to enhance personal professional development, 5) to express personal perspective or identity, 6) to promote oneself or the profession, and 7) to have fun.[17] Notice that sharing, participating, and expressing are high on the list of motivating factors for bibliobloggers.

To his survey question "What have you learned from blogging?" the No. 1 lesson is that the blogging experience affords varying perspectives on the library community—librarians want to help one another, even commiserate; librarians want to network and be "part of a whole." Among other intriguing responses, "Blogging fosters thinking and reflection," and "Blogging requires persistence and hard work."[18]

This final answer would have been at the top of my list. I've started several blogs with the most earnest intentions of sticking with them, yet they were ultimately abandoned. To chronicle my progress writing this book, however, I began the UContent blog at web20librarian.wordpress.com. It is certainly not TameTheWeb, nor is it Free Range Librarian; it's a newbie's attempt at pulling together the values of librarianship, authorship, and personal discipline. I've resolved to post frequently, link to interesting information, and provide topics that, I hope, attract conversation from readers. I enthusiastically invite you to check it out (and *please* leave a comment). I chose the hosted WordPress platform because its blog templates were appealing. I set my blog up in minutes but continue to tweak it by adding widgets and other WordPress-supported features. You can see a good list of blog software options at Blogged Out (www.blogged-out.com/2007/05/26/list-of-blog-soft ware-blog-generators).

If You Don't Have a Blog, Why Not?

A variety of software, both free and fee, is available for creating blogs that are visually appealing and easy to edit. The "2007 Survey of the Biblioblogosphere" found that Blogger (www.blogger.com) was the software that information professionals most frequently chose for their blogs (n = 364, or 46.2 percent of survey respondents), with WordPress (www.wordpress.com) being the next most popular (n = 262, or 33.3 percent of survey respondents).[19] My random inspection of library and librarian blogs supports the findings of the 2007 survey. A free blog takes only 5 minutes to create with Blogger or WordPress, although that blog will require continual nurturing.

Libraries That Blog

It's as natural and logical for libraries to publish blogs as it is for corporations such as Ford Motor Company (blog.ford.com) and Microsoft (www.microsoft.com/communities/blogs/portalhome.mspx). Blogs give companies—and libraries—a voice and a face.

Academic, public, and special libraries that have adopted blogging use their blogs in various ways. They may communicate issues such as water leaks in the stacks or an early library closing. They may provide web searching tips, a calendar of events, or a list of new books. Individual departments within a library may also want to use a blog to develop and nurture a relationship with their clientele. A librarian involved in an instruction program may frequently blog about educational opportunities or new tutorials; a reference department might use a blog to raise awareness of new services or databases (or canceled services and databases during cutbacks). A library manager who values transparency might start an internal blog to communicate with staff. And it is hoped that someone is reading those blogs!

You may have surmised that I link blogging success with the sense of community that it cultivates. In other words, do the postings generate readers' comments? If people aren't talking back (or perhaps at least linking to a post now and then), you could be blogging in a void. Earlier I described my examination of several nonlibrarian blogs. I attempted similar examinations of librarians' blogs and blogs published by libraries for their patrons.

My first exploration was to look at public library blogs (I used the Blogging Libraries Wiki at www.blogwithoutalibrary.net/links/index.php?title=Public _libraries to identify the libraries). Though my study was unscientific, some observations may prove interesting. Specifically, I tabulated the posts from 50 randomly chosen public library blogs for the month of March in 2008, 2009, and 2010. Taken together the public libraries published 1,019 posts and received a total of 300 comments, for an average of .29 comments per post. (You can see how the libraries ranked at web.ccsu.edu/library/tomaiuolon/publiclibrariesblogs1.htm.)

Next I checked the Blogging Libraries Wiki (www.blogwithoutalibrary.net/ links/index.php?title=Academic_libraries) and randomly selected 50 academic libraries. In the same time frame, the academic libraries had published 588 posts, fewer than their public library counterparts. But the academic libraries also had more total comments (379) than the public libraries, for a better average of .64 comments per post. (To view this list, please see web.ccsu.edu/library/tomaiuolon/UContent/blogcomments1.htm.)

At the top of the list for most comments on any one specific post was the Pensacola Junior College Library Blog (psclibraryblog.blogspot.com/2009/ 03/top-10-surf-colleges-check-it-out-dude.html), which attracted 24 comments for an article at Surfline.com about the "Top Ten Surf Colleges in America." The Pensacola Junior College Library Blog also gets top honors for overall interaction. During the months of March 2008, 2009, and 2010, Pensacola posted 46 entries and had 186 comments, for a list-topping 4.04 comments per post.

If a library's blog is open for comments, it may be wise to create a policy for potential postings from the general public. Here is an example excerpted from the New York Public Library's website (www.nypl.org/policy-patron-generated-web-content):

> Please also remember to exercise good judgment when contributing written material or other content. In the NYPL blogs, for example, the Library prohibits comments that are offensive or objectionable to others, that use inappropriate language, or that are off-topic. In most instances, we will not have the resources to review patron comments/content, but we do reserve the right to edit or delete user comments/content in a manner consistent with our mission and policies. We also ask that you do not insert your own or a third party's advertising, branding or other promotional content into any of your comments/content.[20]

Librarians Who Blog

The second section of my mad scientist exploration sought to learn more about librarians who blog. I chose at random 50 blogs written by individual librarians. The lists I used came from Blake Carver's "Ten Librarian Blogs to Read in 2010" (www.lisnews.org/10_librarian_blogs_read_2010), Walt Crawford's list from his June 2009 *Cites & Insights* (walt.lishost.org/blogs-in-the-liblog-landscape-2007-2009), "The Top Fifty Librarian Blogs" from Get Degrees (www.get degrees.com/articles/career-resources/the-top-fifty-librarian-blogs), and LISWiki's list of individual librarians' blogs (www.liswiki.org/wiki/weblogs). I needed to combine the lists because I had specific criteria for selection: blogs that had been up since 2008 and had at least five posts. You might not think those criteria would be difficult to satisfy, but a significant number of blogs from the LISWiki list have been abandoned, and a few from Walt Crawford's list are also MIA. In addition, many of the blogs hadn't posted in March 2010, which was the month I wanted to include. In fact, if I had a nickel for every blog link that landed on an error page, blogger that hadn't posted in March 2010, or blog that had been taken down because of a breach of terms and conditions, I'd have enough for a venti at Starbucks.

But you will be happily surprised when you look at the list of individual librarians' blogs at web.ccsu.edu/library/tomaiuolon/UContent/librarians blogs1.htm and see the considerable interaction between bloggers and their readers. The Annoyed Librarian (blog.libraryjournal.com/annoyedlibrarian) attracts the most comments per post. For the 3 months I inspected, there were a total of 35 posts and 2,497 responses, for an average of 71 comments per post! Meredith Farkas's Information Wants to Be Free (www.meredith.wolfwater.com/wordpress) was second with 14 posts and 120 comments in 3 months (an average of 8.6 responses per article). Only three individual librarians' blogs (in my random sample) had cumulative posts with no comments. So there's a good deal of demonstrable community created by librarians' blogs. Moreover, the average number of comments per post for all individual librarians' blogs is three. This indicates high general interest and collegiality among librarians. What do librarians blog about? In a thorough content analysis of 30 librarians' blogs, professor Noa Aharony of Israel's Bar-Ilan University categorized 33.62 percent of 455 unique tags as general, 20.21 percent as technology-related, 19.12 percent as library-related, 14.60 percent as information-related, and 12.90 percent as social-web-related.[21]

FYI: Some of the more prolific biblioblogs, at least according to my random 3-month count, are iLibrarian, TameTheWeb, Phil Bradley, Stephen's Lighthouse, and Librarian in Black (all with more than 100 posts during the interval). Table 3.1 shows the top 15, but I urge you to take this ranking with a grain of salt: I am not a statistician (more at web.ccsu.edu/library/tomaiuolon/UContent/librariansblogs1.htm).

As one would expect, there is a significant spike in comments whenever a librarian blogs about a hot topic. For example, Ellyssa Kroski blogged about "10 Websites for Book Lovers" at iLibrarian and received 19 comments on that post alone. On March 18, 2008, Michael Stephens of TameTheWeb blogged about a public library banning access to Facebook and Myspace; his post racked up 41 responses. And when Stephen Abram at Stephen's Lighthouse asked "Do librarians use smartphones much?" 23 readers supplied answers.

Table 3.1   This list of librarian's blogs is ranked by the average number of comments per post. The numbers are a result of a tally of posts/comments during 3 randomly chosen months in 2008, 2009, and 2010.

Rank	Blog title	Listed by	# of posts	# of comments	Average # of comments per post
1	Annoyed Librarian (blog.libraryjournal.com/annoyedlibrarian)	Get Degrees	35	2,497	71.3
2	Information Wants to Be Free (www.meredith.wolfwater.com/wordpress)	Get Degrees	14	120	8.57
3	Judge a Book by Its Cover (www.judgeabook.blogspot.com)	Get Degrees	19	159	8.36
4	In the Library With the Lead Pipe (www.inthelibrarywiththeleadpipe.org)	Get Degrees	11	91	8.27
5	Free Range Librarian (www.freerangelibrarian.com)	Get Degrees	23	179	7.78
6	A Librarian's Guide to Etiquette (www.libetiquette.blogspot.com)	Get Degrees	49	343	7
7	The Ubiquitous Librarian (www.theubiquitouslibrarian.typepad.com)	LISWiki	9	58	6.44
8	Cool Librarian (www.coollibrarianblog.blogspot.com)	Walt Crawford	9	52	5.77
9	Librarian.net (www.librarian.net)	Get Degrees	23	117	5.08
10	Swiss Army Librarian (www.swissarmylibrarian.net)	LISWiki	14	65	4.64
11	Walt at Random (walt.lishost.org)	Get Degrees	21	81	3.85
12	David Lee King (www.davidleeking.com)	Get Degrees	74	277	3.74
13	Library Garden (www.librarygarden.net)	BCarver	23	70	3.04
14	Never Ending Search (blog.schoollibraryjournal.com/neverendingsearch)	Walt Crawford	46	141	3.06
15	Virtual Dave ... Real Blog (quartz.syr.edu/rdlankes/blog)	Get Degrees	21	56	2.66

Things I Learned From an Experienced Blogger

On my UContent blog, I discussed the possibility that one may be "blogging in a void" if one's blog does not attract dialogue. I did this after noticing that a blog called AWOL: The Ancient World Online (www.ancientworld online.blogspot.com) rarely had comments even though the blogger posted frequently. My post quickly received a comment from AWOL's creator Charles Jones, librarian at the Institute for Study of the Ancient World at New York University. Stating that his blog was mainly informational, he wrote, "I get a great deal of response offline and on the Twitter and Facebook iterations of AWOL, and the fact that AWOL has attracted 1,100 feed by email subscribers in less than a year is a sign of serious interest in a small discipline."

This exchange, brought about by my blog post, later resulted in Charles Jones becoming my friend on Facebook, where he elaborated on the methods he uses to manage and promote AWOL:

1. I use StatCounter (www.statcounter.com) to analyze use. I'm very open about this and have a link in my right-hand sidebars to "View My Stats." Have a look via www.ancientworldonline. blogspot.com. This utility allows me to track who is doing what and when they are doing it. The utility also lets me discover which postings have a greater or lesser impact or interest. It also allows me to track "came from" data, which provides me with an idea of who is linking to the blog and whether it brings any traffic. I generally get only an impressionistic view of this data. I imagine there are ways to analyze it more thoroughly.

2. My community—or at least the community I think of as mine— is mostly academic. I know that for all its members' apparent adeptness at the use of the web, things such as RSS, Atom, and associated newsreaders remain a mystery—or at least underutilized by the academic community—so in the last year or two, I have been using a news feed by an email utility. FeedBurner is the one I use (feedburner.google.com). This allows people to opt into receiving the feed by email. I deployed this last summer for the Ancient World Online blog, and at the moment I have 1,109 addresses subscribed by email. An additional 26 are getting the FeedBurner feed in various newsreaders. This is interesting because my FeedBurner feed sends the full text of each posting to the subscribers. To follow up on the links, they are not obligated to click back through to AWOL—they can use the hyperlinks in the emails to go to the content I am presenting. This

means that some proportion of the AWOL-by-email population never gets reflected in the StatCounter data. I can also review the subscriber emails to get a sense of who is there and what sorts of addresses are subscribed (heavily .edu, for instance).

3. I'm pretty transparent about how people can contact me off-list, and I've been an active participant in online communities relating to the ancient world since the early 1990s, so people know how respond to me.

I recently wrote about some of this in a short piece, "Going AWOL: Thoughts on Developing a Tool for the Organization and Discovery of Open Access Scholarly Resources for the Study of the Ancient World." It's in the *CSA Newsletter*, Vol. XXII, No. 3 (csanet.org/newsletter/winter10/nlw1001.html).

The Twitter and Facebook manifestations (and I see you do them too) are interesting but not, I think, very important, except for the fact that people in Facebook at least seem more inclined to comment—though most comments are terse and uninformative. In the end AWOL is not really a blog in the traditional sense of the thing, but I use Blogger as a convenient free content management system to organize and deliver useful data in ways the scholarly community finds useful.[22]

Other Perspectives on Measuring Blog Success

While having a StatCounter or Google Analytics package set up to allow tracking of visits to your blog is a good idea, and while calculating the number of comments is another method, neither is foolproof. Blogger Steffen Moller, a business consultant, writes, "I can assure you that excellent blogs that are getting obscene amounts of traffic can get as little as one to five comments per month, despite plenty of efforts on our side to encourage commenting, such as via questions or provocative remarks in posts. At the same time, blogs where the content is less interesting and the traffic less impressive are kick-starting week-long conversations via comments. Trust me, it's not a reflection of the blog itself, but of your readership. So what's the best measure of success? I think it's the 'time spent on site' metric."[23] Avinash Kaushik, author of *Web Analytics 2.0* and *Web Analytics: An Hour a Day*, blogged his metrics for a successful blog, and they include Citations/Ripple Index, Audience Growth, and Conversation Rate.[24] Jim Turner, of Business Blog Consulting, also doesn't rely on statistics alone but provides a nice linked list of statistical packages (www.businessblogconsulting.com/2006/08/measuring-a-blogs-success).

Blog Promotion

Blogging may be a personal and reflective endeavor, but the blogosphere is lonely if no one is reading your blog. If you've just created a blog, here are a few ways you can get the word out:

1. Send an email to friends and colleagues asking them to spread the word.

2. Determine which discussion lists are related to your blog's content, and submit posts to those listservs.

3. Link your blog to a dedicated Facebook page in such a way that the Facebook page will update whenever you post.

4. Send a tweet about your updated blog whenever you post.

5. Be sure that you give your audience an easy way to subscribe to your blog by creating a button that leads to your RSS or Atom feed. Of course, if your readers use a nifty browser such as Apple Safari 5, Internet Explorer 9, or Firefox 7 or higher, the RSS button will be right in the browser bar.

6. Turn your RSS feed into JavaScript and embed the link on webpages: Your posts will show up on the page. (Figure 3.2 shows the way a library blog looks when embedded on a library wiki page.) They will also update whenever you publish new posts. This RSS-to-JavaScript translation can be done at free utilities (e.g., Feed2JS at www.feed2 js.org). Google also offers a free Dynamic Feed Control Wizard (see Figure 3.3) that will generate code, and it offers a news ticker-style display at www.google.com/uds/solutions/wizards/dynamicfeed.html.

Caveat Blogger

Michael Stephens's doctoral dissertation provided another insight: Blogging requires discretion. Reporting on a survey he had administered to blogging librarians, he wrote, "Blogging is not a private act. There is potential for conflict within a blogger's organization or with superiors. … Respondents [to his survey] reported it is 'less anonymous than you realize' and that 'small mistakes

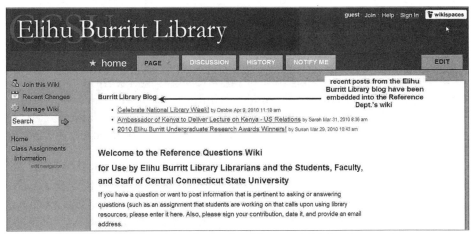

Figure 3.2   Promote your blog by embedding its RSS feed on webpages. [Courtesy of Wikispaces]

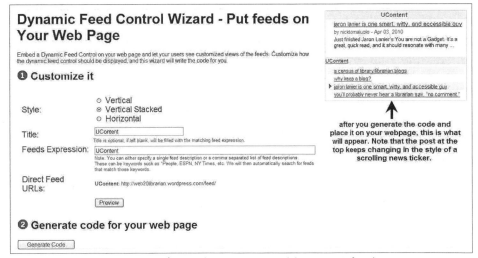

Figure 3.3   Step 1: Google's utility turns your blog's RSS feed into a smart looking box (customizable). Step 2: Google generates the code. Step 3: You embed it on your webpages. [Courtesy of Google]

get caught by everyone.' These descriptors and phrases included 'people you don't expect to be reading are' and 'do not post too quickly.'"[25]

Indiscrete posting is precisely why Mark Jen was fired from Google on January 28, 2005. In his blog Ninetyninezeros, he gave a day-by-day account of his activities at Google, which included praise as well as criticism. *PC World* reported, "It turned out that his superiors at Google, which owns the popular Blogger service, also read Ninetyninezeros. On January 26, Jen disclosed in his blog that he had been asked to remove some information from prior postings that Google considered to be sensitive information about the company's finances and products. Then more than a week passed without his posting anything. Rumors abounded among tech industry bloggers over Jen's fate. On February 9, Jen finally disclosed that Google had fired him on January 28—11 days after he had started on the job—and that his blog had 'either directly or indirectly' been the reason."[26]

Fake bloggers are also a problem. Plain Layne, a defunct blog that was the online journal of a bisexual woman, is widely thought to have been a hoax site that was written by a man.[27] Another well-known case is the blog of Kaycee Nicole Swenson, a 19-year-old woman dying of cancer. The *New York Times* later exposed this as a hoax blog written by a 40-year-old woman.[28] While that particular blog probably did no one any harm, people in the marketing industry, as well as the general public, reacted very negatively to what was thought to be a manipulative counterfeit blog posting of a video praising the automobile manufacturer Mazda on a shill site.[29] The blog quickly disappeared only 2 days after drawing fire from various individuals.[30] A similar set of circumstances surrounded the idont.com blog early in 2006. The website, which appeared to be the work of average end users, criticized owners of Apple's iPod. After some investigation, site visitors discovered that idont.com was actually created by the SanDisk Corp.—to promote its digital music player.[31]

Finding Blogs

Earlier in this chapter was a list of URLs you can use to find individual library and librarian blogs. But searching for blogs and posts is another option. An excellent deployment of the Google Custom Search Engine is available at www.liszen.com. The LISZEN Library and Information Search Engine searches more than 750 blogs. LibWorm (www.libworm.com), which searches more than 1,500 library and librarian blog newsfeeds, is also very useful. For blog searches outside the library realm, the most popular search engines include Bloglines (www.bloglines.com), Icerocket (www.icerocket.com), EatonWeb Blog Directory (portal.eatonweb.com), BlogPulse (www.blog pulse.com), Google Blogs (www.google.com/blogsearch), and Technorati (www.technorati.com/search).[32]

Conversation With Walt Crawford

Walt Crawford is a semi-retired library systems analyst, writer, speaker, and editor with more than a dozen books (plus several self-published books), more than 500 columns and articles, and a monthly ejournal to his credit. Check out his ejournal *Cites & Insights* (www.citesand insights.info) and his blog Walt at Random (walt.lishost.org).

Nick Tomaiuolo: *Your blog, Walt at Random, has been around since 2005. It's obvious that you've worked very hard at it. What tools, if any, do you use to find new topics to write about? How many of these tools do you employ? Do you find any more fruitful than others? If you aren't deploying any formal "tools," how do you come upon the topics you discuss?*

Walt Crawford: Walt at Random has been around since 2005, which is not really all that long—roughly 40 percent of the blogs discussed in But Still They Blog (at least 195 out of 514) are older. It's an informal adjunct to my ejournal, Cites & Insights, which has been around for a long time, since December 2000.

I've worked hard on the ejournal. The blog is composed of miscellany, random thoughts, and other things that don't fit in the ejournal. The tools I use for the blog are the same as those for the ejournal: Bloglines (www.bloglines.com) to monitor more than 500 other blogs, FriendFeed (www.friendfeed.com) for discussions with several hundred library people and a few dozen others, lots of print media, and general awareness.

I'd say Bloglines or any good RSS reader is the most useful tool, but it's hard to discount the informality and honesty of FriendFeed participants.

NT: *Your insight regarding this question will be especially important to new librarians, library and information science students, and others just starting to blog: Because blogging is such a stern taskmaster—that is, one puts a lot of work into it and should expect a "payoff," at least in terms of readers—what is the best way to promote one's blog to make the effort pay off for the blogger?*

WC: I don't agree with the first clause, and I don't have an answer for the second. I don't believe blogging is or needs to be a "stern taskmaster"—particularly now that most people (I believe) get posts either through RSS feeds or through social networking notices. That is, they're not coming to your blog every day, so the key is to have interesting posts when you have something to say, not to have a steady stream of posts. I certainly don't—I can have three posts in a day (rare) and then go a week or more without a post (not rare).

I've never done any formal promotion for the blog. If I were doing explicit promotion, it would always be for the ejournal. RSS is a fundamental tool for any blog, and it's built into WordPress and other major blog platforms, so that's a given (or should be— a blog without RSS is a failure waiting to happen). It does make sense to list your new blog in the LISWiki weblogs list and to let your friends and acquaintances know about the blog. Include it in your Facebook profile and consider having post headlines show up on your Facebook wall automatically (I don't, but it's not a bad idea). If you're on FriendFeed, *absolutely* have your blog feed headlines into FriendFeed (I do that). The same probably goes for Twitter, but I don't use that.

NT: *Walt, please clarify the distinction between liblogs and library blogs.*

WC: Liblogs [blogs done by library people] and library blogs [official blogs from libraries] are very different animals.

NT: *When blogging was still a nascent phenomenon, Laurel Clyde, in a 2004 article in* Library Management, *observed that there were not a sufficient number of library blogs to call blogging a "natural" for librarians; of course, this has certainly changed. In your book* The Liblog Landscape, *you write that the number of librarians' blogs probably peaked in 2006, yet people are still creating new blogs. What new librarian bloggers on the scene have gotten your attention? What do you like about their blogs?*

WC: I'm not sure that blogging is a natural for librarians any more than, say, article writing (and relatively few librarians write more than one article in their careers). The "shiny" for blogging—the time when it was a hot new thing—probably peaked in 2006. It's moved from shiny new thing to just another tool, but it continues to be a great tool for those who can use it well. Some people who would have had blogs in the past now just tweet, and if you're just highlighting websites or tossing out single sentences, that's sensible.

Others still have longer things to say; I believe most of the best new blogs consist of essays, either longer or shorter.

It's easier to say what I like about new (and old) blogs than to provide examples. Good liblogs have personality (the writing is in the blogger's own voice), interest (the posts are interesting), and at least a little substance (the blogger has something to say that's worth reading, which does not mean every post or any post has to be Deeply Serious).

NT: *The reasons for creating and sustaining a blog can range from "having fun" to "expressing yourself" to "archiving information or experience" to "sharing insight." I know the primary reason for my blog is to chronicle my progress on my book. You're a prolific blogger. What initially made you want to blog? What sustains your interest in blogging?*

WC: I'm not really that prolific as a blogger. I've averaged one post every other day over 5 years. I *am* a fairly prolific writer and have been for a long time (at one time, I had three print magazine columns in addition to my books, blog, and monthly ejournal). The blogging is just a piece of that.

I started a blog because I thought it would be amusing and that I might have things to say that didn't belong elsewhere. I've kept doing it because it's still fun and because I still have readers and, every so often, comments. I'd say having fun, expressing myself in a more informal and shorter manner than elsewhere, and sharing insights are all good reasons.

NT: *Would you like to offer any words of encouragement, guidance, or direction for new bloggers? Any caveats?*

WC: If you have something to say, you will reach an audience—and if you run out of things to say, there's no shame in letting a blog go fallow for a season or cease entirely. I recommend WordPress as a platform—either hosted at wordpress.com or as software on your own platform; you'll find a steady migration to WordPress by libloggers and others, for good reasons. If you think you're going to be serious about blogging, you might want a domain name and a good host (LISHost is a great place to be), although I didn't bother with my own domain name.

There's always room for another voice—but don't expect a huge audience out of the gate and don't expect lots of comments on most posts. Oh, and don't expect big bucks from ads in your blog. I'm sure it must happen somewhere, but when I had Google

AdSense ads, the revenue was so tiny as compared to the nuisance of having those ads in the window that I discontinued them—and, in fact, there were so few clickthroughs that the only check I ever received was after shutting down ads.

Endnotes

1. Interactive Advertising Bureau, "IAB Platform Status Report: User Generated Content, Social Media, and Advertising—An Overview," April 2008, accessed August 3, 2011 www.iab.net/media/file/2008_ugc_platform.pdf.

2. Debbie Weil, "Top Twenty Definitions of Blogging," WordBiz Report, accessed August 3, 2011, www.wordbiz.com/archive/20blogdefs.shtml.

3. Jay Rosen, "The Weblog: An Extremely Democratic Form in Journalism," PressThink, March 8, 2004, accessed August 3, 2011, archive.pressthink.org/2004/03/08/weblog_demos.html.

4. Ellyssa Kroski, *Web 2.0 for Librarians and Information Professionals* (New York: Neal-Schuman, 2008), 16.

5. David Sifry, "Sifry's Alerts: The State of the Live Web, 2007," Sifry's Alerts, April 5, 2007, accessed June 16, 2011, www.sifry.com/alerts/archives/000493.html.

6. Phillip Winn, "State of the Blogosphere 2008: Introduction," Technorati, August 21, 2009, accessed August 3, 2011, technorati.com/blogging/article/state-of-the-blogosphere-introduction.

7. "User Generated Content Draws Fans," eMarketer, February 3, 2009, accessed August 3, 2011, www.emarketer.com/Article.aspx?R=1006895.

8. Winn, "State of the Blogosphere 2008."

9. Marshall Kirkpatrick, "Technorati Numbers Indicate Blogging Is Niche and Slowing," ReadWriteWeb, September 22, 2008, accessed August 3, 2011, www.readwriteweb.com/archives/state_of_the_blogosphere_2008.php.

10. Walt Crawford, "The Liblog Landscape 2007–2008: A Lateral Look," *Cites & Insights: Crawford at Large* 9 (June 2009): 1.

11. Harry McCracken, "25 Best Blogs 2011," *Time* magazine, June 6, 2011, accessed August 3, 2011, www.time.com/time/specials/packages/article/0,28804,2075431_2075447,00.html.

12. Dave Navarro, "The Dark Side of Blogging: When Free Gets Ugly," Launch Coach, February 25, 2010, accessed August 3, 2011, www.thelaunchcoach.com/the-dark-side-of-blogging-when-free-gets-ugly.

13. Paula Hane, "Blogs Are a Natural for Librarians," NewsLink, October 2001, accessed August 3, 2011, www.infotoday.com/newslink/newslink0110.htm.

14. Laurel A. Clyde, "Library Weblogs," *Library Management* 25, no. 4/5 (2004): 183.

15. Laurel A. Clyde, "Weblogs? Are You Serious?" *The Electronic Library* 22 (2004): 390.

16. Karen Schneider, email message to author, April 9, 2010.

17. Michael Stephens, "Modeling the Role of Blogging in Librarianship" (doctoral dissertation, University of North Texas, 2007), p. 74.

18. Ibid., 79.

19. Meredith Farkas, "2007 Survey of Biblioblogosphere: Blog Demographics," Information Wants to Be Free, September 7, 2007, accessed August 3, 2011, meredith.wolfwater.com/wordpress/2007/09/07/2007-survey-of-the-biblio blogosphere-blog-demographics.

20. New York Public Library, "Policy on Patron-Generated Content," accessed August 3, 2011, www.nypl.org/policy-patron-generated-web-content.

21. Noa Aharony, "Librarians and Information Scientists in the Blogosphere: An Exploratory Analysis," *Library & Information Science Research* 31 (2009): 177.

22. Charles Jones, email message to author, May 12, 2010.

23. Steffen Moller, "Measuring Blog Success: Not Necessarily in the Comments," Steffen Moller, April 17, 2009, accessed August 3, 2011, steffenmoller.wordpress.com/2009/04/17/measuring-blog-success-not-necessarily-in-the-comments.

24. Avinash Kaushik, "Six Recommendations for Measuring Your Success," Occam's Razor, November 19, 2007, accessed August 3, 2011, www.kaushik.net/avinash/2007/11/blog-metrics-six-recommendations-for-measuring-your-success.html.

25. Stephens, "Modeling the Role of Blogging," 79.

26. Juan Carlos Perez, "Three Minutes: Fired Google Blogger," *PC World*, February 16, 2005, accessed June 16, 2011, www.pcworld.com/article/119715/three_minutes_fired_google_blogger.html.

27. "Plain Layne (and Other Fake Bloggers)," Museum of Hoaxes, June 22, 2004, accessed August 3, 2011, www.museumofhoaxes.com/hoax/weblog/plain_layne.

28. Katie Hafner, "A Beautiful Life, an Early Death, a Fraud Exposed," *New York Times*, May 31, 2001, accessed August 3, 2011, www.nytimes.com/2001/05/31/technology/a-beautiful-life-an-early-death-a-fraud-exposed.html?pagewanted=all.

29. "Fake Mazda Blog Site Pulled," Marketing Vox, November 1, 2004, accessed August 3, 2011, www.marketingvox.com/fake_mazda_blog_site_pulled-017277.

30. See, for example, "Mazda's Blog+Viral Campaign Falls Flat," Marketing Vox, www.marketingvox.com/mazdas_blogviral_campaign_falls_flat-017206, and B.L. Ochman, "Mazda Pulls Fake Blog. Was It a Response to Bloggers' Criticism?" What's Next? Blog, www.whatsnextblog.com/2004/10/mazda_pulls_fake_blog_was_it_.

31. Frank Ahrens, "Puppets Emerge as Internet's Effective, and Deceptive, Salesmen," *Washington Post* (October 7, 2006): D1.

32. Ann Smarty, "Blog Search Engines: The Complete Overview," *Search Engine Journal*, October 24, 2008, accessed August 3, 2011, www.searchenginejournal.com/blog-search-engines-the-complete-overview/7856.

Chapter 4

Wikis

Information professionals have been quick to adapt to and employ many Web 2.0 tools, but one that hasn't quite caught fire is the use of wikis. Meredith Farkas's Library Success: A Best Practices Wiki (www.libsuccess.org) is probably one of the most successful, and Meredith is a prominent proponent of wikis. In *Social Software in Libraries* (Information Today, Inc., 2007), she tells us, "At their most basic, wikis are spaces for quick and easy web editing and publishing. At their best, they can be true community resources that position a library as an online hub of its local community."[1] It's true, wikis have many features that should make them one of the most frequently used tools in information centers. Wikis are web-based and can be accessed from anywhere on the internet. Work done in a wiki is asynchronous (a good thing inasmuch as individuals can work independently and still collaborate). Also, the learning curve is not very steep; users don't need to be technically proficient, a feature that certainly lowers barriers for contributions.

Yet Samuel Kai-Wah Chu's research on wikis in academic libraries (a survey with a sample of 60 libraries and an 80 percent response rate) showed that 16 libraries (33.3 percent) used wikis for intralibrary work, four (8.3 percent) were experimenting with wikis, and 13 (27.1 percent) were considering using wikis. The remaining 15 libraries (31.3 percent) had no intention of implementing a wiki. The 16 users listed the following reasons for using wikis for intralibrary work: to co-construct webpages, to enhance information sharing among librarians, to archive different versions of work online, and to expedite updating of webpages.[2]

Web 2.0 tools, as seen through librarians' lenses, can help us interact with our community and, in so doing, reinforce the relevance of libraries. Unfortunately, wikis do not appear to be seen as the appropriate tool for accomplishing this. Matthew Bejune's investigation into library wikis demonstrated that, of the 35 libraries in his study, 16 (45.7 percent) used wikis for interlibrary collaboration, 11 (31.4 percent) for collaboration among library staff, five (14.3 percent) for collaboration between library staff and patrons, and three (8.6 percent) for collaboration among patrons.[3]

These last two categories seem hopeful, don't they? I was eager to see the wikis that supported collaboration between library patrons, but of the three Bejune listed on the website companion to his article (www.librarywikis. pbworks.com), Online Computer Library Center, Inc.'s (OCLC's) was defunct, another (www.seedwiki.com/wiki/butler_wikiref) yielded a blank webpage, and the remaining wiki's most recent 500 entries had been edited by the wiki administrator.

Bejune's group of wikis that represented collaboration between library staff and patrons, although expanded since he published the article, was similarly lugubrious. The first on the list was a subject guide that could be edited only by librarians. The second was a library homepage. The third wiki, which actually had some good content, had not been edited since July 2009. The fourth landed on a blank page. The next three were subject guides (one apparently a well-kept secret inasmuch as there were a few recurring usernames), followed by another homepage. I suppose in a very liberal interpretation of collaboration, subject guides and homepages rendered by librarians using wiki software could be considered collaborative because they are *intended* to be used by patrons.

Information professionals can successfully use wikis within their organizations as knowledge bases and for other internal purposes, but wikis do not appear to be the best vehicle for an active conversation with their clientele. Perhaps this is as it should be—after all, isn't there potential liability in allowing anyone to edit the wiki (think spam and misinformation)? Bejune sums it up this way: "Historically libraries have been repositories of information, and this remains a [concept that is] pervasive and difficult … to change—libraries are frequently seen simply as places to get books. In this scenario, the librarian is a gatekeeper that a patron interacts with to get a book. … It is also worthy to note that the relationship is one-way—the patron needs the assistance of the librarian, not the other way around. Viewed in these terms, this is not a collaborative situation."[4]

The Library Success wiki is not just an exemplary gateway to content about libraries and librarianship; it also provides us with a good sampling of library wikis (it links to 44 of them). I explored some of those listed at www.lib success.org/index.php?title=Wikis and found that most of them are effectively sharing information. Some of the liveliest include the San Diego Librarians Wiki (www.snozzcumber.com/wiki/index.php?title=San_Diego_ Librarians_Wiki), the Michigan Libraries Wiki/Indiana Libraries Wiki (www.mlcnet.org/wiki), Archivopedia (www.archivopedia.com), and John Hubbard's LISWiki (www.liswiki.org); John is also known for his website Library Link of the Day (www.tk421.net/librarylink). For another list, try the Tarver Library 2.0 Program website (www.tarverlibrary.wetpaint.com/page/

Examples+of+libraries+using+Wikis). If you are considering implementing a wiki, check out WikiMatrix (www.wikimatrix.org), where you can compare wiki software. My personal choice is Wikispaces (www.wikispaces.com), which is free.

Even though wikis may not work for collaborating with library patrons, we can still use them to leverage more use of our collections, and we can do it by becoming collaborators with the most well-known wiki in the world: Wikipedia.

Conversation With Meredith Farkas

Courtesy of Adam Farkas

The general public probably associates the word *wiki* with Wikipedia, but librarians probably associate the term with Meredith Farkas, author of *Social Software in Libraries*. Farkas is a librarian; a blogger (www.meredith.wolfwater.com/wordpress); author of the monthly "Technology in Practice" column in *American Libraries*; winner of several commendations, including the Library and Information Technology Association/Library Hi Tech Award (2009); and an enthusiastic advocate of Web 2.0 technologies in libraries. I had the opportunity to ask her some questions in a recent email exchange.

Nick Tomaiuolo: *Meredith, I want your perspective on wikis and their use in libraries. Tell me about Library Success (www.libsuccess. org), the wiki you started. I noticed it has more than 1,000 registered users, who include software developers, businesspeople, library school students, and information professionals from the National Institutes of Health, as well as public and academic librarians. And they aren't just from the U.S. and Canada; they are from New Zealand, the U.K., Portugal, Malaysia, and Australia. What attracts so many people from so many different places to the Library Success wiki?*

Meredith Farkas: The wiki has more than just 1,000 registered users, though it's difficult to gauge exactly how many are legitimate users adding content. When users register, we hope that they will add their name to the Wiki User List (www.libsuccess.org/index.php?title=Wiki_User_List), but many do not do so and simply edit the wiki without identifying themselves. There are 7,464 registered users total, though many of those are spambots.

A lot of people see the wiki as a useful place to collect knowledge on their topic(s) of interest. If librarians are interested in collecting a list of all the libraries that do something (have mobile websites, offer gaming programs, etc.), the wiki is a great place to do that because anyone can contribute. While some other library wikis have cropped up over the years, it makes a lot more sense to contribute to a large, thriving wiki since the whole purpose of a wiki is to have a central repository of knowledge. I think it also helps that the wiki wasn't created by an organization or company. Because of that, people feel as if it belongs to the profession as a whole, and I do everything I can to convey that message in the way the wiki is moderated.

NT: *When I first registered at Library Success, I immediately went to (and created and edited text in) the Search Engines in the Information Sharing and Education category. I was pretty enthusiastic. Please talk about some of the areas of the wiki that you feel are well-used. Could you also talk about some of the areas that you personally find especially interesting or helpful?*

MF: I find so many useful resources created by others on the wiki, but there are a few pages that have received a tremendous number of contributions and have become the go-to resources for those subjects. The Online Reference page (www.libsuccess.org/index .php?title=Online_Reference), and its many subpages that have cropped up as the topic grew, is the authoritative guide to who is providing online reference services and what products are available to provide those services.

As libraries have become increasingly interested in mobile library services, the M-Libraries page (www.libsuccess.org/index. php?title=M-Libraries) has grown to become an oft-cited resource in many presentations on the subject.

Many passionate teen librarians have made the pages linked from the Services for Teens page (www.libsuccess.org/index.php? title=Services_for_Teens) a valuable resource for librarians looking to provide services for their teenage population. The Urban Fiction/Street Lit page (www.libsuccess.org/index.php?title=Urban_ Fiction/Street_Lit/Hip_Hop_Fiction_Resources_for_Librarians) is one of the largest and most visited on the site.

As different topics come into vogue, I have seen pages receive lots of attention and contributions from users. As those topics are replaced by new "hot topics," I see the contributions dwindle. You can see that with the gaming-related pages. In 2006 and 2007, there were hundreds of contributions to those pages, but since that time, the contributions have slowed to a trickle.

NT: *In your book* Social Software in Libraries, *you say librarians should build an online presence because that's where our patrons are. We probably all agree that wikis, which allow rapid creation, editing, and publishing, would be one place to meet our patrons online. Yet I've been looking at the literature on wikis and librarians, and I've decided that librarians frequently collaborate with one another via wikis, but there appears to be a challenge in attracting our patrons' participation in library wikis. I believe you mentioned this concerning Chad Boeninger's Biz Wiki (www.library.ohiou.edu/subjects/bizwiki) at Ohio University. In a 2007 article, Matthew Bejune reported that only 14.3 percent of the libraries he surveyed noted collaboration between patrons and librarians. Why is this such a big challenge?*

MF: The vast majority of libraries are using wikis behind the scenes to collaborate organizationally or to collaborate with others in the profession. Some others have been created as an easy way for libraries to create resources for their patrons, since people do not need to know HTML to edit a wiki. Very few libraries have created wikis designed to collect knowledge from patrons. There are a few reasons for this. Some libraries worry about the moderation burden that would come with such a resource; librarians would have to ensure that patrons were adding appropriate content. I believe the biggest reason, though, is that not every patron population would be interested in contributing to such a resource.

Chad Boeninger's Biz Wiki was initially designed with the hope that business students and faculty would add content, but he eventually ended up closing it to contributions because there was no interest. I don't think that means that collaboratively developed wiki resource guides can't work; I think that we have to work with a motivated population. If you see a population that is already sharing resources through discussion boards or some other electronic means, they already have interest in that activity, and providing a wiki gives them a better organized and more permanent tool for doing that. To ask a group of people who have no interest in sharing resources with one another to take the time to add content to a wiki is a futile task. It's important that we look at the culture of the group we want to work with and see if the sharing of resources is something they value.

NT: *Why has Wikipedia caught on with the general public and the hardware and software world (Ward Cunningham's Portland Pattern Repository [www.c2.com/ppr] enjoys success), but library patrons appear reluctant to contribute to library wikis? Meredith, perhaps you totally disagree with this assertion, and if so, correct me and provide insight for the readers.*

MF: There have been very few wikis that were actually created to solicit content from patrons, so I'm not sure that we can say that patrons are reluctant to contribute content to library wikis. You can certainly say that previous attempts to get patrons involved in content creation using wikis have failed. That being said, I think there's a very good reason why a library patron would rather contribute content to Wikipedia than to a wiki for his or her library. When you are contributing to Wikipedia, you are contributing to a large, thriving community, and you know that your contribution will be seen by people all over the world. You are contributing to something for the world, not just for your library. A library wiki is going to have fewer contributors and less content, and most people don't want to waste their time contributing to a wiki that doesn't have a large community. While people might see value in a library wiki that collects uniquely local information—like things to do in the community, community history, and so forth—I don't know of any wikis like that that have been created by libraries (though many of the local wikis that have not been created by libraries are thriving).

NT: *In addition to the Library Success wiki, what are some of the most important librarian-to-librarian wikis?*

MF: A lot of wikis have been created to share knowledge among librarians, but very few of them are still being updated regularly. One of the most successful was the Palinet Leadership Network, which thrived under the editorial directorship of Walt Crawford, who has worked with OCLC; it was a first rate resource for three years before becoming defunct in June 2010. The Michigan Libraries Wiki (www.mlcnet.org/wiki) and the San Diego Librarians Wiki (snozzcumber.com/wiki/index.php?title= Surf,_Sand,_Books,_Stuff_Wiki) are good examples, too. There may be other great examples out there that I'm unaware of. There have been instruction wikis, digitization wikis, and other niche wikis created that don't exist anymore or haven't been updated in years. I think this lends credence to the notion that beyond large repositories (like Wikipedia or Library Success), wikis focused on local concerns are the only ones that have a good chance of being successful. For issues that impact the entire professional population, it makes more sense to use a single repository.

UContent, Information Professionals, and Wikipedia

Information professionals probably know of many sources that have criticized Wikipedia, but such a litany provides a good backstory. This free online collaborative encyclopedia constantly takes heat from both scholars and the general public. One information scientist wrote, "Wikipedia poses as an encyclopedia when by no stretch of the definition can it be termed such, therefore it is subject to regulation."[5] One health professional entitled her editorial, "When searching for the evidence, stop using Wikipedia!"[6] and a Middlebury College professor mandated that his students refrain from citing the wiki.[7]

Conversely, one author called for scholarly publications to modernize their peer-review methods to emulate Wikipedia.[8] And in one study pitting Wikipedia against *Encyclopaedia Britannica*, reviewers called the clash of the titans a stalemate.[9] One writer has even reminded us that the venerable *Oxford English Dictionary* began as an old-school, paper-based wiki.[10]

There are undoubtedly a number of reasons to be skeptical of wikis in general. One view is that a handful of editors may be "tag teaming" articles, using different logins to make it seem as though collaboration is occurring. Furthermore, computer scientist Jaron Lanier asserts, "Wikipedia, for instance, works on what I call the Oracle illusion, in which knowledge of the human authorship of a text is suppressed in order to give the text superhuman validity. Traditional holy books work in precisely the same way and present many of the same problems."[11] And as computer engineer Uche Ogbuji says, "It's a darling of those who believe that opening up data for free use, reuse, and contribution by users advances society and civilization. It's the very devil to those who believe that such open data leads to a mess of unreliable and uneven knowledge, and it's a gift to outright kooks and spammers."[12]

Through-the-Roof Usage

Farhad Manjoo, a journalist for the *New York Times*, *Time* magazine, and Slate online magazine, noted that computer scientists studying Wikipedia found the site's growth had peaked in March 2007; editors were beginning to drop out of the project.[13] But a month later, the Pew Internet & American Life Project found the site "popular among the well-educated" and reported that 36 percent of American adults with computers use Wikipedia.[14] As recently as March 2010, a paper in the peer-reviewed online journal First Monday stated that college students continued to frequently use the free encyclopedia.[15]

Wikipedia may not be the No. 1 site on the web, but it's consistently near or in the top 10. Internet traffic-measuring firms also ranked it high throughout 2010 and 2011: Hitwise at 17, comScore at 12, and Alexa at 7.[16,17,18] I teach library skills classes, and during the past several years, I've asked more than 100 students to compare a Wikipedia article with an online *Encyclopaedia Britannica* article; their preferences split right down the middle.

Analyze these numeric findings and you can see why teachers who try to keep the lid on student use of Wikipedia are engaged in a fool's errand. Looking at it another way, imagine what it would be like to contribute to some of the most widely read articles in the world. Imagine writing for an audience of well-educated computer users who potentially access English Wikipedia contributions 5.4 million times a month.[19,20]

If you believe that Wikipedia holds a great deal of potential, you're in good company, because no less a luminary than Joseph Janes, *American Libraries* columnist and founder of the Internet Public Library, agrees with you.[21] In 2010, the Stanton Foundation of New York City, which had given funds to the Wikimedia Foundation in the past, awarded a $1.2 million grant to the overseeing body of Wikipedia so that the free encyclopedia could attract scholars to write and edit articles in the complicated subject area of public policy. In October 2011, the Stanton Foundation followed this up by awarding Wikimedia $3.6 million—its largest grant ever.[22]

Subscribers to the "Got lemons? Make lemonade!" maxim can count themselves among many who urge us to use Wikipedia as a point of departure for teaching information evaluation skills to our communities. The late Roy Rosenzweig, American historian at George Mason University, went one better, not only calling on his colleagues to use the encyclopedia to teach students better research skills, but inviting them to make the existing free resources better.[23] And that is exactly what some librarians have been doing.

Libraries Using Wikis

University of North Texas Libraries

Dreanna Belden works at the University of North Texas (UNT) Libraries (www.library.unt.edu), which offers the digitized collection Portal to Texas History. Methods of outreach being what they are, Belden observed that librarians are often consigned to promoting their materials via newsletters, press releases, and workshops. Considering these vehicles somewhat less than optimal, Belden had a quintessential "emperor has no clothes" moment when she asked, in an article for *Internet Reference Services Quarterly* (*IRSQ*), "Are we just kidding ourselves?"[24] She continued, "Social networks provide powerful mechanisms for connecting libraries with information seekers." Though it's undecided whether social networks in general can facilitate user–library connections (the University of Wisconsin's Digital Collections Center, described later, rejected Facebook and YouTube), Wikipedia stands out as a resource with which libraries can cooperate.

The UNT Libraries began its involvement with Wikipedia in October 2005. Belden noticed that if she executed Google searches for subjects in the Portal to Texas History, she usually encountered a Wikipedia article on the subject in the first page of results. This logic followed: 1) Users invariably search Google, and 2) for any given search, these users quickly find a link to a Wikipedia article in Google's results. Knowing that users embrace Wikipedia and would follow the Google reference to the online encyclopedia, Belden deduced that the next logical step was to use Wikipedia to connect users with the Portal to Texas History. She accomplished this by placing links to the Portal to Texas History in the appropriate Wikipedia articles. This would potentially promote the library collection, with the reciprocal benefit of infusing Wikipedia content with more authority.

The result? Belden edited 700 Wikipedia articles, placing external links that referred to digitized items in the Portal to Texas History. These links effectively added authority and content to the Wikipedia articles. Additionally, Belden reported that click-through traffic referred by Wikipedia accounted for a staggering 48 percent of visitors to the portal; Google referrals accounted for only 16.68 percent. So the links not only helped the Wikipedia articles but also helped the Portal to Texas History's usage. Belden provides more answers about her work with Wikipedia in a sidebar in this chapter.

University of Washington Libraries

Ann Lally and her colleagues at the University of Washington Libraries (www.lib.washington.edu) also recognized that Google searches frequently drive users to Wikipedia. To push information to a resource that individuals will likely use when doing research, the University of Washington Libraries' Digital Initiatives (UWDI) program (www.lib.washington.edu/digital) started a project explicitly meant to "integrate the UW Digital Collections into the information workflow of our students by inserting links into the online encyclopedia Wikipedia."[25] In May 2006, UWDI began to methodically match its 120,000 image, text, and audio files to Wikipedia articles. After determining precisely what subjects were represented by items in its collection, librarians searched Wikipedia for related articles. The UWDI established a standard format for its links, adding them to the appropriate section of a corresponding article. Lally stated, "In a few instances, there were no articles in Wikipedia that corresponded to the subject matter of a collection or the subject was not adequately covered, so it was necessary to write a new article."

UWDI's effort is particularly noteworthy because it both added links and created articles. Moreover, it cross-referenced articles to related articles within Wikipedia. The report by Lally and colleague Carolyn Dunford (www.dlib.org/dlib/may07/lally/05lally.html) describes a number of recommended practices, as well as pitfalls to avoid, when adding content to the online encyclopedia. The staff at UWDI learned several important lessons: Users should officially register (i.e., create a login account), the links added should be described concisely, and the Watchlists and User Talk pages should be monitored.

Initially, the staff began editing pages as unregistered users, but unregistered users often find their links deleted. Registering seems to be a simple demonstration of one's commitment to the project. The article by Lally and Dunford also recommends—and other librarians who have edited pages agree—that if you edit an article, you should put it on your Watchlist. Watchlists are available only to registered users. Putting an article on your Watchlist allows you to monitor changes initiated by others. Although a User Talk page is not restricted to registered accounts, registering will help you keep your User Talk in one place in case you use several computers and visit Wikipedia from different internet protocol addresses. At the User Talk page, others, including people who may have problems with your submissions, can leave messages for you.

Although Lally didn't report the dramatic increase in traffic that the UNT Libraries experienced, she did cite sustained traffic originating from Wikipedia over the summer months, when most students are away from campus, as a credible indicator of Wikipedia's positive role in driving traffic to the UWDI collections.

University of Wisconsin Digital Collections Center

The University of Wisconsin Digital Collections Center (UWDCC; uwdc. library.wisc.edu) stores 57,000 images, 296 hours of audio (which may actually be less than my son's or daughter's iTunes libraries), and 1.6 million pages of text. Like Belden at UNT and Lally at the University of Washington, Melissa McLimans, UWDCC's digital services librarian, suspected that using Web 2.0 sites could place those materials before a worldwide audience. Her team considered, but rejected, reaching users through YouTube, Facebook, and Myspace. In 2005, they decided to place links in Wikipedia by identifying items in the Collections Center and adding links to existing Wikipedia articles.[26]

McLimans says, "We have written some articles, or parts of articles, but we spend most of our time adding links of the External Links sections of existing articles. For instance, UWDCC has a Carson Gulley Cookbook Collection that we've digitized. In the external links of the Carson Gulley article in Wikipedia, we edited the page and inserted a link so Wikipedia users can click through to our digitized cookbooks."

Six percent of visitors who arrive at the UWDCC begin their searches at Wikipedia. From December 1, 2007, to December 1, 2008, this accounted for 26,700 visitors. But everything didn't always go smoothly. McLimans stated that early in the experience, she was blocked from adding links and was even accused, in an exchange with a vitriolic Wikipedian, of using the online encyclopedia as a link farm. She learned quickly that one way to avoid having her edits deleted was to register at the site by creating a user account.

University of California's California Digital Library

Calisphere (www.calisphere.universityofcalifornia.edu) is the University of California's collection of more than 150,000 digitized items depicting California history. It includes digitized photographs, documents, newspaper pages, political cartoons, works of art, and transcribed oral histories—all designed for K–12 classrooms and free for anyone to use. Following in the University of Washington's footsteps, Camille Cloutier, an intern at California Digital Library, began her project by performing an in-depth subject analysis of carefully considered items in the collection. Her approach to Wikipedia was only to add links to the encyclopedia's articles if the California Digital Library items filled a unique gap. This overarching rule—to insert links where they are truly appropriate and serve a purpose distinct from any other link within an article—is pertinent, plus it satisfies the demands of those strident Wikipedians.

As for measuring the success of one's contributions, Cloutier and colleague Lena Zentall commented, "Longevity is one measure, and explicit approval or disapproval communicated by fellow editors is another. In the case of links, use is a third measure."[27]

Conversation With Dreanna Belden

Dreanna Belden is the University of North Texas (UNT) Libraries' assistant dean for external relations.

Nick Tomaiuolo: *Dreanna, would you please help clarify for our readers exactly what role you play at the UNT Libraries? How is placing links in Wikipedia and other social networking sites related to what you primarily do at the UNT?*

Dreanna Belden: I do a wide variety of work at the UNT Libraries: I write the grant applications for the digital projects unit, manage relationships with our 95 collaborative partners, handle new partnership inquiries, and create and launch any promotional items or ideas for the Portal to Texas History. I see adding Wikipedia links as a way of increasing awareness and providing access to our digital collections while providing people with relevant, authoritative content.

NT: *In the introduction to your IRSQ article, you do a good job of convincing librarians that press releases and other mechanisms such as partnerships with like-minded websites aren't optimal ways of driving traffic to library websites, because digital collections, which are often hidden in the deep web, are not as transparent as we'd like. What made you decide to start looking at social networking sites as possible places to help extend the reach of libraries?*

DB: The internet provides the greatest opportunity to grab people at the point that they are looking for information and to direct them to a place that can answer their question or provide more in-depth resources. I just decided to start experimenting with some different social networking sites to see what was most effective. Some of them proved to be more worthwhile than others.

NT: *In your article you often refer to the "staff at UNT." For example, you wrote that "Staff at UNT noticed that Google searches relevant to the material offered in the Portal to Texas History almost always turned up a Wikipedia article about the same topic ..." and you go on to say that "UNT staff edited more than 700 articles in Wikipedia ..."*

DB: Well, we are a "we" kind of department in digital projects, but for adding the Wikipedia links, it was more like me sitting at my computer at home and adding links! Some people play video games (well, I do that too), but for a few months I invested time in adding a lot of links to Wikipedia, especially when we saw the results from my early efforts.

The whole thing really started when I noticed Wikipedia results turning up in my Google searches. When we started the portal, I searched for websites or forums that I wanted to link to it. I emailed a lot of folks to let them know we were here offering free access to lesson plans and thousands of historical documents and to let them know they were welcome to link to the portal. I noticed Wikipedia results showing up in my searches and my research for grant applications. I wondered what would happen if we added some links from Wikipedia into the digital content offered on our site.

NT: *How formalized is the project?*

DB: It is not formalized at all! Early on I just decided to add some Wikipedia links to our content. It was fun, so I added several hundred links in the first 6 months or so. Through our web traffic software, we saw some significant impact on visits to our site.

NT: *How formalized is the commitment?*

DB: Well, after the first year of experimenting with this and viewing the great results we had, we added it to my performance agreement. My task is to "explore the use of Social Networking websites for opportunities to increase access to the Libraries' digital collections." The Method of Assessment is web traffic analysis, and following are the results for our 2009–2010 fiscal year:

Visits referred from Wikipedia and GenWeb (the U.S GenWeb Project, a genealogy site that has a page for every county in the U.S. with links to genealogy research materials at www.usgen web.org):
To the Portal to Texas History: 401,922
UNT Digital Collections: 813,567

These numbers represent a more than 100 percent increase over fiscal year 2007–2008, which was before placing the links in Wikipedia.

NT: *How was/is the work divided up?*

DB: I'm the only person in the library adding the Wikipedia links, but we reached a "saturation" stage a long time ago, in that I've linked to our collections in any way that seems useful and relevant and just add new collections as they are uploaded. It doesn't take very much time anymore.

NT: *Was the real work of the project (placing links in Wikipedia) done systematically, or was a "go for it" feeling driving it (with individuals placing links wherever and whenever they could)?*

DB: Definitely "go for it," which is pretty much the character in our unit. You try something, it works, you build on it—if it turns out to be a lame idea, that's OK too. I want to emphasize that I do put a lot of thought into whether linking things is useful to most Wikipedia users—and sometimes other editors will disagree or delete entries. But when adding links, I always try to ensure that we really have enough information about a topic to make it worth the user's time to click through.

NT: *How many human hours have been devoted to the project?*

DB: Wow, a lot. Early on I spent a significant amount of time doing it, but it takes much less time now. I'm guessing, but total time investment is perhaps 150 hours, with most of that coming up front in the first year. Now all I do is add links to new collections and materials we upload if a link makes sense. For instance, I already have a link to historic photos from Austin in the "Austin" Wikipedia article. If we upload another 1,000 images of Austin, the link is already there, so there is nothing for me to do. At this point I am only adding links for material that is new and unique or in a new geographical area for us.

NT: *I consider the project at UNT to be on a large scale. Besides this experience and the one reported by Ann Lally at the University of Washington, do you know of other libraries that are really work-ing on doing the same thing on any scale? If so, where are they and what types of collections do they have?*

DB: I'm not sure who else might be doing it, but I have talked about it with a number of people in digital libraries and suggested they try it. I know that the Chronicling America historic newspaper site at Library of Congress made a decision not to add any Wikipedia links because they know that Wikipedians may interpret these types of links as "spam." You would think that people editing articles would be looking for authoritative sources to bolster their usefulness! I can't figure out why people editing at Wikipedia are not doing more to link to digital library content and great resources such as Google Books.

NT: *In the* IRSQ *article, you reported that Wikipedia accounts for 48 percent of referring traffic, while Google (surprisingly) accounts for only 16.68 percent. How have these figures changed since the article was published?*

DB: Our traffic has more than doubled since I finalized that article, and we've done a lot to open up our content to Google and other search engines in the past few years, so the numbers really reflect those changes. The percentages have flip-flopped. Currently, much more of our traffic comes from Google, but the number of click-throughs from Wikipedia is still increasing slightly every year as we add new links. Our overall traffic has increased dramatically.

NT: *You placed valuable links in Wikipedia. I was particularly interested in the UNT Primary Source Adventure called "Iwo Jima: Forgotten Valor." I wanted to take a look at that resource, but I wanted to do it through Wikipedia, and my simple search on the words* Iwo Jima *brought up two possible articles. The UNT primary source site was, appropriately, linked to the second article, "Battle of Iwo Jima," and not the article on the island; this showed that the UNT Libraries staff are diligent about putting the links in the correct articles. After I found the "Iwo Jima: Forgotten Valor" link in Wikipedia, I clicked through to the PowerPoint presentation at UNT and found a transcript of Charles W. Lindbergh talking about his Air Force training. The transcript came from the UNT's Charles W. Lindbergh Oral History Collection. What are some of the other Wikipedia articles that have been edited, and what UNT content do they link to?*

DB: Here are a few examples of the types of links we have added: "Tanning" is a Wikipedia article about processing leather. We created a link to a government publication titled *Home Tanning of Leather and Small Fur Skins.* I guess that would be useful to the ultimate do-it-yourselfer. In the Norman Rockwell article, we provided a link to nine World War II posters that the artist designed. The Fort Wolters article covers the U.S. Army installation in Mineral Wells, Texas. It served as a training facility in World War II and then was the army's primary helicopter training school for several decades. We linked to 23 volumes of *A Pictorial History of Fort Wolters,* which has thousands of pictures in it. The Texas City Disaster is still the deadliest industrial accident in U.S. history. We created a link to over 300 photographs we have online that show the extent of the damage and the aftermath. We've also added in a lot of links that are geography-based at the county or city level.

NT: *In Wikipedia, references to the Portal to Texas History, which refer back to the UNT Libraries, often have two links. The first link goes to a specific part of the UNT digital collection (in the "Battle of Iwo Jima" article, there is a link to Iwo Jima: Forgotten Valor), then there is another link called From the Portal to Texas History.*

Ann Lally's article about the University of Washington's library outreach through Wikipedia said one prominent obstacle to infusing Wikipedia with credible information was that even authoritative links can be construed by Wikipedia editors as "self-promoting." I don't think a link to the entire Portal to Texas History indicates self-promotion, but this is the type of situation Lally describes as an obstacle to libraries.

Why do you think Wikipedia has permitted UNT to include a general link to the Portal in these articles? Have you had any "talks" with Wikipedia moderators or editors?

DB: Oh yes, and Ann is exactly right about that. I've had a few "talks" with Wikipedians, and they often see this type of linking as spam and "self-promoting." For some Wikipedians, it doesn't matter that our site is totally noncommercial and offers authoritative materials that are totally free for the public to use. I believe their official policy is that any linking to a site you are associated with is not allowed, but I disagree with it and add links anyway. I mean, we are a library! The fact that most of the links to our site remain on Wikipedia and are not removed tells me that most people find these to be useful.

As far as putting in two links, I just started formatting them that way and it's stuck. No one has said anything about it to me.

NT: *The UNT Libraries maintain an online government documents collection consisting of 10,200 Congressional Research Service reports. You've embedded 160 links within Wikipedia that refer users to these reports. But the Wikipedia articles you have worked on have widely different subject matter. You've put links to Gov Docs in Wikipedia articles about the spotted owl, teenage pregnancy, and the Gulf War. This is quite different from simply targeting articles in a subject area such as Texas history. It seems as* *though you (or someone) is carefully going through UNT's digital collections, one item at a time, and then locating the relevant article in Wikipedia. Is this the way it is actually done, or is there a less labor-intensive, automated solution to matching the contents of the collection with Wikipedia articles?*

DB: Early on, I did go through our content carefully to determine good matches for Wikipedia articles, but I didn't go through item by item. The Congressional Research Service reports do have a Browse by Subject page, so that made them a lot easier to conceptualize. For the portal and our other digital collections, we have a great metadata analysis tool on the back end that Mark Phillips created and that allows you to easily be able to look at the data in different ways. I can look at word clouds of subjects, titles, or other data fields to discover topical areas in which we have a lot of content. It's a visual representation of the data, so I can see that we have a lot of materials about a certain person or geographic area. I can then investigate whether that would be a good area or topic to link to from Wikipedia.

NT: In the IRSQ article (page 104), you write about many resources on the Alamo (and you say that links to the resources have been placed in Wikipedia). Try as I might, I do not see links to the UNT Libraries in either the article called "Battle of the Alamo" or the article "The Alamo." Did Wikipedia delete the links? Because what you've written about on page 104 ("Schoolchildren in California writing book reports on the Alamo use books, floor plans, and images from the Portal after discovering them through Wikipedia.") certainly indicates that links to UNT should appear in the "Battle of the Alamo" Wikipedia article. What do you think?

DB: Yes, it looks like someone deleted the link and many other links that used to be there. You can never count on the fact that what you put up will stay there. Wikipedia does not delete the links, but every article is up to the interpretation of anyone. If some stray Wikipedian thinks an external link is irrelevant, BAM! They will delete it without a thought. For example, we have digitized every Austin College yearbook from 1899 to 1950. Every page is there, and the entire collection is searchable. Most people would assume that this is a great resource for people who are interested in Austin College, and it is a noncommercial, free resource. Someone decided that all the external links in this article are a "link farm" and deleted all of them except the one to the official Austin College website. The same thing happened to the Abilene

Christian University article, and we have all of its yearbooks from 1916 to 2007 online.

When this happens, I don't even try to fight it anymore. I may go back in a few months and put the links back in, but I don't confront the person who did it. I found that while some people are reasonable, some just like to make it into a drubbing.

NT: *In the "old days," we just counted on old ways of promoting our collections and were satisfied. What is your overall internet traffic like now?*

DB: Google accounts for 47.97 percent of the traffic for the University of North Texas Digital Collections, and Wikipedia accounts for 11.66 percent. For the Portal to Texas History, Google accounts for 46.31 percent and Wikipedia accounts for 12.61 percent.

Grassier Roots

Efforts need not be on a colossal scale. Villanova's Falvey Library employed two graduate students to write brief biographical entries for Wikipedia and then link them to some of the library's digitized items.[28] For example, its Special Collections houses the Sherman-Thackara Collection. We all know General William Tecumseh Sherman, Union general in the Civil War, and may have read his autobiography, of which one historian said, "It was impossible for Sherman to write a dull word." But what about his daughter, Eleanor, and son-in-law, Alexander Montgomery Thackara? Their courtship letters are an interesting read in themselves. Since Wikipedia articles didn't exist for either lovebird, the Falvey Library grad students wrote them and augmented their content by linking to the digitized communiqués in the Falvey collection. (See the articles and external links at en.wikipedia.org/wiki/Alexander_ Montgomery_Thackara and en.wikipedia.org/wiki/Eleanor_Sherman_ Thackara.)

Similarly, Diane Madrigal, at the New York State Library, says, "I've been adding links to some of our digital documents in Wikipedia. In some cases I've just added a link to one of our documents in the External Links section of a related topic." As an example, Madrigal mentioned the external link to the New York State Library (en.wikipedia.org/wiki/John_Rocque). She adds, "In a few other cases, I've used information in one of our documents to contribute to Wikipedia articles, and then cited the document as a reference source. For instance, I added a link to a PDF at the New York State Library in the Notes section on Census Questions for the Wikipedia page called '1850 United

States Census' (see en.wikipedia.org/wiki/United_States_Census,_1850). Obviously this takes more time and effort. My intent is not just to improve Wikipedia content but also to increase use of our resources."[29]

Now I'm Doing It, Too!

I have also begun personal contributions to Wikipedia. They're on a small scale, though, I hope, useful. I work at a library named after Elihu Burritt, the "Learned Blacksmith" of New Britain, Connecticut. There is a Wikipedia article covering Burritt and an Elihu Burritt Archive in the special collections department at my library. My first adventure in editing the online encyclopedia, early in 2009, was to add an external link in Wikipedia to our archive. I went to the Wikipedia page for Elihu Burritt. I had already registered as a user, so I logged in and clicked Edit above the External Links section of the article and added a link to the specific page offering an inventory of primary source materials on Burritt in the special collections department at my library (see Figure 4.1).

I'm not quite certain who, if anybody, was viewing that page prior to my Wikipedia edit, but as Figure 4.2 shows, since I placed that link, 82.26 percent of page views have originated at Wikipedia. Since that edit I've gone to Wikipedia's Lemon Law article and placed links to video and audio files from the Connecticut Lemon Law Records at Central Connecticut State University (Connecticut was the first state to pass a "lemon law"). I've also

Figure 4.1   Register, log in, and begin placing external links that will lead Wikipedia users to other authoritative content—including your library's collection. [Courtesy of Wikipedia]

pointed Wikipedia readers to my institution's Veterans' History Project oral history files.

Consider the Library of Congress's photostream at the Commons on Flickr. With its images on the photo sharing site, traffic to the Library of Congress

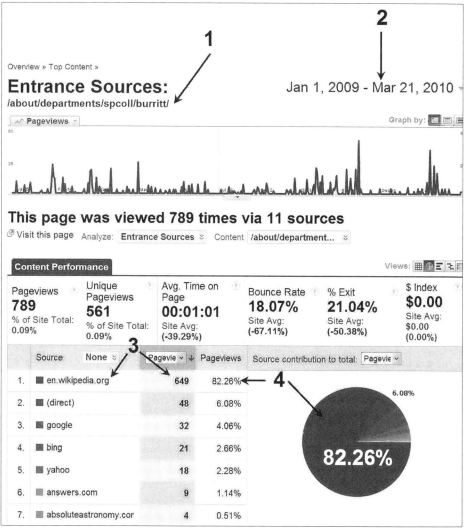

Figure 4.2   This image represents the web traffic going to the Elihu Burritt Special Collections page at the author's library (1). Since the author placed the link in the Wikipedia article in March 2010 (2), 649 hits came from Wikipedia (3), representing 82.26 percent of the overall traffic to the Elihu Burritt Special Collections page (4). [Courtesy of Google]

website increased dramatically—an average of 2,205 percent from 2007 to 2008, the year the Library of Congress uploaded its images.[30]

You may be asking, "If my library doesn't host digitized versions of historic monographs or a file of maps or electronic images of postcards, and even if I don't really have the time to begin writing articles from scratch for Wikipedia, can I still become involved?" After all, not every institution can offer the Langston Hughes Papers (Beinecke Library, Yale) or the JFK Assassination Records (National Archives) or documents concerning the Office of Scientific Intelligence (a precursor agency of the Central Intelligence Agency) or even the Core Historical Literature of Agriculture (Cornell). You can take whatever topics you are interested in, do some searching, discover some worthwhile sites, evaluate them for worthiness, and then add those links to the corresponding articles.

For example, on a trip to London, I toured one of Dr. Samuel Johnson's homes. I found the link to the museum and added the link to a specific page addressing the history of the house to the external links in the Samuel Johnson article in Wikipedia. Be careful not to add links to homepages for museums and similar institutions; add links only to specific content-rich pages. Wikipedians scowl at general links that can be construed as peripheral or promotional and will delete your work.

Quick Start Guide for Editing Wikipedia

1. Register as a user by clicking the Create Account link in the upper-right-hand corner of the English Wikipedia page (en.wikipedia.org). Users who create an account and log in when making edits have much less trouble with the people monitoring the pages, and that means fewer deletions of your work.

2. Consider what is in your collection (or the collections of others that you know about) and search Wikipedia for related articles.

3. Most successful links to library collections are placed in the External Links sections of articles.

4. To enhance your chances of nondeletion, remember to add links only to specific, content-rich pages of museums, libraries, and similar institutions.

Many Wikipedia users scrutinize edits to pages. They look even more closely at newly created articles. Unfortunately, the wiki is inherently subject to vandalism. The experience of librarians who have witnessed firsthand the tendency of some editors to take things to extremes emphasizes several dos and don'ts. Lena Zentall, project manager for discover and delivery at California Digital Library, wrote, "Malicious activity casts doubt on the validity of the information and discourages coordinated efforts by reliable sources to insert references and links."

Some Wikipedia editors concede that links to library materials are valuable but cite the Wikipedia policy that systematically adding links of any sort is considered spam. This is covered under External Link Spamming at the Wikipedia Project Page (en.wikipedia.org/wiki/Wikipedia:Spam#External_link_spamming), which states, "Although the specific links may be allowed under some circumstances, repeatedly adding links will in most cases result in all of them being removed." For more information see Part II, Chapters 5 through 10, in Phoebe Ayers, Charles Matthews, and Ben Yates, *How Wikipedia Works* (San Francisco: No Starch Press, 2008).

Please Have Your IDs Ready

There is at least one more "bibliographic" improvement that you can make to add solid information to Wikipedia with minimal effort. While investigating different ways information professionals might help expand and enhance end users' experiences in Wikipedia, I received a very useful email from Andy Havens, manager of Branding and Marketing Services at OCLC. Havens described appending WorldCat Identities links to existing Wikipedia articles.

Tom Hickey, OCLC Research's chief scientist, describes WorldCat Identities: "The idea of WorldCat Identities is simple: Create a summary page for every name in WorldCat. Since there are some 85 million records in WorldCat and nearly 20 million names mentioned somewhere, this is a large-scale data mining effort that would have been difficult even a few years ago. We are working with both personal and corporate names, so you can see a page for the Beatles, as well as the individual pages for John, Paul, George, and Ringo. Just working within WorldCat, there is a lot of information that can be associated with people. We show lists of the most common works written by the person and those written about them."[31]

What does this have to do with Andy Havens and, moreover, you and me? Havens likes the Beatles and is also interested in writer Neal Town Stephenson. For both entities, Havens has gone to Wikipedia, found the existing article entries, and added a link to a corresponding WorldCat Identities page for these topics. Wikipedia users at either the Beatles' or Neal

Stephenson's articles can click on the Wikipedia External Link that says "Works by or about Neal Stephenson in libraries (WorldCat catalog)" or "Works by or about The Beatles in libraries (WorldCat catalog)." At the bottom of either page, they will find links to WorldCat Identities pages. Figure 4.3 shows that I've gone to Dante Alighieri's Wikipedia article and added a link to his WorldCat Identities record. The WorldCat Identities template also automatically adds a link to the article about WorldCat within Wikipedia.

When I asked Havens if there were any large-scale plans to insert links to WorldCat Identities into Wikipedia, he responded, "We haven't done anything programmatic (since Wikipedia might interpret it as spamming/botting the encyclopedia—and that's forbidden). We'd have to figure out a way to take the millions of Identities and, somehow, put links to them in every matching Wikipedia entry. A colleague in OCLC Research mentioned that there were several thousand Wikipedia pages to which various folks (some librarians, some not, I'd assume) had added links to WorldCat Identities. OCLC Research has a way to count the references to WorldCat Identities in Wikipedia."[32]

Since learning about this maneuver from Havens and Hickey, I've done this to several Wikipedia articles, including articles about Elihu Burritt, V. S. Naipaul, Paul Theroux, David Byrne, Clete Boyer, Don DeLillo, Carrie Fisher, Ralph Vaughan Williams, Jethro Tull (the agriculturalist), Jethro Tull (the musical group), and Stephen Colbert. That covered some of my favorites, but in a nod to contemporary pop culture (and, I hope, younger users who consult Wikipedia frequently), I also added WorldCat Identities to the Wikipedia

Figure 4.3   An external link in the Wikipedia article for Dante refers users to WorldCat Identities to find more information in libraries. [Courtesy of Google]

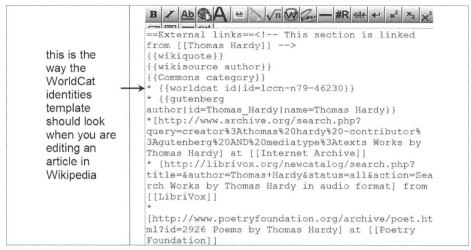

this is the way the WorldCat identities template should look when you are editing an article in Wikipedia

```
==External links==<!-- This section is linked
from [[Thomas Hardy]] -->
{{wikiquote}}
{{wikisource author}}
{{Commons category}}
* {{worldcat id|id=lccn-n79-46230}}
* {{gutenberg
author|id=Thomas_Hardy|name=Thomas Hardy}}
*[http://www.archive.org/search.php?
query=creator%3Athomas%20hardy%20-contributor%
3Agutenberg%20AND%20mediatype%3Atexts Works by
Thomas Hardy] at [[Internet Archive]]
* [http://librivox.org/newcatalog/search.php?
title=&author=Thomas+Hardy&status=all&action=Sea
rch Works by Thomas Hardy in audio format] from
[[LibriVox]]
*
[http://www.poetryfoundation.org/archive/poet.ht
ml?id=2926 Poems by Thomas Hardy] at [[Poetry
Foundation]]
```

Figure 4.4   You can use the WorldCat Identities template to edit your favorite Wikipedia articles. [Courtesy of Wikipedia]

articles for Taylor Swift, Flo Rida, Stephenie Meyer, Miley Cyrus, and (her brother Trace's band) Metro Station. And as soon as I completed these edits, I emailed the instructions to several other librarians. As a result, the Wikipedia articles for Albert Payson Terhune, Margaret Drabble, Rebecca West, Hunter S. Thompson, Steve Martin, and William Safire quickly received an external link to their respective WorldCat Identities.

Information professionals with a few minutes on their hands and favorite authors in mind should get crackin'. Editing a Wikipedia article to include WorldCat Identities is extremely easy. Figure 4.4 illustrates where the WorldCat Identities template should be placed when you're editing a Wikipedia article.

Adding WorldCat Identities and Project Gutenberg Links to a Wikipedia Article

To add OCLC WorldCat Identities:

1. Begin by searching WorldCat Identities at orlabs.oclc.org/identities.
2. Copy the "ID," i.e., the string after the last slash in the URL (for example, Victor Hugo's ID is lccn-n79–91479).
3. Insert it directly after id= in this template: {{worldcat id|id=YOURLCCNHERE}}. (The correct code for adding Victor Hugo is {{worldcat id|id= lccn-n79–91479}}.)

4. Find the relevant article in Wikipedia, scroll to the External Links section, and click [edit].

5. After the last listed external link, insert your updated WorldCat Identities template, preceded by an asterisk, just as it appears from {{ ... to ... }}.

6. Provide a brief edit summary (something like "small addition made; the article now links to an information page about the author in OCLC WorldCat") to appease the Wikipedians who may think about deleting the link.

7. Click Save Page.

If, by chance, you come upon an entity in WorldCat Identities that does not have the id= string in the URL, you can still copy whatever follows the part of the URL ending with /identities/ and add it to the string in the template. For example, flamenco guitarist Paco DeLucia does not have an id=, but instead, retrieving his Identities record yields the URL orlabs.oclc.org/identities/np-delucia,%20paco. I copied /np-delucia,%20paco into the template so that it read {{worldcat id|np-delucia,%20paco}}, edited Paco's page at Wikipedia, and it worked just fine!

You can find similar instructions at en.wikipedia.org/wiki/Template:Worldcat_id.

To add Project Gutenberg links:

1. Find the article for the author in Wikipedia. Scroll down to the Works or External Links section to confirm that the link to Project Gutenberg doesn't already exist.

2. Go to www.gutenberg.org.

3. Search for your author to confirm that his or her works are held by Project Gutenberg.

4. Take note of the correct spelling of the name.

5. Use this template: {{gutenberg author|id=Firstname+Lastname | name=FirstnamespaceLastname}}. The correct code for adding Dante Alighieri would be as follows: {{gutenberg author|id=Dante+Alighieri | name=Dante Alighieri}}.

6. Return to Wikipedia and edit the appropriate section.

7. Add the "optional" edit summary to satisfy whoever might be inclined to delete your link (for example: "Link added that goes to free electronic texts by the author at Project Gutenberg").

8. Click Save Page.

Your Unproctored Final

There are so few restrictions for creating or adding content at Wikipedia that anyone and everyone heeds the siren call to chip in. Junior high school students are doing it. College kids are doing it. Professors are doing it. Information pros are doing it. In addition, doing it creates a win–win situation: The content we place in Wikipedia attracts users and gives our collections or favorite sites more use.

There are at least three types of content we can contribute: 1) links to digitized items in library collections, 2) articles on topics in which we're personally interested and about which we possess some knowledge (or articles on topics represented in our collection but not present in Wikipedia), and 3) links to WorldCat Identities (and, for that matter, full texts at Project Gutenberg).

It makes sense for us to contribute, because not only can we offer access to substantive information, we can also bring our collections back into the spotlight. It takes only a few minutes to add your handpicked link to Wikipedia. So create your login and start editing. There isn't a good reason not to.

Conversation With Phoebe Ayers

Courtesy of Ross Sage

Phoebe Ayers is one of the authors of *How Wikipedia Works*. A major proponent of wikis, she is active on 19 public wiki sites and was the conference chair of WikiSym2010 (an international conference on wikis and other collaborative technologies). She presently specializes in engineering and computer science reference work at the University of California (Davis). [Phoebe's photo is licensed under a Creative Commons Attribution-Share Alike 3.0 Unported License. Photo courtesy of Ross Sage, Wikipedia Commons CC-BY-SA-3.0.]

Nick Tomaiuolo: *Phoebe, as a Wikipedia editor and a librarian, you must have many insights into the project. Please give me your overall impression and thoughts.*

Phoebe Ayers: Wikipedia is an extraordinary project. By any measure, it is the largest reference work ever to be created, undoubtedly the most multilingual, the most free and open, and certainly the most accessed reference site online today, outranking all other websites except for the most popular search portals and social networking sites. And amazingly, all this content has been developed by volunteers, working under a handful of basic behavioral and content guidelines but without any top-down editorial leadership or control. On Wikipedia, the community of editors develops not only content but also, through discussion, trial, and iteration, the standards to which they edit articles. And all of this has happened very quickly. Wikipedia was founded in 2001, but the site didn't really take off until 2003, when successive waves of new editors and the content they contributed helped cement the site as a useful reference resource.

NT: *One thing I didn't like about Wikipedia when I first began to think about it is that the articles could always be under revision and, therefore, weren't necessarily "correct" at any given time. What about that?*

PA: The thing to remember is that the whole site is a work in progress. The openness of Wikipedia is in large part grounded in a belief that not only can everyone contribute something to the endeavor, but also that all content can continue to be improved. Every article is a draft. Some articles are excellent, having been worked over by dozens of committed writers, editors, and researchers who have produced work that rivals the best general encyclopedias, while other articles are simply beginnings, "stubs" that contain little content, or possibly even pieces that don't comply with Wikipedia content guidelines, either because the authors were unaware of [the guidelines] or because the article is still getting there, waiting for an editor to come along and take the page under his or her wing.

NT: *You're an official Wikipedia editor. Tell me about editing Wikipedia.*

PA: Well, the first point is that there are no "official" editors! If you sign up with the site and start working on articles, you're considered an editor. It is this basic task—a volunteer taking up an article that looks interesting, or that [the volunteer is] knowledgeable about, or that simply needs some work, and then improving grammar, adding missing content, and adding and checking references for accuracy—that makes up the heart of what goes on in Wikipedia. And every task can be further broken down. Many editors specialize. (I personally enjoy researching and adding references, even for topics I don't know much about—I am a librarian, after all—and doing some maintenance work, merging articles that are accidental duplicates of one another, or doing copyediting.) Other editors enjoy adopting a single article and bringing it up to the highest standards they can, while others keep an eye on new contributions, while still others add those new contributions, trying to reduce the missing articles lists. Still others work primarily on the "back-end" of the community, working on technical development, discussing policies or doing outreach. All of these individuals, whether they fix a typo occasionally or write pages from scratch, are classed as "editors," and with few exceptions they all have the same privileges—to work on Wikipedia, as long as their changes improve the encyclopedia.

NT: *What about my concerns that the articles are never finished and that so many people have too much input? The old saying goes, "Too many cooks …"*

PA: It's this unevenness that I think gives most librarians pause. We like to be able to say that a source is good or [that] it isn't. We can't do this for Wikipedia. It is not a monolithic source, any more than the community of hundreds of thousands of volunteer editors constitutes a monolithic editorial board. Another common objection is that it's difficult, and usually impossible, to know whether any particular editor knows what he or she is talking about when adding content. Editors aren't vetted for their credentials the way they are in academic publishing; this is seen as part of the site's open culture, less a flaw than a prominent success.

NT: *What are your recommendations for those of us who, as librarians and teachers, want to evaluate an article?*

PA: What anyone who wants to evaluate a Wikipedia article needs to do is go back to the text, to the individual article in question, and ask these questions:

- Is this content accurate? Does it match up with what multiple outside reputable references say is true?
- Are those references good quality? Are they *likely* to know what they are talking about?
- How's the writing style? Does it match Wikipedia's standards?
- Is this the work of only one or of many Wikipedia editors? Can you tell who they are? (This information is provided through the History tab.)

Please note that these bulleted points are a very brief summary of Chapter 4, "Understanding and Evaluating an Article" of *How Wikipedia Works*.

Now, where librarians have an exceptional role to play, in my opinion, is in the first two points. We know how to find and check references better than just about anyone. So why don't we? This peer-review-through-referencing is one of the hardest and most pressing tasks on Wikipedia today, and we are uniquely well-equipped to do it.

NT: *Not sure if it's "If you can't beat 'em, join 'em" or "I want to buttress the content," but I know several librarians and professors who won't even mention the word Wikipedia except in disdain.*

PA: For librarians who want to help out, the question arises, Why work on Wikipedia at all? Why even bother with a project that doesn't meet our standards? And my answer is, Because it's important. Wikipedia is idealistic, a nonprofit organization that aims to do the impossible—collect all human knowledge in all languages—and present it in an accessible, free, and open fashion. Moreover, our patrons are using it, and they are doing so because it is the best quickly accessible store of basic information online today. Why would we *not* want to make that better? And while we're at it, we should teach our patrons about it, about how to evaluate articles, about how to cite properly (hint: the "cite" link on the left-hand sidebar), and other tricks and tips they may not know. Wikipedia is a fabulous laboratory for learning and teaching about research, collaborative work, copyright (and by extension, scholarly publishing), and internet content and culture.

However, it can also be difficult to participate in. As one might expect for a complex project with so many contributors, the site's culture, policies, and even technical aspects have become immensely complicated over the years. So while Wikipedia is entirely open, it's not always transparent. That's why we wrote How Wikipedia Works, to try to make participating easier.

NT: *How about wrapping this up by giving our readers some suggestions as to how we can proceed in getting involved with Wikipedia?*

PA: Here are some things that librarians can do:

- Learn about the site. Start with en.wikipedia.org/wiki/Wiki pedia:About and then move on to any of the many instructional resources available. Your patrons, colleagues, and bosses will and probably do have questions about Wikipedia. And then teach the site. For all of the millions of people who use Wikipedia (including every computer-savvy student I know), few of them actually know how it works or what they are looking at.

- Evaluate articles. Are there especially good ones you can use in research guides? Especially bad ones that need work? Create a free user account, then participate in cleanup and evaluation efforts.

- Add sources. As I said previously, we're uniquely well equipped to do this. Adopt an article about a favorite topic and then think: How would you reference this article, focusing on references that are accessible to as wide an audience as possible, if you were writing the best general encyclopedia you can imagine? Then do it.

- Check references by other people to make sure that they are as complete and accurate as they can be. Books should have their ISBNs listed. Articles should have links to online versions. And so on.

- Add links to primary sources or other excellent resources that are online. Often libraries have developed bibliographies, pathfinders, or digital collections that would be an excellent further reading resource for the readers of an article on that topic. (But do be aware of the strict guidelines on spam; don't add links willy-nilly, but think: Would this resource be educational and helpful for the worldwide audience of this article who wants to find out more on this topic? If so, add a link under the "external links" or "further reading" sections.)

Endnotes

1. Meredith Farkas, *Social Software in Libraries* (Medford, NJ: Information Today, 2007), 67.

2. Samuel Kai-Wah Chu, "Using Wikis in Academic Libraries," *Journal of Academic Librarianship* 35 (2009): 172.

3. Matthew M. Bejune, "Wikis in Libraries," *Information Technology and Libraries* 26 (September 2007): 26–38.

4. Ibid., 33.

5. G. E. Gorman, "A Tale of Information Ethics and Encyclopaedias; Or, Is Wikipedia Just Another Internet Scam?" *Online Information Review* 32 (2008): 73–88.

6. J. E. Lacovara, "When Searching for the Evidence, Stop Using Wikipedia!" *MedSurg Nursing* 17 (2008): 153.

7. Neil L. Waters, "Why You Can't Cite Wikipedia in My Class," *Communications of the ACM* 50 (September 2007): 15–17.

8. Eric W. Black, "Wikipedia and Academic Peer Review: Wikipedia as a Recognised Medium for Scholarly Publication?" *Online Information Review* 32 (2008): 73–88.

9. Jim Giles, "Internet Encyclopedias Go Head to Head," *Nature* 438 (2005): 900–901.

10. Chris Harris, "Can We Make Peace With Wikipedia?" *School Library Journal* 53 (June 2007): 26.

11. Jaron Lanier, *You Are Not a Gadget: A Manifesto* (New York: Knopf, 2010), 32.

12. Uche Ogbuji, "Real Web 2.0: Wikipedia, Champion of User-Generated Content," September 4, 2007, accessed August 3, 2011, www.ibm.com/developerworks/web/library/wa-realweb4/?S_TACT=105AGY01&S_CMP=PODCAST.

13. Farhed Manjoo, "Is Wikipedia a Victim of Its Own Success?" *Time* magazine, September 28, 2009, accessed August 3, 2011, www.time.com/time/magazine/article/0,9171,1924492,00.html.

14. Lee Rainie and Bill Tancer, "Data Memo: 36% of Online American Adults Consult Wikipedia: It Is Particularly Popular With the Well-Educated and Current College-Age Students," Pew Internet & American Life Project, April 2007, accessed August 3, 2011, www.pewinternet.org/~/media/Files/Reports/2007/PIP_Wikipedia07.pdf.pdf.

15. Alison J. Head and Michael B. Eisenberg, "How Today's College Students Use Wikipedia for Course Related Research," First Monday 15, March 1, 2010, accessed August 3, 2011, www.uic.edu/htbin/cgiwrap/bin/ojs/index.php/fm/article/view/2830/2476.

16. "US—Top 20 Websites—March 6, 2010," Hitwise, accessed August 3, 2011, www.hitwise.com/us/datacenter/main/dashboard-10133.html.

17. Mark Walsh, "Wikipedia: A Decade of Ad-Free Information," Online Media Daily, January 14, 2011, accessed August 3, 2011, www.mediapost.com/publications/?fa=Articles.showArticle&art_aid–143022.

18. "Wikipedia.org," Alexa, accessed August 3, 2011, www.alexa.com/siteinfo/wikipedia.org.

19. Torsten Kleinz, "Wikipedia: 10 Billion Page Views a Month," The H, October 21, 2008, accessed August 3, 2011, www.h-online.com/newsticker/news/item/Wikipedia-10-billion-page-views-per-month-737737.html.

20. Erik Zachte, "Wikipedia Page Views," accessed August 3, 2011, stats.wikimedia.org/EN/TablesPageViewsMonthly.htm.

21. Joseph Janes, "Pedias, Familiar and Otherwise," *American Libraries* 36 (October 2005): 76.

22. Jennifer Valentino-DeVries, "In Effort to Boost Reliability, Wikipedia Looks to Experts," *Wall Street Journal*, May 13, 2010, accessed August 3, 2011, blogs.wsj.com/digits/2010/05/13/in-effort-to-boost-reliability-wikipedia-looks-to-experts. See also "Stanton Foundation Awards Wikimedia $3.6 Million for Technology Improvements," accessed October 14, 2011, wikimediafoundation. org/wiki/Press_releases/Stanton_Foundation_Awards_Wikimedia_$3.6_Million_ for_Technology_Improvements.

23. Roy Rosenzweig, "Can History Be Open Source?" *Journal of American History* 93 (2006): 117–146.

24. Dreanna Belden, "Harnessing Social Networks to Connect With Audiences," *Internet Reference Services Quarterly* 13 (2008): 99–111.

25. Ann M. Lally and Carolyn E. Dunford, "Using Wikipedia to Extend Digital Collections," *D-Lib Magazine,* May/June 2007, accessed August 3, 2011, www.dlib.org/dlib/may07/lally/05lally.html.

26. Melissa McLimans and Leah Ujda, "Selecting the Right Web 2.0 Tools for Your Library: The UWDCC's Experience," presented at the Annual Conference of the Wisconsin Association of Academic Librarians, 2008, accessed August 3, 2011, www.wla.lib.wi.us/waal/conferences/2008/postconference/Web2.0.pdf.

27. Lena Zentall and Camille Cloutier, "The Calisphere Wikipedia Project," *CSLA Journal* 32 (2008): 27–29.

28. Teri Ann Incrovato, "The Digital library at Villanova and Wikipedia," *Compass* 5 (2007), accessed August 3, 2011, newsletter.library.villanova.edu/story.php?id= 220.

29. Diane Madrigal, email to the author, December 15, 2008.

30. Michelle Springer et al., *For the Common Good: The Library of Congress Flickr Pilot Project*, October 30, 2008, p. 50, accessed August 3, 2011, www.loc.gov/rr/ print/flickr_report_final.pdf.

31. Tom B. Hickey, "WorldCat Identities: Another View of the Catalog," *OCLC Newsletter* 6, April 2007, accessed August 3, 2011, www.oclc.org/nextspace/006/ research.htm.

32. Andy Havens, email to the author, December 20, 2008.

Chapter 5

Podcasts, Slideshows, Screencasts, and Video

One of parenthood's joys is attending your young adult's college orientation. I had the pleasure of doing this in the summer of 2010 and was treated to a 2-day program of nonstop presentations by faculty and administration on every possible topic from peer counseling to course placement. Engaging the audience with wit and verve, some speakers were excellent. Others plodded lamely along, using slides as a crutch.

When I first encountered PowerPoint, it seemed that it had endless possibilities. It could be employed for just about any task on my daily calendar. Whether the occasion was a staff meeting, library instruction, or a tenure and promotion interview, the answer was a slideshow. Although slideshows remain in the presentation toolbox, today's end users and information professionals have more choices. Which medium we use to make our point depends on the content being conveyed and the audience.

How do individuals learn? There are many theories, but information presented via the web is usually limited to auditory or visual methods, with a steady sprinkling of tactile interaction. Some part of using technology is almost always tactile. Toggle switches, volume levers, keyboards, and buttons help us interact with information. If we wish to teach the auditory learner, we can employ podcasts. If we need to teach the visual learner, we can employ video or slides. Or we can combine sound with video or slides for a comprehensive approach to making our point to a wide audience. Regardless of the method, we can choose from several no-cost resources that require minimal technical expertise to get ourselves into podcasting.

Podcasts

Meredith Farkas, administrator of Library Success: A Best Practices Wiki (www.libsuccess.org), defines podcasting as "a simple means of distributing audio content over the internet, taking advantage of the power of RSS.

Content consumers (end-users) can subscribe to a feed of a producer's audio content and receive automatic downloads of new content as it is made available online."[1] The term *podcast* also applies to videos (vodcasts) that are syndicated with RSS. The RSS subscription aspect of the audio or video content distinguishes a podcast from a one-shot audio or video file uploaded to the web. Podcasts may be watched or listened to on the user's computer or MP3 device at any time. The Online Business Guide adds, "The term podcasting is technically a misnomer as it combines two words: iPod and broadcasting. It does not require an iPod or over-the-air broadcasting. The 'pod' name association stemmed from the popularity of the iPod digital audio player during the time that podcasting began."[2]

Podcasting, which began to become popular in 2004, is not limited to those who can produce professional programs, although executives and experts from a wide range of subject areas create and publish them. For example, the *Journal of Medical Practice Management* podcasts on financial management; CNN podcasts on several topics, including business and politics; and many podcasts originate at the White House, including Your Weekly Presidential Address, Speeches and Events, Whitehouse Press Briefings, and West Wing Week.

Despite the prevalence of podcasting by commercial media, it originated as a means for amateurs to share their enthusiasm for various interests such as sports or television shows. My brief examination of amateur podcasts on random topics discovered excellent work from Jonathan MacFarlane and "Rob," who produce a biweekly podcast called Bat-Radia (batradiae.blogspot. com). In a telephone call, I asked MacFarlane if he was connected with DC Comics in any way; he chuckled and said no, and we continued having a chat about the true nature of the Joker (i.e., menacing or playful?). Another excellent amateur podcaster is Scott Monty, who takes a break from being the head of social media at Ford Motor Company to podcast at www.ihearofsherlock. com, where he has discussed all things Sherlockian since 2007.

Podcast subscribers have a wide choice of content to which they may subscribe. If one likes to hear sports fans talk about Chicago White Sox baseball, there is Adam's and Jeff's Oral Sox (www.oralsox.blogspot.com), but if one prefers professional commentary, ESPN (espn.go.com/espnradio/podcast), among other traditional media outlets, can provide the necessary material.

Libraries and Podcasting

Librarians have adopted podcasting as an efficient, effective, and inexpensive way to push information and programming to their communities. At public libraries, podcasts get teenagers and children involved with books and media. The County of Los Angeles Public Library features a number of teen

poetry podcasts, along with reviews of movies created by teens (www.events.
lapl.org/podcasts). At the Denver Public Library, parents can find numerous
podcasts featuring stories, folk tales, and songs for kids (podcast.denver
library.org). Public libraries haven't forgotten their mature users: In addition
to RSS feeds for teens and tweens, Ohio's Worthington Libraries offers a feed
for adults (www.worthingtonlibraries.org/interact/av). And libraries still produce programs about books: The Mount Kisco (NY) Public Library has several
interviews with authors (mountkiscolibrary.podomatic.com), and the
Lincoln City (NE) Libraries provide a podcast page of bookchats (www.lincoln
libraries.org/podcasts/podcasts.htm).

Information professionals, policymakers, medical librarians, and the general public should be aware of the ambitious podcasting efforts of the
National Institutes of Health, which has been producing biweekly since 2006,
covering numerous topics, including stroke, H1N1 vaccine, gestational dia-
betes, and infant learning (www.nih.gov/news/radio/nihpodcast.htm).

Originally a federally funded program to connect the public to the internet
in California, the Infopeople Project now provides a wide variety of training to
those who work in California libraries. Its podcasts (feeds.feedburner.com/
InfopeoplePodcasts) should interest librarians and information professionals, with topics including J. D. Salinger, censorship, and children's literature.

The Albert R. Mann Library at Cornell University has produced an average
of eight podcasts per year since 2005, available as MP3 audio or MP4 video
(www.mannlib.cornell.edu/podcasts). These podcasts have included poetry
readings, as well as lectures on environmental art, sustainable forest farming,
and healthcare reform. Librarians at Central Connecticut State University's
Burritt Library (www.library.ccsu.edu) have produced various informational
podcasts and have also teamed up with instructional faculty from the English
department to create assignment-specific episodes.

Individual librarians also create podcasts. In Longshots (www.library
beat.org/longshots), Sarah Long, executive director of the North Suburban
Library System in Wheeling, Illinois, interviews leading figures from the world
of library and information science. She has published nearly 300 podcasts
since 2006, and her site Library Beat (www.librarybeat.org) is home to the podcast, as well as news and video. Kate "The Knitting Librarian" Kosturski, from
the Middlesex (NJ) Public Library, has her podcasts distributed via iTunes
(itunes.apple.com/us/podcast/the-knitting-librarian-podcast/id375658588).

If you wonder why I have not mentioned podcasts from the Library of
Congress or its neighbor, the Folger Shakespeare Library, and why I have neglected to discuss Yale's Sterling and Beinecke libraries, the reason is that their
programs, along with those from the British Library, Bodleian Library, New
York Public Library, and nearly 400 additional educational institutions, are
available through the iTunes proprietary software in a separate area called

iTunes U. Just launch your iTunes software and look for iTunes U along the top or right of the main navigation menu.

iTunes U

Launched in May 2007, iTunes U was originally a pilot program aggregating podcasts from Brown, Duke, Stanford, and the Universities of Michigan, Missouri, and Wisconsin at Madison. According to Apple, about half the total number of institutions participating in iTunes U post both audio and video podcasts without any charge to the consumer. Some of the prestigious participants are the Brookings Institution, Brooklyn Museum, Carnegie Endowment for International Peace, Educause, Goldwater Institute, Harvard, Massachusetts Institute of Technology, Metropolitan Museum of Art, Pratt Institute, Princeton University, and RAND Corp.[3] iTunes U also offers institutions the option of controlling access to their podcasts through password authentication, but a tremendous amount of free material is available: more than 350,000 free lectures, videos, films, and other resources (see www.apple.com/education/itunes-u/whats-on.html). Here is a small sample of what is offered:

- The Library of Congress offers more than 500 webcasts and 81 podcasts, including Music and the Brain, America at Work, America at Leisure, and Origins of American Animation. For librarians, the Library of Congress also offers more than 100 free podcasts on cataloging, serials, preservation, and the digital library (see Figure 5.1). It also offers apps for the iPhone and iPad.

- Pepperdine University Libraries offers more than 60 podcasts on various topics, including poetry, books, and Black History Month.

- Columbia University Libraries' titles include Barnard Library Tour, Call Number Guides, Reference Symposia, Murder in the Stacks, and an 11-episode Fundamentals of Copyright.

- Arizona State University's Library Channel offers 158 podcasts, including Academic Libraries in Transition, Banned Books Week, and a series of introductory episodes called The Library Minute.

- Texas A&M University Libraries offers eight video podcasts focusing on practical library information such as Search for Books and More, Renew Books Online, and Keyword Searching.

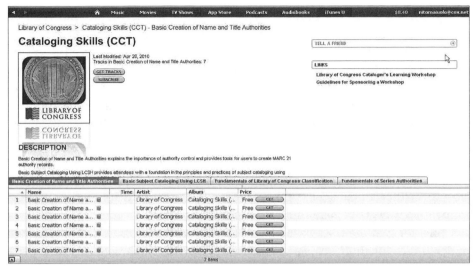

Figure 5.1   The Library of Congress's Cataloging Skills podcast is featured on iTunes U. [Courtesy of iTunes and the Library of Congress]

The Pros and Cons of iTunes U

Could free content from leading universities have the negative effect of discouraging students from formally pursuing a college degree? Pedagogy specialist Leslie Madsen Brooks, who is admittedly skeptical that employers would ever accept a piecemeal iTunes U plan of study, blogged, "Users of iTunes U could patch together a college education, taking courses from different institutions as was convenient and affordable, but not in the end earning a degree."[4] Jim Groom, instructional technology specialist from the University of Mary Washington, opined, "iTunes U is not a place for community, context, or collaboration. What is interesting about the web is not that you can get something, but that you can participate and dialogue around something."[5] While this may be accurate regarding context (one might be listening and watching the lectures oblivious to the appropriate mise-en-scène), community and dialogue are not necessarily hampered: American University professor Patrick Thaddeus Jackson uploads supplemental lectures for his international relations classes. Not only do his students listen, but people from all over the globe listen in, too. He has received feedback from as far away as Scotland. Jackson sees the iTunes U experience as cathartic: "If you're an academic, in terms of producing knowledge, what's better than having the knowledge that you produce be listened to? … People I don't know in Scotland can listen to my stuff, can contact me and tell me, 'You know, the next time you talk about James I, you might want to know there's this controversy about his religious affiliation. …' That kind of accessibility is really quite interesting."[6] But, Groom continues, "iTunesU on campus is really no different from bringing Taco Bell or Starbucks on campus, another sign of the corporatization of the university space that is running rampant in our moment."[7] This point will resonate with anyone working at a medium to large college. Nonetheless, iTunes U offers an abundance of audio and video information for the taking; it's a great resource, even if enjoyed only extramurally.

Institutional participation is largely motivated by philosophy and altruism. Liz Essley, of the *Washington Times*, reported, "Mara Hancock, director of educational technologies at the University of California at Berkeley, said the school gives away lectures on iTunes U and other platforms as part of its mission to further global access to knowledge."[8] At Stanford it's about creating innovative ways to engage millions of people.[9]

Consider that the U.K.-based Open University (www.open.ac.uk), a leader in distance education, gives away an average of 375,000 downloads of its content per week. Its 20 millionth track was downloaded in June 2010.[10] (For comparison, iTunes U's total downloads surpassed 100 million in December 2009.[11]) Martin Bean, Open University's vice chancellor, challenged academia to emulate the Open University's largesse, saying, "There are still a lot of universities in the world that define the value of their experience as somehow locking up their content and … giving people access to the content [only] when they enroll in the program. The courage comes from taking the next leap of faith. Universities no longer define themselves by their content but the overall experience: the concept, the student support, the tutoring and mentoring, the teaching and learning they get and the quality of the assessment."[12] The desire to expand education to all, regardless of ability to pay, seems to drive the participation of many at iTunes U.

Participating in iTunes U

It is not necessarily easy to join the elite of iTunes U; it takes hard work. Apple requires that your institution have a team with technical competence, content (a minimum of 150 audio and video files ready to unveil upon your launch), and a marketing plan. But approximately 370 institutions, both large and small, have brought podcasts online. If your institution is ready, see www.apple.com/education/itunes-u/apply.html.

Other Essential iTunes Information

To subscribe to a podcast in iTunes (with an RSS feed from a podcast you found outside of iTunes), do the following:

1. Start iTunes.

2. Click on Podcasts (left-hand column).

3. Click on the Advanced option in the top menu.

4. Select Subscribe to Podcast and enter the URL for the RSS feed you found outside of iTunes. Click OK.

You have now subscribed to the podcast. iTunes will regularly check for updates and download them for you to hear, watch, or transfer to your MP3 player.

To submit a podcast feed for possible inclusion in the iTunes Podcast Directory, do the following:

1. Open iTunes. Click iTunes Store (in the left menu). Then click Submit Podcast under Podcast Quick Links.

2. Enter the URL for the RSS feed of the podcast you'd like to see listed in the iTunes directory. Click Continue.

You will receive a confirmation from iTunes concerning your submission.

For detailed information on podcasting and iTunes, go to www.apple.com/itunes/podcasts/specs.html.

Finding Podcasts

Before you begin searching for podcasts, please consider my experience. My attempts often led to lists of podcast search engines that have gone to "Error 404 land" (and variations thereon). Danny Sullivan, of SearchEngine Watch.com, sighed, "As someone who produces a podcast—and who has enjoyed searching for podcasts when going on roadtrips—I don't get why podcast search isn't more supported by the major search engines. Yahoo! Podcasts, rolled out with promise back in October 2005, … [began displaying] a message at the top of the page saying 'Yahoo! apologizes deeply, but we will be closing down the Podcasts site on Oct. 31, 2007.'"[13] Podcast search engines and directories including Pluggd and Podcast.net sleep with the fishes. In 2007, the acclaimed PodZinger changed its name to RAMP. RAMP now produces media indexing tools for enterprise content owners, leaving end users to find other ways to discover podcasts.[14]

Precision in podcast retrieval may be tougher to achieve than typical web search retrieval because many podcast search engines have difficulty analyzing the audio within the podcast (or cannot analyze it at all); search results, therefore, depend on the text surrounding the podcast link.

Existing useful sites for locating podcasts include the following:

- Blinkx (www.blinkx.com/videos/podcast)

- Digital Podcast (www.digitalpodcast.com)

- Podcast Alley (www.podcastalley.com)

- Podcast Bunker (www.podcastbunker.com/Podcast_Feeds/Podcast_Feeds/The_Big_List)

- Podcast Directory (www.podcastdirectory.com)

- Podcast Pickle (www.podcastpickle.com)

- Podscope (www.podscope.com)

If searching and browsing for podcasts stresses you out, consider the popular option of downloading the proprietary iTunes software at www.apple.com/itunes/download, then browsing or searching its repository of thousands of free (and for fee) podcasts. According to information consultant Ellyssa Kroski, iTunes is the web's leading "podcatcher": "Its Top 100 Podcasts list accounts for 75 percent of all podcast traffic on the web. Roughly half of those top podcasts are authored by mainstream media companies."[15] Users can search, subscribe, and listen to podcasts within the iTunes application. Once you are in the iTunes Store and you click Audio Podcasts—See All, iTunes will show you only a featured list of about 200 items. If you want something specific, such as SAT preparation materials, you should follow Apple's instructions for executing a podcast power search (see www.apple.com/itunes/podcasts).

Creating Podcasts

To gain experience in podcasting, I created podcasts using two different software packages: Audacity (for PCs and Macs) and GarageBand (for Macs). GarageBand is not a free application, but it comes loaded on newer Apple computers. Audacity is a popular free software program for creating podcasts using a PCs and Macs; it has a very gentle learning curve and allows users to quickly and easily create and edit content. The Audacity software must be downloaded, but once you have it on your computer, you can create a podcast, preview it, and edit it. Then you can convert it into an MP3 file with the LAME MP3 encoder.

Once it's converted, you need to find a host for it. I have used Podbean.com (www.podbean.com) and the Internet Archive (www.archive.org). Once your podcast is hosted, you need to produce an RSS feed for it and validate the feed. At that point, all you need to do is promote your feed and periodically add content. Visitors to your podcast site will subscribe to the feed in their RSS reader or iTunes. There are numerous podcast tutorials on the web; here are some I have previewed:

- GarageBand, Apple (www.apple.com/support/garageband/podcasts)

- Learning and Scholarly Technologies: Podcasting/Vodcasting, University of Washington (www.washington.edu//lst/help/web/ podcasting)

- How to Podcast (www.how-to-podcast-tutorial.com/00-podcast-tutorial-four-ps.htm)

- TechUniversity Freebie: Intro to Recording a Podcast (www.ihas apple.com/2010/08/12/techuniversity-freebie-intro-to-recording-a-podcast) [Note: This screencast is 17 minutes in length but is exceptionally detailed and includes information on saving Mac podcast files as MP3s.]

- Audacity Tutorial for Podcasting, YouTube (www.youtube.com/watch?v=IC3VZkfdgV8)

To create or publish a podcast on a PC or Mac, you'll need:

- A microphone: Low-cost microphones do a great job. Condenser microphones possess greater transient and frequency response and have louder output. They require external power (some have a battery, some require a preamp), and prices begin at around $99.00. Dynamic microphones do not require external power but have a lower frequency response. The price of these mics begins at about $50.00. As an alternative, consider a headset with headphones and a built-in microphone. The price range is $50 to $200.

- A computer (PC or Mac).

- Recording software: I can't argue with free, and if you don't mind a very brief audio company logo being appended to the beginning of your podcast, the AVS Audio Editor (www.avs4you.com/AVS-Audio-Editor.aspx) works well, seamlessly saving recordings as MP3s. The acclaimed Audacity 1.2.6, which has received an average of 4 stars out of 5 from 600 CNET review readers, is also free (download the PC version at www.audacity.sourceforge.net/download/windows). Audacity does not automatically save recordings as MP3s, so be sure to also download the LAME MP3 Encoder (available on the same webpage as the Audacity download) to convert your recorded files into MP3s for podcasting.

Step-by-step instructions on how to create a podcast for a PC and for a Mac can be found on the accompanying UContent webpages at web.ccsu.edu/library/tomaiuolon/UContent/toc.htm.

Slideshows and Slidecasts

Saving slide presentations as HTML or PowerPoint files and uploading them to your own institution's web server has always had advantages. Can't get into the meeting room until just before your presentation? Upload it to your web host. Can't find your flash drive and you're out of burnable CDs? Place your slideshow on your web server.

Slideshows are great, but saving them to our own servers is the old-school method of archiving our presentations. When SlideShare (www.slideshare.net) launched in 2006, it became *the* destination for slideshows. The site sought to outdo itself on July 24, 2007, when it unveiled a new multimedia format called SlideCasting, which its blog describes as a combination of slideshows and podcasting. Several other resources have joined SlideShare in offering end users the ability to contribute narrated presentation content to the web. Because the learning curve is not steep, anybody with access to presentation software and a microphone can make a slidecast, register at one of the sites, and post the presentation. Of course, we assume that these sites will always exist and, therefore, our work will be archived. But if we set aside the gloomy prospect that a site may become defunct, having a slide sharing site host your presentations (slideshows or slidecasts) has several benefits:

- Files are accessible via the web; no need to carry files to meetings.

- Each presentation has a unique URL that you may share with associates.

- Presentations may be embedded on webpages.

- Viewers can add descriptive tags and make comments; this fosters collaboration.

- Most sites offer a "basic" membership and host slidecasts for free; paying subscribers enjoy additional features.

- You can use the slide sharing site to locate other files that you may use or learn from.

- Most sites offer user rights management options (e.g., decide who may see your presentations, make presentations downloadable or restrict downloading).

Slideshows and slidecasts have uses across the professions. Attorneys use them to make closing arguments; marketers pitch ideas to clients; teachers create presentations for a parents' night and send the URL to absentees; physicians explain treatment options; speech pathologists review the examination of a patient with a speech disorder; information professionals view and review specifics of searching databases; and librarians create and post presentations on traditional topics such as banned books or current issues such as open source library system software.

Although slide sharing resources possess components of social media (e.g., tagging, commenting, favoriting, finding contacts), they have not acquired the wild popularity many UContent social websites enjoy (e.g., Facebook, YouTube, Blogger, and Wikipedia are often in Alexa's top 10 UContent sites visited in the world). SlideShare, by comparison, was ranked at 254 in June 2011, yet it is the top slide sharing site on the web, attracting 25 million visitors each month.[16] Although slide sharing sites represent communities and have social features, they are more concerned with topics related to knowledge transfer. If the type of content on slide sharing sites is relatively limited to expository or instructional materials, the popularity of these sites will reflect niche audiences.

SlideShare

Although a few presentation websites preceded SlideShare's debut in 2006, an early positive review by TechCrunch's Michael Harrington saying SlideShare had ironed out problems that were present at other sites gave the site a strong foothold on the market. SlideShare was "clean, fast and functional and supports various copyright claims, including creative commons."[17]

SlideShare comes in several flavors: A free account entitles you to uploads and downloads, the Basic Pro account ($19.99/month) includes analytics. There are two other accounts priced at $49 and $249 per month.

Being Sociable

SlideShare supports uploading of PowerPoint, OpenOffice, Apple Keynote, Word, and PDF files. But before you can use SlideShare for presentation hosting, you must register for a free membership. After uploading a presentation to SlideShare, the user has several administrative choices to make: deciding on a category under which to list the show (this helps users who browse), setting the presentation to public viewing or private viewing, deciding whether to allow others to download the project, and giving the presentation one of six Creative Commons licensing options (or invoking "all rights reserved"). The original contributor may also add tags to the presentation (other people who view the presentation may add tags only after they have made the slideshow a Favorite). For more information about Creative Commons licenses, visit creativecommons.org/licenses.

SlideShare's additional social components include adding members as contacts (contacts may also be imported from popular email services) and being able to form groups, join groups, leave comments, and create events. Users can embed SlideShare content on webpages and email presentations to associates. RSS subscriptions are available for Latest, Most Viewed, Featured, and Most Favorited slideshows; you may also subscribe to tags. You can even insert a YouTube video into a slideshow (comments on the SlideShare site indicate that this is best done with Firefox as your browser).

Testing, One, Two, Three

When a PowerPoint presentation contains narration, the file will lose the audio upon upload to SlideShare. SlideShare developed a fix for this when it announced the ability for users to create slidecasts, but, although the site made it possible to synchronize audio MP3 files with slideshows in 2007, the vast majority of content on the site is static PowerPoint presentations.

If you decide to take the slidecast route, be prepared to follow a slightly tricky procedure. First, upload your PowerPoint presentation. Then upload a separate MP3 file with your narration. (*Note:* SlideShare allows narration only—no music.) The next step is linking your presentation with the MP3 file. Synchronizing your slides to the MP3 file is the final step (and the one I consider tricky). As shown in Figure 5.2, you need to manually set the slide timings, and this is not as straightforward as one would hope. Still, many users

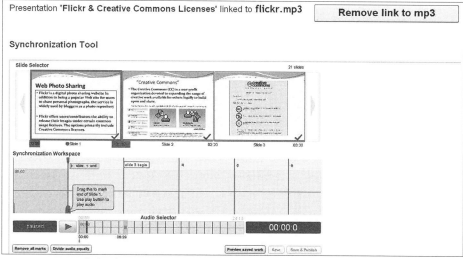

Figure 5.2   SlideShare's slidecast synchronization tool now allows users to upload audio MP3 files. [Courtesy of SlideShare]

have posted a wide variety of excellent slidecasts, including Thoughts on Digital Scholarship (www.slideshare.net/mweller/thoughts-on-digital-scholarship), Case Study: The Audio-Enhanced Learning Environment (www.slideshare.net/amiddlet50/audio-enhanced-learning-environment), Commas Are for Fascists (www.slideshare.net/iansage/punctuation-lecture), and The Rubbaiyat of Omar Khayyam (www.slideshare.net/terraxaman/omar-khayyam-el-rubbaiyat).

Give Us the Business

SlideShare offers an option called LeadShare. LeadShare helps you collect customer leads through the uploaded presentations or documents of other users.

Finding Slideshows

Search SlideShare by keyword or browse its categories to locate content. When browsing a category, a tag cloud of the most-used tags for that category will appear. (Attempting to search within a category you are browsing does not restrict your results to that category.) Once you have identified a relevant item, SlideShare will display its tags and show you a preview list of related presentations. In June 2011, a search for the keyword *cil2011*, for example, retrieved 291 results. If you look closely at a few of the presentations from the Computers in Libraries 2011 conference, you'll see they may be tagged *cil2011* or *cil11*. Clicking the *cil11* tag retrieves 21 presentations; clicking *cil2011* retrieves nine. Only two presentations were tagged with only *cil2011* (the other seven bore both the *cil11* and *cil2011* tags). Using the search box and entering *tag:cil2011* or *tags:cil2011* doesn't seem to work. (The only way to search for tags is to find an item with a valid tag and click on the tag.) Though it lacks a sophisticated search interface, SlideShare is a repository for many presentations on library and information science topics, as shown in Table 5.1.

Dark Horses With an Edge: authorSTREAM and SlideBoom

In terms of popularity, authorSTREAM (www.authorstream.com) and SlideBoom (www.slideboom.com) rank far behind SlideShare. During May 2011, Alexa placed authorSTREAM's global popularity at 4,847 and ranked SlideBoom at 25,624. In terms of usefulness, however, these two resources have a huge advantage: Presentation uploads with narration are possible without the linking–synching rigmarole SlideShare imposes. This means your presentations become slidecasts without breaking a sweat. I placed a PowerPoint presentation on both sites in minutes, and the audio worked without a hitch; I cannot overemphasize the importance of being able to do

Table 5.1   Sample searches of the SlideShare.net database

Search term	Number of items	First three most relevant titles and number of times viewed (June 2011)
Information literacy	932	What Does Information Literacy Mean? (12,382 views) Information Literacy: Tools and Resources (2,457 views) Theory and Practice of Case Study Methodology for Information Literacy (280 views)
Library instruction	166	Podcasting for Library Instruction (2,324 views) Assessing for Improvement: Learning Outcomes Assessment for Library Instruction (1,832 views) What We Can Learn From Library Instruction Research (1,328 views)
Research skills	300	Introducing Research Skills (1,594 views) Developing Research Skills (1,000 views) Research Skills for Science Fair Projects (4,272 views)
Social media	23,072	Social Media Strategy (38,640 views) Social Media Master 2012 (40,006 views) Strategic Social Media Marketing (10,395 views)
Cloud computing	2902	I'm Cloud Confused (20,000 views) Cloud Computing + SAAS + Collaboration = Collective Team Intelligence (9,010 views) Cloud Computing in the Enterprise (25,506 views)
Digital natives	1,517	Digital Natives (5,794 views) Engaging Digital Natives (27,300 views) Digital Natives: Is There Evidence? (657 views)
Intellectual property	2,910	Intellectual Property and Copyrights (6,990 views) STOP—Stop Tolerating Online Plagiarism (1,465 views) Valuing Intellectual Property (1,286 views)

this quickly and without frustration. (Please visit tinyurl.com/2uawk3r and view several embedded examples of my slidecasts and presentations.)

authorSTREAM

After you sign in to your free authorSTREAM account, the first thing you may notice is that the "most viewed" tags and "active users" are displayed without your having to hunt around the site. Although the site supports only PowerPoint uploads (up to 1 gigabyte), it handles them with ease. Features include marking items as public or private and downloading presentations in a variety of video file formats, which facilitates posting on YouTube, including MP4, WMV, AVI, and FLV. Presentations can be any length, but videos must be shorter than 5 minutes or you'll need to buy video credits at 10 cents each (minimum purchase is 20 credits). The ability to embed coding and unique URLs are available for all presentations. You may browse categories or search by keyword (with an advanced option to search by Creative Commons license for items that may be modified or used commercially), and subscribe via RSS to tags, contributors, Most Liked, Featured, and Most Viewed. Other social components include the option to Favorite a presentation and to leave comments. Also, remember the early days of the web, when ecards were free? They are still free at authorSTREAM (see www.authorstream.com/greeting-cards).

Although advertising appears on presentations uploaded with a free account, the free account should serve most individuals and institutions well. It offers 500 MB of storage and two levels of private sharing. The Pro membership ($2.50 per month) features ad-free browsing and presentation analytics. The Business membership ($39.95 per month) permits unlimited presentation-to-video conversion and customizable embed-coding. authorSTREAM also offers a desktop PowerPoint add-in, shown in Figure 5.3, that helps you find images from Bing and video from YouTube for insertion as you work on your presentation (www.authorstream.com/desktop).

The authorSTREAM site appears to be underused by information professionals and librarians (26 presentations are tagged *librarians*, 133 are tagged *libraries*, 13 are tagged *library instruction*, and 24 are tagged *information literacy*). One presentation from the Computers in Libraries 2009 conference (viewed 304 times) and one presentation from the Cincinnati Chapter of the Special Libraries Association (viewed 200 times) have been posted.

SlideBoom

This second overshadowed slide sharing site, shown in Figure 5.4, is also impressive. Like authorSTREAM, it immediately takes your presentations—complete with sound—and uploads them without a hiccup. SlideBoom supports PowerPoint presentation (.ppt/.pptx) and slideshow (.pps/.ppsx) uploads and offers embedding, unique URLs for presentations, tagging, favoriting, comments, ratings, creating and joining groups, RSS, social bookmarking, and posting to blogs. If you can export your OpenOffice or Apple Keynote presentation into a PowerPoint format, you can use SlideBoom, too. Other niceties include an add-in called iSpring Free, which transforms PowerPoint presentations into Flash files, and a graphical annotation tool that allows you to make comments on presentations, which you can then save to your own account or share with others.

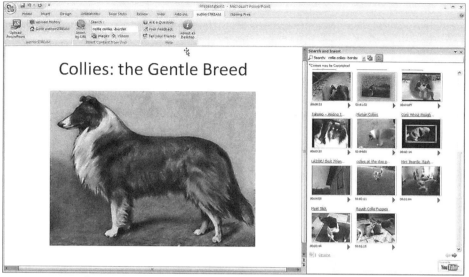

Figure 5.3   The authorSTREAM desktop add-in for PowerPoint facilitates searching in Bing for images and YouTube for videos. Note the YouTube retrieval on the right of the PowerPoint application and the authorSTREAM add-in menu above the slide.

A free account may be all an individual needs (it allows up to 100 presentations for noncommercial use), but Pro accounts are available for $195 per year. The Pro account allows 500 uploads per year, nixes any advertising on your presentations, and provides statistics.

I have used SlideShare, authorSTREAM, SlideBoom, and blip.tv (www.blip.tv) to embed several presentations at tinyurl.com/2uawk3r. Take a look at them and assess the visual and sound quality of each.

An Opportunity for Expanded Collaboration: VoiceThread

VoiceThread (www.voicethread.com) is an exciting site that breaks away from linear slideshows and slidecasts. An example of computer-supported collaborative learning primarily geared toward educators, VoiceThread is free (you must register) and provides web-based software that allows you to create cooperative slidecasts. Using the site's tools, a user could create a VoiceThread by uploading a sequence of photographs and inviting viewers to add narrative to the images; other users may insert PDFs or links to related webpages, and while watching playback, viewers can click a microphone icon to record comments, which the original contributor may elect to moderate. Comments can even be made via cell phone. The majority of presentations are authored by teachers or students, and some have received 20,000 views.

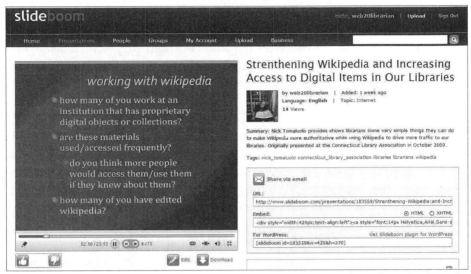

Figure 5.4   SlideBoom is a free slide sharing resource with a clean look and many social features. [Courtesy of SlideBoom]

Contributors from outside the K–12 realm include the New York Public Library (NYPL), which has opened up its Digital Gallery (digitalgallery.nypl. org), containing 700,000 images, to VoiceThread users. NYPL staff have created 15 VoiceThreads at nypl.voicethread.com.

Screencasts

Librarians engage in many do-it-yourself projects; a common one is creating tutorials designed to show, in a step-by-step manner, how specific computer-related tasks must be done. These tutorials include searching online library catalogs, navigating specific database interfaces, and performing routines such as requesting interlibrary loans. Screencasts, which often contain voice-over narration, are digital video recordings that capture actions taking place on a computer desktop.[18] They are useful for demonstrating how to use specific operating systems, software applications, or website features. Screencasts have another advantage: They appeal to the newer generation of information consumers who expect video. Requiring only a microphone and screen capture software, a screencast is the perfect choice for web-based instruction tasks, and because they can combine audio, video, and interactivity, social media advocate Meredith Farkas points out that screencasting possesses important elements of a face-to-face class and closely approximates hands-on instruction.[19]

The Google Business Channel (www.youtube.com/user/GoogleBusiness), Yahoo! Developer Network (developer.yahoo.com/yos/screencasts/mysocial_screencast.html), Apple Computer (gigaom.com/category/screencasts), and others involved in a variety of enterprises, including search engine optimization, programming, and artificial intelligence, have been producing slick screencasts for years.

Many libraries, including the Nashville Public Library (www.library.nashville.org/services/ser_training.asp) and the Virginia Tech Libraries (www.lib.vt.edu/help/screencasts), offer informative screencasts demonstrating everyday tasks end users may need to execute. More specialized libraries, such as the Cushing-Whitney Medical Library at Yale (cwml-tutorials.blogspot.com), have produced screencasts on some relatively arcane topics, such as using Journal Citation Reports to find journal impact factors and citation analysis with the Web of Science and Scopus.

Once you have obtained the necessary software (most practitioners recommend using TechSmith Camtasia or Adobe Captivate) and have consulted a few tutorials, you'll be well on your way to producing your own screencasts. Library Success: A Best Practices Wiki lists helpful links at www.libsuccess.org/index.php?title=Online_Tutorials. Incidentally, check out Screencast-O-Matic (www.screencast-o-matic.com) for free screen capture software. The site will host your screencasts for free as long as they last less than 15 minutes. A Pro account ($12 per year) lets you create screencasts as long as an hour. The Masten Library at the County College of Morris in New Jersey has used it (see its screencast for Gale Nursing Reference at www.screencast-o-matic.com/watch/cQftoeep3).

Remember, you may need five to 20 hours to create a storyboard, write a script, record your screens and voice, and tweak and re-tweak as necessary to produce a 15-minute screencast.

Video

In 2010, researchers at the Pew Internet & American Life Project released a report called *The State of Online Video*. Its survey of 763 internet-using adults found that 70 percent had watched a video on the web; they are watching 19 percent more humorous videos than they viewed in 2007, as well as 16 percent more educational videos than they did in 2007. Affluent young men who had attended college were more likely to watch than any other demographic. Regarding video uploading, the same survey discovered that one in seven (14 percent) adult internet users has contributed a video to the web for others to view or download. That's up from the number of adults who had contributed video in 2007 (8 percent). Social networking sites (e.g., Facebook) were the most likely destination for uploads, with video sharing sites (e.g., YouTube) the next most popular. Home videos were the most uploaded content.[20]

The attributes of video and video sharing sites are a good fit with end users' desire to comment on, rate, tag, embed, and share content. Web developer Jason A. Clark comments, "Widespread broadband, simplified video editing and creation tools, and a perfect storm of people wanting to watch other people being creative on a computer screen have also contributed to the ubiquity of digital videos on the web."[21]

You're Nobody 'Til Somebody YouTubes You

YouTube (www.youtube.com) transcends being a mere website. It has become part of our culture. The global digital marketing intelligence firm comScore declared that YouTube had achieved an all-time high of 14.6 million videos viewed in the month of May 2010.[22] Consider this juxtaposition: Noah Kalina, a photography student, took a picture of himself every day between January 11, 2000, and July 31, 2006. He strung the 2,356 photos together into a video, placing one copy on YouTube and one copy on Vimeo. On June 20, 2011, his YouTube video had been viewed almost 20 million times (see www.youtube.com/watch?v=6B26asyGKDo), while the same video on Vimeo had been watched 101,000 times (see vimeo.com/99392).

But YouTube is not the ideal place to watch videos. Although some of its content is high definition, most is distributed in low resolution so the videos will load faster. When *PC World* compared YouTube to other video sharing sites, YouTube came in at No. 7. But the criticism that the video quality is not optimal is offset by the site's ability to draw the widest audience.[23] Conversely, a more recent review gave YouTube the highest rating and added, "The best part about YouTube is being able to watch videos, any video, without being a member, but the real strength of YouTube is the community members that interact, comment, and post videos for specific interests. It's possible to find a video on YouTube for any interest, occupation, hobby or pastime, along with a lot of other videos that anybody can love."[24] Why did CSPAN broadcast all three 2008 presidential debates on YouTube? Because that's where people were watching: The videos have received a total of 4,739,470 views and 72,945 comments.

Perhaps mainstream internet users are crazy about YouTube, but what about the erudite educator, the cybernetic computer technician, the laconic librarian, and the tough tax auditor? It seems they are all tuned in as well. When the Library of Congress got its own YouTube channel, its expressive director of communications Matt Raymond titled his April 7, 2009, blog posting, "YouTube and Now We Do Too." The Library of Congress's YouTube channel began with 70 videos and has expanded to 857. Inaugural ceremony footage is there, along with quaint clips of sledding and skating in Central Park. The channel at www.youtube.com/user/LibraryOfCongress had 9,747 subscribers in June 2011.

If the Library of Congress doesn't confer sufficient credibility, consider that the Federal Judiciary created its own YouTube channel (www.youtube.com/uscourts) in spring 2010. In addition, the *New York Times* reported that YouTube and the Guggenheim Museum were teaming up to "short-circuit that exclusionary art-world system" by inviting anyone with a video camera to vie for a place in the museum's video-art exhibition called "YouTube Play," which opened in October 2010.[25] See the Guggenheim's YouTube Play videos at youtube.com/user/playbiennial.

Before I offer a selected list of libraries that have embraced YouTube, I want to direct your attention to a newspaper article that explored the extent to which children are keyed into video. A youngster working on a school project on the platypus began his information search *not with Google* but with YouTube. According to Miguel Helft of the *New York Times*, "The explosion of all types of video content on YouTube and other sites is quickly transforming online video from a medium strictly for entertainment and news into one that is also a reference tool. As a result, video search, on YouTube and across other sites, is rapidly morphing into a new entry point into the web, one that could rival mainstream search for many types of queries."[26]

Institutions That Tube

Arizona State University's Library Channel (www.youtube.com/user/ASU) has uploaded excellent tutorials, including Searching Google Scholar, Connecting to Full Text, and an overview of information literacy. Other institutions with their own channels include the Smithsonian Institution Libraries (www.youtube.com/user/SmithsonianLibraries), which have created videos for both user and staff training, and the Arlington Heights (VA) Memorial Library (www.youtube.com/user/LibVlog), a dedicated video producer with 150 uploads. Library marketing videos are common (check out the humorous "hop on a book truck tour" of Harper College Library at www.youtube.com/watch?v=JHljR4LYmOA). The New York Public Library (www.youtube.com/user/NewYorkPublicLibrary) and the London Public Library (www.youtube.com/user/LondonPublicLibrary) also regularly contribute videos. Vendors are getting into the action. Elsevier has the Library Connect channel (www.youtube.com/user/LibraryConnect), featuring news on publications, ebook readers, and the Medical Library Association's Librarians Without Borders program. PsycINFO appears as a channel with four training videos (www.youtube.com/user/PsycINFO). ProQuest uploads training videos at www.youtube.com/user/timproquest.

Sean Robinson, author of the 2010 book *Library Videos and Webcasts*, is the bibliographic and information technology service manager at Allen County Public Library in Fort Wayne, Indiana. He is also the prime mover for all things visual at his library. YouTube is home to his library's channel (www.youtube.com/user/askacpl), where Robinson and colleagues have uploaded nearly 200 videos (and have over 300 subscribers). When I asked him about his library's prolificacy, Robinson offered the following response:

> I am not entirely sure why video has caught on here. One thing we do is train staff on how to film and edit, and that empowers them. You noticed we are frequent uploaders, and I think that is key. We try to have fresh, current content, and this attracts subscribers. Melissa Kiser, our information technology librarian, creates a weekly "What's happening at the Library" video where we highlight the community and programs we're running. We have also started a WIAR (*What I Am Reading*) blog at acplwiar.word press.com—the blog has videos, too. I am constantly thinking about how to develop our staff's technical skills and grow the organization. Here we had a group of people that loved to read and wanted to share their experiences, but they didn't know how to create videos. So we sat down and showed them how easy it was and stepped them through the process. The idea is once you know how to do something, you have to share that knowledge with others and then ask them to share it. I don't think there is any secret, you just have to keep on creating videos and work really hard at it while having fun.[27]

Why has YouTube become everyone's video destination? Robinson replied, "I think that it is a certainty that a technology will come along and supplant YouTube. YouTube will probably go through stages of trying to reinvent itself, but our desire for the latest and greatest will probably be the YouTube killer." After a pause, he added, "This brings up all the questions of archiving digital content. In my opinion only things that are institutionalized in this country have any chance at longevity."

YouTube.Edu

In the spirit of democratizing education (and meeting clientele on all possible fronts), more than 100 colleges have set up channels at a dedicated space called YouTube.Edu (www.youtube.com/EDU). Like iTunes U, YouTube.Edu features free video lectures. Participants include Stanford University, with more than 1,300 videos and more than 2.7 million views, and Dartmouth College, with 720 videos and 237,132 views.

blip.tv: An Attractive Alternative

Although YouTube is the "800-pound gorilla of video sharing sites," *PC World*'s Danny Allen judged rival blip.tv superior in terms of video quality and embedded player design.[28] More than 22 million people a month visit the site to watch a video. blip.tv features several Web 2.0 components, including tagging, commenting, RSS feeds, and sharing through embedding and emailing.

The site specializes in homegrown shows and handles the distribution of contributed videos, too, by syndicating its content to other sites, such as AOL, iTunes, Yahoo! Video, and MSN. And because anyone is welcome to upload any number of videos without charge, it's well suited as a distribution platform for library and business videos. David Lee King, digital branch and services manager at the Topeka and Shawnee County (KS) Public Library (and frequent conference presenter), has several technology videos at the site. "Em the Librarian" (a NextGen librarian in Kentucky) has a channel of videos capturing the social side of librarianship; the San Jose State University School of Library and Information Science's lengthy episode list includes lectures on the evolution of controlled vocabularies and tips for contributing to journals. Librarians Debbie Herman and Susan Slaga at Central Connecticut State University (my home base) have a blip.tv channel called Burritt Library Adventures in Research (burrittlibrary.blip.tv); the series contains 21 episodes and is always expanding. Our videos, which feature librarians, students, and faculty, include screencasts, instruction, lectures, and a movie called *The Sisterhood of the Lost Girls: Finding Their Way Through Burritt Library*.

Other Video Sharing Sites

eConsultant lists 62 video sharing sites (web2.econsultant.com/videos-hosting-sharing-searching-services.html), and Wikipedia lists 67 (en.wikipedia.org/wiki/List_of_video_hosting_services). Certain features should come standard in all good video sharing sites: a search box and a way to browse by category, screenshot previews of videos, a brief description of each video's content, and user-submitted ratings. See Table 5.2 for a comparison of standard features for six popular video sharing services.

If you have uploaded a video to any of the popular video sites, you know it is a simple process. Most digital cameras, even many inexpensive ones, will record video and sound. Once the recording has been made, you need only connect the camera to your computer, save the file on your desktop, access the video sharing site, and upload it. The remaining "work" is actually fun—choose a category for the video and provide a description and some tags. If you are a newcomer to YouTube, a video called *The Medieval Helpdesk* should give you a chuckle (www.youtube.com/watch?v=pQHX-SjgQvQ).

Table 5.2   Features of popular video sharing sites

	blip.tv (www.blip.tv)	Dailymotion (www.daily motion.com)	Metacafe (www.meta cafe.com)	TeacherTube (www.teacher tube.com)	Vimeo (www. vimeo.com)	YouTube (www. youtube.com)
Site description	Mission: Make independent web shows sustainable	Find or upload videos about your interests and hobbies; get feedback on your clips and creative work	Specializes in short, original content	Online community for sharing instructional videos	A friendly community of video creators	A forum for people to connect, inform, and inspire others across the globe
Memberships	Free, Pro account ($8/month)	3 types of user: Free, Motionmaker, Official User	Free	Free	Free, Plus account ($9.95/month)	Free; sponsors pay to have content featured
Revenue sharing	Yes	Yes (with partners)	No	No	No	Yes (with partners)
High definition available	Yes	Yes	Yes	Yes	Yes	Yes
Search box	Yes	Yes	Yes	Yes	Yes	Yes
Advanced search	No	No	Yes	Yes	Yes	Yes
Search by category or browse	Yes	Yes	Yes	Yes (by channels)	Yes	Yes
Uses tags	Yes	Yes	Yes	Yes	Yes	Yes
Audience rates video	No	Yes	Yes	Yes	Yes	Yes
Audience or contributor comments	Yes	Yes	Yes	Yes	Yes	Yes
RSS feeds	Yes	Yes	Yes	Yes	No	Yes
Embed code	Yes	Yes	Yes	Yes	Yes	Yes
Make public or private	Yes	Yes	Yes	Yes	Yes	Yes

Table 5.2 (cont.)

	blip.tv (www.blip.tv)	Dailymotion (www.daily motion.com)	Metacafe (www.meta cafe.com)	TeacherTube (www.teacher tube.com)	Vimeo (www. vimeo.com)	YouTube (www. youtube.com)
Maximum file size or other limits	1 GB	150 MB	8 minutes	None	500-MB weekly limit	15 minutes
Supports AVI[1]	Yes	Yes	Yes	Yes	Yes	Yes
Supports ASF[2]	No	No	Yes	No	Yes	No
Supports MOV[3]	Yes	Yes	Yes	Yes	Yes	Yes
Supports WMV[4]	Yes	Yes	Yes	Yes	Yes	Yes
Supports MPG[5]	Yes	Yes	Yes	Yes	Yes	Yes
Supports Flash[6]	Yes	Yes	Yes	Yes	Yes	Yes
Email support	Yes	Yes	Yes	Yes	Yes	Yes
FAQs	Yes	Yes	Yes	Yes	Yes	Yes
User forums	No	No	Yes	Yes	Yes	No
Knowledge base	Yes	No	Yes	No	Yes	Yes
Tutorials	Yes	No	Yes	No	Yes	Yes
Rights protection options	Yes (Creative Commons)	Yes (see site)	Yes (see site)	Yes (see site)	Yes (see site)	Yes (Creative Commons)

Key to software terms:
[1]AVI—Audio Video Interleave: a multimedia format by Microsoft that allows the synchronized (interleaved) playback of audio and video.
[2]ASF—Advanced Systems Format: Microsoft's digital audio and digital video software, often used for streaming media; ASF files may also contain metadata.
[3]MOV—MOVie file: a multimedia file format used for Quicktime movies, compatible with Macs and PCs.
[4]WMV—Windows Media Video: a video compression format; WMV is a subset of Microsoft's Advanced Systems Format.
[5]MPG or MPEG—Moving Pictures Expert Group: represents a series of audio/video recording formats for displaying a wide range of multimedia items at good resolution.
[6]Flash: Adobe multimedia software that adds interactivity to webpages; FLV refers to Flash Video, a small multimedia file that uploads easily to the web, and is good for rendering full motion video, while SWF or Shockwave Flash creates much larger files that are better for producing graphics.

Endnotes

1. Meredith G. Farkas, "Podcasting," Library Success: A Best Practices Wiki, accessed August 3, 2011, www.libsuccess.org/index.php?title=Podcasting.

2. Danny Wirken, "Podcasting Search Engines—The Good and the Not So Good," ArticleDashboard, May 22, 2010, accessed August 3, 2011, www.articledash

board.com/Article/Podcasting-Search-Engine-The-Good-And-The-Not-So-Good/91842.

3. "A Wealth of Knowledge From Top Institutions," iTunes U, accessed August 3, 2011, www.apple.com/education/itunes-u/whats-on.html.

4. Leslie Madsen Brooks, "iTunes U: Disruptive Education—In More Ways than One," BlogHer, November 28, 2009, accessed August 3, 2011, www.blogher.com/itunes-u-disruptive-education-more-ways-one.

5. Jim Groom, "5 Reasons I Don't Like iTunes U," Bavatuesdays, November 22, 2009, accessed August 3, 2011, bavatuesdays.com/5-reasons-i-dont-like-itunesu.

6. Liz Essley, "Citizen Journalism: The iTunes Classroom," *Washington Times*, July 6, 2009, accessed August 3, 2011, www.washingtontimes.com/news/2009/jul/06/the-itunes-classroom.

7. Groom, "5 Reasons I Don't Like iTunes U."

8. Essley, "Citizen Journalism."

9. "Apple Announces iTunes U on the iTunes Store," Apple press release, May 30, 2007, accessed August 3, 2011, www.apple.com/pr/library/2007/05/30itunesu.html.

10. "The Open University Is the First University Worldwide to Reach 20 Million Downloads on iTunes U," Open University, June 29, 2010, accessed August 3, 2011, www3.open.ac.uk/media/fullstory.aspx?id=19109.

11. Jim Dalrymple, "iTunes U Breaks 100 Million Downloads," CNET News, December 18, 2009, accessed August 3, 2011, news.cnet.com/8301-13579_3-10418611-37.html.

12. Brad Stone, "The Argument for Free Classes Via iTunes," *New York Times*, November 17, 2009, accessed August 3, 2011, bits.blogs.nytimes.com/2009/11/17/the-argument-for-free-classes-via-itunes.

13. Danny Sullivan, "Yahoo! Podcasts to Close; the Sorry State of Podcast Search," Search Engine Land, September 27, 2007, accessed August 3, 2011, searchengineland.com/yahoo-podcasts-to-close-the-sorry-state-of-podcast-search-12288.

14. Liz Gannes, "$10 Million for EveryZing (nee PodZinger)," GigaOM, June 12, 2007, accessed October 30, 2011, gigaom.com/video/10-million-for-everyzing-nee-podzinger.

15. Ellyssa Kroski, *Web 2.0 for Librarians and Information Professionals* (New York: Neal-Schuman, 2008), 174.

16. "SlideShare Launches Channels for Marketing to Professionals," BusinessWire, February 3, 2010, accessed August 3, 2011, www.businesswire.com/news/home/20100203005810/en/SlideShare-Launches-Channels-Marketing-Professionals.

17. Michael Arrington, "Introducing SlideShare: Powerpoint + YouTube," TechCrunch, October 4, 2006, accessed August 3, 2011, techcrunch.com/2006/10/04/introducing-slideshare-power-point-youtube.

18. "Screencast," WhatIs?, accessed August 3, 2011, whatis.techtarget.com/definition/screencast.html.

19. Meredith G. Farkas, *Social Software in Libraries* (Medford, NJ: Information Today, 2007), 198.

20. Kristen Purcell, *The State of Online Video*, Pew Internet & American Life Project, June 3, 2010, accessed August 3, 2011, www.pewinternet.org/~/media//Files/Reports/2010/PIP-The-State-of-Online-Video.pdf.

21. Jason A. Clark, "YouTube University: Using XML, Web Services, and Online Video Services to Serve University and Library Video Content," in *Library 2.0 Initiatives in Academic Libraries*, ed. Laura B. Cohen, 156 (Chicago: American Library Association, 2007).

22. comScore, "comScore Releases May 2010 U.S. Online Video Rankings," Press Release, June 24, 2010, accessed August 3, 2011, www.comscore.com/Press_Events/Press_Releases/2010/6/comScore_Releases_May_2010_U.S._Online_Video_Rankings.

23. Danny Allen, "Online Video Shoot-Out: blip.tv Beats YouTube," *PC World*, August 22, 2007, accessed August 3, 2011, www.pcworld.idg.com.au/article/192011/online_video_shoot-out.

24. TopTenREVIEWS, "Video Share Websites 2011," accessed August 3, 2011, video-share-review.toptenreviews.com/index.html.

25. Roberta Smith, "The Home Video Rises to Museum Grade," *New York Times*, October 21, 2010, accessed August 3, 2011, www.nytimes.com/2010/10/22/arts/design/22youtube.html. See also Carol Vogel, "Guggenheim and YouTube Seek Budding Video Artists," *New York Times*, June 13, 2010, accessed August 3, 2011, www.nytimes.com/2010/06/14/arts/design/14video.html.

26. Miguel Helft, "At First Funny Videos. Now, a Reference Tool," *New York Times*, January 17, 2009, accessed June 20, 2011, www.nytimes.com/2009/01/18/business/media/18ping.html.

27. Sean Robinson, email message to author, April 16, 2010.

28. Allen, "Online Video Shoot-Out."

Chapter 6

Facebook

Whether a new internet service, resource, or utility tanks or takes off is a question best asked of a crystal ball. AOL looked like a rocket to the moon in the early days of the web, but now it's just one more face in a huge crowd of services vying for our attention. Who knew Google—just a white page with a search box and a handful of words—would achieve such eminence? In 2004, Facebook had just started up at Harvard. By September 2006, it was open to anyone. It had 1 million members in 2004. As of July 2011, Facebook's Timeline (www.facebook.com/press/info.php?timeline) states that it had 500 million users. But the Facebook statistics blog Socialbakers says the number is nearing 700 million (see www.socialbakers.com/blog/171-facebook-is-globally-closing-in-to-700-million-users). In terms of how often the site is visited, Facebook is ranked No. 2 by Alexa (www.alexa.com/siteinfo/facebook.com), right behind behemoth Google, both in the U.S. and worldwide.

Though librarians and information professionals may not exactly consider Facebook the proverbial elephant in the room, several sources warn us not to be indifferent toward it. Educause says Facebook is generally considered the leading social networking site among college students and has become a leading space for UContent.[1] In 2010, comScore Data Mine noted that the 25- to 34-year-old demographic was the largest group of Facebook users (20.9 percent).[2] One writer, calling social networking an age-neutral phenomenon, states that the key message of his research is "the desire for people to network is not a transitory fad. It is here to stay."[3]

Research on Libraries and Social Networking

According to the Pew Internet & American Life Project, "A social networking site is an online place where a user can create a profile and build a personal network that connects him or her to other users."[4] Strictly speaking, that doesn't necessarily seem like something in which libraries need to become involved. But because Facebook and other social networking sites see such heavy use, the Online Computer Library Center, Inc., (OCLC) commissioned the American market research company Harris Interactive to execute a blind study into social networking and libraries. Assessing the perspective of the general public in six countries and library directors from the U.S., the survey, done between December 7, 2006, and February 7, 2007, gathered answers from 6,545 total respondents. A total of 6,163 respondents were from the general public (1,801 were from the general U.S. public). The rest were U.S. library directors. Here are some of the most interesting findings: Not surprisingly, 90 percent of the general public uses web search engines. Unfortunately, library website use decreased between 2005 and 2007 from 30 percent to 20 percent.[5] Another important finding is that the general public does not see a role for libraries in their socially networked world. In fact, the report stated, "The general public respondents do not see a role for libraries in constructing social sites, and most would not be very likely to contribute content, self-publish or join discussion groups if a library were to offer these services." If there is a place for libraries in a socially networked world, respondents thought an online book club was the best service a library could offer. The respondents from the general public were not alone. Library directors from the U.S. felt about the same.[6] Here are some of the top responses to the question, "Why *don't* you think it should be the library's role to build social networking sites for your community?"

General Public (six countries)
Library is for learning or information (25 percent)
Not the role of the library or librarian (16 percent)
Personal or individual matter (7 percent)
Library is not for socializing (7 percent)

Library Directors (U.S.)
Not the role of the library or librarian (30 percent)
Enough social networking sites exist already (16 percent)
Library is for learning or information (14 percent)
No time or resources (9 percent)

The report also concluded:

- The library brand has put boundaries around the expectations of libraries on the social web. Overwhelmingly, neither the general public nor librarians see a role for libraries as providers of social sites.

- Offline, libraries are vibrant social spaces. They are hubs of community activities and provide a venue for open exchange and dialogue. Yet neither users nor librarians can envision such a role for libraries online. Fewer than 15 percent of the users or library directors think libraries should construct or sponsor social networking sites. An equally small percentage of users say they would be very likely to contribute content, view others' collections, or become involved in a social site if one was provided by a library.

- Of the roughly 15 percent of both the general public and library directors who saw a role for their libraries in social networking, the top suggestion for services their library should provide was predictable: book clubs. "But, unfortunately, librarians are not pioneering the social web. Whether it is a privacy concern, a lack of resources or the expectations of their users, librarians are lagging, not leading. Even when it comes to the social networking activity most easily associated with the library—book clubs—the digital pioneers are being out-innovated."[7]

If both library users and library directors agree that the library shouldn't build social sites, so be it. This still leaves the question, Should libraries piggyback onto existing social networks in an effort to meet their clientele online? You may think yea or nay, and the literature answering this question is also divided.

Noting that students are far more likely to use Facebook than any library's website, State University of New York (Stony Brook) librarian Darren Chase reasoned that establishing a Facebook page offering access to library resources while providing notifications of library events was desirable.[8] Meredith Farkas, head of Instructional Services at Portland State University (Oregon), and others have affirmed the theoretical advantages of libraries' presence on Facebook.[9,10] But are libraries pursuing this connection? One article looked at 483 public library websites and noted a connection to Facebook in only 2 percent of the sites and to Myspace in 6 percent of the sites.[11] In health sciences libraries, researchers analyzed the responses of 72 colleagues to the question, Does your library have a Facebook page? to which 12.5 percent (9) said yes, while 85 percent (61) said no.[12] Early in 2009 a study surveyed 222 librarians (148 completed the survey) to gauge their use of social media, and although Facebook was selected as the "most used" technology by 71.4 percent of respondents, many libraries had not adopted Web 2.0 for various reasons. This survey reported several key responses to survey questions:

- "Web 2.0 is where today's generation is living, working, studying. We need to incorporate these elements into our library services to meet the needs of our users."

- "We are still investigating staff time necessary to participate in these online promotional materials."

- "Our administration has not yet embraced the technology."

- "We cannot jump on every tool that comes our way."

- "We just don't have the staff or time to do an effective job with these tools."[13]

In an early report describing his outreach effort using Facebook, Brian S. Mathews, an outreach librarian at Georgia Tech, sent 1,500 individual emails over 10 days to graduate and undergraduate mechanical engineering students. In all, 48 students replied to Mathews' email, in which he characterized himself as approachable and asked about library renovations, software, and group study space. Although he conceded the response rate was low, he was "friended" by several students and concluded, "Rather than waiting for students to approach us, it is perhaps more beneficial to be proactive and approach them. By using online social networks, librarians can increase campus visibility and update the stereotypical image, but, most importantly, we can let students know what the library is really all about."[14] Still other researchers reported a positive experience with Facebook in 2006 in which one Penn State University librarian established a Facebook profile and promoted it during library instruction sessions. As the weeks of the fall semester progressed, the librarian tracked interactions with students via email, phone, instant messenger, Facebook, and in person. By mid-December, interactions via Facebook (126) surpassed all other types of contact. These researchers also commented that librarians' concern for their patrons' privacy was, in fact, not mirrored by the patrons themselves. Consequently, the concern with protecting privacy is a "potential hindrance to our ability to provide and effectively utilize tools that students need and want [in order] to connect with others, share information and learn."[15]

Several years later, in 2009, the results of another survey of 100 libraries were published, in which the authors stated, "When asked how successful they felt that their presence on Facebook was, the libraries' responses were inconclusive. ... The answers ranged from unsuccessful to highly successful, but a significant number of [those] responding (27.5 percent) also reported feeling ambiguous in regard to whether ... having a profile on Facebook actually accomplished anything."[16] The question of the place of libraries with regard to social networking sites, and particularly Facebook, is one about which librarians, libraries, and the general public have widely varying perspectives.

Although the number in her research sample was low (n=12), Terra Jacobson, Prairie State College Library's public services manager, tried to determine exactly how libraries were using their presence on Facebook. Using a "Site Observation Form," she collected information on the number of page revisions, use of photos, presence of reference help, frequency of Wall posts, and posts by page visitors. She reported that 11 out of the 12 libraries posted information about events; 10 also had a box for searching the online catalog, eight announced research services, and four provided an Ask-a-Librarian option. Only two of the 12 libraries offered a link to actual databases. She also found a positive relationship between the number of updates and the number of users (then called "fans"), and a positive relationship between the number of add-on applications a library provided and the number of users (but she stated that neither relationship was statistically significant).[17]

The Creep-Out Factor

I realize the terms *creepy* and *creep out* are supposed to make our skin crawl, so when those words are used to describe how students might feel if they were approached by a librarian on Facebook, it really gets our attention. Librarians on Facebook could have a creep-out factor, and that's not just an opinion held by a small group: There are several published cases in which librarians have implied that students would feel a "little weird" if a librarian asked to become a Facebook friend.

Let's take them in reverse chronological order. In the summer of 2009, Kwabena Sekyere, electronic services librarian at the Miami University Libraries, who stated that reaching out to students on Facebook is a "noble idea," contributed a brief but useful article on how libraries could use Facebook as a marketing tool and as a conduit for asynchronous communication. He remarked, "The question remains: are students interested in interacting with libraries and librarians on a social networking site? ... We have to be aware of the fact that the majority of Facebook users are there for reasons not connected to academia or libraries. ... If it has the effect of creeping students out ... it may have the adverse effect of turning students away from the library."[18] Ouch! If you deal with students, you know this is potentially a reality, but it still hurts to hear it, doesn't it?

In a paper submitted to the 14th Annual Conference of the Association of College and Research Libraries (March 2009), David Beitila, Chris Bloechl, and Elizabeth Edwards described an intense effort by George Washington University Gelman Library librarians to mount a campaign titled "The Librarian Is Your Friend," which included establishing Facebook accounts. Unfortunately, it became apparent to the librarians that students don't necessarily want to be friends with librarians. Sensing another door opening, the librarians enlisted the assistance of an anthropologist and constructed a study to critically examine students' Facebook-related behavior, and the 105 responses provided the following insights:

- Facebook is a primarily—and often exclusively—recreational space and is heavily used by students for social purposes.

- Students' "academic" uses of Facebook are still inherently social (e.g., they communicate about assignments, but they perceive that Facebook negatively affects their studies).

- Students generally perceive the presence of non-peers—especially authority figures—on Facebook as an intrusion. ("Interviewees typically described the prospect of student-librarian Facebook interactions as 'weird' or 'awkward.'")

One bright spot is that 63 percent of the respondents stated they would feel comfortable communicating with librarians via Facebook about research or if they had a question (24 percent said no, and others were not sure).[19]

A student intern at Information Today, Inc., also addressed librarians and Facebook in a commentary piece from an issue of *Computers in Libraries*:

> First, never "Friend" someone who isn't one of your library assistants. No matter how good your intentions are, a lot of the same kids who never set foot in a library will be put off by a librarian attempting to contact them online. … It might take a while for kids to warm up to the idea of being friends with their school's librarian. For those students who take advantage of it, your presence on Facebook could prove extremely useful and, if it does, they'll let people know. Wait it out. Just please don't start "Poking" us kids.[20]

The author also mentioned that he disagreed with another article in the same issue in which two librarians advocated using a laptop at freshman orientations to take students' names for subsequent contact on Facebook.[21] All I can add to this is that bringing a fingerprint pad to freshman orientation is also ill-advised.

Another author sums up the situation in this way: "While it might be tempting to seek out some of your students and add them as your friends on Facebook, it is our experience that this is not the best approach. It is great to be where our users are, but let them decide when and where they need you. Encroaching too much on what they perceive as their space may be intimidating to many students and scare them off."[22]

At Valparaiso University, librarians enlisted the help of faculty to distribute 721 surveys to first-year students. The study attempted to determine how the students felt about libraries having a presence on social networking sites. Their analysis of the 366 usable responses found that 63 students (17.2 percent) would be proactive and invite the library to be a friend, 211 (57.7 percent) would accept the library's invitation to become a friend, and 92 students (25.1 percent) would not add the library as a friend. To the question, How would you feel if the library tried to send you announcements and communicate with you via Facebook and/or Myspace? they found that 156 (42.6 percent) would be receptive to this, while 134 (36.6 percent) answered "I would not pay attention but would not mind this communication." Another 45 (12.3 percent) were considerably more in-your-face, stating that they "would not pay attention and would resent the library trying to contact me through the social network," and 30 (8.2 percent) answered "other" and gave written explanations. Here are a few of them:

- "If they sent me messages, I would 'defriend' them."

- "I like to keep my personal life separate from school administration."

- "Good idea, practically every other group/organization has one, you should too."

- "Please do add students to a library Facebook. It is easy for the students to accept the library rather than searching for it. These communication efforts are appreciated."

- "It's probably not worth your time unless the library does new and exciting things."

- "Facebook is to stay in touch with friends or teachers from the past. Email is for announcements. Stick with that!"[23]

How Libraries Use Facebook

In spite of the decidedly mixed results of libraries' involvement in Facebook, it has to be acknowledged that Facebook is a juggernaut. Libraries, colleges, news organizations, and other businesses would be wise to establish a presence, if only to stake a claim and post information.

With this in mind, I decided to visit some pages libraries had constructed on Facebook. Prior to looking at any Facebook pages, I consulted the Libweb list of library servers at lists.webjunction.org/libweb to find academic and public library websites that contained a link to Facebook. For my academic library list, I randomly chose six institutions from each state. My brief exploration would provide me with a sense, albeit unscientific, of the approximate percentage of college libraries with a Facebook presence. After clicking on at least six sites from each state and the District of Columbia (a small number of sites did not load), I tallied the number of academic libraries with and without Facebook pages. Of 306 academic library homepages accessed, 82 (27 percent) had a link to a library page on Facebook, and 224 (73 percent) did not. To compare public library Facebook features with those of academic libraries, I chose one library from each state's capital city: 18 (36 percent) public libraries had an associated Facebook page, 32 (64 percent) did not.

Having no preconceptions about what I might see on these library Facebook pages, I began to keep a checklist of features, which evolved into a list of items that library pages had in common.

Types of Pages

Besides personal profile pages, which individuals create to represent themselves and connect with friends, there are two other types of Facebook pages. The first, called Facebook Pages, is intended for use by public figures, businesses, and brands to create an interactive forum and share information with fans or consumers. The second, called Groups, is intended to bring together people who share a common interest.

Keeping these page types and Facebook policy in mind, it would be inappropriate for a library to create a personal page, although in doing so it could ask people to become "friends." Nevertheless, quite a few libraries have done this; these libraries are usually named after a person, and so they probably pass the superficial scrutiny with which Facebook monitors pages. Individual librarians may, of course, create personal profiles, but libraries observing the service's official policy should choose Facebook Pages. In my random examination of Facebook entries, I noticed that libraries had used all three types of pages (Facebook Pages for businesses and organizations, Groups, and personal profiles).

Author's Note: You may remember some point in the past when you became a "fan" of a band's page, a cruise line's page, or a television show's page. Early in 2010, Facebook ended the fandom phenomenon and provided this explanation: "People will be able to connect with your Page by clicking 'Like' rather than 'Become a Fan.' We hope this action will feel much more lightweight, and that it will increase the number of connections made across the site. When you click 'Like' on a Page, you are making a connection to that Page. The Page will be displayed in your profile, and in turn, you will be displayed on the Page as a person who likes that Page. The Page will also be able to post content into your News Feed." Therefore, although page administrators and others (including Facebook in some of its documentation) still refer to "fans," the status no longer exists.

About the Pages

After scanning approximately 2 dozen pages, I realized there was no "typical" library page; library Facebook pages are as varied as the research results I summarized earlier. Some had just three or four items in the left column (some kind of combination of Wall, Info, Photos, Events, Videos, etc.). Others were much more involved. The Bryant University Library's left column features links for Wall, Info, Research (which expands to provide access to subscription databases), Business Sources (leading to the OPAC and more databases), Ask Us (this link landed on an embedded Meebo widget for messaging the library from the Facebook page), and embedded results from the library's blog (see Figure 6.1).

The Wall

The Wall is used to broadcast the institution's status. For the pages I viewed, this was a place to post announcements that covered anything from advertising library hours for spring break to soliciting applications for a research award to highlighting (and linking to) someone's blog to providing details about a "Meet the Author" day. For example, on June 3, 2011, the frequently updated Columbus Metropolitan Library's Wall (www.facebook.com/ columbuslibrary) featured posts for the kick-off of a summer reading club, a few book reviews, and a dialogue begun by a patron asking for the location of a book she believed was missing—which was answered by a librarian. The patron then posted: "THANK YOU!!! Most useful facebook page everrrrrrrr!"

In addition to the links to online catalogs, Ask-A-Librarian widgets and databases, there is room for more information in the left column. Many libraries use this space to post a profile photo (or any graphic that represents the institution), library hours, and favorite pages. Many academic libraries place links to the JSTOR Facebook page or other university departments' Facebook pages. Public libraries may show links to branch libraries' Facebook pages, authors' Facebook profiles, or town government pages. The Stony Brook University Libraries makes efficient use of its left column (www.facebook.com/pages/ Stony-Brook-University-Libraries/47593645009; see Figure 6.2).

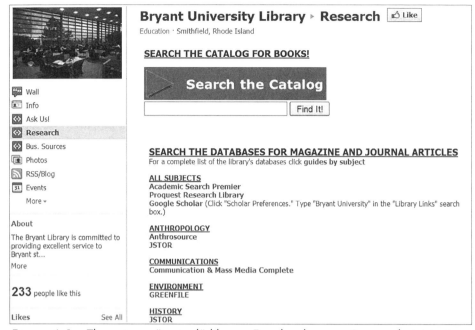

Figure 6.1   There is no "typical" library Facebook page. Page administrators may be as creative as they wish. Note multiple links in the left column; clicking the "Research" link leads to the page above, which includes OPAC and database access. [Courtesy of the Bryant University Library and Facebook]

Does the Library–Facebook Connection Meet a Need?

I received several informal responses to this question from librarians on the Web4Lib discussion list. Emily Harrell, of Gulf Coast Community College in Panama City, Florida, wrote of an unexpected use. "As far as furthering a goal of keeping connected with our students, the Facebook page did enable a faculty member to contact me during spring break, when the college and library were both closed down. The faculty member had a student who was having difficulty accessing databases. I was able to provide the correct information to the faculty member, and the student was able to get to the databases when he or she needed them."[24]

When I asked Jeremy McGinnis at the Alice E. Chatlos Library at Davis College in New York how well Facebook was working there, he sent the following reply:

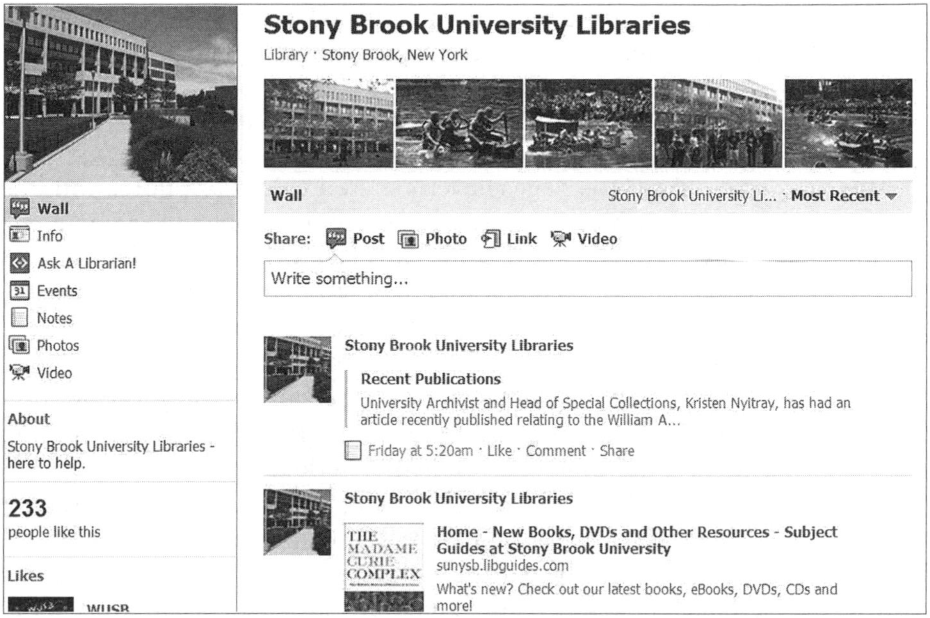

Figure 6.2   On Stony Brook University Libraries' Facebook Wall, announcements occupy the main part of the page, with links and other information appearing in the left column, including "233 People Like This." [Courtesy of the Stony Brook University Libraries and Facebook]

That's the question, isn't it? If answering this question is based on the number of responses or interactions, then the library Facebook account is pretty sickly. There is simply not a lot of interaction with the posts. It's interesting to attempt to gauge while posting what will generate a response and what will not. (We hosted a video game night recently as well as an acoustic musical evening and the posts leading up to those events garnered interaction, but the usual posts about new journals typically fail to elicit any sort of response at all, which is not all that surprising.) At the same time, I have not been dedicating an incredible amount of time to focused development of the account. It has existed more as a lengthy experiment [or] project to see how Facebook might help the library reach out and possibly retain users. One of the interesting happenings that I did not anticipate was that we have had several alumni "friend" the library. I think this is a good thing as this may help the alumni to feel connected to the library in particular and the college in general. Also the fact that they feel the freedom to comment on the library page may indicate there is some degree of effectiveness that the alumni support collection development and even excitement about different issues of various journals.[25]

Based on the dozen responses that my posting on Web4Lib garnered, no abuse of the libraries' pages has ever occurred (that's obviously good), but people who have "liked" the pages haven't shared videos or photos with the libraries' pages either (which is something commonly done on Facebook).

Another positive report regarding the presence of academic libraries on Facebook centered on how the daily student newspaper at Rutgers University in New Jersey had praised the university's libraries in two front-page articles. The first applauded the libraries' ability to add resources at a time of budget cuts, and the second focused entirely on the Facebook initiative the libraries had taken, "disseminating news and information regarding the libraries to students in a manner that will reach them more effectively." The author connected these articles to items distributed through the Facebook news feed.[26]

At the University of North Carolina in Wilmington, Anne Pemberton discovered a way librarians involved in information literacy instruction could use Facebook in teaching library concepts. For example, Facebook is a database; a profile is equivalent to a database record; each bit of information such as one's name, school, and date of birth is a field in the database record.[27]

Writing in *Library Journal*, Alison Kastner, librarian at the Popular Library in the central branch of Portland Oregon's Multnomah County Library (MCL), reported an extremely positive account of the library/Facebook nexus (see www.facebook.com/multcolib). To encourage a connection with the library through social media, Kastner and colleagues initiated a 1-day experiment in June 2010 in which they acted in a Readers' Advisory (RA) capacity. The library's marketing director posted a notice on the library's Facebook page asking people to use MCL's Wall to list a few of their most recently read book titles and, based on these titles, the RA team would recommend the next book for the patron to read. At day's end the librarians had answered 100 readers.[28] (MCL also posted a related question for its patrons asking "What do you think we should read and why?") In the same issue of *Library Journal*, Cuyahoga County Public Library's assistant marketing director Robert J. Rua described a similar RA event at his library (see www.facebook.com/pages/ Cuyahoga-County-Public-Library/61234117754); it attracted 200 patrons.[29]

When I checked MCL's Wall, I saw that a second RA day had taken place in May 2011; I contacted Kastner by email for more details. She replied:

> We made some changes to the way we did the campaign the second time. This time we created a "situation room" and had shifts of reference staff participating. The last session it was mostly just three of us doing the work, and it was a bit overwhelming with 100

questions. This session, we had 137 questions, but were more pre-pared. We also billed it as a way for our reference staff to hone their RA skills because many of them work in busy branches, and don't always get to practice in-depth RA.

As questions came in, people called out the name of the person whose question they wanted to work on, so there was no duplica-tion of effort. When they had composed their answers, they sent them to me and I posted them on the [Facebook (FB)] wall.

We chose FB for a number of reasons. We have close to 14,000 fol-lowers on FB, so we have a built-in audience. Facebook allows for conversation back and forth—it's a more engaging platform than a blog would be, and gets updated very quickly. It also allows for peo-ple who aren't participating in the conversation to view the results—so it gives a sense of community, of many people taking part.[30]

As I scanned the interaction of MCL's second RA day, I noted many positive patron comments including, "This was one of my favorite Facebook things ever," and "I checked out the book you suggested today!"

Things to Consider Before Joining Facebook

You are a committed Library 2.0 information professional, and although the jury is still out on the libraries–Facebook connection, you have decided not to sit on the sidelines. So "damn the torpedoes and full steam ahead!" Here are some important things to consider when starting a page for your library:

- Add appropriate links to library services.

- Add content such as the WorldCat widget.

- Create your pages so that they share the look of your library's homepage (if that is what you desire).

- Commit yourself to being an active page administrator. (Keeping content fresh is one of the most important variables in attracting use.)

The page administrator's role is particularly important. People may write inappropriate comments on your Wall or add unsuitable links, photos, videos, or even spam. Although the administrators at libraries I contacted reported no abuse, it's still a possibility. Facebook also provides a basic statis-tical view of your page's use through its Page Insights module. Page adminis-trators have access to the Insights and can view interesting demographic information about page visitors. I am grateful to Janet Flewelling, of the

Wallingford (CT) Public Library, for sending a sample page of her Insights statistics for our observation (see Figure 6.3). If you forget to check your Insights, it's not a problem because every week Facebook will email you a summary of activity on your pages.

Sinister Side(s) of Facebook?

While researching topics for this book, I've discovered many pitfalls associated with UContent. Anonymity can cause problems with bogus postings; companies may attempt to manipulate potential customers by inserting favorable remarks about themselves. And of course, there's the whole question of who owns the UContent. Nowhere in my research has the possibility of a menacing element been more prominent than in Facebook. As you read the following information, you may be tempted to file some of the data under paranoia and some under prudent vigilance, but I feel it's fair to lay these considerations before the reader.

Figure 6.3   Facebook Page Insights provides basic statistics for administrators. This is a report generated for the Wallingford Public Library. The library's Facebook page quickly became popular, due in part to the teen librarian's rapport with a core group of adolescent library users. [Courtesy of the Wallingford Public Library and Facebook]

Occasionally you'll come upon a news item or broadcast that gives a story about the hijacking of someone's name to set up a nasty Facebook page that discredits the person, their parents, and anyone else they have contact with. It's also a given that some individuals use Facebook to troll for photos. And as members, we sometimes make "friends" with people we wouldn't greet on the street or make eye contact with if it could be avoided. As distasteful as these scenarios are, there is, possibly, greater depth to the foreboding that may accompany indulging in social networking.

Let's begin with a relatively innocuous yet insidious issue. Facebook, it seems, analyzes your profile and then opens the floodgates so that the things you've written about are marketed to you. In a blog post titled "User Generated Content: A Triumph of Democracy or Just Another Way We are Exploited by the Tyranny of Corporations?" a Cornell student went to some effort to capture the number of times he'd mentioned his affinity for music and specifically John Lennon in his profile. Sure enough, he was able to include a screenshot of his Facebook page that was accompanied by an ad for Apple's iPad that began: "Love John Lennon?" This incisive young man also linked to Soren Mork Petersen's article in First Monday titled "Loser Generated Content: From Participation to Exploitation." Petersen wrote: "The examples in this paper outline two different strategies within the architecture of exploitation that capitalism can benefit from: 1) Through a distributed architecture of participation, companies can piggyback on user generated content by archiving it and making interfaces, or using other strategies such as Google's AdSense program. 2) Designing platforms for user generated content, such as Youtube, Flickr, Myspace and Facebook."[31]

In the article "Joining the Party. Eager to Make Friends," Saul Hansell reported that a Facebook member named "Brody Ruckus" created a group on Facebook and said if 100,000 people joined it, his girlfriend would agree to have sex with him and another woman at the same time. The group soon attracted 430,000 members. But the group was actually created by Ruckus Networks, a company involved in setting up wireless hotspots. Hansell's article provided the following account:

> Facebook shut down the group, citing its policy against commercial activities by members (unless, of course, they are paying advertisers). Michael Bebel, the chief executive of Ruckus Networks, … said the promotion was an experiment in guerrilla marketing that grew bigger than the company expected. … Facebook shut the profile down, but not before the marketers got the 430,000 members.[32]

In an article going into much more detail concerning Facebook's assault on its members' privacy, as well as its place as a middleman selling leads to advertisers, author Tom Hodgkinson, writing in London's *Guardian* (where one of his more recent articles is titled "Shakespeare Had No Blackberry and Aristotle Managed Without an iPhone"), methodically picks apart the social networking site's privacy policy. For example, under "How We Use Your Information," he highlights "to serve personalized advertising to you" and rewrites it as "We will advertise at you." He also calls our attention to the statement that "We cannot guarantee that only authorized persons will view your information. We cannot ensure that information you share on Facebook will not become publicly available. We are not responsible for third party circumvention of any privacy settings or security measures on Facebook" and rewrites the heading as "Anyone can glance at your intimate confessions." Under a heading that Hodgkinson renamed "The CIA may look at the stuff when they feel like it," he highlights the following privacy policy language:

> We may disclose information pursuant to subpoenas, court orders, or other requests (including criminal and civil matters) if we have a good faith belief that the response is required by law. This may include respecting requests from jurisdictions outside of the United States where we have a good faith belief that the response is required by law under the local laws in that jurisdiction, apply to users from that jurisdiction, and are consistent with generally accepted international standards.

Of course, certain information about you may be viewable even after you close your Facebook account because "even after you remove information from your profile or delete your account, copies of that information may remain viewable elsewhere to the extent it has been shared with others, it was otherwise distributed pursuant to your privacy settings, or it was copied or stored by other users."

As a final warning, Hodgkinson writes, "At the time of writing Facebook claims 59 million active users, including 7 million in the U.K., Facebook's third-biggest customer after the U.S. and Canada. That's 59 million suckers, all of whom have volunteered their ID card information and consumer preferences to an American business they know nothing about. Right now, 2 million new people join each week. At the present rate of growth, Facebook will have more than 200 million active users by this time next year."[33] Hodgkinson wrote this in January 2008, and his calculations proved conservative; as I have previously stated, there are more than 500 million active members worldwide.

Facebook continually revisits its policies, and as I look at its blog while writing this, I can see, "In the proposed privacy policy, we've also explained the possibility of working with some partner websites that we pre-approve to offer a more personalized experience at the moment you visit the site."[34]

Aside from these criticisms dealing with privacy and marketing, some individuals have identified a personal, social cost of active participation in Facebook. Carly Weeks, a reporter for Canada's *Globe and Mail*, describes the dilemma:

> You've got 741 Facebook friends, a cellphone crammed with numbers and an email inbox that keeps on filling up. You might consider those things indicative of your popularity, but a well-accepted social theory suggests there is a limit to the number of people any given individual can maintain relationships with … "Dunbar's number," named after Robin Dunbar, a British anthropologist popularized in Malcolm Gladwell's *The Tipping Point*, suggests that the maximum number of family, friends, co-workers and acquaintances people can have in their social circle while still being able to recall how everyone is connected to them and the group at large is about 150 … "It becomes a very, very sort of shallow form of communication," said Avner Levin, director of the Privacy and Cyber Crime Institute at Ryerson University's Ted Rogers School of Management. "Although you're obsessed with it, you're not doing anything meaningful with it."[35]

Some of the following perspectives on Facebook may seem unduly cautious, but if you are inclined to think like David Gewirtz, a cyber security specialist who frequently writes analysis and commentary for Anderson Cooper 360, you may wish to pay special attention. Gewirtz warns us that "The bulk of social networkers are between 18 and 49—prime employment years and ages where a mistake today could haunt them for many years to come." His first concern is for the network members' reputations. What's been bandied about as a joke on Facebook may surface in a search done in 2029, when an individual is up for an important job. Gewirtz's second concern is identity theft, malware, and phishing scams because social networks are open to the public and make individual members—and all their contacts—vulnerable. He is also worried about members' physical security: "Kids, women, and other often-targeted potential victims are actively providing a complete roadmap to attack. … If a criminal can easily find out where you are, what stores you frequent, what your daily habits are … you can be targeted with a level of ease never before possible."[36]

Facebook Places, a new development aimed at getting businesses to advertise at the social networking site by creating a Place page, will also permit people to "check in" at locations that have a Place page (e.g., a hotel, restaurant, or bar). Facebook Places will make use of the location-sensing capabilities of certain smartphones to broadcast members' whereabouts to their Facebook friends, but it will also allow people to find others who have recently logged their physical location using the Here Now feature, a default feature that users will have to turn off to deactivate.[37] The People Here Now feature will, of course, make it easier for individuals with questionable motives to ascertain when a person is not at home or is in a vulnerable location.

Finally, there is the unspeakable and unthinkable harm that can be done by humans when acting with a pack mentality. Cyberbullying, for example, has caused tremendous anguish and even cost people their lives.

Additional Observations Concerning Librarians and Facebook

More than a dozen information vendors and library resource brokers have pages on Facebook, including Brodart, Taylor & Francis, Credo Reference, RILM Abstracts, ProQuest, Springer, and Highwire Press. If these companies believe a Facebook presence is a good business move, perhaps libraries have another reason to set up camp there as well.

Facebook participation has another benefit. I've personally found that colleagues I have never met are likely to quickly respond to a message sent through Facebook. I realize that LinkedIn is the preferred platform for this type of communication, but Facebook has helped me meet librarians throughout the U.S. who have helped me research many topics for this book.

Endnotes

1. Educause, "7 Things You Should Know About Facebook," September 2006, accessed August 3, 2011, net.educause.edu/ir/library/pdf/ELI7017.pdf.

2. "Visitor Demographics to Facebook. Persons Age 25–34 Account for the Largest Segment of Facebook Users," comScore Data Mine, September 16, 2010, accessed August 3, 2011, www.comscoredatamine.com/2010/09/visitor-demographics-to-facebook-com.

3. Dick Stroud, "Social Networking: An Age Neutral Commodity: Social Networking Becomes a Mature Web Application," *Journal of Direct, Data, and Digital Marketing Practice* 9 (2008): 289.

4. Amanda Lenhart and Mary Madden, "Social Networking Sites and Teens," Pew Internet & American Life Project, January 7, 2007, accessed August 3, 2011, www.pewinternet.org/Reports/2007/Social-Networking-Websites-and-Teens.aspx.

5. Cathy De Rosa et al., *Sharing, Privacy and Trust in Our Networked World: A Report to the OCLC Membership*, 2007, accessed April 28, 2011, www.oclc.org/reports/pdfs/sharing.pdf: 1-2.

6. Ibid., 5–1.

7. Ibid., 8–5.

8. Darren Chase, "Using Online Social Networks, Podcasting, and a Blog to Enhance Access to Stony Brook University Health Science Library Resources and Services." *Journal of Electronic Resources in Medical Libraries* 5 (2008): 126.

9. Meredith Farkas, "Going Where Patrons Are: Outreach in MySpace and Facebook," *American Libraries* 38 (April 2007): 27.

10. Sophie McDonald and Belinda Tiffen, "UTS Gets Social: Using Social Media to Connect to Users," *incite* 30 (September 2009): 15.

11. Zeth Zietzau, "U.S. Public Libraries and Web 2.0: What's Really Happening?" *Computers in Libraries* 29 (October 2009): 8.

12. Dean Hendrix et al., "Use of Facebook in Academic Health Sciences Libraries," *Journal of the Medical Library Association* 97 (2009): 45.

13. Curtis R. Rogers, "Social Media, Libraries, and Web 2.0: How American Libraries are Using New Tools for Public Relations and to Attract New Users," German Library Association Annual Conference, June 2009, accessed August 3, 2011, www.slide share.net/crr29061/social-media-libraries-and-web-20-how-american-libraries-are-using-new-tools-for-public-relations-and-to-attract-new-users.

14. Brian S. Mathews, "Do You Facebook? Working With Students Online," *College and Research Libraries News* 67, May 2006, accessed October 30, 2011, crln.acrl.org/content/67/5/306.full.pdf+html.

15. Daniel Mack et al., "Reaching Students With Facebook: Data and Best Practices," *Electronic Journal of Academic and Special Librarianship* 8, summer 2007, accessed August 3, 2011, southernlibrarianship.icaap.org/content/v08n02/mack_d01.html.

16. Jamie M. Graham, Allison Faix, and Lisa Hartman, "Crashing the Facebook Party: One Library's Experience in the Students' Domain," *Library Review* 58 (2009): 233.

17. Terra B. Jacobson, "Facebook as a Library Tool: Perceived vs. Actual Use." *College & Research Libraries* 71(2011): 79–90, accessed August 3, 2011, crl.acrl.org/content/72/1/79.full.pdf+html.

18. Kwabena Sekyere. "Too Much Hullabaloo About Facebook in Libraries! Is It Really Helping Libraries?" *Nebraska Library Association Quarterly* 40 (summer 2009): 26.

19. David Bietila, Chris Bloechl, and Elizabeth Edwards, "Beyond the Buzz: Planning Library Facebook Initiatives Grounded in User Needs," Paper presented at the

Fourteenth Annual Conference of the Association of College and Research Libraries, Seattle, Washington, March 14, 2009. Accessed August 3, 2011, www.freedomtoread.org/ala/mgrps/divs/acrl/events/national/seattle/papers/135.pdf.

20. Scott Koerwer, "One Teenager's Advice to Adults on How to Avoid Being Creepy on Facebook," *Computers in Libraries* 27 (September 2007): 40.

21. Sarah Elizabeth Miller and Lauren A. Jensen, "Connecting and Communicating with Students on Facebook," *Computers in Libraries* 27 (September 2007): 18.

22. Mack, "Reaching Students With Facebook."

23. Ruth Sara Connell, "Academic Libraries, Facebook and Myspace and Student Outreach: A Survey of Student Opinion," *portal: Libraries and the Academy* 9 (2009): 25–36.

24. Emily Harrell, email message to author, May 12, 2010.

25. Jeremy McGinniss, email message to author, May 19, 2010.

26. Harry Glazer, "Clever Outreach or Costly Diversion? An Academic Library Evaluates Its Facebook Experience," *College & Research Libraries News* 70 (2009): 13.

27. Pemberton, Anne, "From Friending to Research: Using Facebook as a Teaching Tool," *College & Research Libraries News* 72 (2011), accessed August 3, 2011, crln.acrl.org/content/72/1/28.full.

28. Alison Kastner, "Facebook RA," *Library Journal*, May 1, 2011, accessed August 3, 2011, www.libraryjournal.com/lj/communitylibraryculture/890008-271/facebook_ra.html.csp.

29. Robert J. Rua, "Mission Connect," *Library Journal*, May 1, 2011, accessed August 3, 2011, www.libraryjournal.com/lj/communitylibraryculture/890008-271/facebook_ra.html.csp.

30. Alison Kastbner, email message to author, June 6, 2011.

31. Soren Mork Petersen, "Loser Generated Content: From Participation to Exploitation," First Monday: Peer-Reviewed Journal on the Internet 13, March 3, 2008, accessed August 3, 2011, www.uic.edu/htbin/cgiwrap/bin/ojs/index.php/fm/article/viewArticle/2141/1948.

32. Saul Hansell, "Joining the Party. Eager to Make Friends," *New York Times* (October 16, 2006), accessed August 3, 2011, query.nytimes.com/gst/fullpage.html?res=9402E3DE1E30F935A25753C1A9609C8B63&sec=&spon=&pagewanted=2.

33. Tom Hodgkinson, "With Friends Like These," *Guardian*, January 14, 2008, accessed August 3, 2011, www.guardian.co.uk/technology/2008/jan/14/facebook.

34. Michael Richter, "Another Step in Open Site Governance," March 26, 2010, accessed August 3, 2011, blog.facebook.com/blog.php?post=376904492130.

35. Carly Weeks, "Facebook Face Time Counts," *Globe and Mail*, April 2, 2009, accessed August 3, 2011, www.theglobeandmail.com/life/article977763.ece.

36. David Gewirtz, "The Dark Side of Social Networking," *Frontline Security* 4 (spring 2009): 36–37, accessed August 3, 2011, viewer.zmags.com/publication/d935d279#/d935d279/36.

37. Geoffrey A. Fowler, "Facebook Unveils Location Service," *Wall Street Journal*, August 19, 2010, accessed August 3, 2011, online.wsj.com/article_email/SB10001424052748703649004575438243433457782-lMyQjAxMTAwMDIwMzEyNDMyWj.html.

Online Reviews of Products and Services

Criticism is easy to dish out, but when it's aimed at us, it may not be as easy to take, unless, that is, it's about something that might save us time, trouble, or—best of all—money. Criticism can make you or break you. In Tim Burton's 1994 film *Ed Wood*, Johnny Depp as the title character and his ensemble read reviews of their play and, in turn, ask each other, "Do I really have a face like a horse?" and "What does *ostentatious* mean?" Finally Depp's character says, "Hey, it's not that bad. He's got some nice things to say. See, 'The soldier costumes are very realistic.' That's positive!" The play closes.

The right kind of criticism can save you, too. In Mel Brooks's *The Producers*, shady Max Bialystock, having staked his fortune on the certainty that his musical will fail, hears his talentless director Roger De Bris holler, "Have you seen the reviews? It's the biggest hit on Broadway!" Bialystock moans, "How could this happen? I was so careful. I picked the wrong play, the wrong director, the wrong cast. Where did I go right?"

From movies to moving companies, hot tubs to hotels, automobiles to autobiographies, reviews can help us avoid making mistakes. Because the economy has forced us to make more careful choices, consulting reviews has become almost compulsory. Thanks to the UContent on sites such as Yelp, Kudzu, and BizRate, it doesn't matter if *Consumer Reports* tests only a limited number of products or if the editors at CNET can't evaluate every gadget the technology tsunami washes up. Regardless of the purchase you are contemplating, the doctor you may have to visit, or the community you're thinking about moving to, someone has probably posted a relevant review online.

The same underlying principle applies when we are deciding which books to read or buy. After all, we're only pounding the terra for a finite amount of time, and few of us have unlimited financial resources, even if Amazon thinks we do. With online customer reviews, we're no longer restricted to scanning the *New Yorker*, *Atlantic Monthly*, and *New York Times Book Review*, or subscribing to *Choice*, *Booklist*, or the other standard sources we once consulted for expert editorial reviews. In fact, current research shows that we're likely to eschew the opinions of experts and look to our peers for recommendations.

The Power of Online Customer Reviews

It may take a couple of weeks, but it always comes. You buy a book, a DVD, or a toaster from Amazon and then receive an email that asks—indeed, almost insists—that you "review your recent purchase." The message means Amazon values you as a customer, but Amazon also needs you to contribute to its database of customer reviews. Why? Because research proves that customers are more likely to "convert" (buy) an item if they read positive peer reviews.

Even though a few of our favorite professional book review sites are freely accessible, a Bazaarvoice-Vizu Research poll suggests that people trust the opinions of, well, other people. The survey found that 80 percent of U.S. shoppers place more trust in items that offer customer ratings (signified by numbers of stars) and reviews. Amazon thrives not only because websites that lack reviews are considered passé, but "by amassing one of the world's largest collections of consumer opinions, the site has become a leading source of product reviews. And those reviews are a valuable magnet that lures more consumers to its website."[1] Amazon does itself a huge favor by offering its customers a gigantic database of reviews; when people find a good review at Amazon, they are likely to buy the product at Amazon as well, instead of switching to another retailer's page.

Delving further into the review phenomenon, the Bazaarvoice-Vizu Research survey showed that 44 percent considered ratings and reviews the most important thing on any retail website. Three out of four shoppers held it "extremely important/very important" to read customer reviews and added that they prefer customer reviews to expert reviews by a 6-to-1 margin.[2]

A Lightspeed Research poll of 1,000 internet users in the U.K. indicated that online *professional* reviews were the least trusted by consumers, with just 6 percent of people rating them trustworthy. Furthermore, 75 percent of review readers would decide not to buy a product after reading up to three negative reviews.[3] Kudzu, a search/review engine for local services, surveyed 600 of its users and found that 86 percent read online reviews before making purchasing decisions, and out of those, 90 percent trust online reviews.[4] From personal experience I'd have to agree: I visited an M.D. who spent a total of 5 minutes with me before dismissing me. When I returned home, I searched a site called RateMDs.com. My "caregiver" had scored one star (out of five) and had been reviewed four times. One patient wrote: "This physician spent a total of 10 minutes with me. I had planned my comments for my visit carefully, but this doctor never even attempted to examine me except to ask me where my pain was. He then said he could not help me, and when I asked him if he'd even heard of my symptoms before or if he could provide any insight, he replied in the negative. I'm not sure why he took such a disinterest in my case, but when one is suffering chronic pain, as I am, it is difficult to be dismissed without more attention." The other three reviews were similar. If I had only looked at these reviews sooner, I would have chosen a different physician!

According to the Gartner Group, sites that don't already have review mechanisms in place are planning to add them. Its survey, which polled clients responsible for ecommerce sales via a web channel, found that 33 percent of survey respondents would definitely add community-based, user-generated product reviews to their websites in 2008. Interest in this capability is driven by Amazon. Companies realize "that customers use reviews and that reviews not only drive sales, but they also provide insight into the customers."[5]

A Matter of Trust: The Integrity of Reviews

Early in 2009, the Pointy-Haired Boss in the comic strip *Dilbert* faced the reality that the company was getting killed by bad customer reviews. He told Asok, the intern, "I need you to pretend you are several different customers and write positive reviews."

The question of trust is valid. Randall Stross, a professor of business at San Jose State University, wrote:

> Like others, I used to rely on professional critics for guidance in many domains—restaurants, movies, books. When the web arrived and the opinion of every single customer could easily be published online, we began to listen to one another instead. Amazon was a pioneer in offering customer reviews of books and many other products. But there was a nagging concern. Without knowing reviewers' real identities, couldn't we be misled? In 2004, a computer glitch at Amazon temporarily revealed the real names of its reviewers, including, in at least one instance, a book author who had submitted rave reviews of his own books.[6]

Everyone should be concerned about potential fake and biased reviews. An October 2007 *PC World* poll reported 48 percent of respondents believed that fake reviews were being planted on consumer sites; 57 percent said they wouldn't buy a product if the reviews were suspect. This dark side of online reviews was also evident when the *San Francisco Register* claimed that Yelp was charging businesses to bury bad customer reviews.[7] (Yelp is an online city guide with reviews of local services; see www.yelp.com.)

Yet consider the following logic: According to Patty Smith, Amazon's director of corporate communications, fake reviews are little more than an annoyance: "There's no way to vet thousands of reviews on Amazon. But we don't need to. When readers see 35 negative reviews and one glowing one—well, they can figure it out."[8] So while we can continue to ponder whether user-generated reviews are trustworthy, the excerpted research stats suggest that the issue shouldn't concern us too much.

The Rise of eWOM

Back when information professionals searched databases on stand-alone CD workstations, news traveled only as fast as the U.S. mail or a telephone conversation. We chose our doctors, cars, and colleges based on their reputations as passed on by friends and neighbors. Although many studies have considered online reviews,[9] two are particularly interesting. The first focuses on how consumers are affected by review content. According to artificial intelligence specialist Jumin Lee and colleagues, "The importance of word-of-mouth (WOM) communications is widely accepted in traditional marketing research. … The WOM phenomenon has been transformed into various types of electronic WOM (eWOM)."[10] With WOM, both good news and bad news were rapidly disseminated; eWOM spreads this good and bad news at an unprecedented rate and range.

Lee's team attempted to quantify the effect of review quality. Using Amazon's review system, which permits users to "vote" on the "helpfulness" of reviews, they noticed that "high-quality reviews" (those which users voted as helpful) tended to fit the criteria of having relevance, reliability, understandability, and sufficiency, whereas the content of a low-quality review was not germane and insubstantial.[11] They hypothesized that as the number of high-quality negative reviews increased, the attitude of consumers became less favorable. The experiment had its subjects interact with a replicated internet shopping page for an MP3 player, complete with both high-quality and low-quality reviews. The study concluded, "First, consumers conform to online consumer reviews and their attitudes become unfavorable as the proportion of negative online consumer reviews increases. Second, high-quality negative online consumer reviews influence attitude more than low-quality consumer reviews." In essence, they added, "Negative information is also more powerful than positive information."[12] Figure 7.1 shows a typical display of customer reviews at Amazon.com. Notice that the most helpful favorable review can be viewed along with the most helpful critical review.

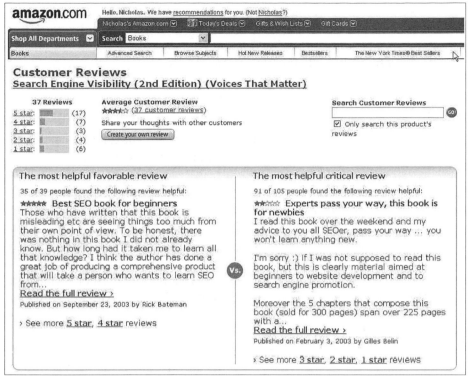

Figure 7.1   Amazon provides well-organized and diverse opinions when customers seek book reviews.

"Helpfulness" is defined by the number of users who state they "found the review helpful."

This implies that when items are accompanied by positive reviews, people are more apt to accept the item. In a sales context, they are more apt to purchase the item. This is precisely what researchers verified in an experiment that tracked books at Amazon.com. The experimental design included choosing books (and other materials) at random and collecting data about their price and sales by using Amazon's "Sales Rank" as a proxy for product sales information. At 3-day intervals, the researchers took note of positive reviews, negative reviews, and the sales ranks of the books. (Keep in mind that the top-selling book is No. 1. The investigators in this study considered, for example, a book moving from sales rank 10 to sales rank 3, an instance of a decrease in sales rank. Enigmatically, a decrease in sales rank means a book or DVD is selling more copies. The lower the sales rank, the better, from the researchers' point of view.[13]) The researchers looked at both book reviews/sales rank and DVD reviews/sales rank. At the conclusion of the study, they determined that favorable reviews decreased the sales rank of DVDs by a mean of 195.7. Over the course of several months, the authors noted that unfavorable reviews for books increased their sales rank by a mean of 4,828.4. Librarians could make the easy mental leap and imagine that, in a library context, books accompanied by good reviews might circulate more often.

Back to the Books

If we accept that users' book reviews affect sales at Amazon.com and agree that user interaction is a desirable component of the social web, how could these facts be leveraged to benefit libraries? If we incorporated more social features, such as book reviews, into our library websites, would online traffic to libraries increase? ChiliFresh and LibraryThing for Libraries (LTFL) are online public access catalog (OPAC) add-ons that provide subscribing libraries with a database of reviews, along with the ability for library users to add reviews to the OPAC.

Is there any correlation between well-received books with increased circulation? Could LTFL demonstrate this connection? I asked Tim Spalding, the creator of LibraryThing, whether the review/circulation relationship had been studied. He replied, "The stats we generate can't prove people took the book out, but they can prove people are using LTFL to find new books. You can lead a horse to water and then go away; they usually drink." His colleague at LibraryThing, Sonya Green, added, "I agree with Tim that the function of LTFL is to create an easier experience for the patron to search the OPAC. Whether this ends in an increase in circulation seems to be difficult to quantify."[14] David Kane, systems librarian at the Waterford Institute of Technology in Ireland, also addressed LTFL's possible role in increased book circulation, saying, "In terms of an academic library, the times when LTFL recommendations might most be used is during peak borrowing times, before papers are due. Restrictions in the availability of key texts may dispose students to look for alternatives. I don't know how to quantify this though."[15]

UContent Meets eWOM in the OPAC

There is a cadre of librarians who would rather suffer the fate of the doomed, gentle bookseller in the lavish 1989 film *The Cook, The Thief, His Wife & Her Lover* than permit UContent to find its way into their OPACs. Spalding said as much in *Library Journal*, at least with regard to public librarians, when he stated, "Unfortunately, public libraries are also more scared of user-contributed data than academic ones."[16] Bibliomation's Kate Sheehan, who blogs for ALA TechSource (www.alatechsource.org/blogger/17), worked at the Danbury (CT) Public Library when it became the first institution to begin working with LTFL. She sees library adoption of social software as a necessity:

> There is a huge online push for social software. The *New York Times* website will let you email a news item, post it on Facebook, or bookmark it on Delicious. That's an example of how one website has hooks into other websites. There is no reason for library websites to be any different. It goes beyond user demand. It's an expectation; it's what websites are doing now. Libraries can't afford to ignore those expectations. Adding a social component to your website makes it more engaging and more interesting. Not offering a social component, at this point, makes a website outdated. It's a matter of "with-it-ness." At the Darien Library, where I have also worked, they've reached out to people online and invited patrons to participate, and this has been extremely well-received and successful. A library website that engages users teems with activity. Here's another example: When they launched their redesigned website with more social options, they had so many more IM [instant message] reference questions. There was no change in the number of clicks-in to ask a question, but an explosion of IM reference questions accompanied the redesigned site launch.[17]

Ken Chad, executive director of Talis, a U.K. library and educational software company, conveyed a similar message. Citing a 2006 Talis survey of 2,000 internet users that found only 27 percent had visited the website of a public library, Chad said, "To avoid disintermediation, libraries must compete for attention, partly through their own web presence but also by innovative interaction with other web applications and services. The increasingly comprehensive nature of search engines creates an impression (and expectation) that anything is discoverable online."[18]

Having a well-designed site is common sense, but encouraging patrons to add information to the OPAC is another matter. Sheehan observed the patron-review phenomenon while she was at Danbury and later at Darien Library, where the Social OPAC (SOPAC 2.0; www.thesocialopac.net) is in operation. When asked whether patrons found the feature noticeably exciting or just another glitzy option, she responded, "People like to write reviews, and they want to see what other people are thinking about what they are reading. It really took off. Whenever patrons were shown the review capability, they reacted positively. I talked to people who found the review option on their own. They contribute reviews, and really enjoy doing it. The Darien Library has a lot of regular reviewers."[19]

There's an element of "genuineness" in user-generated reviews, too. "Librarians who *get it*," says LibraryThing's Sonya Green, have "gone on Amazon and looked at the professional review for a book, then scrolled down to the user reviews to really figure out if they'd like it. There are only one or two professional reviews per item, but many more user reviews. It's a different kind of experience. You're reading some guy's words (misspellings and all) and getting an idea about how a person feels about the book. If one of the reviews resonates with you, talks about the things you think are important in a book, then that review helps you—more than the dense, stoic professional review. The difference between *any* OPAC and Amazon is embarrassing. Bringing more usability to the OPAC is what we're doing."[20]

Incidentally, this chapter isn't a commercial for LTFL or ChiliFresh. Other resources, such as the previously mentioned SOPAC 2.0, can also furnish reviews and allow users to contribute reviews to the catalog. At the very least, a competent systems librarian should be able to use an existing OPAC framework to link to reviews from Amazon. Figures 7.2 and 7.3 are illustrations of well-deployed OPACs. Figure 7.2 shows the Seattle Public Library's OPAC, which includes 1) a link to reviews from LTFL, along with the capability to let the current user add a review (no sort on "helpful" votes); 2) the AnswerTips feature (double-click any word on the page for a definition, which appears in a bubble without opening a new browser); 3) a link to a book description (and more informative links) at Google Books; 4) links to reviews at Amazon.com, LibraryThing (this link actually goes to LibraryThing, where you can sort reviews by the number of times they were voted "helpful"), and WorldCat; and 5) a tag cloud of reader-contributed descriptors for the item. Figure 7.3 shows a review in an OPAC that uses ChiliFresh, in which the user can sort the reviews by newest, oldest, highest, lowest, and most useful. Note that at the bottom, the user can vote on the usefulness of the review.

For the still-hesitant librarian, the question is not "Will you?" but rather "When will you?" Take the lessons that businesses have learned and apply them to your information center.

The Fine Print

What commentary on anything involving money would be complete without the usual legal matter? Generally, online reviews are judged by readers who assess them as noteworthy, banal, or grousing. In some circumstances, however, the bellyaching can be construed as libelous, and remember, ostensible anonymity is no guarantee of privacy. Service providers may be subpoenaed to track down review writers.

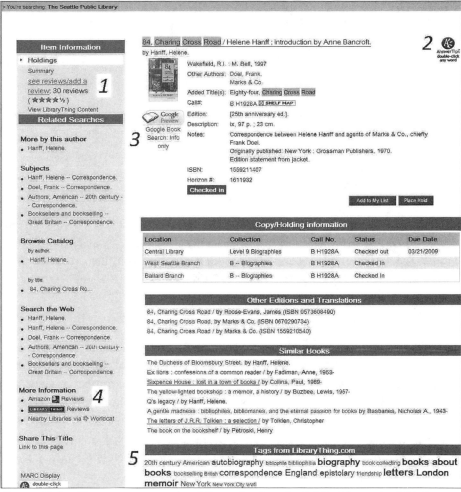

Figure 7.2   This natty item record from the Seattle Public Library's OPAC includes various helpful links. [Courtesy of the Seattle Public Library]

Here are some examples of cases in which reviews were perceived to have crossed the line. A chiropractor initiated a lawsuit when a former patient's review at Yelp suggested that the chiropractor's charges bilked insurers. The patient later published an apology on the chiropractor's Yelp page. The same article reported that a dentist sued Yelp for refusing to remove a negative posting from her page. Michael Blacksburg, an attorney involved in a Yelp lawsuit, said, "Yelp and other bulletin board sites … need to think about how to protect the reviewer and reviewee from flame wars or potentially libelous statements."[21] A plastic surgeon in Florida filed a lawsuit against a patient

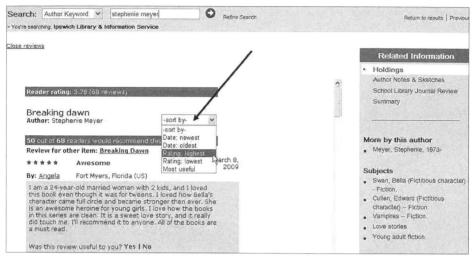

Figure 7.3   In this review in an OPAC that uses ChiliFresh, the arrow indicates the sort feature. [Courtesy of the Ipswich Library]

who gave the physician bad grades online and also against patients who canceled procedures because of reviews.[22]And a country club in Florida is seeking damages from an online reviewer for "posting a defamatory review that caused a noticeable drop in business."[23] Yelp's legal problems continued with a veterinary hospital joining the list of plaintiffs. The vet's complaint has become a class action suit, which nine additional small businesses have joined.[24] There are others; a quick search in Google News, Google News Archive, or LexisNexis should reveal more.

These types of incidents may increase, but it's unlikely Daniel Defoe's heirs will seek out "Sylvester" for beginning a one-star review of *Moll Flanders* with, "I had to read this for a book club, and a fifth of the way into it, I began to wish I were blind." Nor will Cormac McCarthy become rabid over the review "Blimp" gave *All the Pretty Horses*, which begins, "An OK book with distracting grammar."

Take note that Yelp does remove some reviews. If it believes businesses are "trading reviews" (giving a positive review in exchange for a positive review), it will delete both users' accounts. Yelp's position is that in order to preserve review integrity, it must delete accounts of any entity it thinks circulates fraudulent reviews. One businessperson is hoping to mount a class-action suit. She has created two websites asking people who have been yanked by Yelp to sign up.[25]

On the Subject of Buying and Selling

Reviews and ratings are not the only ways consumers can make an impact in the marketplace. Two examples show that companies trying to gain customer goodwill should be cautious. Nike allows customers to personalize some of their goods with a name or slogan, but in late 2000, when Jonah Perritti requested that the company print the word *sweatshop* on his training shoes, the company balked. The email exchange between Nike and Perritti, then a graduate student at MIT, was published in the *Village Voice*.[26] Similarly, Chevrolet rolled out a "write your own ad" campaign in 2006, allowing customers to select music and text to accompany existing 30-second video clips showing off the 2007 Chevy Tahoe. But the SUV promotion took a turn for the worse when the user-generated copy began to emerge. One clever wag submitted, "This powerful V8 engine gets only 15 miles per gallon. In a world of limited resources, you don't need GPS to know where the road leads" and another japed, "If you want a gas-guzzling, road-hogging, global warming-causing ride, buy a Tahoe."[27]

Other Thoughts

In *American Libraries*, Bradford Lee Eden's "Ending the Status Quo" is a piercing rebuke of the traditional OPAC. He asserts that people aren't using it because they construct and organize information on their own terms.[28] The responses to his article ran under the title "The Library Is Not a Business." The library, in our most pristine vision, may not be a business, but in reality, it does have to run like one. The conclusions of a 2008 Gartner Group business survey apply equally to libraries: "41 percent of the U.S. customers [businesses] surveyed will definitely add community capabilities. The company insiders said, 'Successful organizations will master the art of user-contributed content and communities as part of the consumer experience. ... Opinions matter. Members of communities value user-contributed content—more than content provided by the seller.'"[29] The survey results added, "Web reviews carry weight with buyers: With the web, buyers have more available to them than just the product information by the seller; they have access to reviews by professionals and users of the products. Buyers can use these reviews to determine whether a product meets or exceeds their personal requirements. As a result of this trend, many sites offer their own product reviews to avoid having buyers leave the site to investigate the product."[30]

That last sentence is significant. Why make a user dash off to another website for a book review when the OPAC can offer multiple reviews? If we substitute the words *library* for *seller*, *patrons* for *buyers*, and *library materials* for *product,* this concept applies to libraries as well as any other institution with a presence on the web.

We cannot claim that the library remains the center of research, thought, and knowledge if we simultaneously resist change. Many articles that deal with improving the image of libraries dwell on promotion. Others emphasize the need for feedback. But if librarians are serious about inviting the patron to the table, more work needs to be done. For example, let's try to quantify the effects of social networking. No one I asked, including Tim Spalding, had tried to establish a connection between item reviews and circulation statistics. Establishing this link would make social software options more acceptable to all librarians.

Similarly, considering the business research that reports high-quality reviews as more helpful than others, I have yet to see a critical mass of this type of voting (that is, I haven't seen many readers giving a "thumbs up" to the reviews of others) done in LibraryThing or ChiliFresh, even though both allow people to "vote" on the helpfulness of reviews, as shown in Figure 7.4. Note in the figure that there are a total of 84 reviews of the book, and the user can sort by the number of "helpful" votes. In this book's case, the first review

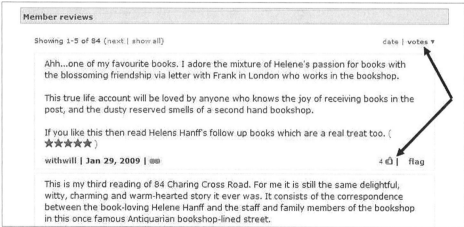

Figure 7.4   This sample LibraryThing page shows that *84 Charing Cross Road* has been reviewed by (coincidentally) 84 LibraryThing members. The arrow pointing at the word votes, the arrow pointing down toward the number 4, and the thumbs-up graphic indicate that four people have found this review "helpful." Because this review appears first in the list, it is the most helpful review of the total 84 reviews (note the top arrow indicates you can also sort by date). [Courtesy of LibraryThing]

that displays is the one that has been deemed "helpful" more often (by only four users) than the other 83 reviews.

ChiliFresh also has the ability to have its reviews sorted by highest or lowest starred rating, but neither it nor LibraryThing takes the online review task as seriously as Amazon, which presents helpful positive and negative reviews side by side. Permitting OPAC users to read reviews and write them shouldn't just be "all in good fun." Online reviews matter; let's use them purposefully.

A Scorecard on Reviews: Excerpted Research Statistics

The following are selected survey results on UContent (reviews) from Bazaarvoice (www.prophit.posterous.com/archive/10/2009).

According to "Web Users and Web Community" (Rubicon Consulting, Inc., October 2008), online reviews are second only to personal advice from a friend as the driver of purchase decisions, and user reviews are more influential than third-party reviews.

"Most Consumers Read and Rely on Online Reviews; Companies Must Adjust" (Deloitte & Touche, Accounting & Consulting, September 2007) reports that seven in 10 consumers who read reviews share them with friends, family, or colleagues, thus amplifying their impact. The same report states that more than eight in 10 (82 percent) of those who read reviews said that their purchasing decisions have been directly influenced by those reviews.

Another report, "Purchase Behavior Subsequent to Online Review Consultation" (comScore/The Kelsey Group, Global Information Provider, November 2007), noted that reviews generated by fellow consumers had a greater force than those generated by professionals.

"Consumer Feedback Survey" (BizRate, October 2007) reported that 59 percent of users considered customer reviews to be more valuable than expert reviews.

More Free Book Review Sites

For those of us who aren't quite ready to embrace user-generated book reviews, this section lists several recognized book review sites. Some of the reviews at these sites might be partially considered "user" reviews. Many of the sites use networks of reviewers with interests in certain types of books. The only prerequisite for most reviewers is that they are given a free copy of the book they've agreed to review, but this probably does not bias their critiques.

AcqNet (Acquisition Librarians Electronic Network) Book Review Sites on AcqWeb
www.acqweb.org/book_review
This gathering place for collection development librarians and acquisitions librarians has a page serving up dozens of links to reputable review sites. Most resources are free, but some require payment.

Arts & Letters Daily
www.aldaily.com/#bookreviews
Arts and Letters Daily is a resource underwritten by the *Chronicle of Higher Education*. The site maintains links to numerous book review pages including the *Boston Globe*, *Times Literary Supplement*, *Financial Times*, *Christian Science Monitor*, and many others.

Book Page
www.bookpage.com
The free online version of *Book Page* is the web equivalent of the print, subscription-based monthly review publication. Reviews are searchable and browsable back to 1996.

Book Report Network
www.bookreporter.com
This site offers readers book reviews and excerpts, author interviews, and biographies. Content updates are made weekly, and the site is searchable and browsable. Other sites in the Book Report Network include www.kidsreads.com, www.teenreads.com, www.faithfulreader.com, and www.readinggroup guides.com.

BookWire
www.bowkersupport.com/bookwire/reviews.asp
The homepage states, "BookWire offers reviews of titles you won't find anywhere else!" BookWire specializes in topics ranging from alternative medicine treatments to murder mysteries. The database covers 2004 to the present and contains more than 600 reviews.

Education Review
www.edrev.info
Education Review is made available to the public for free as a service of the National Education Policy Center at the University of Colorado (Boulder). Search or browse reviews of books covering the broad range of education scholarship and practice.

Favorite Teenage Angst Books
www.grouchy.com/angst
   Cathy Young writes the book reviews organized by categories such as Sex &
Love, Fitting In, Diary-Ish, Healing, Trouble, and Mixed-Up Families (among
others).

H-Net Reviews
www.h-net.org/reviews
   Search or browse for book reviews in the social sciences and humanities.

Library Journal
www.libraryjournal.com
   Library Journal reviews many different types of materials. If you are browsing, be sure to hover over the word *reviews* in the red horizontal menu bar at
the top of the home page, and then click Book or one of the other genres or
formats offered. You may also search reviews by using the form on the homepage. Type your keyword, click Reviews over the search box, and then click
Search.

The Modern Word
www.themodernword.com
   This site provides book reviews and essays on 20th-century modernism,
surrealism, postmodernism, and magical realism.

Nancy Pearl's Book Reviews
www.kuow.org/program.php?id=12912
   Nancy Pearl, author and librarian, reviews books via podcasts from Seattle
Public Radio KUOW.

National Public Radio Book Reviews Podcasts
www.npr.org/templates/topics/topic.php?topicId=1032
   Here you'll find book reviews, news, and author interviews from National
Public Radio.

New York Review of Books
www.nybooks.com
   Selected recent book reviews are free to view, but access to archived
reviews is pay-per-view or subscriber-only.

New York Times Book Reviews
www.nytimes.com/pages/books/index.html

This site offers free access to book reviews back to 1981. Find weekly podcasts from 2006 to the present at www.nytimes.com/ref/books/books-podcast-archive.html.

Overbooked
www.overbooked.org
Created by Ann Chambers Theis, collection management administrator for the Chesterfield County (VA) Public Library, Overbooked is recognized for excellence in book reviewing and covers all genres of fiction and "readable non-fiction" for the "ravenous reader."

Publishers Weekly
www.publishersweekly.com
Only recent reviews are free and must be browsed. To search reviews or view the reviews archives, you must subscribe. To see recent reviews, use the horizontal bar at the top of the homepage and then select a type of review or click all reviews. The categories include fiction, nonfiction, children's, religion, web exclusives, comics, and audio.

Salon
www.salon.com/books/index.html
On Salon, you can find book reviews that go back to 1995.

SF Site
www.sfsite.com
For science fiction and fantasy, this searchable and browsable site includes an extensive list of book review feature articles and author book lists.

Book reviews (and reviews in general) serve many purposes. Because of the proliferation of reviews on the web, no individual need purchase an item, contract a service, attend a concert, take a trip, see a film, or dine at a restaurant without having some foreknowledge of what to expect. In addition to the aforementioned resources for book reviews, some of the web's prominent review sites include CNET.com, an editorial and consumer ratings site for software and hardware; Buzzillions.com, which offers consumer reviews for clothing, power equipment, sporting goods, and toys; ConsumerReview.com, which offers user-generated reviews in hundreds of categories, from office equipment to video games; Epinions.com, which pays some reviewers; and Angie's List (www.angieslist.com), which is a subscription review site for local businesses including carpenters, auto mechanics, workout centers, and other service providers. The last site claims it is better than free review sites because it does not contain anonymous reviews, has a complaint resolution service, and supports its users with live help at its call centers.

Endnotes

1. Spencer E. Ante, "Amazon: Turning Consumer Opinions into Gold," Bloomberg Businessweek, October 15, 2009, acccssed August 3, 2011, www.businessweek. com/magazine/content/09_43/b4152047039565.htm.

2. Dianna Dilworth, "Consumers Prefer Customer Reviews," *DM News* 29 (July 20, 2007): 6.

3. "Three Strikes and You're Out! 75 Percent of Brits Would Change Their Mind About a Purchase After Reading Three Bad Reviews," Lightspeed Research, September 15, 2008, accessed August 3, 2011, www2.lightspeedresearch.com/ uploads/LSR_PR_OnlineReviewing.pdf.

4. "Kudzu.com Survey Reveals Online Reviews Significantly Impact Consumer Spending," Lexdon: The Business Library, December 9, 2008, accessed August 3, 2011, www.lexdon.com/article/kudzu.com_survey_reveals_online_reviews/ 417241.html.

5. Gene Alvarez, "2007 CRM Summit: E-Commerce Survey Findings," Gartner Research, ID Number G00152656, November 2, 2007.

6. Randall Stross, "How Many Reviewers Should Be in the Kitchen?" *New York Times* (September 7, 2008): BU4.

7. Fredric Paul, "Yelp Controversy Exposes Dark Side of Web 2.0," Entrepreneur, August 14, 2008, accessed August 3, 2011, www.entrepreneur.com/technology/ informationweeksmb/article196440.html.

8. Robert Luhn, "Online User Reviews: Can They Be Trusted?" PC World, October 20, 2008, accessed August 3, 2011, www.pcworld.com/article/152380/online_ user_reviews_can_they_be_trusted.html.

9. See, for example, Patrali Chatterjee, "Online Reviews: Do Consumers Use Them?" (eds.), in *Proceedings of the Association for Consumer Research*, eds. M. C. Gilly and J. Myers-Levy, 129–134, 2001, accessed August 3, 2011, ssrn.com/abstract= 900158; Chris Forman, Anindya Ghose, and BatiaWiesenfeld, "Examining the Relationship Between Reviews and Sales: The Role of Reviewer Identity Disclosure in Electronic Markets" *Information Systems Research*, April 30, 2008, accessed August 3, 2011, papers.ssrn.com/sol3/papers.cfm?abstract_id=918978; Nikolaos Korfiatis, "Evaluating Content Quality and Usefulness of Online Product Reviews," July 7, 2008, accessed August 3, 2011, papers.ssrn.com/sol3/papers. cfm?abstract_id=1156321; and Lan Xia and Nada Nasr Bechwati, "Word of Mouse: The Role of Cognitive Personalization in Online Consumer Reviews," *Journal of Interactive Advertising* 9, fall 2008, accessed August 3, 2011, www.jiad.org/ article105.

10. Jumin Lee, Do-Hyung Park, and Ingoo Han, "The Effect of Negative Online Consumer Reviews on Product Attitude: An Information Processing View," *Electronic Commerce Research and Applications* 7 (2008): 341–352.

11. Ibid., 343.

12. Ibid., 349.

13. Nan Hu, Ling Liu, and Jie Jennifer Zhang, "Do Online Reviews Affect Product Sales? The Role of Reviewer Characteristics and Temporal Effects," *Information Technology & Management* 9 (2008): 201–214.

14. Tim Spalding and Sonya Green, email message to author, February 2, 2009.

15. David Kane, email message to author, December 6, 2009.

16. Melissa L. Rethlefsen, "Chief Thingamabrarian," *Library Journal*, January 15, 2007, accessed August 3, 2011, www.libraryjournal.com/article/CA6403633.html.

17. Kate Sheehan, email message to author, January 6, 2009.

18. Paul Miller, "Library 2.0: The Challenge of Disruptive Innovation," Talis, February 2006, accessed August 3, 2011, cmapspublic2.ihmc.us/rid=1211299379745_1806224281_20373/447_Library_2_prf1.pdf.

19. Kate Sheehan, email message to author, January 6, 2009.

20. Sonya Green, email message to author, February 4, 2009.

21. Deborah Gage, "Dentist Sues Over Negative Yelp Review," *San Francisco Chronicle* (January 13, 2009): D1.

22. Jon Burstein, "Web Reviews Can Lead to Lawsuits," *South Florida Sun-Sentinel* (November 12, 2008).

23. "Businesses Sue Over Online Reviews," UPI.com, November 9, 2008, accessed August 3, 2011, www.upi.com/Business_News/2008/11/09/Businesses_sue_over_online_reviews/UPI-91791226261906.

24. Jennifer Fiala, "More Businesses Join in Yelp Class Action Suit," April 3, 2010, accessed August 3, 2011, www.yelp.com/topic/los-angeles-more-businesses-join-in-yelp-class-action-lawsuit.

25. Ellen Lee and Anastasia Ustinova, "Merchants Angry Over Getting Yanked by Yelp," *San Francisco Chronicle* (July 4, 2008): C1.

26. "Making Nike Sweat," Village Voice, February 13, 2001, accessed August 3, 2011, www.villagevoice.com/2001-02-13/news/sports/1.

27. Julie Bosman, "Chevy Tries a Write-Your-Own-Ad Approach, and the Potshots Fly," NewYorkTimes.com, April 4, 2006, accessed August 3, 2011, www.nytimes.com/2006/04/04/business/media/04adco.html. See also Antone Gonsalves, "SUV Haters Vent in GM's Make-Your-Own-Ad Contest," Information Week, April 3, 2006, accessed August 3, 2011, www.informationweek.com/news/184428387.

28. Bradford Lee Eden, "Ending the Status Quo," *American Libraries* 39 (March 2008): 38.

29. Gene Alvarez, "The Business Impact of Social Computing on Web Selling," Gartner Research, ID Number: G00161362, September 26, 2008.

30. Alvarez, "Business Impact of Social Computing on Web Selling," 6.

chapter 8

Self-Publishing

Self-publishing has gone from being the last resort of the desperate and talentless to something more like out-of-town tryouts for theater or the farm system in baseball. It's the last ripple of the Web 2.0 vibe finally washing up on publishing's remote shores. After YouTube and Wikipedia, the idea of user-generated content just isn't that freaky anymore.[1]

Wired's Chris Anderson described what happens when "infinite shelf space" combines with "real-time information about buying trends and public opinion." He explained that an obscure book called *Touching the Void* became a best-seller because it appeared as an Amazon recommendation when readers searched for Jon Krakauer's popular *Into Thin Air*. Anderson defined this phenomenon, which he deemed the Long Tail, with this question from a music company CEO: "What percentage of the top 10,000 titles in any online media store (Netflix, iTunes, Amazon, or any other) will rent or sell at least once a month?" The answer is a surprising 99 percent. The takeaway from this story is that the "hits" sell, but the "misses" sell, too. Anderson summarizes this with an example that resonates with both information professionals and end users:

> What's really amazing about the Long Tail is the sheer size of it. Combine enough nonhits on the Long Tail and you've got a market bigger than the hits. Take books: The average Barnes & Noble carries 130,000 titles. Yet more than half of Amazon's book sales come from *outside* its top 130,000 titles. Consider the implication: If the Amazon statistics are any guide, the market for books that are not even sold in the average bookstore is larger than the market for those that are. … In other words, the potential book market may be twice as big as it appears to be, if only we can get over the economics of scarcity. Venture capitalist and former music industry

consultant Kevin Laws puts it this way: "The biggest money is in the smallest sales."[2]

Although Anderson blogged about the Long Tail in 2004, his words rang true in 2011 when book industry behemoth R. R. Bowker released its April statistics. Under the headline "Print Isn't Dead," its press release stated that traditional print title output in 2010 had a slight 5 percent increase over 2009, but "the non-traditional sector continues its explosive growth, increasing 169% from 1,033,065 in 2009 to an amazing 2,776,260 in 2010. These books, marketed almost exclusively on the web, are largely on-demand titles produced by reprint houses specializing in public domain works and by presses catering to self-publishers and 'micro-niche' publications."[3] Bowker's vice president for publishing services, Kelly Gallagher, remarked, "Non-traditional publishing, especially related to print-on-demand, continues to offer new avenues and opportunities to grow the publishing industry. Given the exponential growth over the past three years, it's showing no signs of abating." Observing that these self-publishing companies accounted for more than half the titles produced in 2009, Gallagher continued, "Today, these companies are opening up new publishing venues by producing titles for very niche markets and also bringing public domain titles back to life. The net effect creates a long-tail that has no end."[4]

A *Wall Street Journal* poll (June 3, 2010) seems to support the sustainability of the nontraditional trend. When it asked, "How big a threat is digital self-publishing to the traditional book industry?" 48.7 percent (424 votes) said it was a "big threat," 32.8 percent (285 votes) said it was a "moderate threat," 13.3 percent (116 votes) said it was a "low threat," and 5.2 percent (45 votes) said it was "no threat."

A closer look at the Bowker statistics reveals that most of the "new" titles were actually produced by companies that specialize in reprints and titles in the public domain. The top seller was BiblioBazaar (owned by BiblioLabs; www.bibliolabs.com), which specializes in "digital preservation of classic material," and the third-top producer was Kessinger Publishing (www.kessinger.net), another company specializing in reprints. Rounding out the top 10 were print-on-demand publishers and micropresses, including CreateSpace (www.createspace.com), Lulu (www.lulu.com), PublishAmerica (www.publishamerica.com), Xlibris (www.xlibris.com), and AuthorHouse (www.authorhouse.com).

When applied to book publishing, the Long Tail theory would say the more specialized a title is, the less likely a large house will pick it up and publish it. The more specialized a title is, however, the more likely it is to be very useful to a certain group of people. But Victoria Strauss, writing in the popular Science Fiction & Fantasy Writers of America Writer Beware blog, notes:

But I have to wonder, who is buying all these books? Or, put another way, how many of these books are being bought at all? In the long-tail digital universe, where books are nothing more than bits and bytes, it really doesn't matter if you offer thousands of books that never sell a single copy, as long as you offer tens of thousands that sell just a few. Which is why I think it would be very interesting to compare sales figures for the POD [i.e., print-on-demand] sector (info that does not seem to be available) to title growth over the past couple of years. It might place that huge increase in titles in a somewhat different perspective.[5]

Although it disproves author Samuel Johnson's aphorism that "No man but a blockhead ever wrote, except for money," there are authors who are not trying to turn a book into a financial bonanza. Professionals in the fields of animation, photography, architecture, and interior design may need just enough copies to showcase their work. Individuals are self-publishing cookbooks, wedding albums, and baby picture books. The relative ease with which one can self-publish books—and I don't mean blogs, Wikipedia articles, or knols (i.e., knol.google.com)—assures that the growth trend of self-published materials will continue, regardless of the number of books actually sold.

The Self-Publishing Continuum

Writers self-publish for a variety of reasons, and even well-known authors have done so. Walt Whitman self-published *Leaves of Grass* in 1855. The poignant novella *Maggie: A Girl of the Streets* was self-published by Stephen Crane in 1892. Among more recent notable authors who have self-published are poet Nikki Giovanni (*Black Feeling, Black Talk* in 1968) and novelist Pat Conroy, who self-published his first book *The Boo*, a novel about life as a cadet at the Citadel, in 1970. Though Conroy said the book was "greatly flawed," it marked his territory and assured readers that he would "be heard from again."[6] Of course there is also William P. Young, the author who self-published *The Shack*, of which more than 10 million copies are in print. Yet the term *self-publishing* has different meanings; the concept may be viewed on a continuum. At one end is pure self-publishing, in which the author has complete control of the project (and reaps all the profits, if any). At the opposite end is vanity publishing, in which the author pays to have the project executed.

Pure Self-Publishing

In the purest form of self-publishing, the author is in charge of all aspects of the book. He or she writes, edits, designs, prints, binds, stores, markets, and sells the book. Certain tasks may be outsourced, such as printing and binding, but the author decides who will carry out these tasks. Furthermore, the author retains all rights to the book and claims all the profits. The chief advantage of this form of self-publishing is the author's complete control, but the major disadvantage is that the author must also find distribution channels and sell the books.

The book *What Color Is Your Parachute?* is an example of this type of self-publishing. In an interview for the website Go Publish Yourself, author Richard Bolles explained his experience:

> I simply typed the manuscript—it ran about 168 pages—pasted in some drawings/lithographs from books that supplied such things, whose copyright date had been exceeded, and took it down to my local copy shop. They printed, for me, about 100 copies at a time, and bound the book with a spiral binding. People could order it directly from my office—it was written primarily for campus ministers, and they all knew my address—but only from there, until Ten Speed Press came along. I charged just a little over the cost (i.e., $6.95 per book). I sold about 2,000 copies until the first commercial edition came out in late 1972.[7]

The success of *What Color Is Your Parachute?*, which is the Bible for job hunters, has been prodigious. Revised annually to keep its content fresh, it is bought by an average of 20,000 people each month. With more than 10 million copies in print, it has cumulatively spent 288 weeks on the *New York Times* best-seller list. *What Color is Your Parachute?* is ranked No. 1 in Amazon's Job Hunting category.

Assisted Self-Publishing

Assisted self-publishing refers to companies that help authors get their books into print and/or digital form. These companies offer a range of services and may or may not charge setup fees, but almost always offer add-on features, which may become expensive. For example, Xlibris offers several packages, beginning at $449 and increasing up to $14,999. Authors choosing the less-expensive packages can add features such as marketing services, copyediting, and copyright registration. Though Xlibris charges authors to create books, it stresses that (unlike vanity presses) it processes and fulfills book orders, pays royalties, and offers marketing support. It is this "give and take" between author and publisher that helps Xlibris and other print-on-demand (POD) services escape the pejorative designation of *vanity* press.

There are different business models. Other popular companies such as Lulu and CreateSpace do not charge the author for creating the book but instead make money by asking for a percentage of the list price and are paid only when a book is sold, printed, and shipped. Some of these companies provide you with an ISBN, or you may need to buy one and provide it for yourself.

Depending on the publishing package the author selects, most companies will also convert a book submission into digital files that can be read by various ebook readers—an attractive feature, with ebook sales growing so quickly. January 2011 ebook sales reports stated that ebook purchases jumped 116 percent over January 2010.[8] Table 8.1 provides details on the offerings of several popular assisted-self-publishing companies.

The state of the art for these self-publishing companies is POD. POD services will print a book only after it has been ordered, thereby saving money on warehousing. Also, neither the publisher nor the author is ever stuck with extra copies. Writing in the *Canadian Library Journal*, Patricia Hayward pointed out another advantage of self-publishing: "One very important aspect of timing is the speed at which the author-publisher can get the work into the marketplace. A commercial publisher tends to work slowly with a manuscript that will be one of several in various stages of development. … Self-publishers who focus all their attention on a single book can get it to the release stage quickly. This is particularly important for time sensitive non-fiction."[9] Library guru Walt Crawford (who has self-published books with both Lulu and

Table 8.1   The best-selling self-publishing companies and their basic features

Publisher	Contract	Distribution	Initial or basic cost	Royalties or sharing	Added-value-package costs	Digital version
CreateSpace	Nonexclusive	Author's estore, Amazon.com, other outlets depending on package	None	Yes; percentage depends on plan and list price	Begins at $758	Yes, through Amazon's Kindle Direct Publishing
Lulu	Nonexclusive	iBookstore, eBay, Amazon Marketplace, Amazon.com, BN.com, Ingram	None	Yes; percentage depends on list price	$369 to $4,499	Yes (for a fee), through ePUB, for Mac, PC, iPhone, Sony, and Stanza
Xlibris	Nonexclusive	Xlibris online bookstore, Baker & Taylor, Ingram; certain books at Amazon.com and BN.com	$399	Royalty: 25 percent of retail price of book	Up to $13,999	Yes, with eAdvantage package and other packages
AuthorHouse	Nonexclusive	AuthorHouse online bookstore, Ingram, Baker & Taylor, BN.com, Amazon.com	$599	Payment depends on book's selling price, cost to print, and percentage author wants to claim as royalties	$599 ($399 for poetry)	Yes, included in all packages
PublishAmerica	7-year exclusive contract	Baker & Taylor, PublishAmerica online bookstore	None	Negotiated	None	Depends on contract

CreateSpace) verifies this by adding that POD "makes it feasible to do an unusually timely book."[10] POD companies do a respectable job producing a handsome end product. I have a copy of Crawford's *But Still They Blog*, which he self-published using Lulu. It's a well-made, attractive paperback book.

POD's potential disadvantages must be considered as well. Michael Owens, author and filmmaker, reminds self-published writers that major media outlets will not review POD books. He adds, "People will judge your book by its cover. … If graphic design is not your area of expertise, wait until you have enough capital to hire a professional."[11]

Vanity Press

A vanity press is a publishing service that charges the author in advance for printing books. Vanity presses do not screen for quality (although some state that they exercise a degree of selectivity). They rarely engage in any proofreading and may require the author to agree to certain other conditions (such as purchasing a quantity of books). The charges include a markup, which makes vanity publishing more expensive than pure self-publishing. Basically, vanity presses assume no financial risk, whereas commercial publishers usually provide the author an advance against the monies they hope the book will earn. Three vanity presses I explored in an information sciences context are Dorrance Publishing (www.dorrancepublishing.com), Ivy House (www.ivyhousebooks.com), and Vantage Press (www.vantagepress.com).

Subsidy Press

A subdivision of vanity presses, subsidy presses charge the author to print and bind a book but theoretically contribute some amount of money toward the preparation of the book or provide services such as copyediting, warehousing, and marketing. The writer may still earn income in the form of a royalty. According to Victoria Strauss, writing in the "Writer Beware" section of the Science Fiction & Fantasy Writers of America blog: "The lines have blurred over the past few years [between vanity presses and subsidy presses]. What you'll most often find nowadays is neither a vanity publisher nor a subsidy publisher in the classic sense, but a hybrid of the two—following the vanity model in terms of pricing and selection (building a fat profit into its fees and publishing anyone who will pay), and the subsidy model in terms of book ownership and income to the author (the publisher owns the finished books, and the author earns royalties on sales)."[12]

Services Make Publishing Easy

With the sales of self-published books growing, one could logically assume that the number of individuals producing manuscripts is also growing. In September 2002, a survey of more than 1,000 Americans found that 81 percent "think they have a book in them." Following that survey's release, Neva Grant, a correspondent for National Public Radio, undertook a quick live poll at a bookstore in Washington, DC. She asked 100 people if they had thought they could write a book, and 63 percent answered affirmatively.[13] Writers, however, could not be self-publishing at this rate if digital publishing companies were not making it easier and easier to do.

According to Bowker's statistics for 2009, the five top "Author Solutions Services" (and their title output) are CreateSpace (21,819), Lulu (10,386), Xlibris (10,161), AuthorHouse (9,445), and PublishAmerica (5,698).[14]

My Experience With CreateSpace

To really learn what needs to be done to self-publish with a POD publisher, you've got to do it yourself. So I did. I like buying my books from Amazon, so I chose CreateSpace, Amazon.com's POD company. Before you can get to the fun of creating a book, you've got to do all the prerequisites: 1) Create an account and password, 2) agree to terms and conditions, 3) enter your bank account number (for direct deposit of royalties, or pay an $8 handling fee every time CreateSpace sends you a check), and 4) enter your Social Security number (CreateSpace has to report your royalties to the Internal Revenue Service). Remember, no porn or offensive material is allowed, and a minimum of 24 pages is required. Now that you have dispensed with all the preliminaries, you can focus on how to allocate the money from sales.

CreateSpace has a Standard Plan and a Pro Plan. You pay $39 per book title the first year you enter the Pro Plan, and $5 per title per year every year after the first year. You pay nothing with the Standard Plan. The advantages of the Pro Plan are that you get a bigger cut of the sales price and can use CreateSpace's Expanded Distribution Channel, which includes possible sales to libraries, certified resellers, and bookstores. Here's the rough difference between royalties from the Standard Plan and the Pro Plan. With the Standard Plan, a book priced at $16.00 with 150 pages earns Amazon $10.90 and nets the author $5.10. With the Pro Plan, Amazon gets $9.05 and the author earns $6.95 (see www.createspace.com/Products/Book/ProPlan.jsp).

Being a parsimonious fellow, I went with the Standard Plan. It gives you a free ISBN and an eStore front from which to sell your books, and it enables you to sell on Amazon.com (see the Free Self Publishing articles at www.face

book.com/free.self.publishing). Plus, you can buy your own book at a discounted price and sell the copies yourself. Also, there is a nonexclusive agreement, so if a publisher offers you a contract after seeing your CreateSpace book, you are free to sign it.

Now the fun begins. At www.createspace.com/Products/Book, click Create a Book. Name your project. Click the Paperback radio button. Let CreateSpace guide you through the process—just click Guided Setup Process. Enter the title, the subtitle, the author, and a description of the book. Click Save and Continue, and choose your paper color. Next, tell CreateSpace whether you are providing your own ISBN or if you'll accept the ISBN it will assign to your book (for free). If you own the ISBN, you can designate a name for your own imprint; if you take the freebie, your book will be published by CreateSpace. Select a Book Industry Standards and Communications category. I decided to put my book, which I called *Inscribed by Author*, in the Reference-Quotations category.

The creative part comes next. Upload a PDF of what you've written. But before you upload your PDF, play with the fonts and add some original illustrations or images in the public domain from Wikimedia or elsewhere. When it looks good, go on and upload it. CreateSpace will tell you immediately that it was successful. Next, you get to build your own cover. You may upload cover art, play with the fonts, and even include a photo of yourself for the back cover. CreateSpace presents an ample number of eye-catching templates from which to choose (see Figure 8.1).

The next page asks you to provide more information for the cover. When you are done it's time to set a list price for your book and enable your eStore and sales on Amazon.com. I didn't want to be greedy, so I started with a list price of $5.00, only to learn that if I went that route on the Standard Plan, I was going to lose money because CreateSpace charges a small flat fee to print the book and wants its cut first. It wasn't until I upped the price to $15.99 that I was "making" about $6.00 per book. After examining all of your files, CreateSpace will print a proof and provide a link to your own eStore. With a service this easy to use, you can see why self-publishing is catching on.

There is no pressure to do so, but CreateSpace offers packages beyond the basics that I have described. There are four Total Design Freedom Solutions, which include extras such as a custom cover, copyediting, marketing tools, and phone support. These range from $758 to $4,999. But you don't have to buy a package if you know which à la carte add-ons you need. For example, the Publicity Kit is $499 (www.createspace.com/Services/PublicityKit.jsp), and a professionally rendered unique illustration for your book cover is $1,499 (www.createspace.com/Services/IllustratedBookCover.jsp).

A compendium of the most imaginative inscriptions by authors to their readers.

"When a man writes from his own mind, he writes very rapidly. The greatest part of a writer's time is spent in reading, in order to write; a man will turn over half a library to make one book." -- Samuel Johnson

"Inscribed by Author"

Nick Tomaiuolo

Publisher logo
1.25" x .8"
(width and height)
300 DPI recommended

Barcode Area
We will add the barcode for you.
Made with Cover Creator

Figure 8.1   This cover was created for a self-published book using CreateSpace's Cover Creator. [Courtesy of CreateSpace; cover photo by Kristin Tomaiuolo, copyright 2011, all rights reserved]

Other Options at Amazon.com

Authors can have their books printed by any company and still sell them through Amazon.com's Advantage Program (www.amazon.com/gp/seller-account/mm-product-page.html?topic=200329780). To enroll an item, you need a valid ISBN. You set the price, pay Amazon 55 percent of that amount, pay to ship to the Amazon warehouse, and pay a $29.95 annual membership fee (www.amazon.com/gp/seller-account/mm-product-page.html?topic=200329770).

Self-published authors can also sell their books on Amazon Kindle. By using Amazon's Kindle Direct Publishing (kdp.amazon.com/self-publishing/signin), writers can upload electronic versions of their books to Amazon's ebook reader store. Kindle Direct Publishing supports MobiPocket, Adobe PDF, plain text, Word, or Zipped HTML. Authors set their own price and receive 35 percent of the sales (kdp.amazon.com/self-publishing/help?topic Id=A29FL26OKE7R7B).

... And One at Barnes & Noble

Barnes & Noble unveiled its own economical method for self-published writers to easily upload and distribute their works, called PubIt!, in October 2010 (pubit.barnesandnoble.com). Authors are able to create an account, specify payment options, and upload titles for any work for which they hold the rights. PubIt! accepts ePUB files for direct sale (ePUB is the free and open ebook standard agreed upon by the International Digital Publishing Forum). PubIt! also has a free converter tool to convert popular file formats into ePUB. (See the PubIt! FAQ at pubit.barnesandnoble.com/pubit_app/bn?t=support.)

Self-Publishing and Traditional Publishers

Though hardly eager to accept unsolicited manuscripts, traditional publishers don't want to miss out on a good thing. In addition to monitoring the catalogs of author solution service companies, some traditional publishers have established websites that encourage authors to post their work. This affords the publishers a preview of the works of unpublished authors and the prospect of signing the most talented participants to book contracts. At HarperCollins, the writing community is called authonomy (www.authonomy. com), and the mantra is "Get Read. Get Noticed. Get Published" (www.authonomy.com/about.aspx). The company's digital publisher Clive Malcher said authonomy was created because HarperCollins did not wish to overlook any self-published gems. HarperCollins signed Steve Dunne, who had posted his self-published novel *The Reaper* on authonomy, after he'd already sold several thousand copies, but Malcher says they wouldn't have discovered him without the site.[15]

An alternative version of the HarperCollins scenario is WestBow Press (www.westbowpress.com). WestBow is the POD service of Thomas Nelson, the well-known Christian book publishing company. Rather than asking potential authors to post their work, Thomas Nelson promises to monitor a self-published work executed through WestBow. Enticing authors with "discovery opportunities," a WestBow page states, "As a Division of Thomas Nelson, WestBow Press titles will be regularly reviewed by the parent company. For authors who hope to one day be signed by a traditional publisher, this is an opportunity to get your foot in the door. While there is no guarantee of the number of titles to be signed each year, Thomas Nelson will monitor the WestBow Press catalog for talented authors that rise to the top." Authors can self-publish here for a fee beginning at $999 for the Essential Access package and topping out at $3,999 for the Online Platform bundle.

Yet another variation is Harlequin Enterprises's Dellarte Press (www.dellartepress.com). Known for its romance novels, Harlequin offers Dellarte as an assisted self-publishing solution. There are no intimations about possible book deals, only straightforward self-publishing packages that begin at $599 and go up to $4,499, depending on the features the author decides upon.

Websites Related to Self-Publishing

- Aaron Shepard's Publishing Page (www.newselfpublishing.com): Shepard is a self-published author. This site does try to sell you books, but it also contains helpful articles for other self-publishing authors.

- The Book Designer: Practical Advice to Help Build Better Books (www.thebookdesigner.com): Veteran book designer Joel Friedlander maintains this site brimming with practical information, including mistakes to avoid as a self-publisher, and information about ebooks and ebook readers. Friedlander has designed books for clients that can compete head-to-head with books from major publishers. He supplies files for Lightning Source, CreateSpace, and other digital printers.

- An Incomplete Guide to Print-on-Demand Publishers (www.books andtales.com/pod): While not comprehensive, this index offers evaluative comments and lists the features and costs of dozens of POD publishers.

- IndieReader.com (www.indiereader.com): This website is a frequently updated blog with posts of interest on various aspects of self-publishing.

- MediaShift (www.pbs.org/mediashift): Not exclusively about self-publishing, this PBS blog frequently considers topics on the provision of digital content.

- POD, Self-Publishing & Independent Publishing (mickrooney.blogspot.com): Mick Rooney keeps this blog fresh with news on book events, statistics on self-publishing, and reviews of publishing services.

- Print-on-Demand (POD) Printers and Publishers (www.bookmarket. com/ondemand.htm): This site contains another long list of links to POD services.

- Science Fiction & Fantasy Writers of America: Writer Beware (www.sfwa.org/for-authors/writer-beware/pod): Full of

cautionary information, case studies, and basic education
material for self-publishers, this is one of the most incisive blogs
for writers considering self-publishing.

- Self-Publishing Discussion Group (groups.google.com/group/
self-publishing): With more than 351 members, it may be worth
looking into if you have a question you'd like to post.
- Self-Publishing Pointers (www.self-publishing-pointers.com): This
site contains many informative articles for self-publishing novices.
- Self-Publishing Resources (www.selfpublishingresources.com): Run
by a consulting firm, this site contains informative entries in many
categories of self-publishing, including social media, writing
tutorials, editing, and book promotion.

The Google Book Project and the Self-Published Author

Google's quest to make every book available via its Book Project does not distinguish between books published by commercial publishers, books in the public domain, and books published by the end user. In a Google Books help article (books.google.com/support/bin/answer.py?hl=en&answer=43782), an individual asked, "I'm an author. How do I add my books to Google Books?"

There are really two answers. For a traditionally published book, Google encourages authors to nudge their publisher to join the "Partner Program." Becoming involved with the Partner Program allows publishers (and the self-publishing author) to promote books for free. According to Google (books.google.com/partner), Google "helps users discover your books," "keeps your content protected," and "drives book sales" by providing links to bookstores and online retailers.

But even if you are not represented by a publisher, you can promote your books. The Google Author FAQ (books.google.com/googlebooks/author_faq. html) says, "Just sign up here" to get links through books.google.com/partner/signon?apply=Click+Here+to+Apply. To register for a Google Partner account, go to books.google.com/partner/signon. When you have completed all the initial steps and agree to the conditions of the program, you will be able to access the Add Books form (books.google.com/partner/add-books-form), which outlines the steps for adding your titles to the Google Books program.

Identify your book; specifically, enter one ISBN for each book. The cost of a single ISBN is $125. ISBNs are distributed and sold through Bowker. You can learn more about ISBNs (including buying them with add-ons or in bulk) by visiting the self-publisher services link at www.bowker.com/index.php/component/content/article/34/264. The identification step also requires the author's name and the book's title.

Next, decide whether you want to upload a PDF file of your book or ship physical books to Google in California.

You will earn money from the context-sensitive ads (sponsored links) posted alongside your book. Other links take potential buyers to sites to buy your books and increase your revenue.

Google has posted testimonials from several self-published authors who posted their work with Google Books. For example, author Susan Foote Wagner said, "When my book appeared in Google Books, I had a wave of new orders I didn't expect, and started receiving email from buyers who said they found my book on the internet … I hadn't been doing any other kind of marketing for about a year, so I knew they found me through Google" (read more at books.google.com/googlebooks/author_wagner.html).

Google eBooks and the Self-Published Author

Formerly known as Google Editions, Google eBooks (books.google.com/help/ebooks/overview.html) was launched in December 2010. Because Google has already scanned millions of titles from commercial publishers and self-publishers, the new venture positions Google to become the world's largest bookseller. At launch, Google reported its database held 3 million books, but since most are in the public domain and are free, only about 200,000 were for sale.[16] When a consumer buys a Google eBook, the work will be available in the consumer's personal library on Google's "cloud" (its phalanx of servers); the consumer may access this personal library on any platform. You could begin reading a work on your iPhone, continue it on a tablet reader, go back to it on a desktop computer, and then access it from another smartphone. In fact, almost any internet-connected device will be able to access the books in the consumer's personal library on demand. (Although Amazon's Kindle was originally unable to use Google's eBooks, companies like RetroRead at www.retroread.com are converting public domain titles in Google's collection to the Kindle-compatible mobi file format.)

Everyone is invited to place the books they've written (or hold the rights to) on the "cloud"—self-published authors included. In fact, when self-published authors attempt to enroll in the Partner Program, they will be ushered to an addendum to their Google Partner agreement called Terms & Conditions for Google Editions (for some reason, Google hasn't changed the name to Google eBooks at the Terms & Conditions page, even though you must select the Google eBooks tab to read the terms). To be included in Google eBooks, the author (or rightsholder) must agree to these appended terms (books.google.com/partner/google-edition). The implications for the self-published author are enormous. Of course, readers will still consult book reviews, but they will also use Google Book search (books.google.com/advanced_book_search) and Google eBook search (books.google.com/ebooks) to find interesting titles. This could put a newly self-published author on almost equal footing with established writers.

Libraries and Self-Publishing

Laura Dawson, an independent publishing consultant, describes multiple dilemmas surrounding self-published works and libraries. She points out that the Library of Congress does not accept cataloging in publication data from self-published authors. This gives mainstream publishers an edge since their cataloging data is accepted, and therefore, these publishers dictate what publications get taken seriously in the library world, with most self-published works never catalogued at the Library of Congress. She also observes that when library budgets decrease and book purchases decline, considering self-published books becomes a low priority. She suggests that librarians make an effort to add self-published works to their collections by searching and browsing the catalogs of self-publishing services.[17] Another librarian, Pat Hayward, shares this view: "Good writers are writing and publishing good books on specialized subjects that trade publishers will no longer produce because of limited financial returns possible on these books. Libraries that want to build well-rounded, relevant subject collections will increasingly be forced to purchase from the small presses and self-publishers."[18]

Librarians have not generally sought out self-published books to add to their collections, although, as demonstrated, there are some gems in the digital slushpile. But given the increase in self-publishing, this behavior may change. In May 2010, a letter in *Library Journal* questioned the practice of reviewing self-published books. A public librarian wrote, "While I don't in any way impugn the quality of some self-published works—especially given that the large publishers are primarily motivated by dollar currency and not idea currency—I really don't think reviews of self-published works are useful or helpful for collections librarians working with limited budgets and for clientele whose reading choices are largely driven by whatever is reviewed in the mainstream media."[19] A month later a collection development librarian responded, "I heartily disagree. Selectors need all the help that we can get, and reviews of quality self-published titles are crucial in this ever-growing

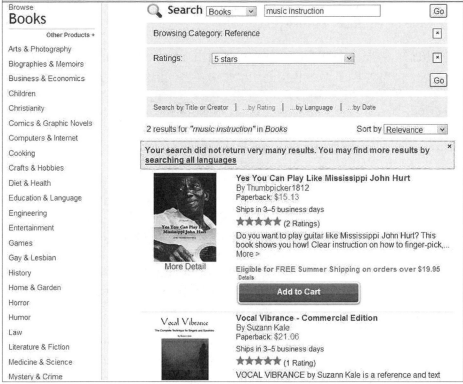

Figure 8.2   Should acquisitions professionals consult the catalogs of self-publishing companies? [Courtesy of Lulu]

self-publishing environment."[20] Figure 8.2 shows the results of a search for *music instruction* in the database of self-publishing bookseller Lulu.

Reviews of self-published books in mainstream publications are rare. When asked by a reader why the *New York Times* doesn't review self-published works, its senior book review editor Sam Tanenhaus explained:

> For the time being, we don't review self-published or print-on-demand books. Even excluding such books, the number of published titles is growing each year; the latest number I heard was in the neighborhood of 200,000 titles released annually. Since we can cover only a small fraction—about 1,500 titles a year—we have no choice but to make distinctions, for instance, reviewing only books that our readers can find in bookstores. Your point about merit is well taken, and it's one we share. Our thinking, which may be old-fashioned, is that with so great a volume of books being published each year by traditional publishers, and with so many imprints

available, every book of merit is almost certain to find a home at one or another of those presses.[21]

Hans Roes, of the Tilburg University Library (Netherlands), touched on library involvement in self-publishing by outlining a project in which his library cooperated with faculty and launched an electronic journal. He asserted, "Given the ever increasing prices of journals and the not-always increasing university budget it was clear that, although we could at least stabilize collection development in the short run, in the long run we would—and will—inevitably face ever deteriorating journal collections. So why not try and find out how difficult self-publishing would be? To see whether we could do the job at lower cost. To gain control over—after all—our own work again and to introduce some countervailing power in the publishing industry."[22] He explains how the *Electronic Journal of Comparative Law* came about and describes the problems that setting up a digital peer-reviewed journal present. In this case, self-publishing simply means bypassing the publisher—and doing the work of creating, promoting, and disseminating content.

In the only study that makes an effort to quantify the number of self-published books appearing in libraries, University of Toronto professors Juris Dilevko and Keren Dali focused on seven self-publisher firms. Three were subsidy or vanity publishers: Dorrance Publishing, Ivy House, and Vantage Press. The other four provide POD "author services": AuthorHouse, iUniverse, PublishAmerica, and Xlibris. By using WorldCat's advanced search and limiting it to the years 2000 through 2004, the researchers found that libraries that were OCLC members held 14,061 titles published by the seven self-publishers. The top four self-publishing firms represented in WorldCat were AuthorHouse (5,223 titles held by 1,905 libraries), Xlibris (3,351 titles held by 2,589 libraries), iUniverse (2,945 titles held by 1,998 libraries), and PublishAmerica (1,250 titles held by 676 libraries). Note that the top four publishers are businesses that provide POD services.

The subsidy and vanity press item counts were much lower: Dorrance Publishing (525 books held by 462 libraries), Vantage Press (698 titles held by 989 libraries), and Ivy House (69 titles held by 316 libraries). The research suggests that self-published books from POD firms are much more acceptable to librarians than those produced by vanity presses. Only three titles appeared in more than 400 libraries, and these three were produced by two of the POD companies (*If I Knew Then*, by Amy Fisher and Robbie Woliver, published by iUniverse; and *Abortion and Common Sense*, by Ruth Dixon-Mueller and Paul K. B. Dagg, and *American Western Song: Poems From 1976 to 2001*, by Victor W. Pear, both published by Xlibris).

Ninety-three percent of all 14,061 self-published titles were in fewer than 10 libraries, but even Harvard owned some (60, including eight from Dorrance Publishing, six from Vantage Press, and one from Ivy House). Yale owned 57 (including one from Dorrance Publishing and seven from Vantage Press). Dilevko and Dali recommended, "Librarians should remember that self-publishers often release titles that would not typically find a home with a profit oriented publisher … public and academic librarians should reevaluate their negative preconceptions about self-publishers, especially AuthorHouse, iUniverse, and Xlibris, because [they are] catering to segmented, niche, and individualized markets … collection development librarians should make a conscious effort not to exclude self-published titles … because the stigma traditionally associated with self-publishing is quickly disappearing."[23]

The Dark Side of Self-Publishing

A library assistant self-published a book through POD publisher PublishAmerica in 2008: *Library Diaries* chronicles a fictitious worker's time at a library in Denialville. According to her library director, Sally Stern-Hamilton (whose *nom de plume* is Ann Miketa) described fictionalized characters in such detail that she violated the privacy rights of actual library patrons of the Mason County (MI) District Library, on whom the fictionalized characters were based. Chapter titles include "Greedy, Unenlightened Patrons" and "Lying Patrons." Library officials initially suspended Stern-Hamilton but then fired her, a decision she did not appeal, although she felt the dismissal was ironic inasmuch as libraries typically protect free speech. The library director contends he did not violate Stern-Hamilton's First Amendment rights.[24] WorldCat shows that the book, which carries the subject headings Public Libraries—Michigan and Libraries and Community—Michigan, is held in 86 libraries.

PublishAmerica has been alternately criticized and praised by the authors it represents. According to an Associated Press report, "Even authors happy with the company said there are problems. Billy Edd Wheeler, for example, took care of his own editing and promotion for his compilation of bawdy humor, *Sultry Magnolias*. Wheeler said he was his own biggest customer."[25] Another author, Robert Mayer, said that he's happy his book was finally published, but "what bugs him is that there are no author's copies, and the book is priced by PublishAmerica at what Mayer considers an 'outrageous' price: $34.95."[26] But Paul Olson was delighted when PublishAmerica picked up *Dogpire*, his collection of short stories, even though the contract stated that PublishAmerica retains all rights to the book for 7 years.[27] The 7-year contract is one of PublishAmerica's most unpopular conditions. Author Sam Proof, who has mounted numerous YouTube videos on publishing, growls, "My biggest gripe with this particular company is that they attempt to lock you into a 7-year contract over something that they cannot guarantee you will sell a single issue of. … 7 years is a long time to have nothing to show for it. You've spent a lot of time putting this thing together. … If you put it out there and for 7 years nothing happens, that's devastating. … So again, they are not paying you up front, they should not be locking you in to a 7-year contract."[28]

   Publishers Weekly has also reported hearing from several authors aggrieved by PublishAmerica.[29] The Better Business Bureau of Greater Maryland has had dozens of complaints about the company.[30] But as of February 2010, book distributing giant Baker & Taylor had made an agreement to print and fulfill orders of PublishAmerica's extensive catalog of 40,000 authors.[31]

Summing Up Self-Publishing

Self-publishing has several benefits, even for individuals who have already had one or more books traditionally published. Control over the work—how it will read, how it will look—is one compelling benefit. A self-published book will go to market far more quickly than one that goes the route of traditional publishing, and this is a large plus, especially for topics of an emergent nature. I also found that if one begins a project with a self-publishing resource but does not finish it quickly, the company will probably offer live help and send emails that gradually discount the original prices encountered on the website.

Conversation With Steff Deschenes

Courtesy of Rick Bouthiette

Steff Deschenes is the gastronomically obsessed, award-winning self-published author of *The Ice Cream Theory*; involved in many culinary projects, Steff blogs at www.steffdeschenes.com.

Nick Tomaiuolo: *What are some of the important factors an author should consider when deciding to self-publish?*
Steff Deschenes: I had always wanted to be a writer, and after finishing my book *The Ice Cream Theory* I knew the next step was to publish it. Before I did that, I let five or six of my closest friends and family read and comment on it.

If it was rubbish, I wanted to hear it from them before attempting to publish it. Outside of the additional grammatical and editorial help, they all proved to be excellent sources of honesty.

I finished writing the book in January 2008 and gave myself 1 year to try to be published traditionally. I sent hundreds and hundreds of query letters via email and snail mail and got rejection after rejection. The following January, after having spent a year filled with no interest, I did what I said I was going to do and began the self-publishing process, which is a huge commitment, especially timewise and financially. But this was something I wanted to do—I knew I had a really good thing, and it was important to me that it didn't just sit and collect dust, but that it get in the hands of people.

NT: *What does the self-publishing process consist of, from the moment of creation to seeing the book in print? What did you have to do to self-publish* The Ice Cream Theory?

SD: I researched the different companies that offered self-publishing. And there are tons, not all of them totally legit. I went with [the folks at] BookSurge (now called CreateSpace); their parent company is Amazon.com. I chose them because they seemed the most professional; they offered the most flexibility, the most support, and best options for me personally. Most importantly, their connection to Amazon.com also seemed like it would be really important down the road. ... They helped me tailor-make a package of things I wanted: an editor, a press release, etc.

The total cost for me from that *original* package was close to $2,500, because I had some *major* editorial changes, which ended up costing me quite a bit to change. But that was just for the publishing part—that price estimate doesn't include all of the contests which I entered (which cost anywhere from $50 to $150 each), purchasing books to send to reviewers, marketing materials, etc. As far as how much time I've spent on the project, it's basically a part-time job for me. I spend anywhere from 20 to 30 hours per week on the book.

But again, I'm a big believer that you'll get out what you put into something. Other self-publishers may have spent only a couple hundred dollars and a couple hours on their book. This was my dream—to be a writer—so I wasn't about to slack on making it all come to fruition. There was no price point or time limit to making that happen.

NT: *How satisfied were you with BookSurge?*

SD: When I self-published through BookSurge, it was a year before they had merged with CreateSpace. I have no idea how CreateSpace operates from a publishing point of view, so I have no comment to make on that. BookSurge was *wonderful* to and for me. I was treated like royalty! I told BookSurge everything about what I wanted for and from the book, my dreams and fears regarding the huge undertaking of self-publishing, … and they were more than accommodating to me. They took a genuine interest in my book and in me as a person.

NT: *Did you manage all the editorial tasks: laying out the book, the proofreading, designing the cover? Or did BookSurge provide assistance? Did they charge for the assistance?*

SD: I had total control over every aspect of my book. BookSurge did provide assistance, and when I had a question or a doubt or a concern, I turned to them. As far as the layout of the book, I had total design freedom. I chose everything from how the internal chapters were set up to where the numbers on the bottom of page were located. For proofreading, I [hired] an editor to help me go through the book … I wanted a fresh pair of eyes to not only point out mistakes I might've missed, but to also give me general writing assistance (as a result, I am more aware of my faults as a writer). And, finally, part of BookSurge's publishing package was that they created a cover for you. I didn't like either of the options I was given, so I hired a freelance graphic designer, and he helped take my pitifully drawn picture and make it into the exact cover I had pictured in my head.

NT: *Why did you choose to go with a POD publisher?*

SD: POD is an excellent option, because it appeals to my eco-friendly heart. There are no extraneous copies … floating around unnecessarily. When I want copies of the book, I purchase them … for a nominal fee.

NT: *Your book is available at Barnes & Noble and Amazon.com in traditional print format, and it's readable on Amazon's Kindle. What do you think are the advantages and disadvantages of print and electronic formats?*

SD: We live in the digital age. To be able to put one's entire book collection in one light-weight technical gadget is brilliant. However, it's important to remember that technology has a way of failing us: the power runs out, viruses infect systems, etc. The book you hold in your hand isn't going to randomly turn off or go blank on the inside for no reason. Call me old-fashioned, but there's something charming and wonderful about the smell of an old book!

NT: *The Ice Cream Theory has been awarded honors at least 10 times, including at the DIY Book Festival, the 2009 Nashville Book Festival, and the New England Book Festival, and it has even been acclaimed internationally at the Paris Book Festival. For a self-published author, are such accolades a stepping stone to a contract with a major publisher or is that something that self-publishing writers won't consider once they have had the kind of success you have had independently?*

SD: Awards grant instant credibility to your book. They also influence book sellers, distributors, and reviewers. For me, I wanted my name and book everywhere it possibly could be, getting as much recognition as possible. And, by entering every single contest I could (and subsequently winning a lot of them), I feel like my book was able to expand out of my local area to regions of the country I might not have been able to market to (given that I'm a self-published author with limited funds). They've certainly opened the door to local bookstores, which started selling my book sight unseen, because of its obvious success.

I certainly hope those awards are a stepping stone to a contract with a major publisher! I didn't become a self-published author to stay a self-published author. There's only so much a one-man machine can do, so to be picked up would mean the opportunity to spend less time on marketing and public relations and more time on what I'm supposed to be doing: writing.

NT: *I noticed you're raising funds using a service called Kickstarter (www.kickstarter.com). How does Kickstarter work?*

SD: Kickstarter is a company that supports creative endeavors through grassroots funding. The company screens each project before deciding whether it's a viable idea, one that people would support. When they approve your project, you decide how much you need and how many days you'd like to raise it in. And then you offer incentives, so that people who pledge to your project get something in return. The catch with Kickstarter is that they have an all-or-nothing policy. If you don't raise the funds you requested in the amount of days you chose, you don't get any of the money, and the pledgers don't get charged.

I had funded everything about my book on my own, and I had finally reached my financial breaking point, so I began looking for writing grants or investors. And I stumbled on Kickstarter, which seemed like the perfect option for me. It was better than a writing grant, because it seemed that grants were really specific and exclusive; and it was better than finding investors, which you eventually have to pay back.

NT: *How will you use the funds you receive from Kickstarter? Will they be used to continue to promote your book (for example, television advertisements, newspaper ads)? Will you use them to push your book toward major publishers? To enter more contests? Or do you have other plans for the funds?*

SD: Advertising is definitely the major focus point of the funds I received from Kickstarter. Nothing nearly as costly as TV, which I don't think is a good option for me, for my book, or as a writer. Neither are newspapers. My primary focus will be advertising on the internet. There's also the potential for a virtual booktour. The Kickstarter endeavor was primarily to be able to push the book toward major publishers. Could I continue to do the self-published thing? Sure. I've been relatively successful so far. But I don't have the network or connections that a major publisher has, which would catapult the book into an entirely new realm.

NT: *Is* The Ice Cream Theory *a book that you wrote because you "knew you had a book in you," or is it a product of certain circumstances, events, or individuals interacting with you?*

SD: *The Ice Cream Theory* is not a typical self-help book. It's an exploration of the parallels between human personalities and ice cream flavors, a tongue-in-cheek celebration of the variety inherent in a well-lived life. The book strives to use that all-comfortable, all-inclusive, all-relatable dessert, ice cream, as the nonthreatening medium to share insight into life when it comes to friendships, hardships, and overcoming obstacles. It neatly brings together anecdotes from my own adventures with broader-reaching social commentary to help others recognize the wisdom and joy inherent in a beloved dessert. If you've been bruised by life's tough lessons and are in need of a cheerful pick-me-up, you'll enjoy the book.

I wrote the book, because it's what came out. When I sit down to write, I may have an idea of what I want to say, but what usually comes tumbling out onto paper is far from what I originally thought was going to. The book is a result of living; it's full of people from my life, the experiences I've had, and my thoughts ... on all of it. I am a true believer that fact is better than fiction.

NT: *Are you the same Steff Deschenes from the 2007 indie film* Freaky Farley? *If you are, how involved are you with social media? Do you upload to YouTube? Twitter? What about Flickr?*

SD: I am the Steff from *Freaky Farley*! In 2006, I dabbled in modeling and indie films and had an absolutely excellent time working on the set of *Freaky Farley*! I played "The Witch" and also got to work behind the scenes in a variety of different roles. I learned a lot [from that movie] about how difficult and unbelievably rewarding it was to be an independent artist. ...

I think social media is integral in this day and age. It's an excellent marketing resource and is key for networking, too. Social media itself is sustainable, although the specific social websites out now may not be. But we're a society that's constantly evolving to fit our ever-expanding needs and demands, so there'll always be some new and exciting social website to take over when another one grows taboo or ancient.

I do have a YouTube account, but there are only a couple videos on my site. They were shot on the official release date of *The Ice Cream Theory*. My sister and I celebrated the day by eating ice cream at all 10 ice cream stores in town, so we created a two-part video entitled "The Ice Cream Bender." I do have a Twitter as well. Again, I use it mostly for networking and also as a way of staying up to date with my favorite companies or general interests.

NT: *What's a lucrative genre self-publishing authors should consider?*

SD: For fiction it's romance novels. According to the Romance Writers of America, "Romance fiction continued its reign as the largest share of the consumer market at 13.2 percent, beating other market categories such as mystery, science fiction/fantasy, and religion/inspirational. According to R. R. Bowker's Books In Print, there were 9,089 romance titles out of 832,253 new titles published in 2009. Romance fiction has long been the mainstay of the mass-market paperback format. However, the genre has been gaining ground in the ebook format, where romance fiction was the number three category in 2009 and number two category in 2010" (www.rwanational.org/cs/the_romance_genre/romance_literature_statistics/industry_statistics).

I truly think that the self-help genre is probably the most lucrative for nonfiction. People are constantly trying to figure themselves out and grow as individuals. As a result, there's a vast array of self-help books on the market available for all aspects of one's life.

NT: *Is the current growth in self-publishing just a hiccup or will self-publishing increase in the coming decade?*

SD: I think that publishing houses aren't taking on new authors because of the shifty economy. People don't have money to put into arts and entertainment the way they do when the economy is a little more stable, and as a result I think that independent artists, including authors, are taking advantage of using other platforms. After all, if indie movies are winning Oscars, and indie musicians are more successful than ever, then it was really only a matter of time before indie writers overtook their industry as well.

Endnotes

1. Lev Grossman and Andrea Sachs, "Books Unbound," *Time International* 173 (February 2, 2009): 50.

2. Chris Anderson, "The Long Tail," Wired, October 2004, accessed August 3, 2011, www.wired.com/wired/archive/12.10/tail.html.

3. "Print Isn't Dead, Says Bowker's Annual Print Production Report," Bowker, May 18, 2011, accessed August 3, 2011, www.bowker.com/index.php/press-releases/633-print-isnt-dead-says-bowkers-annual-book-production-report.

4. "Bowker Reports Traditional U.S. Book Production Flat in 2009," Bowker, April 14, 2010, accessed August 3, 2011, www.bowker.com/index.php/press-releases/616-bowker-reports-traditional-us-book-production-flat-in-2009.

5. Victoria Strauss, "Lies, Damned Lies, and Statistics," Science Fiction & Fantasy Writers of America, May 23, 2010, accessed August 3, 2011, www.sfwa.org/2010/05/lies-damned-lies-and-statistics.

6. Pat Conroy, *My Losing Season* (New York: Bantam-Dell, 2002), 383.

7. "An Interview with Richard Bolles," Go Publish Yourself, accessed August 3, 2011, www.go-publish-yourself.com/community/interview-bollesr.php.

8. "eBook Sales Increase Nearly 116% in January, Paperback Book Sales Plunge Nearly 31%," Huffington Post, March 17, 2011, accessed August 3, 2011, www.huffingtonpost.com/2011/03/17/book-sales_n_837138.html.

9. Pat Hayward, "The Trend Towards Self-Publishing," *Canadian Library Journal* 49 (1992): 289.

10. Walt Crawford, "Publishing It Yourself: Experiences with POD," *Online* 32 (May/June 2008): 59.

11. Michael Owens, "10 Things to Know Before You Self-Publish," *Writer* 121 (June 2008): 37.

12. Victoria Strauss, "Vanity and Subsidy Publishers," Science Fiction & Fantasy Writers of America, accessed August 3, 2011, www.sfwa.org/for-authors/writer-beware/vanity.

13. "Study Says 81 Percent of Americans Say They Could Write a Book," National Public Radio (Morning Edition With Bob Edwards, October 21, 2002), transcript available at Lexis-Nexis Academic Universe.

14. "Bowker Statistics 2009: Non-Traditional Means Now the Majority Path for Authors," POD, Self-Publishing & Independent Publishing, April 14, 2010, accessed August 3, 2011, mickrooney.blogspot.com/2010/04/bowker-statistics-2009-non-traditional.html.

15. Felicity Wood, "Digital Focus," The Bookseller.com, September 4, 2009, accessed August 3, 2011, www.thebookseller.com/feature/digital-focus.html.

16. Kurt Schiller, "Google Opens eBookstore," *Information Today* 28, (January 2011): 8.

17. Laura Dawson, "The Role of Self-Publishing in Libraries," *Library Trends* 57 (Summer 2008): 45.

18. Hayward, "The Trend Towards Self-Publishing," 290.

19. Eddie Paul, "Self-Published Donations," *Library Journal* 135 (May 15, 2010): 12.

20. Lorraine Burdick, "Review the Self-Published," *Library Journal* 135 (June 15, 2010): 10.

21. "Talk to the Newsroom," NewYorkTimes.com, December 11, 2006, accessed August 3, 2011, www.nytimes.com/2006/12/11/business/media/11asktheeditors.html.

22. Hans Roes, "Libraries Facilitating Self-Publishing: A Case Study of the Electronic Journal of Comparative Law," Spring 1998, accessed August 3, 2011, www.hroes.de/articles/ejcl_98.htm.

23. Juris Dilevko and Keren Dali, "The Self-Publishing Phenomenon and Libraries," *Library and Information Science Research* 28 (2006): 233.

24. "Director Fires Library Diaries Author Over Patron-Privacy Concerns," *American Libraries* 39 (October 1, 2008): 31.

25. Hillel Italie, "Critics and Supporters Debate Success of Fast-Rising PublishAmerica," *Associated Press Newswires*, January 27, 2005.

26. Kate McGraw, "Times Change in Publishing World; Author Finds Home for Books in Publish-on-Demand Industry," *Albuquerque Journal* (June 21, 2010): 1.

27. Jane Laskey, "Minnesota Authors Turn to E-Books, Other Methods," *St. Paul Pioneer Press* (January 31, 2010).

28. Sam Proof, "Path to Publication," November 18, 2007, accessed August 3, 2011, YouTube, www.youtube.com/watch?v=eS8v8Q53pHA&feature=fvsr.

29. Steven Zeitchik, "Authors Allege Publisher Deception," *Publishers Weekly* 251 (November 11, 2004): 13.

30. "Publish America, LLP," Better Business Bureau of Greater Maryland, accessed August 3, 2011, www.bbb.org/greater-maryland/business-reviews/publishers-book/publish-america-llp-in-frederick-md-32010985.

31. "Baker & Taylor Inks Deal With PublishAmerica for Digital Printing, Distribution," PR Newswire, accessed August 3, 2010, www.prnewswire.com/news-releases/baker—taylor-inks-deal-with-publishamerica-for-digital-printing-distribution-83541172.html.

Chapter 9

Citizen Journalism

Citizen journalism (CitJ) goes by many names—participatory, open source, grassroots, networked, or distributed journalism—but it always combines technology and the internet to not only disseminate news, but to expand upon, critique, and fact-check items written by individuals working for both the crowdsourced media (i.e, user-generated) and legacy media (e.g., *New York Times* and *Wall Street Journal*). Dan Gillmor, who runs the Knight Center for Digital Media Entrepreneurship at Arizona State University and authored *We the Media* (O'Reilly, 2004), traced the roots of citizen journalism to the 18th-century pamphlets of Thomas Paine.[1]

Jumping from the 18th century to the past 5 decades, manifestations of CitJ include the Zapruder film of John F. Kennedy's assassination (1963), videotape of police beating Rodney King (1991), Mary Lou Fulton's launch of the Northwest Voice in 2003 (now called the Bakersfield Voice, it is a community website run solely on photos and stories submitted by the public; www.bakersfieldvoice.com), videos transmitted at the scenes of four coordinated attacks on the London Underground and bus systems (2005), and the cell phone video of the attack that left 32 people dead on the campus of Virginia Tech (2007). With the exception of Fulton's site, these are examples of impromptu citizen journalism created by "accidental journalists," as John Savageau, technology guru and president of Pacific Tier Communications, calls them. He blogged, "Then we have the enthusiast citizen journalist (ECJ). Armed with a digital camera, digital voice recorder, laptop computer, and desire to seek out events (and record them), the ECJ wants to fill in the gaps left when traditional news media edits or determines what the reader/viewer community needs to know."[2] Both types of citizen journalists are valid contributors.

Citizen journalists are all over the world. Look back to the June 2009 election protests in Iran. Reports coming from the people in Tehran's streets differed significantly from the accounts given in the state-controlled media. Asked about traditional news outlets relying on people in the street in Iran, New York University professor Clay Shirky said, "This is the first revolution that has been catapulted onto a global stage and transformed by social media. I've been thinking a lot about the Chicago demonstrations of 1968 where they chanted 'the whole world is watching.' Really, that wasn't true then. But this time it's true."[3]

CitJ tends to be associated with hyperlocal events (a community where a tornado has struck, inland wetlands zoning meetings, etc.), but it's also important when traditional media organizations can't get at the news. Revisiting the Iran election protests from June 2009, CNN's user-generated iReport signed up 3,000 new contributors from in and around Tehran in a 4-day period (see Figure 9.1).[4] In a report for *Time*, James Poniewozic wrote that Twitter may not have been a replacement for TV news coverage during the protests, but carried a great deal of weight in real-time media criticism.[5]

The current upsurge in CitJ is rooted in the fact that people lacking formal journalism experience or education can use computers and the web to comment on anything from the transactions of a local school board meeting to bias in the mainstream media. Citizen journalists can often go where mainstream journalists cannot. When traditional news organizations can't get at the news, CitJ becomes a viable alternative medium. It can also cover more stories because citizen journalists outnumber professional journalists and provide "extra eyes."

Pundits often claim that today's CitJ got its start with blogging; some charge that because blogs are often nothing more than links and opinions,

Figure 9.1   In this user-submitted iReport video, note the following: "Not Vetted by CNN" and also "Vetting Explained." [Courtesy of CNN iReport]

CitJ cannot be objective. Although many CitJ sites allow contributors to submit links and comment on them, CitJ is distinguished from blogging in that the critical mass of content is generally original and, when contributions are mainly video or images, the content is entirely original.

Boon or Bane? It Depends on the Source

Critics of traditional journalism often point to the time limitations that force professional journalists to cover only mainstream stories and rely heavily on routine sources. Citizen journalists, because of their numbers and varied interests, have fewer constraints and more opportunities to seek out and report on a variety of news. Because they aren't mandated to subscribe to a traditional news organization's goals or values, citizen journalists can either be more objective or infuse a story with their own ideas.

Participation in both consuming and creating CitJ content has a high positive correlation with participation in a community, including volunteerism. Serena Carpenter, who teaches at the Walter Cronkite School of Journalism and Mass Communication (Arizona State University), suggests this is one of CitJ's positive characteristics. Her research revealed that while traditional journalists are more likely to behave as observers, citizen journalists are more likely to interpret content. She theorized that this presence of opinion may mean that citizen journalists are willing to challenge the status quo in their communities and affect change.[6] Hyperlocal media pioneer Mary Lou Fulton, speaking about her publication Northwest Voice back in 2004, said, "We are the traditional journalism model turned upside down. Instead of being the gatekeeper, telling people what's important to them 'isn't news,' we're just opening up the gates and letting people come on in. We are a better community newspaper for having thousands of readers who serve as the eyes and ears for the [Northwest] Voice, rather than having everything filtered through the views of a small group of reporters and editors."[7]

Detractors usually take umbrage with citizen journalism simply because it is done by nonprofessionals. The criticism sometimes becomes vitriolic. In 2006, Nicholas Lemann, dean of Columbia's Graduate School of Journalism, flippantly wrote, "The content of most citizen journalism will be familiar to anybody who has ever read a church or community newsletter—it's heartwarming and it probably adds to the store of good things in the world, but it does not mount the collective challenge to power which the traditional media are supposedly too timid to take up."[8] More recently *Seattle Times* columnist Jon Talton ventured, "The notion that hundreds of part-time gadflies, blowhards, tub-thumpers, students and well-meaning good-government types can replace real journalism is silly."[9] Though both Lemann and Talton have decided that CitJ undermines traditional journalism, the two need not be at odds. The optimal scenario is working together. (Even the author of *The Cult of the Amateur*, Andrew Keen, agrees.)[10]

How Some Professional Journalists View CitJ

David Domingo, whose research concluded that professional journalists are generally reluctant to interact with users, found that the professionals interpret online user participation mainly as an opportunity for readers to debate current events.[11] Insights gained from interviews with numerous journalists at the *Guardian* demonstrated a significant degree of concern with users placing content on the newspaper's website. Here are some highlights from the article "Comment Is Free, But Facts Are Sacred," from a section with the heading "User Comments: Trouble or Benefit"[12]:

- The extent to which user-generated content challenges or undermines personal and institutional credibility was a major concern. Journalists felt confident that they took adequate steps to ensure what they wrote was credible, but they felt helpless to either assess or improve the credibility of what users provided. An editor said she had no expectation that users would be credible, citing issues of "what they know, what they don't know, what motivation they have, and what views they bring with them." The *Guardian* understands the value of open discourse—"Comment is Free"—yet it also values a traditional approach to ensuring credibility and accuracy—"Facts are Sacred."

- Respondents saw anonymity as a user-generated content characteristic that distinguished by-lined *Guardian* writers from those who merely commented. Indeed, almost all the respondents who mentioned anonymity suggested it was a factor in the too-often uncivil tone of online discourse. Because they are anonymous, "people feel licensed to say things in content and style that they wouldn't own if publishing as themselves," an online editor said.

- Overall, journalists indicated the presence of user-generated content on "their" website was spurring a reconsideration of what the relationship with the public has been, is, and might be. One online journalist said, "It takes time working out what the best way is to respond. People who raise interesting points, it's nice to acknowledge that." Several other interviewees also indicated that they were coming to see that the encouragement of cogent public contributions was beginning to outweigh the discouragement of the less cogent.

I discussed the connection between CitJ and the closings, downsizings, and reorganizations of numerous newspapers over the past few years (e.g., *Baltimore Examiner, Cincinnati Post, Rocky Mountain News, Seattle Post-Intelligencer, Ann Arbor News, Miami Herald*) with Rich Hanley, graduate director of journalism and interactive communications at Quinnipiac University. Hanley said, "Citizen journalism has had no impact on the collapse of the newspaper industry. Newspaper management is solely to blame for this, as they failed to see or understand how the internet would destroy their existing structure in the mid-1990s when they could have accelerated the transition to online."[13]

As to the theory that craigslist has caused newspaper revenues to suffer (craigslist allows free classified ads and makes money only through paid advertisements from companies in major cities), craigslist CEO Jim Buckmaster told the *San Francisco Chronicle*, "It's possibly a cynical cop-out by the moneyed interests at newspapers to point fingers at Craigslist. ... Newspapers are cutting their investment in reporting. They're running more Associated Press wire stories and increasing the percentage of the product they devote to advertising. ... But it's much easier to point the finger at a site like Craigslist."[14]

During a 2009 interview with Ed Keating, vice president of the Software & Information Industry Association Content Division, he was asked, "Are your users looking for 'good enough' or 'perfect' information?" Keating answered, "It used to be said that in order to succeed in the information industry, you needed to provide timely, accurate, and comprehensive information. As the price for these products increased through forced bundling and other tactics, consumers sought out substitutes that offered most of what they needed. Customers might trade off some content or functionality for a substantial drop in price."[15]

Traditional media sites, bloggers, academics, and citizen journalists often link to the Pew Project for Excellence in Journalism's 2009 "The State of the News Media" report.[16] The report methodically discusses the successes and shortcomings of citizen news sites and legacy media. The report analyzed the content of 145 CitJ sites and 218 traditional media sites. These statistics are among the report's findings:

- The report found that 89 percent of the CitJ sites include links to external news stories and other external content. Legacy news sites are more self-contained, offering external links a total of 77 percent of the time. CitJ sites also tended to publish stories with multiple links more often than the legacy sites. The irony is that the CitJ sites linked to legacy sites in 29 percent of their stories, while the reverse was true in about half the cases (14 percent).

- The CitJ sites are more open to reader participation: 34 percent allowed users to upload video, 28 percent allowed audio uploads, and 45 percent allowed photo uploading. In contrast, the same actions were permitted at 12 percent, 4 percent, and 34 percent of the legacy sites, respectively.

- CitJ sites and legacy sites also differ in their sourcing. At legacy sites, 48 percent of the analyzed stories included two or more sources; this was true in 36 percent of the articles on the CitJ sites. Single-sourced accounts were more common on CitJ sites (36 percent) than on the legacy sites (27 percent).

- The report found that 89 percent of the legacy media's articles were original reporting compared with 56 percent of the stories at CitJ sites. CitJ sites also included opinion (16 percent) and calendar items (28 percent).

These findings may not be especially surprising. Legacy sites produce the professional news—there's no need to host users' links, comments, or images, agreed? But the line dividing CitJ sites and certain areas of the most popular traditional news sites, such as CNN and Fox News, has blurred.

Multiple Personalities

CitJ sites vary tremendously in scope, slant, arrangement, and features. There are at least four varieties. The first type is websites where citizen journalism represents the majority of the content. Following are some examples:

- Allvoices (www.allvoices.com): Allvoices is an open media site where "anyone can report from anywhere." Users direct what news gets noticed by ranking reports up or down. As more related media, comments, and positive rankings are added to a posting, it rises in the list of stories. Stories are broken into "Contributor Reports" and "Mainstream News."

- Bakersfield Voice (www.bakersfieldvoice.com): Online since 2003; contributing to the site is as easy as registering and posting.

- Global Voices (www.globalvoicesonline.org): Two-hundred volunteers translate news items into 15 languages. They look for citizen journalism news content that may have been overlooked by mainstream news outlets.

- NowPublic (www.nowpublic.com): Stories come from people witnessing the news, insiders, and community leaders. Footage comes from eyewitnesses. *Time* named it one of the Top 50 Coolest websites in 2007.

- YourArlington (www.yourarlington.com): Community journalism that is dedicated to reporting news about Arlington, Massachusetts, by its residents.

The content at a vanguard CitJ website such as Allvoices is overwhelmingly dominated by citizen journalists' contributions. Allvoices follows a familiar participation process. It lets users file reports from the field via email, multimedia messaging service (MMS), and short message service (SMS).

South Korea's OhmyNews International (OMNI; international.ohmynews.com), which the *Guardian* called "the news equivalent of Wikipedia,"[17] was once a leader in publishing citizen-produced news, but changed its format in 2010 from a wiki with 70,000 nonprofessional contributors to a blog format with information created by a much smaller group of "curators." It transformed from an "edited citizen journalist news site" to a "blog dedicated to covering and discussing the world of citizen journalism itself." Devoting itself entirely to coverage of the development of citizen journalism throughout the world, OMNI is a prime resource for citizen journalists. Typical blog entries include "How to Get Started in Citizen Journalism," "Debate on Citizen Journalism," and "Your Story Will Be Better With Multiple Sources."

A second variety of CitJ sites exist as sections of CNN, BBC, MSBNC, Fox News, and similar traditional news outlets. From a marketing point of view, these websites expand their reach and their audience by encouraging users' submissions. They also capitalize on the citizen journalist's ability to complement traditional information gathering. Reduced to the lowest common denominator, these professional news sites have their readers contributing content for free. Individuals may post text, audio, and video in separate sections at these sites, but these organizations are careful not to mingle user content with the "official" news—unless the report is particularly polished and significant. Following are examples of some of these sites:

- Citizen Journalist, MSNBC (www.msnbc.msn.com/id/6639760): Here, news stories are "assigned." Users accept assignments on topics such as "returning home after Katrina" and upload their text, images, and video.

- EyeMobile, CBS (www.cbseyemobile.com): This site is video and image intensive, accepts video and photos from most mobile phones, and displays video on the web and mobile phones.

- Have Your Say, BBC News (www.bbc.co.uk/news/have_your_say): This section of BBC News contains uploaded photo essays with brief textual interpretations, but also offers opportunities to comment on intriguing topics.

- iReport, CNN (www.ireport.cnn.com): iReport is entirely user-generated. Stories submitted by users are not edited, fact-checked, or screened before they post. Some individual contributors at iReport are very active, uploading hundreds of reports and commenting on thousands of stories.

- The Local: Fort Greene and Clinton Hill (fort-greene.blogs.nytimes. com) and The Local: The East Village (eastvillage.thelocal.nytimes. com), NYTimes.com: These sites are excellent examples of coverage of local news by writers living in those towns and neighborhoods.

- Newsvine (www.newsvine.com): Owned by MSNBC, it takes reports from legacy news publishers and posts them, but it also has a UContent component: Every registered user has a "column" and can publish.

- uReport, Fox News (ureport.foxnews.com): uReport includes user-uploaded media. Users view, vote, and comment on clips.

CNN's iReport, which like CitJ site Allvoices accepts users' stories, images, and videos sent by computer or cell phone, states on its homepage: "iReport is a user-generated section of CNN.com. The stories here come from users. CNN has vetted only the stories marked with the 'CNN' badge." The description continues, "Everything you see on iReport starts with someone in the CNN audience. The stories here are not edited, fact-checked or screened before they post. CNN's producers will check out some of the most compelling, important and urgent iReports and, once they're cleared for CNN, make them a part of CNN's news coverage. (Look for the red CNN iReport stamp to see which stories have been vetted for CNN)."

The *New York Times* also appears among the traditional media that have adopted citizen journalists' content. Early in 2009, it took a bold step by launching two projects designed to give citizen journalists a voice in reporting about specific neighborhoods and towns in proximity to Manhattan (the sites are subdomains of NYTimes.com). One site is still in existence: The Local: Fort Greene/Clinton Hill, which covers two prominent Brooklyn neighborhoods. Another site, The Local: Maplewood/Milburn/South Orange, which covered the news for three New Jersey suburbs near the metropolitan New York area (maplewood.blogs.nytimes.com) ran from March 2009 until

June 30, 2010. In September 2010, along with the Carter Institute of Journalism at New York University, the *New York Times* established The Local: East Village (eastvillage.thelocal.nytimes.com). Contributors to both sites are area residents and include bookshop owners, graduate and undergraduate students, schoolteachers, professional writers (e.g., from the *Village Voice*), and freelancers. Both sites feature a Virtual Assignment Desk, which lists potential topics and gives readers instructions on how to "Be the Journalist." The Virtual Assignment Desk also asks readers for story ideas. The content is solid local information ranging from news on regulating 24-hour businesses to features on local merchants and columns called "The Stoop" and "IMHO." Other examples of citizen journalism content linked with traditional news outlets are the *Dallas Morning News*' highly interactive CitJ annex called Neighborsgo.com (www.neighborsgo.com) and the *Chicago Tribune*'s extensive network of citizen-contributed news combined with staff reporting at its TribLocal sites (www.triblocal.com). But these ventures are not always successful. In August 2009, the *Washington Post* shut down its experiment in citizen journalism called the Loudon Extra, stating that the "separate site was not a sustainable model" (see www.loudounscene.com/2009/08/washington-posts-loudounextracom-experiment-is-over.html).

Following are some locally focused and professionally managed news sites that invite readers to upload stories and photos on a more restricted basis:

- iTowns, *Hartford Courant* (www.courant.com/community): This online and in-print section of the newspaper is published once per week and accepts submissions with a local focus from anyone.

- MinnPost (www.minnpost.com): This site provides news and analysis based on reporting by professional journalists. It also includes commentary pieces from the community and comments from readers on individual stories.

- NewWest (www.newwest.net): Dedicated to life west of the Rocky Mountains, this site is staffed by professionals, but works with citizen journalists on specific projects. Unregistered users can comment on any story. NewWest also considers work by freelancers and has an "Unfiltered" section that is entirely written by the public.

Finally, a few legacy sites have cautiously begun letting individuals comment on published articles, while not yet inviting users to actually submit news content to the main site.

Low-Key Participation Options

Large-scale news operations usually keep their CitJ reports separate from their main webpages (e.g., CNN iReports, Fox News uReports) because of the possible inaccuracies, doctored photos, and occasional malicious missives inherent to user submissions. That's one level of caution. Influential newspapers with huge readerships exercise an even higher level of circumspection. Not wishing to appear excessively stodgy or unprogressive, a few publications have created features that afford readers a modicum of interaction. Compared with full-scale CitJ, these are very tame, and their popularity with users varies; none furnishes users with a real opportunity to share anything substantive.

Henrik Ornebring, a research fellow at the Reuters Institute for the Study of Journalism, validated this attitude of circumspection when he studied the user-generated sections of two European news websites for 6 weeks. His "overall impression is that users are mostly empowered to create popular culture-oriented content ... rather than news/informational content. Direct user involvement in newsgathering, news selection and news production is minimal."[18] The *New York Times*'s TimesPeople, *Wall Street Journal*'s Community, and the *Guardian*'s Comment Is Free sections are examples of sites with opportunities for low-stakes participation (to participate, you must register with the sites):

- Comment Is Free, *Guardian* (www.guardian.co.uk/commentisfree): This site consists of the user comments that are published by the *Guardian* and *Observer* newspapers, plus a web-only group blog with hundreds of regular contributors from Britain and around the world. It also provides "instant commentary on British and world current events, and a forum for debate for topics of interest to a liberal, progressive readership online."

- Journal Community, *Wall Street Journal* (online.wsj.com/community): This site contains three components: Discussions, Connections, and Answers. Registered users may also comment on articles.

- TimesPeople, *New York Times* (timespeople.nytimes.com): TimesPeople offers an opportunity for registered users to follow their favorite *New York Times* authors and other *New York Times* readers (other TimesPeople). TimesPeople can recommend stories, comment on stories, and comment on the recommendations of other readers. User can import contacts from other sites, and a Facebook app is available. Readers may recommend comments made by other readers.

TimesPeople offers robust and varied activities. The ability to recommend articles is one of the main attractions, and members may also comment on others' recommendations. When you log in to TimesPeople, you'll see a list called "The Latest." This list is continually updated in real time and shows the articles being recommended by members. Just below that window appear three columns: Most Recommended, Most Commented, and Most Tweeted. The ability to see the news that others believe is important provides incentive to instantly become a *New York Times* pundit. You may follow the paper's writers (and get their articles and recommendations upon signing in), and if you find yourself interested in what specific readers are saying, you can stay abreast of their activity by following them, too.

TimesPeople has some good points, but a professional journalist I interviewed wasn't impressed. Rich Hanley remarked, "It's a tool for *Times* readers to reach other *Times* readers, but the evidence clearly suggests people would rather use a more robust social networking application such as Facebook to recommend articles to each other."[19] (Incidentally, you can configure your TimesPeople account to update your Facebook page when you recommend an article from the *New York Times*.)

The Journal Community at the *Wall Street Journal* site has three main areas. It hooks users with Join Discussions (join and interact with a group of people sharing an interest in a topic), Find Answers (ask the Community frank questions, such as "Will the recession worsen?" which attracted a respectable 50 answers in 5 days), and Make Connections (Find someone's postings insightful? Click "make a connection" to send a personal message.). I've lurked, asked a few questions, and participated in a discussion. Generally speaking, it's a pithy, erudite group.

The (U.K.) *Guardian*'s Comment Is Free site is exactly that—comments on news articles published on its site and in its paper. The exchange is brisk. An article entitled "Have Faith in Atheists" prompted 182 comments within 24 hours of publication, yet it was outpaced by "A Night in Riyadh," which received 102 comments in 10 hours. Like TimesPeople, Comment Is Free allows users to recommend one another's comments.

Citizen Aggregation Sites

Sites promoting social networking by allowing users to submit links to news stories and then providing a forum for users to comment on those stories include the major aggregators Digg, Reddit, and Topix. These sites allow users to "vote" news stories "up" or "down." The votes contribute to a ranking of the most important (or most popular) news stories. Of the three, Reddit and Topix are more skewed toward citizen journalism (i.e., the tagline for Topix is

"Your Town. Your News. Your Take." Reddit's is "User generated news links."). Because most of the web's news sites have hooks into these aggregation sites, it's easy to submit links to places like Digg, Reddit, and Topix. You can read an article at the *New York Times* or at a CitJ site such as Allvoices or CNN's iReport and submit the link to an aggregation site by clicking the Share button (see Figure 9.2). The following provides a quick comparison of these resources:

- Digg (www.digg.com): Users submit content and rate that content by "Digging" what they see and like best. A submission that earns a larger number of Diggs, and therefore is more popular with users, is promoted on the Digg webpage for the category of content it belongs in. Digg was launched in November 2004. Graphical representation of search results helps users refine search by date, digital media type, and content (topic area).

- Reddit (www.reddit.com): Users can post links to content, and other users may then vote the posted links up or down, causing them to become more or less prominent on the Reddit homepage. Easy link submission is available from internal and external pages.

- Topix (www.topix.com): Users can choose to display items that default to a specific ZIP code. Number of user comments affects the popularity of a news item.

Reddit organizes its user-submitted links with five tabs: what's hot, new, controversial, top scoring, and saved (available for registered users to save links). In the Politics category on July 5, 2011, the top-scoring story was an item that had received 2,000 "up" votes and 1,666 comments from site members within 13 hours. In the Technology category, a story about IP addresses had 1,138 "up" votes and 76 comments. I noticed users submitting links to blogs as well as legacy sites. I also encountered a few links to CitJ sites such as NowPublic, CNN iReports, and Global Voices, but these links had not attracted many votes or comments.

Digg has topic categories too, and its interface has an appealing look and feel. Registered users can easily submit links to news, images, and video links. Items are ranked by "Diggs," which are "up" votes by other registered users. Stories from CitJ sites were well-represented among Digg users when I checked by entering site names in the search box.

Topix collects its information from 50,000 news sources. Users cannot submit links to stories, but it qualifies as a citizen aggregation site because users may leave comments on any of the stories, and the number of comments determines the "Most Popular" items on the site. While there is no "up and

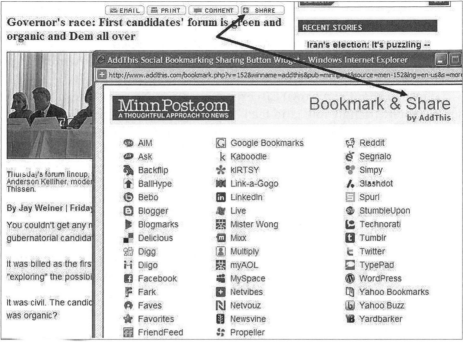

Figure 9.2   A Share button makes it easy to distribute news links to Digg, Reddit, Topix, and many others. [Courtesy of MinnPost.com]

down" voting per se, news items can rise in the standings on pages—or become buried—depending on how much discussion they generate. Because its news engine grabs information from so many sites, Topix can offer an intensely local focus—just enter a ZIP code, and you're looking at stories relevant to that location.

DIY Bylines

Individuals can quickly become citizen journalists at Newsvine (www.newsvine.com). Owned by MSNBC, the site features both user content (known as the Vine) and professional content (the Wire). It's a huge hit with the 25-to-44-year-old demographic. With a U.S. Alexa rank of 1,200 (July 2011) and 60,000 sites linking in, it's as well-used as NowPublic, a similar CitJ site, and actually more popular than Global Voices, which earns praise for translating CitJ reports into 15 languages and boasts a link on Andrew Sullivan's Daily Dish at the *Atlantic Monthly*'s site. The Newsvine site has two main divisions: the Wire and the Vine. You may read continually updated news from the Associated Press via the Wire, but within the Vine you'll find original user-written articles and "seeded links" (user-submitted pointers to other material). As with the citizen aggregation sites Reddit and Digg, both Wire and Vine articles move up or down in the site, depending on how often an article is read and how many users vote for it. Users may also comment on articles. It's a great portal for fresh news.

I chose to conduct my own CitJ experiment with Newsvine because it has an extremely friendly look and feel. In contrast to sites that seemed home-grown, Newsvine's direct organization quickly appealed to me. The site has some nice features, including a Leaderboard, which shows the most active contributors, and a section called Newsvine Live, which provides a ticker of stories added to the site as soon as they are published. You can also search by tags.

If you want to publish, you must register. All registered users are issued a workspace where they may compose articles, maintain watchlists of tags, invite friends, and initiate seeding. The workspace's address is a subdomain of the site (mine is webtut.newsvine.com). While everything shown in the workspace is editable when the user logs in, others can visit your subdomain address directly to see what you've authored, as well as information that you post about yourself.

Content is created with Newsvine's user-friendly editing tools. When you log in, a toolbar will display at the top of the page. As soon as you feel inspired, just click Write Article and begin composing (see Figures 9.3 and 9.4). For submitting links and making comments, a Seed Newsvine button appears on most pages. Right-click the button and add it to your book-marks/favorites. Whenever you're on a webpage you feel others should know about, click the bookmark, write your annotation, give it relevant tags, and click the Seed This Link button, and the Vine snaps it up.

New users have their work featured in the Greenhouse, but, according to the FAQ, you must write a "few articles or seed a few links" before your stuff makes it to the live Vine. Three days elapsed between my first contribution and Newsvine's email telling me I had been promoted from the Greenhouse to the Vine; I'd written two articles and submitted five annotated links.

Once bitten by the CitJ bug, I couldn't quite shake the urge to publish. Although I didn't witness a jumper or survive an earthquake, I donned my reporter's cap again when I uploaded a brief story to the iTowns section of the *Hartford Courant*, my state's largest newspaper. Launched in May 2008, iTowns provides a channel for readers to electronically submit photos and text about local business, politics, education, seniors' events, clubs, religion, or anything. Electronic versions of submissions are available almost immediately on a moderated site (www.courant.com/community). Equivalents are usually published in the Sunday edition of the print newspaper.

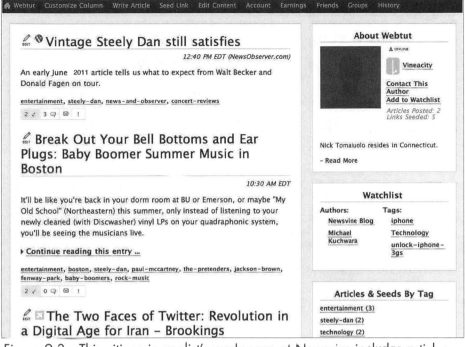

Figure 9.3   This citizen journalist's workspace at Newsvine includes articles the user has contributed or "seeded," tags the author has used, and a Watchlist of favorite Newsvine searches. [Courtesy of Newsvine]

When five co-workers at the Central Connecticut State University Library recently accepted the State of Connecticut's "RIP," or Retirement Incentive Program (Connecticut has a huge deficit, and getting state employees to leave the payroll was one of many strategies used to balance the books), I decided their combined 176 years of service was noteworthy. So I accessed the *Hartford Courant*'s website and quickly learned that CitJ, as far as the *Courant* is concerned, is as easy as writing an email to iTowns and attaching a photo.

I enjoy seeing readers comment on my articles and links. I especially enjoy having my work voted up, so much so that I don't mind the risk of negative feedback. If you think you may want to connect with a CitJ project, check out the Knight Citizen News Network's map and list of 1,000 websites (www.kcnn.org/citmedia_sites). There's always a story to tell, an issue to consider, a problem to probe, and a little Fred Friendly in all of us.

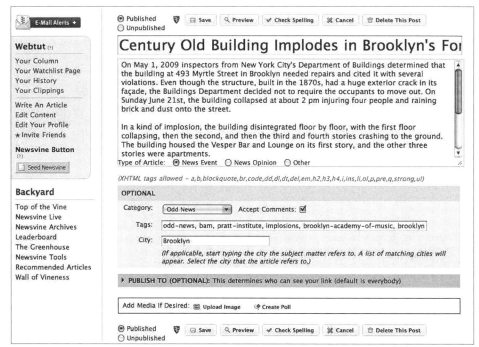

Figure 9.4   This citizen journalist's editing space at Newsvine makes it easy for users to generate and publish text, upload images, and create polls. [Courtesy of Newsvine]

The Darker Side of Citizen Journalism

While professional journalists have leveled criticisms at citizen journalists based on credentialing and standards, detractors of CitJ mention several other factors. Citing the unwholesome voyeuristic nature of society, Trevor Cook, a doctoral student at the University of Sydney who blogs on politics, international relations, and literature, found a compelling example of this dark side in the videos of the moments leading up to Saddam Hussein's execution (in late December 2006), which surfaced on YouTube and Google Videos. Cook, referring to the potential desensitizing effect this material has on its viewers, called into question the responsibility that Google, owner of YouTube, had as a publisher in permitting this footage to reside on its sites.[20]

Another concern is in people posting misinformation to manipulate events. A vivid example of this occurred in late 2008 when the Securities and Exchange Commission launched an investigation into an anonymous and erroneous posting on CNN's user-generated iReport.com. The posting, which was quickly removed by CNN, claimed that Apple's then-chief executive, the late Steve Jobs, had been rushed to a New York City hospital, having suffered a major heart attack. Apple shareholders, who were already jittery about Jobs's general health throughout 2008, saw shares fall 5 percent after the posting.[21]

A more recent example of real-time web reporting demonstrates how easily misinformation may be uploaded and spread. During the tragic shooting spree at Fort Hood, Texas, Paul Carr, blogging at TechCrunch, commented on the tweeting being done inside Fort Hood during the massacre while the facility was in lockdown. Carr listed some of the tweets, which were graphic, and included at least one that contained false information: a tweet saying that the alleged perpetrator, Major Malik Hasan, had been killed. In fact he wasn't killed; he was captured. A twitpic of a wounded soldier was also uploaded. Carr pointed out that while the U.S. Army was doing its best to process the situation and release informed reports, its efforts were being undermined by a selfish informant who, in the name of "getting the word out," was simply indulging in egotism.[22]

Disregard for privacy and abdication of morality were also the subjects of a short video clip from *This American Life* in which, in an elementary school art class, one child made a fake TV camera and the rest of the class quickly became a series of competing news organizations. The culmination was their "coverage" of a fistfight. When teachers broke up the fight, the "cameras" were taken away and banned. Animator Chris Ware observed, "People act different when they are behind the camera, even if they [i.e., the cameras] aren't real."[23]

The Rest of the Story

The late Paul Harvey, the National Association of Broadcasters Hall of Famer who always saved an unexpected detail for the conclusion of his syndicated commentaries, would have appreciated the irony in the CitJ phenomenon. Many organizations and independent websites have taken long strides to give nonjournalists a voice in reporting the news, but they have neglected to do very much to facilitate easy retrieval of archived information. CitJ sites are big on author resources but fall short on options for researchers. Anyone looking for hyperlocal news should be able to easily locate it, but this is one area of the web in which search retrieval is not akin to drinking from the proverbial fire hose.

The Google News Advanced Archive Search (news.google.com/archivesearch/ advanced_search), with its Source search option, is sometimes able to find information from CitJ sites. For example, searching for all dates revealed that OhmyNews International is actually searchable as a source (13,300 articles were retrieved when I checked). The Archive Search retrieves news about NowPublic as a topic but never as a source; this is also true in the case of Allvoices. Neither were there any occurrences of Global Voices in the current news or Archive Search. Not surprisingly, there is relatively good coverage of Comment Is Free, most likely because it originates from the mainstream *Guardian*. Yahoo! News didn't pick up any of the tested CitJ sites.

If you desire comprehensive retrieval, you must search the individual CitJ sites. There's no metasearch engine for these entities, nor are they indexed by LexisNexis or Factiva. (This deficit would be a great opportunity for some forward-thinking data mining concern.) Most sites—but not all—listed on page [9-8] are searchable back to their respective inceptions. Global Voices presented systematic access to its older articles (entering www.globalvoices online.org/2006, for instance, will take you straight to the archived stories from the year 2006). NowPublic is searchable back to its inception in 2004. Similarly, Allvoices, founded in April 2007, appears searchable only back to the beginning of 2008.

Just what we professional searchers need—another "round the mulberry bush" search process. Here's an idea: Read Chapter 11 on custom search engines, and build your own metasearch for CitJ sites.

Conversation With Rich Hanley

Courtesy of Quinnipiac University

Rich Hanley is associate professor of Journalism and the graduate director of Journalism and Interactive Communications at Quinnipiac University in Hamden, Connecticut. Recently a panelist at the National Press Club's discussion on "The Merits of Social Media Driven Journalism," he is a frequent guest and contributor on National Public Radio, the Public Broadcasting System, Fox News, and MSNBC.

Nick Tomaiuolo: *In the article "How Online Citizen Journalism Publications Utilize the Objectivity Standard," author Serena Carpenter points out that "Controversy exists regarding the informational value of online citizen journalism content because many citizen journalists have little or no journalism training." Rich, you teach journalism students, but notwithstanding, do you believe Carpenter has a valid concern, and to what extent is the concern* *an actual problem? What are some ways citizen journalists differ from professional journalists?*

Rich Hanley: The concern is valid but has nothing to do with training, and the actual problem forecast in the article has yet to emerge. The points are self-interest and sustainability from the actual practice of citizen journalism and the motivation of news organizations to deploy unpaid or thinly paid residents in place of paid, professional journalists. Journalism existed long before it became the subject of professional training in higher education. In fact, when I first joined the profession in 1978, I worked with a number of journalists whose formal education ended at their high school commencement. They had learned the craft on the job and had been practicing it for 30 years or more. So the definition of a *professional reporter* needs to be clarified. It is simply defined as one who is paid to cover something as a proxy for the larger public.

Citizen journalism involves coverage of local events by generally unpaid or thinly paid local residents who wish to contribute to the public discourse. But because one does not make a living at doing this, and reporting takes a lot of time and energy given that it requires attendance at events such as public meetings and access to documents available only during normal business hours, it is highly unlikely that it can be sustained on an individual basis. What's more, it's unlikely that a citizen journalist without a personal ax to grind would expend energy and time on investigative reporting that requires sustained effort and financial outlays.

That leads to the self-interest concern. What is the citizen journalist's stake in the outcome of something? Take, for example, a common area of coverage: local zoning boards of appeal. Why would a disinterested citizen, without a stake in the outcome, sit through hours of testimony and review complex plans and documents? If the matter at hand concerned a project in the citizen journalist's neighborhood, it makes sense that coverage would happen this way. But what about objective reporting? It's not to say that high-minded people with a stake in the community cannot be objective; it's just to say that it is difficult to do from the perspective of the volume of time and effort it takes to do this job properly.

The second concern is sustainability. Despite the wonders of the internet, the practice of journalism requires boots on the ground. One has to attend meetings, cultivate contacts in the community, develop sources, and pay attention to detail at the molecular level to accurately and effectively reflect activities in a given community.

It is possible that a citizen journalist with time and independent financial support can do this, but it is unlikely that swarms of citizen journalists, operating only in the public interest, would be able to sustain coverage over an extended time and be consistent in that coverage. The upshot is that citizen journalism probably works best when it concerns coverage of one-off events that would be considered to be soft news in the context of professional journalists.

The third motivation is that of paid media. The balance sheets of newspapers are in tatters, and publishers continue to look to squeeze costs out of the system. Because journalism doesn't require a license or even professional training, it is possible to deploy citizen journalists in place of paid staff to drain costs out of the system. Its attraction to corporate interests is thus clear: free or extremely inexpensive labor. The trade-off, of course, rests in the first two concerns: the self-interest of the citizen journalist and sustainability.

News organizations tend to use citizen journalists according to long-established patterns of coverage common to legacy publications. A resident interested in the garden club will write about garden club events, for example. Citizen journalism's value is that it extends and enhances the news organization's role in community as opposed to investigative journalism. The best citizen journalism sites are those whose focus is on local communities and are not necessarily interested in developing a wider profile.

NT: *Many people are skeptical about the fact that these days anyone, and anyone can include the malicious, has the ability to upload content. There have already been several embarrassing moments for citizen journalists and citizen journalism sites: In October 2008, there was a false posting at CNN's iReports saying Steve Jobs had a heart attack. Around the same time, CBS's EyeMobile, which allows users to send video to its site directly from their cell phones, aired some sexually explicit content according to Michael Learmonth's "Media Morph: CBS Gets a Rude Lesson in Citizen Journalism" in* Advertising Age. *Recently I surfed over to EyeMobile and saw what appeared to be a lot of homemade self-promotional videos—like those you'd see on YouTube. In the era of UContent and Web 2.0, what are your best recommendations for dealing with these problems?*

RH: Professional news media organizations get things wrong, too, but generally do so because of omission, not commission. I recommend that the audience allow local citizen journalism time to establish its reputation for reliability but view the more national or global sites with a touch of skepticism because of the ease with which information can be manipulated to suit a self-interest, including self-promotion.

NT: *You've said many professional journalists got their starts right out of high school; let's talk about the educational preparation of today's journalist. What about the Reporting for the Web course that you teach at Quinnipiac University? I imagine there are a number of unique topics that distinguish reporting on the web from traditional reporting. What are they? How does technology play a role in the differences in reporting? What types of projects do your students in this course undertake?*

RH: Reporting for the web requires students to report single stories through multimedia conveyances and assemble these conveyances in a narrative that plays to the strength of each. Students need to know how to shoot and edit video, how to acquire and edit audio, how to shoot and edit images, how to create Google maps and polls, and how to piece all these elements together.

The technology allows a reporter to present more information across media forms and thus give the audience a chance to more fully and visually understand the information. Even though we train students in the use of technology, our focus is on the decisions that need to be made regarding the type of information that is best carried by the specific media form. What works best in video? What works best in text? And so on.

For example, one of our students pursued a multimedia report on the so-called freshman 15, the propensity of new college students to gain weight. The student performed the routine common to traditional print journalists: interviewed dietitians, students, and university cafeteria administrators. That piece of the story would be carried in text, spread across what we call individual modules or "chunks" so that the audience would not be confronted with a wall of text. That means the traditional reportage would be formatted for reading on a screen. In this case, the story, accessed by "back" and "next" paddles at the end of each chunk, would be perfectly rendered for the pattern of reading online.

The student decided to use video in two ways to provide a visual sense of the choices college students face in a cafeteria. He used a 45-second tracking shot to go from one end of the serving area to the other, using natural sound under the video illustration. He introduced the subject via a text slate at the beginning. The audience heard students ordering food and [the video] showed, without telegraphing it, that the healthy stuff—the salads—could be reached only after the student navigated through the grill and pasta areas and then exited only after traversing a wall of candy.

The second video focused on an interview with a student whose food tray was brimming with food. The student explained why she made the selections, thus giving insight into the individual process. A brief 30-second audio segment featured a student who gained weight and struggled to lose it.

[My] student then deployed a Google map with placement markers to show the vast number of fast-food restaurants arrayed within five miles of the campus. But he didn't stop there. We teach students how to use the street-view feature to create a video tour. The student used this tool for a tour on the street, with just about every chain of fast-food restaurants represented.

The student created a slideshow of images of food considered to lead to obesity available in the cafeteria and created a graphical chart that indicated the calories in each entrée available. Finally, the student deployed a poll asking the audience to decide whether college cafeterias should restrict their offerings to healthy foods.

In all, the student used text, video, audio, images, graphics, and interactivities to create a robust news story that fully covered the issue. Our students use WordPress pages to create their multimedia sites.

Other students pursued multimedia projects on a cheerleading competition, abandoned homes, student radio DJs, mixed martial arts, the debate over legalization of marijuana, suburban sprawl, job searches, and so on. The key decision is to determine the subject that works best when presented as a multimedia story.

NT: *Your students obviously bring a proclivity for technology to your course. I've been reading a great deal about citizen journalists' adroit use of Twitter. During the Iran election protests in June, CNN's Errol Barnett noted that Twitter was receiving 2,000 tweets per hour with the hashtag #iranelection.[24] Even this activity was eclipsed on June 26 as 100,000 tweets per hour spread news of popstar Michael Jackson's death and brought down Twitter's servers. According to Ethan Zuckerman, a fellow at Harvard's Berkman Center for Internet and Society, neither the tweets for swine flu nor Iran ever got close to generating that amount of traffic on Twitter.[25] In July 2011, Twitter claimed that there were*

200 million tweets a day.[26] *How large is Twitter's role in citizen journalism?*

RH: Twitter is an exceptionally efficient tool to connect communities in groups of followers around an individual subject or issue. It permits citizen journalists to use residents as sources with one post instead of several calls. For example, if a citizen journalist who has an established Twitter presence with many local followers wishes to get comments on the local strawberry festival, a tweet requesting such views can be posted. It's also a great tool for promoting upcoming stories and for requesting immediate reaction to breaking news. However, it doesn't work with only a handful of followers. Twitter is useful only if the citizen journalist has enough followers to reflect the community as a whole instead of a tiny, discreet group of technologically savvy people.

Endnotes

1. Dan Gillmor, "1) From Tom Paine to Blogs and Beyond," We the Media, accessed August 3, 2011, www.authorama.com/we-the-media-2.html.

2. John Savageau, "Formalizing Citizen Journalism," SYS-CON, March 31, 2011, accessed August 3, 2011, www.sys-con.com/node/1776543.

3. Chris Anderson, "Q and A with Clay Shirky on Twitter in Iran," TED [Technology, Entertainment, Design] Blog, June 16, 2009, accessed August 3, 2011, blog.ted.com/2009/06/16/qa_with_clay_sh.

4. Mike Shield, "iReport Submissions From Iran Soar," Adweek, June 18, 2009, accessed August 3, 2011, www.adweek.com/news/technology/ireport-submissions-iran-soar-112602.

5. James Poniewozic, "Iranians Protest Election, Tweets Protest CNN," Time.com, June 15, 2009, accessed November 1, 2011, entertainment.time.com/2009/06/15/iranians-protest-election-tweeps-protest-cnn.

6. Serena Carpenter, "How Online Citizen Journalism Publications and Online Newspapers Utilize the Objectivity Standard and Rely on External Sources," *Journalism and Mass Communication Quarterly* 85 (2008): 540.

7. Mark Glaser, "The New Voices: Hyperlocal Citizen Media Sites Want You (to Write)!" USC Annenberg Online Journalism Review, November 17, 2004, accessed August 3, 2011, www.ojr.org/ojr/glaser/1098833871.php.

8. Nicholas Lemann, "Amateur Hour," NewYorker.com, August 7, 2006, accessed August 3, 2011, www.newyorker.com/archive/2006/08/07/060807fa_fact1?currentPage=all.

9. Jon Talton, "When I Hear the Term 'Citizen Journalist,' I Reach for My Pistol!" Encylopaedia Britannica Blog, April 8, 2008, accessed August 3, 2011, www.britannica.com/blogs/2008/04/when-i-hear-the-term-citizen-journalist-i-reach-for-my-pistol-the-blogging-rage.

10. Oliver Lindberg, "Andrew Keen" (interview), .net Magazine, October 16, 2007, accessed August 3, 2011, www.netmagazine.com/interviews/question-answer/andrew-keen.

11. David Domingo, "Interactivity in the Daily Routines of Online Newsrooms: Dealing With an Uncomfortable Myth," *Journal of Computer-Mediated Communication* 13 (April 2008): 694.

12. Jane B. Singer and Ian Ashman, "Comment Is Free, But Facts Are Sacred: User-Generated Content and Ethical Constructs at the *Guardian*," *Journal of Mass Media Ethics* 24 (2009): 3–21.

13. Rich Hanley, telephone conversation with author, January 10, 2009.

14. Dan Fost, "All the News That's Fit to Post: Newspapers Figure Out a Future," SFGate.com, April 19, 2005, accessed August 3, 2011, articles.sfgate.com/2005-04-19/business/17370243_1_newspaper-association-competitive-strategy-nations -newspaper-publishers.

15. "Interview with Ed Keating," *Information Today* 26 (Dec. 2009): 41.

16. Pew Project for Excellence in Journalism, "State of the News Media: An Annual Report on American Journalism," Pew Research Center, 2009, accessed August 3, 2011, www.stateofthemedia.org/2009/special-reports-summary-essay/citizen-based-media.

17. Bobbie Johnson and Michael Fitzpatrick, "Korean Website's 40,000 Citizen Journalists Get Shot at Byline in Herald Tribune," Guardian.co.uk, May 31, 2006, accessed August 3, 2011, www.guardian.co.uk/media/2006/may/31/pressand publishing.business.

18. Henrik Ornebring, "The Consumer as Producer—of What?" *Journalism Studies*, vol. 9 (2008): 783.

19. Rich Hanley, telephone conversation with author, January 10, 2009.

20. Trevor Cook, "Video and the Dark Side of Citizen Journalism," Trevor Cook, January 5, 2007, accessed August 3, 2011, trevorcook.typepad.com/weblog/2007/01/video_and_the_d.html.

21. "S.E.C. Investigates Web Report on Apple," NYTimes.com October 3, 2008, accessed August 3, 2011, www.nytimes.com/2008/10/04/business/4bizbriefs-SECINVESTIGA_BRF.html.

22. Paul Carr, "NSFW: After Fort Hood, Another Example of How Citizen Journalists Can't Handle the Truth," TechCrunch, November 7, 2009, accessed August 3, 2011, www.techcrunch.com/2009/11/07/nsfw-after-fort-hood-another-example-of-how-citizen-journalists-cant-handle-the-truth.

23. Ira Glass, "Chris Ware Talks About His Work" (video), *This American Life*, March 22, 2007, accessed August 3, 2011, www.youtube.com/watch?v=WbVeN13wGFc.

24. Elise LaBott, "Officials: Social Networking Providing Crucial Info From Iran" (video), CNN.com/Technology, June 16, 2009, accessed August 3, 2011, www.cnn.com/2009/TECH/06/16/iran.twitter.facebook/index.html?iref=newssearch#cnnSTC.

25. Ethan Zuckerman, "My Twitter Search Script" (twitter post), June 25, 2009, accessed August 3, 2011, twitter.com/EthanZ/status/2333139296.

26. "200 Million Tweets Per Day," Twitter Blog, June 30, 2011, accessed August 3, 2011, blog.twitter.com/2011/06/200-million-tweets-per-day.html.

Chapter 10

Tagging, Folksonomies, and Social Bookmarking

One of the first things we reflexively do when we begin reading a book, viewing a presentation, watching a movie, listening to a podcast, or seeing a play is determine what it is "about" and where we would categorize it in our minds. The novel is historical fiction, the presentation is a tutorial, the movie is a romantic comedy, the podcast is an interview, the play is a comedy of manners. It seems natural to want to label these things, because labeling not only gives us a degree of control in our interpretations, but also enhances our ability to store the information in our brains for later recall. The same rules apply when we browse a website, open a PDF, look at a group of images, or retrieve an article in an online database; we want to associate the item with a label so we can cognitively deal with it and, we hope, remember something useful about it at a later time.

Tags and Tagging

Let's revisit the first set of hypothetical items through a "zoom" lens. Perhaps a more comprehensive set of labels will emerge for each item. The novel is historical fiction set during the Civil War at the battle of Gettysburg; the presentation is a tutorial about embedding a Meebo widget in a blog; the movie is a romantic comedy about a man who loves a woman with short-term memory loss; the podcast is an interview with Sergey Brin discussing Google and the stock market; and the play is a comedy of manners written by Moliere that satirizes the French aristocracy. As I've demonstrated, any given entity may be "about" multiple "things." I've also demonstrated that the labels depend on how the items are perceived. For instance, to a Library of Congress-trained cataloger, Cervantes's *Don Quixote* is about "Knights and knighthood—Spain—Fiction and Don Quixote (Fictitious character)—Fiction" (which seems a bit redundant). A reader more personally involved with the text may have decided that the novel is about irony, truth, old age, deception, chivalry, moral values, dementia, and loyalty. These two lists describing *Don Quixote* form an apt contrast between using a controlled vocabulary and letting users "tag" items in their own words.

Jennifer Trant, writing in the *Journal of Digital Information*, states that the current interest in studying tagging is attributable, in part, to the phenomenon that Chris Anderson, editor of Wired, calls the Long Tail (discussed in Chapter 8). She observed that in the social web landscape, there is a mandate to reach micromarkets, in addition to mainstream end users. She also pointed to the success of keyword access to textual sources (as in Google searches).[1] Several writers tell us that tagging has been around for a long time.[2,3,4] An early manifestation of tagging is author-supplied keywords for journal articles. One prominent difference between user-supplied tags (*exo-tagging*) and author-supplied tags (*endo-tagging*) is that while user-supplied tags are usually descriptive, they may also provide information about the user's personal interaction with the information, whereas endo-tags are almost always an author's attempt to describe content.

The activity we call tagging began to gain popularity when Joshua Schacter rewrote a computer program he called Muxway and launched del.icio.us (now called Delicious) in 2003.[5] Tagging, folksonomies, and social bookmarking are interdependent: Folksonomies are the result of individuals consuming information and tagging items for later retrieval, and social bookmarking takes place when link management resources permit users to save and annotate items both for their personal use and to share with other users.

Tags and tagging have the following attributes:

- Tags are descriptive words (i.e., keywords) that computer users apply to items they encounter on the World Wide Web (e.g., photos, URLs, computer games, podcasts, music, videos, presentations, and documents). They are considered metadata and are applied to items that the user wants to be able to find again.

- Tags may describe an item's content according to the information consumer's perception and knowledge and may even describe the user's relationship to the content.

- Although some tagging resources provide users with the option of publicizing their tags or keeping them private, tagging is usually done in a social environment (shared and open to others).

- Unlike browser Bookmarks and Favorites, most social tagging resources permit users to also add descriptive summaries to tagged items.

- Unlike browser Bookmarks and Favorites, which are native to individual computers, tagging resources reside on the web, and one person's tags (and bookmarked items) can be accessed from any computer on the web.

- Tags are democratic; anyone can contribute and share tags. This starkly contrasts with exclusionary, hierarchical, controlled vocabularies, in which descriptors are formulated by authorities. Tags allow users to organize the vastness of web on their own terms.

Folksonomies

Thomas Vander Wal coined the term *folksonomy* (a mashup of *folks* and *taxonomy*) while participating in a round of dialogue on the Asilomar Institute for Information Architecture listserv. When a colleague posted, "Some of you might have noticed services like Furl, Flickr and Delicious using user-defined labels or tags to organize and share information. … Is there a name for this kind of informal social classification?" Vander Wal rejoined, "So the user-created bottom-up categorical structure development with an emergent thesaurus would become a Folksonomy?"[6] Vander Wal declared that in a folksonomy, the "cumulative force of all the individual tags can produce a bottom-up, self-organized system for classifying mountains of digital material."[7]

Folksonomies have the following attributes:

- They improve with use; as more people contribute tags, the folksonomy grows and gains strength. Although individuals serve their own needs by adding tags, a consensus vocabulary ultimately emerges.

- They are flexible and easily adapt to current word usage, quickly reflecting new concepts and terms. This is in contrast to controlled vocabularies, which may contain obsolete and arcane descriptors.

- They facilitate the establishment of online communities for sharing information.

- They cost almost nothing to maintain, whereas expensive taxonomies and hierarchical classification systems require experts to monitor and maintain.

- They offer information professionals a way to observe how end users interact with content.

Social Bookmarking

Social bookmarking refers to the activity of storing, classifying, sharing, and searching links by attaching tags to information. In a social bookmarking system, participants store lists of internet resources that they find useful, and other people with similar interests can view the links by category, tags, or randomly.[8] The application of tags results in a user-directed, "amateur" method of classifying information.[9] Link management sites that host social bookmarking usually include features that allow users to view and use the bookmarked resources of other users. Most social bookmarking sites also offer the user the option of making bookmarks public or private.

Shortcomings of Tagging, Folksonomies, and Social Bookmarking

Though ubiquitous at this point, tags and folksonomies are still criticized for several reasons. This disapproval emanates from librarians, information architects, and other technology professionals. According to the "hype cycles" of the Gartner Group, which indicate the point at which there is over-enthusiasm with technology, the popularity of folksonomies peaked in 2006.[10] That was just around the time the Pew Internet & American Life Project declared 7 percent of computer users tagged something on any given day.[11] Critics contend that folksonomies are not viable because there is no oversight or consensus on the vocabulary that users employ as they tag. Folksonomies can't handle polysemes, words spelled and pronounced the same way, but having different meanings (e.g., *bark* can be the abrupt explosive sound made by a dog, but also the external covering of a tree and a sailing vessel). Folksonomies don't do well with synonyms (words that have similar meanings, such as *car* and *automobile*) either. Plurals also present a problem. If one person tags an item with the word *apples*, will that item ever be shared with the user who is searching for *apple*?

Aside from these obvious mainstream shortcomings, critics argue that tagging may suffer from "basic level variation." Basic level variation relates to the continuum of meaning from general to specific (e.g., one user might use the tag *animal*, another might use the tag *cat*, and yet another might use the tag *cheetah*). Tags also may sometimes consist of unhelpful, non-subject-related terms, which Marcus Heckner, Tanja Neubauer, and Christian Wolff called "time," "task," and "affective" labels. For example, how helpful to anyone else is the tag *vacation* when applied to an item that someone read and enjoyed *while on* vacation? Similarly, someone might tag an item *funny* because it was either humorous or ironic, but the tag *funny* might mean peculiar or odd to another individual; likewise, the task/time tag *readsoon_August2011* is meaningful only to the individual who created that tag as a reminder to "read a particular item soon—by August 2011."

But this criticism may not be valid. In a very large study of 18,904 unique tags, Margaret Kipp, a professor at the University of Wisconsin's School of Information Studies, stated, "A total of 3,049 unique tags [16 percent] were identified as being time or task related."[12] But this finding could not be replicated in a study of 1,010 tags taken from Delicious, in which researcher Marcus Heckner's group classified only 2.9 percent as being related to time, task, or affect. Heckner noted, however, that many users entered strings of words that the link management resources processed as separate tags.[13] Consider, for example, *OK Go Here It Goes Again*. That string of words makes sense to a YouTube user who has just watched a video of a pop music group performing a song. Unfortunately, because the words are not connected to each other, each word becomes a discrete, meaningless tag. In another example, the following word string becomes eight tags: *Joanne tickling newborn Richard in front of webcam*. In this example, the words might mean that a newborn named Richard was being tickled by his 5-year-old sister Joanne while being filmed by a webcam. The sentence makes sense, but the individual words, entered separately as tags, do not convey the essence of the sentence.

This and other tagging problems may be solved by what some authors call "tag literacy." A tagging-best-practices blog article posted by Ulises Mejias (State University of New York, Oswego) suggests the following guidelines: Always use plurals rather than singulars, always use lower case, keep words that make up a phrase together by using underscores, follow tag conventions started by others, and add synonyms.[14]

As far as considering folksonomies bottom-up classification systems, as Vander Wal claims, Tom Reamy, chief knowledge architect at the KAPS Group, responds, "Folksonomies are not a classification system; they are an unordered, flat set of keywords that are ranked by popularity. Ranking words by their popularity can tell you a great deal about how groups of people are thinking. That information can be extremely useful, but it does not tell you much of anything about the relationships between words or concepts. In other words, there is no 'onomy' in folksonomy."[15]

This semantic incongruence isn't a big problem for Stewart Butterfield, co-founder of Flickr, who said, "One of the unfortunate consequences of the term folksonomy is, whether it was intended or not, people assume that tags are meant to be a replacement for controlled vocabularies for describing taxonomic space or for categorizing things when they [tags] are not necessarily [that] at all. They can be just for noting aspects of things and helping to find things … things that share one or more aspects."[16]

A Rose by Any Other Name, or "Do Our Tags Agree?"

If you think that it is easy to produce the same metadata for an item that will also occur to the next human being who might find the item useful, Sean Gorman concisely summed up the difficulties in the Off the Map blog: "Your users will not always implement tags in ways that are productive for the community—in the extreme resulting in Flickr's 20 million unique tags ... many of those 20 million tags are misspelled words or so off the path they never get found."[17] His point is clearly illustrated by Liz Lawley, a librarian writing on the social consequences of social tagging who brought my attention to the ESP Game depicted in Figure 10.1. After you read this excerpt from her post, check the likelihood that you can match your tags with those of other players at GWAP (Games With A Purpose; www.gwap.com/gwap/gamesPreview/espgame):

> The ESP Game is a site developed by researchers at CMU [Carnegie Mellon University], intended to create a set of descriptors for images indexed by Google. But the unintended consequences of this approach are nontrivial, as I found when I spent a few hours playing with it yesterday and today. The way the site works is that [when] you register as a game player you're paired at random with another player, and presented with the first in a series of images. [You are trying to describe an image with the same word(s) your anonymous partner is using.] The clock in the top right corner shows how much time is left. The thermometer along the side shows how many matches you've made, and how many images are left to describe. ... You start typing words associated with the image, one at a time. When you and your partner have both typed the same word, you're told it's a match and you move on to the next item. The goal is to come to agreement on a word for every picture before time runs out. ... When I started playing the game, my scores were very low. I kept trying to assess the context and content of the image, and choose descriptors based on that. So if I saw a woman in a bathing suit walking down a runway wearing a sash and a crown, I'd type pageant or contestant. But it turns out that's a lousy strategy for winning the game, because it's unlikely that you'll be matched with someone doing the same thing."[18]

Figure 10.1   The ESP Game approximates the task of matching tags with other humans. It isn't always as easy as you would think. [Courtesy of Games With A Purpose]

The Tag Cloud

Using a site's tag cloud is one of several ways to find information at a social bookmarking site. A tag cloud is a visual representation of the most popular tags in use at any given time at a social bookmarking website. Of course, we often encounter tag clouds elsewhere (in our own blogs, at Amazon.com), but the tag cloud is a characteristic of folksonomies because it allows a site visitor to visualize frequently tagged topics, and the tag cloud navigation/browsing option offers an alternative to searching. Many link management resources will display a tag cloud for the whole site as well as a tag cloud of the individual user's keywords. Figure 10.2 shows the tag cloud Popular Tags for the entire Delicious community for a day (I elected to sort them by size, which refers to how frequently the tags are used). Note that many site users are tagging items with the words *design*, *blog*, and *video*. Note also that members of the Delicious community employ the convention of connecting multiple word terms by running the words together (e.g., *webdesign* near the top and *socialnetworking* near the bottom). Figure 10.3 shows the tag cloud for my personal account (that I elected to sort alphabetically), with the following items noted: 1) title of tagged item; 2) number of users who share that tag; 3) a description that the user has given to the bookmark as a reminder of the item's content; 4) the user's tags listed alphabetically (note that larger/darker tags, as contrasted with the smaller grayed-out tags, indicate the most frequently applied tags; the author has used 405 separate tags and places an underscore between words when employing multiword phrases); 5) edit and delete buttons; and 6) tags applied to that bookmark. Notice that I used quasi-synonymous phrases to make the item more easily shared and findable. Clicking on any tag in a tag cloud will display all items that have had that tag applied to them throughout the site.

Tag clouds are featured at many folksonomy-based websites, including Flickr (photo hosting), Technorati (blog search engine), Diigo (a social bookmarking site similar to Delicious), and others. Some subscription databases are beginning to adopt navigation and browsing via the tag cloud, as shown

---

Tag Cloud: Popular

KEY: green tags are tags you have in common with everyone else.   Sort: Alphabetically | By size

design   blog   video   software   tools   music programming webdesign reference tutorial art web howto   javascript   free   linux   web2.0   development google inspiration photography news food flash css blogs education business technology travel shopping books   mac   tips   politics   science   opensource   games culture research java windows security internet movies online search   humor   funny   social   community   fun   mobile   recipes cool marketing health php tutorials cooking resources history portfolio   audio   download   graphics   media   library   toread python photo article ruby ajax learning film maps photoshop youtube   architecture   rails   computer   wordpress   freeware plugin home hardware firefox apple mp3 illustration photos email twitter socialnetworking api ubuntu language database fashion   osx   tv   blogging   network   html   book   typography

---

Figure 10.2   This tag cloud of popular Delicious tags is sorted by size, which actually refers to the number of times users have tagged items with a particular keyword. [Courtesy of Delicious]

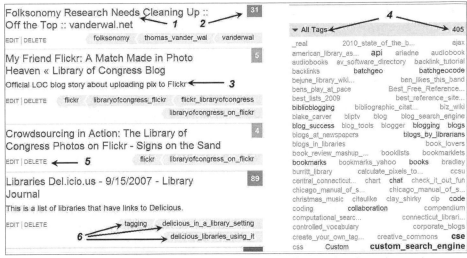

Figure 10.3   This is a glimpse of the author's Delicious bookmarks and tags. [Courtesy of Delicious]

at Engineering Village in Figure 10.4. Note that the protocol for entering tags containing more than one word is to combine the words (see *waynestate* near the bottom of the cloud) or to separate tags with commas; this is why *thermal management* is a single tag and not two separate tags, which is how it might be treated at other social bookmarking sites (e.g., YouTube).

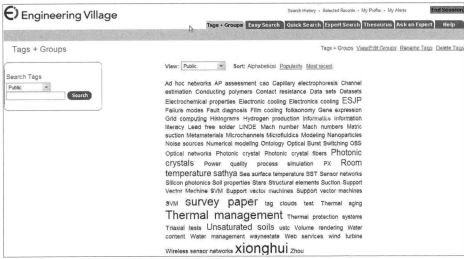

Figure 10.4   Subscription databases have started to facilitate tagging and tag clouds. [Courtesy of Engineering Village]

In a mordant aside, Vander Wal wrote that tag clouds are "the things that are cute but provide little value."[19] Referring to a once fashionable but now passé hairstyle, web designer L. Jeffrey Zeldman called tag clouds "the new mullets" because "as tag clouds come to replace expert taxonomies in common practice, carefully constructed hierarchies vanish. In their place is a flattened world where every idea, at any level, is a topic as worthy as any other. *Eight Mile* is a topic at the same level as *Detroit*, which is a topic at the same level as *cities*, which is a topic at the same level as *United States*, and so on."[20]

But clicking on keywords in a tag cloud is easy, though not every word in a link management database can be depicted in a tag cloud. The more a tag is used (i.e., the more popular it is), the more it increases in size. Speaking relatively, this is going to necessitate that some tags drop out of the cloud entirely. In an experiment aimed at determining whether tag clouds are useful, Australian National University researchers Sinclair and Hall asked 89 participants to tag 10 articles apiece. Following this step, each participant was asked to answer 10 questions by using either the tag cloud that the group had just created or a traditional search box. In all, 48 percent of the questions were answered by individuals' use of the tag cloud, and 41.2 percent were answered by using the search box. In interviews, eight respondents indicated that their choice of interface depended on the question at hand (i.e., the information-seeking task), and 10 participants commented that the search box afforded greater specificity. The researchers concluded, "The tag cloud has a number of positive attributes. … The tag cloud does indeed provide value. … It is particularly useful for browsing or non-specific information discovery. … However, it is clear that the tag cloud is not sufficient as the sole means of navigating a folksonomy dataset."[21]

Different Tags for Different Folks

People primarily tag items to keep themselves organized, so that "found resources will stay found." Delicious offers an example of finding some item on the web and then saving, annotating, and sharing it, complete with tags you assign. This is sometimes considered exo-tagging. You usually save the links to websites and the tags you have assigned for your own reasons, but other Delicious users may benefit also. Some users participate by endo-tagging (i.e., they tag to promote their own content). A blogger will assign several tags to a posting in order to attract readers, or users uploading videos to YouTube may tag their videos with as many access points as possible in the hope that someone will view them. This is also true in the case of SlideShare and blip.tv. If you want your presentation seen, give it plenty of tags. Endo-tagging differs from *tag spam*, which is the practice of giving items tags that have nothing to do with the tagged items in order to lure searchers to inappropriate destinations.

One group of researchers hypothesized, "When applying the concept of familiarity in our current context of social tagging, we contend that users' familiarity with different concepts of social tagging is likely to influence how users select keywords, which ultimately affect their [the chosen tags'] effectiveness for content sharing." Their survey of 262 college students confirmed that people with a good understanding (i.e., "high familiarity") of the concepts of tagging, social tagging, and web directories perform better in terms of creating effective tags for content sharing. The researchers added, "Apparently, this does not seem to fully support the Wisdom of Crowds theory which suggests that the quality of tags created by a community is thought to be better than that provided by an expert."[22]

It requires only nominal experimentation to understand that individuals use tags differently depending on the type of link management resource involved and the individuals' motives for tagging. For example, Flickr, a wildly popular photo sharing site, offers social bookmarking, but people using Flickr often choose tags that reflect dates and the devices; many photos are tagged with the month and year the photo was taken and the type of camera used to take the photo. In fact, in a study of 4,000 tags applied in YouTube, Connotea, Delicious, and Flickr (about 1,000 tags per system), Flickr contained the most non-content-related tags (229).[23]

In a separate study of Delicious, Flickr, and YouTube, researchers examining 1.3 million tags in Flickr determined that locations, dates (including years and seasons), and colors were the most popular tags. "Flickr taggers frequently assign informal tags to photographs (e.g., 'me'), indicating that users may be tagging photographs for purposes of storing and retrieving them for their own use rather than with any intent to share them with others," the team headed by Ying Ding, Elin K. Jacob, and Zhixiong Zhang wrote. Flickr users primarily tag for "selfish" reasons—so they can easily find their own uploaded images and, secondarily, to direct friends to them.[24]

Ding et al.'s analysis of YouTube tags found that the most popular tags for 2005, 2006, and 2007 were, respectively, *music* (in 2005), *the* (in 2006), and *the* (again in 2007).[25] Obviously the last two tags reflect naïve users' attempts to enter multiword tags without connecting them with underscores. Nevertheless, the exploration also found that tags assigned to items in YouTube were not always non sequiturs but also included content, medium, and genre. YouTube also had the highest number of tags per item (4.81).

In Connotea (a resource offered by the Nature Publishing Group that is mostly used as a bookmarking site for saving and organizing journal articles), tags per item averaged 4.22; 81.25 percent of 1,000 tags studied by Heckner and his colleagues were attributable to creators' names.[26] Ding's research team analyzed more than 9 million tags in Delicious and concluded, "When comparing these three social networks [Flickr, YouTube, and Delicious], [we found that] Delicious demonstrates the tightest connection to the use of tags as extended information about resources. In Delicious, users can tag an available online resource with the tag or tags of their own choice, and an object can be tagged many times and by multiple users, thereby indicating that it 'belongs' (or is more relevant) to the Delicious community as a whole."[27]

Librarians and Tagging

Some members of the information profession hold the belief that subject authority (or "aboutness") is exclusively the purview of information professionals. This group views tagging, folksonomies, and social bookmarking with skepticism. Others feel just as strongly that users should have a voice in how materials are labeled. After all, the whole endeavor is for the users.

In early 2009, a study was published in the *Journal of the Medical Library Association* that provides a window into the way information professionals perceive the social tagging zeitgeist. Cecile E. Bianco originally distributed surveys to 348 medical librarians in the U.S. and Canada. When all was said and done, she had 156 complete surveys to work with—a 45-percent response rate—and found that 47 percent of respondents (73) used social tagging. Of the 53 percent who did not use social tagging, the most common reason expressed for eschewing the practice was "I don't see any need."[28]

To the question "Why do you use tagging?" (to which more than one response could be checked), 67 percent (49 of the 73 who tagged) said they used it to keep found resources found, 60 percent (44) tagged to discover new information, and 41 percent (30) employed tagging in order "to share." Among the top social bookmarking sites mentioned by tagging librarians were Delicious, Flickr, and LibraryThing.

I tapped into the wisdom of the crowd at the LibRef-L listserv (a moderated discussion of issues related to reference librarianship) and asked some of the same questions via an email to the list. The response was not overwhelming, and after a week I decided to "crunch" the numbers. Here are the results:

Do you currently use a social bookmarking resource?
   Yes: 50
   No: 12

Do you use the social bookmarking resource primarily to keep track of items you've found on the web that you intend to revisit, or

do you use it primarily with the intent of sharing the items that you have found with other users (including library patrons)?
Primarily for myself: 18
Primarily to share: 0
For myself *and* to share: 32

Do you think *tagging* and *folksonomies* are:
A fad: 0
Here to stay: 49
(There was one write-in answer: "somewhere in the middle")

Have you ever used your social bookmarking resource as a web search engine (that is, have you ever searched by tags to find information that others may have bookmarked)?
Yes: 30
No: 20

What is your favorite social bookmarking resource?
Delicious: 47.5
Read It Later: 1
Diigo: .5
MyHq: 1

According to Alexa, the worldwide traffic rank for Delicious fluctuates between position 300 and 400 (depending on when you look at the rankings). Delicious has a loyal following of 5 million registered users, according to Loren Baker at SearchEngineJournal.com.[29] One search shortcut is to enter www.delicious.com/url in your browser's address bar. That will take you directly into a Delicious URL search. Once there, enter a URL and you'll see if anyone has tagged it (or how many people have tagged it), as well as the first person to tag it. If you are a Delicious user, you may be interested in some of the following shortcuts:

- To retrieve bookmarks with a specific tag, use www.delicious.com/tag/keyword (e.g., www.delicious.com/tag/oilspill)

- To retrieve bookmarks with more than one tag, use the plus sign between tags: www.delicious.com/tag/keyword+keyword (e.g., www.delicious.com/tag/college+tuition or www.delicious.com/tag/college+tuition+grants)

- To retrieve the most popular sites in any category, use www.delicious.com/popular/tagname (e.g., www.delicious.com/popular/music)

The Classification Controversy

If librarians are tagging, and end users are tagging, would it be appropriate to begin allowing end users to help describe content in a library setting? Two issues lie at the core of disharmony over tagging, folksonomies, and social bookmarking. One centers on whether tags are, in fact, a good way to describe resources. The other is whether libraries should provide a virtual space for end users to introduce their own system of labeling.

One of oft-cited internet expert Clay Shirky's main objections to top-down hierarchies is that, depending on the authorities who developed them, such hierarchies might have huge gaps in what they describe. In "Ontology Is Overrated," Shirky really digs in when he talks about our systems of subject classification:

> The experience of the library catalog is probably what people know best as a high-order categorized view of the world, and those cataloging systems contain all kinds of odd mappings between the categories and the world they describe. … This is the Dewey Decimal System's categorization for religions of the world, which is the 200 category:
>
> **Dewey, 200: Religion**
> 210 Natural theology
> 220 Bible
> 230 Christian theology
> 240 Christian moral & devotional theology
> 250 Christian orders & local church
> 260 Christian social theology
> 270 Christian church history
> 280 Christian sects & denominations
> 290 Other religions
>
> How much is this not the categorization you want in the 21st century?
>
> This kind of bias is rife in categorization systems. Here is the Library of Congress's categorization of History. These are all the top-level categories—all of these things are presented as being co-equal:
>
> **D: History (general)**
> DA: Great Britain
> DB: Austria

DC: France
DD: Germany
DE: Mediterranean
DF: Greece
DG: Italy
DH: Low Countries
DJ: Netherlands
DK: Former Soviet Union
DL: Scandinavia
DP: Iberian Peninsula
DQ: Switzerland
DR: Balkan Peninsula
DS: Asia
DT: Africa
DU: Oceania
DX: Gypsies

I'd like to call your attention to the ones in bold: The Balkan Peninsula. Asia. Africa. Yet, for all the oddity of placing the Balkan Peninsula and Asia in the same level, this is harder to laugh off than the Dewey example, because it's so puzzling. The Library of Congress—no slouches in the thinking department, founded by Thomas Jefferson—has a staff of people who do nothing but think about categorization all day long. So what's being optimized here? It's not geography. It's not population. It's not regional GDP.[30]

And why are there individual categories for Great Britain, Italy, France, Germany, and Greece, but only one category for all of the continent of Africa?

Kate Sheehan, formerly of the Darien (CT) Public Library, is a librarian at Bibliomation in Connecticut and a blogger for ALA TechSource. When I asked her to contrast subject headings with tag clouds as they relate to books in the online public access catalog (OPAC), she provided some insight with an alternate perspective:

It's apples and oranges. The subject headings are, as we all know, a controlled vocabulary assigned by experts. What's nice about the tags is that they are assigned by people who have read the books. Everybody can think of examples of having a book in hand and, when they looked at the subject headings said, "hmmm, not quite." A tag cloud lets people who have read the books talk about the content. True, there is an inherent messiness, but there is also an inherent genuineness, because this is valuable information coming from the end user. The end user has invested time with the book, invested time with the plot—these people care about these books, whether they loved the book or hated it. Plus, tag clouds are useful to librarians. Take the list of tags in the Darien Public Library's online catalog that accompanies Stephenie Meyer's *Twilight*, which I've used frequently because I am an adult librarian. When teens ask, "I've read all the Stephenie Meyer, what's next?" because I haven't read *Twilight* yet, I couldn't say. But the informal yet genuine user-generated tag cloud is really helpful when I need to help someone who wants to read something like it.[31]

Catalog librarian Peter Rolla undertook a study to look at both user tags and subject headings. He compared the LibraryThing tags for a group of 45 books with the library-supplied subject headings for the same books and noted that users and catalogers described the items very differently. Among his discoveries was that LibraryThing records had an average of 35.16 tags (after discarding time/task/affect tags), whereas the library records had about 3.8 Library of Congress Subject Headings each. Rolla stated, "The fact that the users of LibraryThing assign tags … representing concepts not brought out by [Library of Congress Subject Headings] does indicate that catalogers, by following the Library of Congress guidelines, may omit concepts that are important to users. … Conversely, the librarian-assigned subject headings in twenty-five records (55.6 percent) brought out concepts that the user tags did not."[32]

Rolla concluded that user tags cannot exclusively provide the best subject access to the materials in library collections, but they do offer librarians alternative ways of thinking about how patrons perceive content, and this information should be added, via user tags, to OPAC displays.[33]

Nobody is suggesting that we use the 8,222 entries from the *Thesaurus of Psychological Index Terms* as kindling. Nor should we toss the six "big red books" containing 308,000 Library of Congress Subject Headings into a bonfire, along with the 26,142 descriptors in the 2011 Medical Subject Headings, while we issue pink slips to the 12 members of the Medical Subject Headings staff. Several information professionals have advocated a middle ground and have given their reasons.

A Combination of the Two

Taxonomies worked well within the walls of libraries and library media centers, but in the present world of blogs, texting, and Google, a more eclectic approach to teaching literacy skills is required. "While traditional classification systems are concise, exact, and accurate, metadata from the web cannot be incorporated into such a system," writes Dr. Phyllis Snipes, a professor of media technology at the University of West Georgia. "In order to manage the web's massive amount of data, the process of social networking, through tagging, becomes an appealing option, especially since this tagged information is practically labeled by the user and can be shared."[34] She recommends that librarians find good web resources and tag them in Delicious with the objective of sharing the links with faculty and students who would otherwise have to struggle with thousands of web search results.

Explaining that metadata has traditionally been contributed by content creators and/or professionals trained in content classification, Jessamyn West, librarian and blogger, makes the case that "When we ask users how they would classify and organize content (ours or theirs), their choices and decisions often surprise us." Because tagging offers a way for end users to remember where they found digital content, librarians should consider tagging as a beneficial activity: "Anything that can help our users find information should be a net gain to librarians." West also believes a "combination of the two" is a plausible approach. "While a free tagging system is no substitute for an authoritative taxonomy, it can be a worthwhile, simple, and eminently useful addition to any system that aims to successfully store and retrieve digital information."[35]

Imagine you are an information professional working at an institution that publishes content on the web. The content is important public information, and the website is open for anyone to search and use, but the information in it is categorized in formal jargon. This is exactly the case Katje Snuderl, from the Statistical Office of the Republic of Slovenia, describes at the National Statistical Institute. Since its database went online, she noticed, "Making all data freely available on the web significantly changed not only the quantity, but also the diversity of users. Many users don't know where to exactly look for data and they often don't know the exact statistical term." Opening the database to user tagging provided another layer of metadata, which enhanced the discovery process; the search engine could look for both "official" keywords and "unofficial" tags. Snuderl cited other benefits of opening the system to user tags, including getting to know site users better and more user engagement.[36] Dalhousie University's Louise Spiteri endorsed folksonomies in a library setting, citing their growing popularity and potential to add value to the online catalog by supplementing existing controlled vocabularies.[37]

Helping Out at the Reference Desk

The Dig-Ref listserv provides a convincing example of how patrons can help librarians by tagging items. In this case they aren't tagging in the library catalog; they are tagging at LibraryThing (www.librarything.com). Via a blog posting, Dr. John Jaeger, a reference librarian at Dallas Baptist University, described how his associate Scott Jeffries answered a reference question using LibraryThing. In December 2008, a student asked Jeffries for a book but knew neither the author nor the title. She did know it was about a collection of letters between a London book dealer and an American female author. Searching various combinations of the terms *London literature antiques dealer collection writing letter*, the librarian tried, unsuccessfully, to locate the item using Google, Amazon, and WorldCat. Jaeger reported that Jeffries wrote, "My search experiences with LibraryThing have been good (quick and accurate results). Still, those experiences had been with books where I knew the title or author. What could I do in LibraryThing to locate the book? On the search page they have a way to search for tags. I realized that if you were going to tag this book you would probably use some of the terms that I had been searching with no luck in Google. So I tried the tag string of *London, letters, literature, New York, classics*. Their tagmash search feature gave me as a first option the book *84, Charing Cross Road* by Helene Hanff. The reviews and descriptions of the book identified the book as the one I was looking for."[38]

When the online catalog permits it, librarians can add tags to item records, too. This not only helps patrons find materials but also works as an in-house strategy to coordinate librarians' service efforts. For example, when a patron accesses the online catalog at the Darien Library, a long list of tags in a tag cloud runs down the right-hand side of the page. The list is headed by the words *Popular Tags*. Kate Sheehan explained:

> Here's my favorite story about tags. At the Darien Library catalog you can see the huge tag in the cloud that says *Middlesex autobiography* and a slightly smaller tag that says *Middlesex memoir*. Those tags were applied multiple times by the librarians because the local middle school had an assignment to read an autobiography of someone from Middlesex and write a paper on it. Actually, there were two assignments—to find an autobiography or to find a memoir—with the obvious subtle distinctions between the two. Because it was a middle school assignment, the librarians in four departments were involved: the adult and children's reference departments along with teen services and the reader's advisory were getting these questions. We wanted to consult with each other because we didn't want to recommend things willy-nilly. Rather

than emailing each other back and forth trying to discuss books that were appropriate, we found that, collectively, tagging was a fast and easy way to identify books that would be good for that assignment, and it saved us a lot of wandering through the stacks. Everybody jumped in and tagged books, and we quickly had a good list. When the 20th student on a given day walked up and said, "I'm writing a report on a memoir," we just clicked on the *Middlesex memoir* tag. And when the same assignment is given again, that tag will lead us back to that list, and we'll be ready to go.[39]

Implementing Tagging, Folksonomies, and Social Bookmarking on Library Pages

The Library of Congress Working Group on the Future of Bibliographic Control has articulated that libraries would be wise to open up their catalogs to user reviews and tagging. It declared in a 2008 report at Section 4.1.1 (Link Appropriate External Information with Library Catalogs):

> 4.1.1.1 Encourage and support development of systems capable of relating evaluative data, such as reviews and ratings, to bibliographic records.

> 4.1.1.2 Encourage the enhancement of library systems to provide the capability to link to appropriate user-added data available via the Internet (e.g., Amazon.com, LibraryThing, Wikipedia). At the same time, explore opportunities for developing mutually beneficial partnerships with commercial entities that would stand to benefit from these arrangements.[40]

But according to the Denver Public Library's Zeth Lietzau, only about 1 percent of public libraries allow patrons to tag items in their online catalogs.[41] Libraries aren't eager to open the OPAC to end users' vocabularies, yet we can still leverage tagging and folksonomies to help our patrons and ourselves by offering links to bookmarks created by librarians. Many libraries are doing this, and there are several ways to facilitate implementation.

The easiest, though not necessarily the most elegant, way to link your patrons to librarian-created bookmarks is to save a copy of the image file that represents your social bookmark manager, drop it into one of your library's webpages, and link it to your bookmark resource's account. If your library has settled on using Delicious as your social bookmarking tool, three additional, simple approaches exist: setting up a linkroll to a page, adding a tag cloud to a page, and embedding an RSS feed into a page. Browse the links at angelacw.wordpress.com/2007/06/04/delicious-libraries for a representative list of libraries that use Delicious and how the bookmarks are published at different library websites.

The Hubbell Library in New Orleans has set its bookmarks up as a linkroll; the benefit of mounting a linkroll is that it lists your bookmarks on one webpage. If you have a manageable number of links and have bundled them into logical categories, a linkroll is a good choice. Figure 10.5 shows the beginning of the Hubbell Library's linkroll, which has 39 links nicely divided into three categories (or Delicious tag bundles): Community, Government, and Library-Related. Bundles could also be arranged in Dewey or Library of Congress classification. Note that the Hubbell Library gives patrons the option of suggesting a link or to share bookmarks and "join our network." Having patrons join your network enables you to see their bookmarks and add any you deem appropriate.

Here's a quick primer for setting up a Delicious linkroll (Yahoo! recently sold Delicious. As AVOS restyles the site, features may change. As it becomes available, updated information will be published on the UContent website at web.ccsu.edu/library/tomaiuolon/UContent/tags.htm):

1. Choose one of your library's webpages, use your personal webpage, or open a new webpage in an application where you can save your work as an HTML document.

2. Log in your Delicious account.

3. Enter www.delicious.com/help/linkrolls into your browser's address bar.

4. As directed, you will ultimately be copying the HTML code that the help page automatically creates for you; but before you copy the code, experiment with the settings that the page offers you for customization. For example, you can rename the linkroll, specify the number of tags to display, add bulleting, sort by most recent or alphabetically, and so on. Figure 10.6 is an example of a preview for my Delicious bookmarks.

5. Copy the resulting code and paste it into your webpage.

If you opt for placing a tag cloud on your pages, it's a snap. Repeat steps 1 and 2 from the previous list, and then do the following:

• Enter www.delicious.com/help/tagrolls into your browser's address bar. You will immediately see the HTML that will set up the tag cloud,

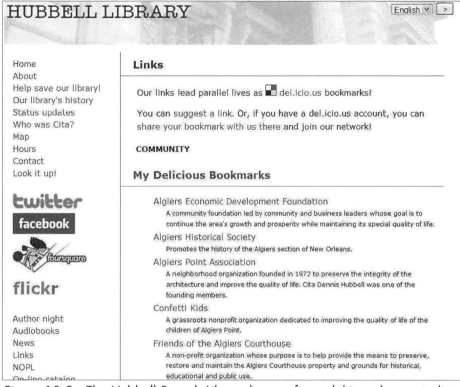

Figure 10.5   The Hubbell Branch Library has configured this webpage to list its links. It also invites users to suggest links and join the library's network so links can be shared. [Courtesy of the Hubbell Library]

but before you copy it to your webpage, play with the settings. With tag clouds, you'll also be able to select colors and tag counts.

- Preview your tag cloud, and continue to adjust it to suit your design and informational requirements. Figure 10.7 is a preview of a tag cloud for my Delicious bookmarks. Figure 10.8 shows the tag cloud from the MIT Libraries' Virtual Reference Collection.

- When you are satisfied with the look of your tag cloud, copy and paste the HTML code into your webpage.

A third option is to embed your bookmark's RSS feed into a webpage. If you want to feature an RSS feed of your bookmarks (or another user's bookmarks) on a webpage, just log in to your Delicious account and scroll down to the bottom of the page you'd like to embed. You will see a link for "RSS feed for this page." Click the link. From there you can copy the URL for the feed from

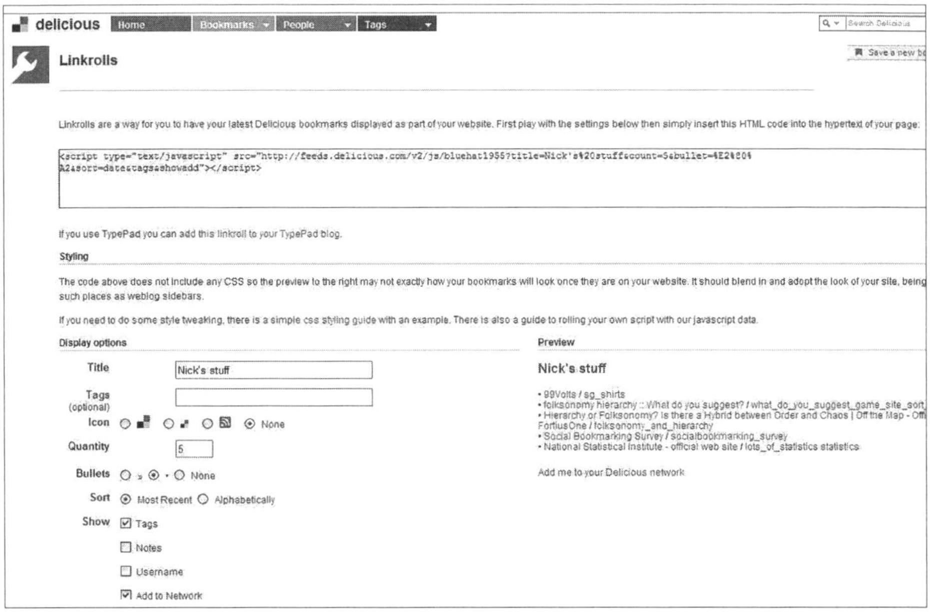

Figure 10.6   On Delicious, you'll find the tools to customize the way your
linkroll will appear on your webpage. [Courtesy of Delicious]

your browser's address bar, head over to a utility such as Feed to JavaScript
(www.feed2js.org), and build the code to embed on your webpage.

If your library subscribes to Springshare's LibGuides (demo.libguides.
com), you can easily change that mundane list of websites on your subject
guide pages to more appealing tag clouds. Log in to your LibGuides account
and choose one of your guides to edit. At the Command Bar, choose Add a
New Page. You'll be prompted to name and describe your page. When your
page is laid out, click Add New Box. Among the many choices, you will see
Delicious Tag Cloud. Click there and type in your Delicious username, and
a tag cloud of your bookmarks will appear on that LibGuides page (see
Figure 10.9).

If you are adept at programming, read the informative article published in
Information Technology and Libraries by Andrew Darby and Ron Gilmour to
learn about more ways to embellish your webpages by working with the
Delicious Application Programming Interface.[42]

Other Social Bookmarking Resources

Although Delicious is one of the most popular link management resources,
there are certainly other noteworthy bookmarking services that offer great

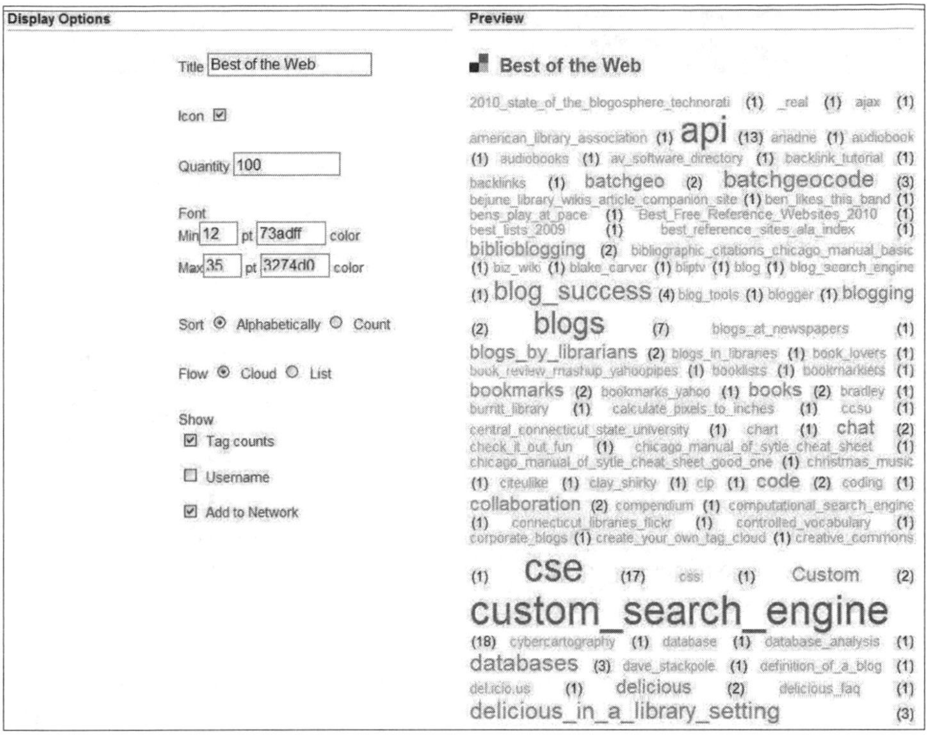

Figure 10.7   Customize everything about your webpage's tag cloud, including color and more. [Courtesy of Delicious]

Figure 10.8   The MIT Libraries website features tasteful deployment of the Delicious tag cloud. [Courtesy of the MIT Libraries]

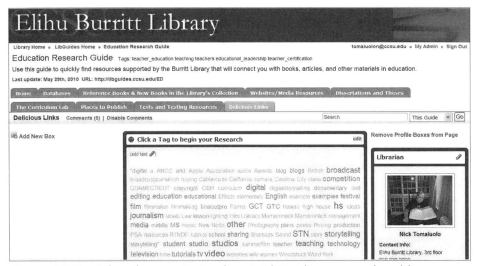

Figure 10.9   Subscribers to Springshare's LibGuides can easily add a
Delicious tag cloud to subject guides. [Courtesy of Central
Connecticut State University]

benefits. Table 10.1 is a roundup of several I've used, along with a summary of
their notable attributes. Please bear in mind that Digg, Reddit, and Slashdot
are not listed there because they are social news bookmarking services and
exist more to share and promote news stories than to preserve information
and tag it for later reference. Similarly, although Flickr and YouTube are discussed in this chapter with regard to tagging, these resources essentially
enable individuals who upload content to tag their contributions for their
own reference (e.g., Flickr) or so that others may easily find and view them
(e.g., YouTube). They are not often used to aggregate general web content to a
user's account.

Vendors and Social Bookmarking

Xan Arch, collection development librarian at Reed College in Portland,
Oregon, reminds us that articles in licensed databases can also be tagged
(and are accessible to patrons through the institutional proxy server). Arch
endorsed the idea of librarians using social tagging to make subject guides
that combined quality web resources, including difficult-to-find gray literature, with subscription database content.[43] Though offering a bridge to popular social bookmarking tools hasn't caught on with every database vendor,
several services have successfully configured their interfaces to include ways
to submit tags directly to link management resources such as Delicious.

Table 10.1   Noteworthy bookmarking resources

Resource and producer	Special features	Tagging advice
CiteULike, Springer (www.citeulike.com): Add a CiteULike button to your browser.	▪ For journal articles, automatically extracts bibliographic information; has this capability for more than 50 sites specializing in online sources of journal and scholarly papers. ▪ Optional methods of posting include DOI and ISBN (CiteULike fetches bibliographic information).	▪ Connect multiple word tags with underscores (or run words together).
Connotea, Nature Publishing Group (www.connotea.org): You may want to use its bookmarklet in your browser's favorites/ links bar.	▪ Enters bibliographic information into your saved bookmark records if it recognizes the website (e.g., PubMed). If this is not possible, Connotea can still use a valid DOI to find and post the bibliographic information. ▪ Entire database is keyword searchable and finds matches in tags, title of article, description, comments, or bibliographic information. Connotea is also searchable by article author. ▪ "Rename Tag" option allows global renaming of your tags—no need to individually edit tags. ▪ Apps for mobile devices are available.	▪ Place multiple-word tags in quotation marks.
Diigo (www.diigo.com): Formerly Furl.net; you may want to use its bookmarklet with your browser's favorites/links bar.	▪ Permits highlighting, sticky notes, taking a "snapshot" of webpages or PDFs for personal archive. ▪ Option to group bookmarks by "section." ▪ Play bookmarks as an interactive slide presentation. Search your bookmarks by tag, full text, annotations, URL. ▪ Apps for mobile devices are available.	▪ Place multiple-word tags in quotation marks.
StumbleUpon (www.stumbleupon.com): You may want to use its bookmarklet in your browser's favorites/ links bar.	▪ A recommendation engine that becomes smarter each time you use it. What it recommends depends on the web items you have viewed and rated "thumbs up" or "thumbs down." ▪ You can manually save items to your StumbleUpon account, and these are counted toward bringing you recommendations, as long as you've rated the items. ▪ Apps for mobile devices are available.	▪ User may enter up to five tags per bookmark; tags may be as long as three words (separated by spaces). Use commas to separate tags.
Note: DOI—digital object identifier; ISBN—International Standard Book Number		

In 2007, Elsevier launched a free social bookmarking tool called 2collab (www.2collab.com). At that time Elsevier's ScienceDirect and Scopus databases included integrated buttons that automatically added bibliographic data to a user's 2collab account. But the service is now closed to new users because it was receiving too much spam. An Elsevier associate told me, "With 2collab we experimented with social media in a more controlled way, but have learned that the best policy in this space is to integrate with any social reference management tools our users might be using. Thus, our current strategy is to work to support all social reference management tools as well as we supported 2collab as far as integration with Scopus and ScienceDirect. We are looking at how we can integrate with third party social reference management tools (e.g., CiteULike, etc.)."[44]

Free web resources for finding articles, such as Scitopia.org and HubMed.org (an alternative access point to PubMed), allow users to tag and comment on articles, as does the American Chemical Society's SciFinder Scholar database. Ebsco, Gale, and ProQuest also offer the option to save articles to social bookmarking services. And while local OPACs may not yet be permitting external tags, ratings, and reviews, Open WorldCat (www.world cat.org) has been allowing registered users to add tags, ratings, and reviews for several years; it also prompts users to "Bookmark and Share" (see Figures 10.10 and 10.11).

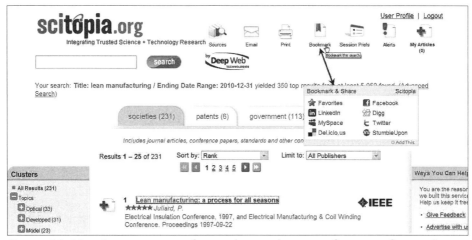

Figure 10.10   Scitopia.org, a free web search engine for scientific articles, makes bookmarking easy. [Courtesy of Scitopia]

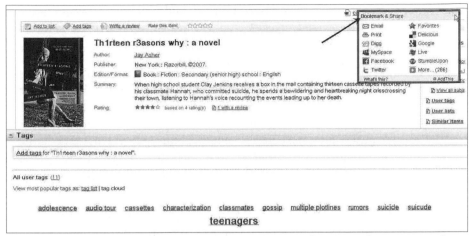

Figure 10.11   Open WorldCat, which implemented tagging for registered users in 2008, contained 78,000 tags as of mid-2010. It also allows bookmarking to external social websites. The record for this book has been tagged (note tags at the bottom of the image) and rated by four users. [Courtesy of OCLC]

No Shortage of Alternatives

Although employing tagging, folksonomies, and social bookmarking does not involve users in content creation, it actively involves them in a popular, quick, and simple way of contributing to the infrastructure of content discovery. Both end users and information professionals have numerous alternatives to explore while they endeavor to organize and share important items found on the web.

Endnotes

1. Jennifer Trant, "Studying Social Tagging and Folksonomy: A Review and Framework," *Journal of Digital Information* 10 (special issue, 2009), accessed August 3, 2011, journals.tdl.org/jodi/article/viewArticle/270.

2. Sue Chastain, "What Is Tagging?" About.com, accessed August 3, 2011, graphics soft.about.com/od/glossary/a/tagging.htm.

3. Lisa Reichelt, "First Example of Tagging," Interaction Design Association, December 19, 2006, accessed August 3, 2011, www.ixda.org/node/13142.

4. Chiara Fox, "Tagging vs. Cataloging: What It's All About," adaptive path, November 30, 2006, accessed August 3, 2011, www.adaptivepath.com/ideas/e000695.

5. James Surowiecki, "Joshua Schacter, 32" Technology Review, accessed August 3, 2011, www.technologyreview.com/tr35/Profile.aspx?TRID=432&Cand=T&pg=1.

6. Thomas Vander Wal, "Folksonomy Coinage and Definition," vanderwal.net, February 2, 2007, accessed August 3, 2011, www.vanderwal.net/folksonomy.html.

7. Daniel H. Pink, "Folksonomy." NYTimes.com, accessed August 3, 2011, www.nytimes.com/2005/12/11/magazine/11ideas1-21.html.

8. "Social Bookmarking," Teaching Excellence Network, last modified December 5, 2007, accessed August 3, 2011, tinyurl.com/teachingex.

9. "7 Things You Should Know About Social Bookmarking," Educause, May 2005, accessed August 3, 2011, net.educause.edu/ir/library/pdf/ELI7001.pdf.

10. Phillip Keller, "Tag History and Gartner's Hype Cycles," May 12, 2007, accessed August 3, 2011, www.pui.ch/phred/archives/2007/05/tag-history-and-gartners-hype-cycles.html.

11. Lee Rainie, "Tagging," Pew Internet & American Life Project, January 31, 2007, accessed August 3, 2011, www.pewinternet.org/Reports/2007/Tagging.aspx.

12. Margaret E. I. Kipp and D. Grant Campbell, "Patterns and Inconsistencies in Collaborative Tagging Systems: An Examination of Tagging Practices," *Proceedings of the 2006 Annual Meeting of the American Society for Information Science and Technology*, Austin, Texas, November 3–8 2006, accessed August 3, 2011, eprints.rclis.org/handle/10760/8720.

13. Marcus Heckner, Tanja Neubauer, and Christian Wolff, "Tree, Funny, To_Read, Google: What Are Tags Supposed to Achieve?" *Conference on Information and Knowledge Management, Proceedings of the 2008 ACM Workshop on Search in Social Media* (New York: ACM, 2008), accessed August 3, 2011, portal.acm.org/citation.cfm?id=1458589&dl=GUIDE&coll=GUIDE.

14. Ulises Mejias, "Tag Literacy," Ulises Mejias, April 26, 2005, accessed August 3, 2011, blog.ulisesmejias.com/2005/04/26/tag-literacy.

15. Tom Reamy, "Folksonomy Folktales," *KM World* 18 (October 2009): 6.

16. Stewart Butterfield, "Folksonomy: How I Learned to Stop Worrying and Love the Mess," ITConversations, March 16, 2005, accessed August 3, 2011, itc.conversations network.org/shows/detail464.html.

17. Sean Gorman, "Hierarchy or Folksonomy? Is There a Hybrid Between Order and Chaos?" GeoIQ, April 5, 2008, accessed August 3, 2011, blog.fortiusone.com/2008/04/15/heirarchy-or-folksonomy-is-there-a-hybrid-between-order-and-chaos.

18. Liz Lawley, "Social Consequences of Social Tagging," Corante, January 20, 2005, accessed August 3, 2011, many.corante.com/archives/2005/01/20/social_consequences_of_social_tagging.php.

19. Thomas Vander Wal, "Memephoria," vanderwal.net, May 26, 2006, accessed August 3, 2011, www.vanderwal.net/random/entrysel.php?blog=1829.

20. Jeffrey Zeldman, "Remove Forebrain and Serve: Tag Clouds II," zeldman.com, May 4, 2005, accessed August 3, 2011, www.zeldman.com/daily/0505a.shtml.

21. James Sinclair and Michael Cardew Hall, "The Folksonomy Tag Cloud: When Is It Useful?" *Journal of Information Science* 34 (2008): 27–28.

22. Chei Sian Lee et al., "Tagging, Sharing and the Influence of Personal Experience," *Journal of Digital Information* 10 (special issue, 2009), accessed August 3, 2011, journals.tdl.org/jodi/article/view/275.

23. Heckner, "Tree, Funny, To_Read, Google."

24. Ying Ding et al., "Perspectives on Social Tagging," *Journal of the American Association of Information Science and Technology* 60 (2009): 2399.

25. Ibid., 2397.

26. Heckner, "Tree, Funny, To_Read, Google."

27. Ying Ding et al., "Perspectives on Social Tagging," 2399.

28. Cecile E. Bianco, "Medical Librarians' Uses and Perceptions of Social Tagging," *Journal of the Medical Library Association* 97 (2009): 136–139.

29. Loren Baker, "Delicious.com Relaunches," Search Engine Journal, July 31, 2008, accessed August 3, 2011, www.searchenginejournal.com/deliciouscom-relaunches-enhanced-speed-search-design-with-no-dots/7403.

30. Clay Shirky, "Ontology Is Overrated," Clay Shirky's Writings About the Internet, accessed August 3, 2011, www.shirky.com/writings/ontology_overrated.html.

31. Kate Sheehan, telephone conversation with author, April 4, 2009.

32. Peter J. Rolla, "User Tags Versus Subject Headings," *Library Resources and Technical Services* 53 (2009): 178–179.

33. Ibid., 182.

34. Phyllis R. Snipes, "Folksonomy vs. Minnie Earl and Melville," *Library Media Connection* 25 (April/May 2007): 56.

35. Jessamyn West, "Subject Headings 2.0: Folksonomies and Tags," *Library Media Connection* 25 (April/May 2007): 59.

36. Katje Snuderl, "Tagging: Can User-Generated Content Improve Our Services," *Statistical Journal of the IAOS* 25 (2008): 130.

37. Louise F. Spiteri, "The Use of Folksonomies in Public Library Catalogues," *Serials Librarian* 51 (2006): 75–88.

38. Lauren Stokes, "Web 2.0 Success Story," Virtual Library Notes, December 20, 2008, accessed August 3, 2011, virtualnotes.wordpress.com/2008/12/20/web-20-success-story.

39. Kate Sheehan, telephone conversation with author, June 19, 2009.

40. Library of Congress Working Group on the Future of Bibliographic Control, *On the Record: Report of the Library of Congress Working Group on the Future of Bibliographic Control*, January 9, 2008, accessed July 8, 2011, www.loc.gov/bibliographic-future/news/lcwg-ontherecord-jan08-final.pdf.

41. Zeth Lietzau, "U.S. Public Libraries and Web 2.0: What's Really Happening?" *Computers in Libraries* 29 (Oct. 2009): 8.

42. Andrew Darby and Ron Gilmour, "Adding Delicious Data to Your Library Website," *Information Technology and Libraries* 28 (2009): 100–103.

43. Xan Arch, "Creating the Academic Library Folksonomy: Put Social Tagging to Work for Your Institution," *College & Research Library News* 68 (February 2007): 80–81.

44. Elsevier customer service associate, tech support email to the author, September 2009.

Custom Search Engines

In this chapter I turn again, as in the chapter on tagging and folksonomies, to how users are building the infrastructure to facilitate their discovery of content. As I searched Google for types of UContent to examine, I realized one topic was right in front of me. Google has placed many UContent tools into netizens' hands: Picasa, Google My Places, Google Maps API, and Knol, to name a few. It may seem a droll exercise, but my search for *google* and *custom* and *searching* cut a path to the information I needed: the Google Custom Search Engine (www.google.com/cse). It only took a few clicks to compile a list of several different custom search engines (CSEs) to investigate: Gigablast Custom Topic Search (CTS), Rollyo, Swicki, and Google CSE.

CSEs are also known as *vortals*, *vertical search engines*, and *topical search engines*. A CSE usually focuses on one topic (e.g., a search for information about making beer), though it may focus on one medium (e.g., a search for music video clips). CSEs/vortals/vertical search engines/topical search engines have the potential to provide greater precision than general search engines (e.g., Bing, Google, Yahoo!), because we can control their focus.

Flashback

In the not-so-distant past when InfoSeek, WiseNut, and AltaVista dominated the web, tech-savvy individuals were already creating their own search engines. While working for San Diego State University, Andrew Scherpbier (now the chief technical officer of Blackball, a data management company) gave us Dig (www.htdig.org), the useful open source software for site searching. Professor Peter Jacso configured several custom engines that searched controlled-access and open access journals at science and energy websites; his biography and dictionary engines are still available at Peter's PolySearch Engines (www2.hawaii.edu/~jacso/extra/poly-page.html). In their 2001 book *The Invisible Web*, information professionals Chris Sherman and Gary Price suggested we "build our own toolkit," and they gave us their extensive collections of links to searchable deep web databases.

When end users create CSEs, they combine their personal or professional interests, their knowledge of websites, and their ability to evaluate information; they take responsibility for the retrieval.

Survivors of the Custom Search Wars

Four websites currently offer users the ability to create customized searches. At various times in the past, the field has contained more choices, but custom offerings from Microsoft (called Live Macros) and Yahoo! (called Search Builder) were discontinued in 2008. Yahoo! has a new custom search solution call BOSS (Build your Own Search Service; developer.yahoo.com/search/boss), but it's not user-friendly right out of the box. For end users the field is now composed of (chronologically in order of original launch) Gigablast CTS, Rollyo, Swicki, and Google CSE (see Table 11.1). A note about search results: Retrieval from custom searches provided by these four resources varies; unlike Google and Gigablast, which each use their own spiders to crawl the web, Rollyo and Eurekster Swicki do not crawl the web but use the information indexed by Yahoo! Search.

A fifth service, called Topicle (www.topicle.com), is the creation of former Google product manager Steffen Mueller. Topicle was launched in September 2007 and is based on Google's custom search. Topicle has a social aspect in that users can rate and edit other users' search engines (if the original creator permits). Unfortunately my attempts to create a new custom search at Topicle (over many weeks using different browsers and different computers) were consistently met with "Done but with errors on page," and nothing was created. I asked associates, including Ran Hock, author of the 2010 book *The Extreme Searcher's Internet Handbook*, Third Edition, to try to create new searches at Topicle, but they got the same strange results. My own efforts to find any information about its status were also inconclusive. But apparently users *are* adding searches to the site. When I first checked it in mid-2010, the home page stated that the service had 13,000 custom searches. As of July 2011, the total had swelled to more than 28,000. If any reader successfully creates a search engine there, please notify me by email (nick.tomaiuolo@gmail.com). Although I couldn't design an engine there, I could use search engines others had created. I could also rate the relevance of the websites that were included in existing Topicle custom search engines. In mid-2011, I executed 25 Topicle custom searches at random; they all worked.

Gigablast CTS

Computer scientist and mathematician Matt Wells founded Gigablast (www.gigablast.com) in 2000. Wells began offering end users the option to

Table 11.1   A comparison of CSE sites

Search Service	Pros	Cons
Gigablast CTS	- Easy to add a custom search box to your own webpage or blog - Accepts up to 500 URLs - Searches quickly - Support emails answered quickly	- Fewer results than other CSEs performing the same task - Minimal knowledge of HTML needed to add websites to CTS
Rollyo	- Easy to add a custom search box to your own webpage or blog - Gadget (Rollbar) available for Firefox to "site-search" any URL you are visiting - Gadget available to add sites to "Searchrolls" (collections of custom searches) on the fly - Flexible, easy-to-copy code for different search box "look and feel" for your webpage or blog - Can search for and use others' public Searchrolls	- Site frequently too busy to use - Emails to support go unanswered - Handles a maximum of 25 blogs or websites
Swicki	- Easy to add a custom search box to your own webpage or blog - Several social features, including promoting or demoting search results tag clouds - Monetization opportunities for Swicki creators	- Emails to support go unanswered
Google CSE	- Easy to add a custom search box to your own webpage or blog - Extensive control over results (keywords can be weighted; results can be faceted; specific results promoted) - More control over "look and feel" of the search interface than any other service - May be possible to monetize the engine via AdSense - Usage statistics available for each custom engine a user creates - User controls which pages at a site are searched - May invite others to collaborate - Accepts hundreds of URLs for any CSE	- Most of the ability to use the extensive power of the API is slightly out of the reach of the "plug and play" end-user - No easy way to find others' CSEs
Topicle	- Permits custom search configuration (though this option seems disabled) - Social component: users can rate the search engines in the Topicle community - User collaboration possible; users may add new URLs to existing custom searches (an option controlled by the original search creator)	- Emails to support go unanswered - Site appears to be online, but end-users cannot create new searches; they can only use searches the community has already created

configure their own CTSs late in 2004. Though Wells no longer actively promotes the CTS, the code is still available at www.gigablast.com/cts.html. At that page, end users receive an introduction to the engine and several lines of HTML. The instructions state users can customize the code by supplying up to 500 URLs to be searched. All the end user must do is copy the code, replace the example URLs with those of their favorite sites (up to 500), and paste the code into a webpage. Bam! Now you've got a Gigablast search box on your page, and the search engine you've configured will search only the sites you have asked it to search. You can also use CTS as a site search for your own pages. If you don't have a webpage where you can install the code and search box, you can still execute a CTS by going to Gigablast's advanced search page (www.gigablast.com/adv.html) where you can restrict your search to specific sites.

Gigablast's CTS has impressed some influential information professionals,[1,2] but one critic has written that Gigablast CTSs are difficult to configure because they require users to hand-edit HTML.[3] This doesn't seem like a significant drawback. The more perplexing issue with Gigablast's CTS is the unexpectedly few results it retrieves.

I created a custom search for medical information at Gigablast, Rollyo, and Google CSE. I chose the same high-profile websites for all three services. You can test the three custom medical searches with your own search criteria at web.ccsu.edu/library/tomaiuolon/gig.htm. These are the five websites that each service searched:

- Centers for Disease Control and Prevention (www.cdc.gov)

- National Center for Biotechnology Information (ncbi.nlm.nih.gov)

- U.S. National Library of Medicine (www.nlm.nih.gov)

- WebMD (www.webmd.com)

- Mayo Clinic (www.mayoclinic.com)

Here are the results for my test search for *H1N1 vaccine*:

- Using Gigablast, "about 130" items were retrieved (in the first 10, five were from the CDC, four from WebMD, and one from the Mayo Clinic).

- Using Rollyo, 1,797 items were retrieved (eight of the first 10 originated at the CDC, and two were from WebMD).

- When executing a user-defined custom search, Google does not offer an estimate of the total number of results (but in the first 10 displayed, nine originated at the CDC and one from WebMD).

Rollyo

David Pell, founder of the Roll Your Own Search Engine (Rollyo), announced the launch of Rollyo (www.rollyo.com) on September 28, 2005.[4] Gary Price immediately posted an overview at SearchEngineWatch.[5] Overall, Price's comments were positive, but he pointed out a weakness common to most CSEs (with the exception of Google CSE). Rollyo's instructions, like Gigablast's, state that the searches can be configured to search entire sites, such as www.infotoday.com or library.stanford.edu, but cannot be configured to restrict searches to individual pages on sites or subdirectories. (The ability to limit the searches would allow more precision.) Price summarized his posting by saying, "Very cool and very easy!"

Individuals may navigate to www.rollyo.com and begin experimenting with custom searches (called Searchrolls in Rollyo lingo) by choosing a name for the search, entering web addresses (up to 25 URLs), and clicking Create Searchroll. Users also have the option of categorizing and tagging their Searchrolls. You may also explore others' public Searchrolls, a feature that Gigablast doesn't offer. If you choose to register and create a username, you can keep your Searchrolls private or make them public (see Figure 11.1).

You can return to Rollyo, log in, and use your searches; you can also click Tools and easily grab the code to embed them on a webpage or blog. With Gigablast the user must modify the embed code and insert URLs, but as I said earlier, this, too, is easy. You can see a few of my embedded Rollyo searches at web.ccsu.edu/library/tomaiuolon/cse.htm. There are two other cool tools: If you use Firefox, you can drag a Rollyo bookmarklet (called a Rollbar) to the Bookmarks toolbar. Whenever you are at a site and you want to *search that site*, use the Rollbar.

I don't have a problem with being limited to 25 websites, but I was seriously frustrated on numerous occasions while I was creating a Searchroll, getting code, or going to the Dashboard (where you can see a list of your searches), and Rollyo countered with "didn't connect, too many connections." The site was frequently slow or busy. Rollyo went through some much-needed maintenance early in 2010, and this problem has been addressed.

The greatest challenge was the care I needed to exercise when selecting web resources. I created one Searchroll called Words and Meanings. It originally contained www.m-w.com, dictionary.law.com, thesaurus.reference.com, www.wordsmyth.com, www.talktalk.co.uk/reference/dictionaries/difficult words, and www.urbandictionary.com. To test this Searchroll, I looked up one of my favorite words, *ultracrepidarian*, and was more than a little perplexed to see that the first 10 items Rollyo found came from the Urban Dictionary! I immediately deleted www.urbandictionary.com from the URL list because, for some reason, Rollyo gave it priority. This experience underscores the need for testing and experimentation.

Most end users and some information professionals will be content with Rollyo. The easy interface, the ability to tag and look for others' Searchrolls, and the easy Embed feature make it a good choice. Librarians using it to configure custom searches for students or the public may not, however, appreciate that they cannot opt out of the sponsored links sprinkled throughout retrieval.

Swicki

Headquartered in San Francisco, Eurekster, Inc., calls itself "a pioneer and leader in social search technologies." On November 17, 2005, the company announced the launch of Swicki (www.eurekster.com). Swicki (which internet expert Phil Bradley called "a play on [the] words, roughly speaking"[6] *search* and *wiki*) allows users to create a CSE and then distribute it to the Swicki community. The social component lets users vote on the usefulness of resources returned by Swicki searches. As the Swickis are used, good resources accrue votes, and the individual Swickis become more relevant with use.

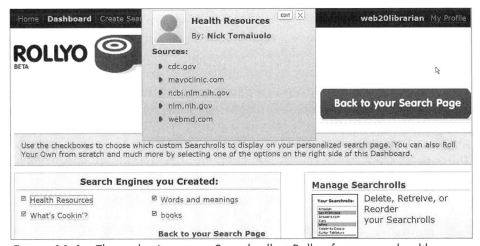

Figure 11.1   The author's custom Searchroll at Rollyo focuses on health
resources. [Courtesy of Rollyo]

For example, there is a Swicki called "Education—a search engine for teacher education." At this Swicki's page (education1234567-swicki.eurekster. com), two modes of search are possible. We can enter keywords in the search form or click on a keyword in the Swicki's tag cloud. Entering keywords or clicking on a word in the tag cloud produces a list of results that may or may not be relevant. The job of the "crowd" (i.e., the people using the search) is to vote on the relevance of individual items in the results. Items that receive positive votes are promoted in the search results (see Figure 11.2).

Although the theory is sound (and works well at a site such as Digg, where users are constantly submitting links to news stories and many people are voting), Swickis don't necessarily deal with the hottest topics; some are outright arcane. A Swicki called Qigong, covering Chi Kung training in Amsterdam, offers a tag cloud that includes words such as *emailadres*, *tips*, and *standing*; this esoteric Swicki probably isn't going to evolve in any meaningful way. I stumbled on many similarly abstruse Swickis.

I created a few Swickis, but I respectfully question their usefulness. If I build a Swicki today and I am the only person using it for several weeks (individual Swickis are added to the database manually, and I never saw any of mine show up even though I emailed the information to the support team as required by the site), it's bound to retrieve a considerable number of irrelevant results until enough users vote the bad links to the bottom. My Swicki is accessible at web.ccsu.edu/library/tomaiuolon/cse.htm.

Do the Swickis ever work? It depends on the Swicki. Here's an example of the strange behavior some Swickis exhibit. Abacus Biotech (New Zealand) published a biotechnology Swicki. Go to that Swicki (abacus-biotech-swicki-swicki.eurekster.com) and click the word *abacus* in the tag cloud. One of the items retrieved is the Wikipedia article on the abacus calculating tool. Similarly, Berkeley (CA) Public Library has a Swicki (berkeley-public-library-swicki.eurekster.com). Click on *Books* or *Databases* or *Internet* in its tag cloud, and in every case you get the message "No pages match the search you requested." The Quotes on Mugs Swicki (quotesonmugs.quotefriends.com) works better. In its tag cloud, click the phrase "political humor quotes on mugs," and the retrieval, which includes links to the novelty businesses Cafepress, Cool Political Coffee Mugs, and Zazzle, is much more relevant.

Even if you are not interested in creating a Swicki, you can use those already published on the site. Eurekster has a directory of categories, and you can perform keyword searches for Swickis. You can also launch a search from the open web for relatively reliable retrieval by entering the word Swicki and your search term.

Building a Swicki seems as simple as 1) naming it, 2) describing the topic, 3) providing five to 15 keywords for the tag cloud, and 4) customizing the code you'll embed on your webpage or blog. Then Eurekster "trains" your

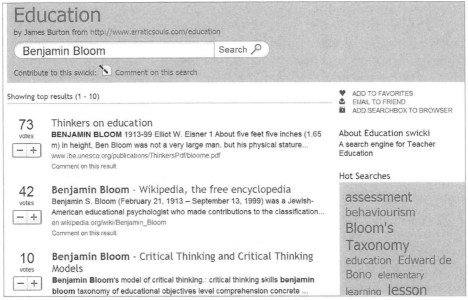

Figure 11.2   Swickis are social searches. Users are encouraged to vote on the relevance of retrieval. [Courtesy of Eurekster, Inc.]

Swicki so it learns which websites are relevant. After this behind-the-scenes feat of prestidigitation, you choose a category in which to list your Swicki and then publish it. The fact that this process takes very long, combined with the lack of support I experienced and the errors I encountered (e.g., the link Take the Quick 30 Second Tour did not take me on a tour), made me eager to look at the next CSE service.

Google CSE

Google CSE was launched in late October 2006. It takes about 3 minutes to get a Google CSE up and running, but you may want to spend more time fine-tuning it after it goes live. Begin at www.google.com/cse and click Create a Custom Search Engine. Give your engine a name and a description. Google then asks if you want to restrict the new engine to search only the sites you select or to search the entire web but emphasize your selected sites. (I have always set my CSEs to search only the sites I chose, but it may be worth experimenting with the other option to determine what the results would look like if you emphasized your sites but let Google search the entire web.) The next step puts your knowledge of websites to work: List the URLs of the resources you want to search. Google then asks whether you want the Standard Edition (which is free, but ads will appear adjacent to and above the search results unless you certify that you are nonprofit or are using the service for education). You may opt for the Business Edition, which Google offers starting at $100 (the Business Edition has no ads). Read the Terms of Service and check the box to indicate you have read them. Click Next.

Then it's time to try out your CSE. This is an important step because if you discover unexpected results, you can edit your search engine. If the search engine works, click Finish, and you will see your new creation listed on your search management page. The management page is key; from there you can click Control Panel to edit your search engine or click Statistics to see whether your creation is getting any usage.

The Control Panel

The control panel houses the links that really give you power over your search engine. You can manipulate the "look and feel" of your CSE and obtain the HTML code to embed your search engine on your own webpage. You can also specify refinements that will add faceted searching to your results pages. The control panel (see Figure 11.3) is also where you should add keywords to your search engine; keywords have a strong effect on your search engine's retrieval. You can also open up your CSE to collaboration if you so desire. One of the newer enhancements is the option to implement autocompletion of queries. You can do this as you set up your search engine by checking the "Enable autocompletions" box in your search engine's control panel.

The Finer Things

The Google Custom Search Blog (googlecustomsearch.blogspot.com) is a good source for tips about tweaking your CSE. In one post, Google software engineer Tom Duerig explained that the keywords you assign your search during its creation can help drive the results you get.[7] For example, consider a Google CSE on *yoga* that searches the entire web but emphasizes specific sites. If its creator does not specify *yoga* as one of the keywords, the first page of retrieval for a search on *mat* includes items about the Miller Analogies Test, wrestling, and a Master of Arts in teaching. If the same search engine has the keyword *yoga* attached to it, Google knows that it should ignore its usual ranking algorithm, and in a search for *mat* results, yoga mats will rise to the top. For a detailed explanation of this, see "Changing the Ranking of Your Search Results" at code.google.com/apis/customsearch/docs/ranking.html.

During the search engine creation process, as you specify the sites you want to search, be sure to read the "Tips for formatting URLs." Knowing how to format the URLs you ask Google to search will affect your engine's performance. Do you want the engine to search an entire site? Just one page on a site? Only one subdomain of a site? Just a single subdirectory? Formatting your selected URLs properly will make a noticeable difference in your

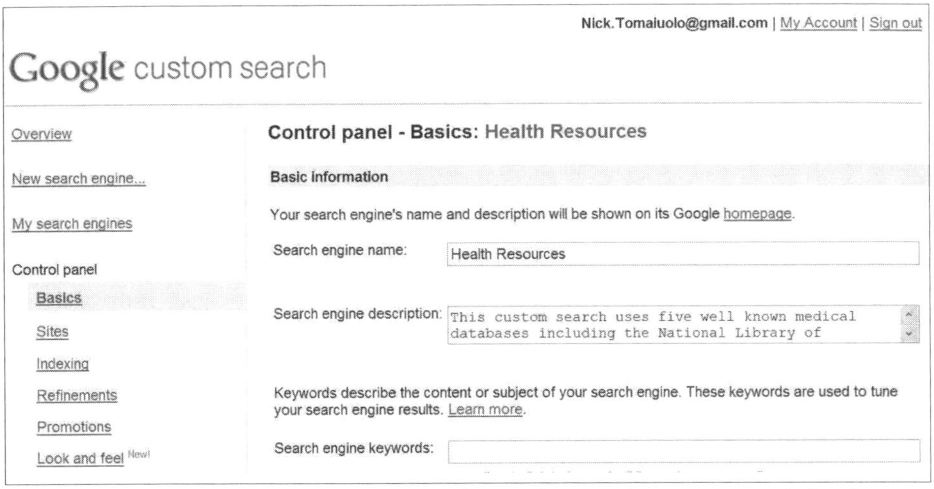

Figure 11.3   On Google CSE's control panel, note the options at left: The user controls the sites to search, the look and feel of the interface, and more. The newest enhancement is the ability to enable autocompletion of queries. [Courtesy of Google]

retrieval. Google community manager Jay Davis points this out in his blog post "Star Power," where he wrote, "you can use an asterisk (or star, in techie vernacular) as a wild card in your pattern to specify a swath of URLs. … Here's how it works: rather than add each page of www.site.com to your search engine, you can merely add www.site.com/* and we will include every URL that begins with www.site.com."[8] In reality, Google will include all the pages of a site by default, but it is good to know that you can exercise a measure of control over your search engine. For example, if you want complete control over which pages are searched from the sites you list, you can select "Include just the specific page or URL pattern I have entered." If you had entered www.loc.gov/law and specified that Google only search that page, your retrieval would come only from that page, and not from any of the subdirectory pages such as www.loc.gov/law/find or www.loc.gov/law/help/current-topics.php.[9]

Formatting URLs and driving results with keywords are just two of the ways you can manipulate search engine retrieval. Technically proficient information professionals should consult the Google Custom Search API Developer's Guide at code.google.com/intl/en/apis/customsearch/docs/dev_guide.html. It will take you far beyond the basics. It explains how to boost, filter, eliminate, and weigh various components of the search engine to further adjust your results.

Trouble in Paradise?

Soon after the Google CSE launch, Ethan Zuckerman, a senior researcher at Harvard's Berkman Center for Internet and Society and co-founder of Global Voices (a multinational citizen journalism project), constructed a CSE to discover content at the thousands of blogs that Global Voices pointed to; he then announced that the Google CSE didn't work well for him.[10] He reasoned that the blogs he'd dropped into the search were very low in Google's ranking algorithm.

Google immediately responded to his post and upgraded Google CSE. Google software engineer Vrishali Wagle referred to Zuckerman in the CSE blog: "After a week of some serious engineering we believe we've made searching on Ethan's Custom Search Engine—and all CSEs for that matter—much, much better."[11] The day the fix was implemented, Zuckerman blogged, "This is great news for me—with a hundred solid results from 3,000 blogs, Google Coop Search [as it was formerly called] is now a reasonable solution to my search problems, removing a particularly thorny problem from my 'to do' list. But it's also good news for Google as a whole, and anyone using [its] tools."[12]

Putting the Custom in CSEs

Google provides considerable flexibility in terms of the code you can grab for your CSEs. You can choose to host the search engine on your own site or have it hosted at Google. Is your blog "shiny"? Is it "espresso"? Google can furnish code to match it! Do you want the search box in one column and the results in an adjacent column? There's code for that, too. Explore my pages at web.ccsu.edu/library/tomaiuolon/cse.htm and web.ccsu.edu/library/tomaiuolon/cse2.htm to see several different customizations of CSEs.

Who Is Using Custom Search?

We often hear that people look at only the first few pages of search results, but that rule doesn't apply when one is trying to seriously analyze search retrieval. Specifically, I wanted to get an idea of the types of end users who are getting involved in creating their own search engines. If you think information professionals lead the way, you're only partially correct. Several types of users appear to be involved and, depending on the search service, we can make an educated guess as to what type of user is responsible for a specific CSE.

Unfortunately it's impossible to determine who is devising and using a Gigablast CTS. I've scrutinized my own Gigablast CTSs, and I don't perceive any pattern in the URL that gives me enough clues to construct a web search that would trace it back to me (i.e., a librarian). My attempts to search for and locate a directory for Gigablast custom searches was unsuccessful.

Because Rollyo users can create profiles and share their searches, it may be possible to determine who is responsible for a Searchroll—if you can trust the profile information. Rollyo has one gimmick afoot concerning its contributors. Searchrolls are browsable by Most Popular, Recently Added, Of Note, and High Rollers. This last category contains Searchrolls authored by actor Debra Messing, *Google Pocket Guide* co-author Rael Dornfest, *Forbes* columnist Steve Rubel, writer and media expert Jeff Jarvis, designer Diane von Furstenberg, and others.

Swicki inventors have the option of signing their searches also. According to Eurekster, there are more than 120,500 Swickis, and because CSEs are invariably created to serve a specific purpose, any attempt to declare a dominant user group would be invalid without looking at a large number of searches. Just glancing at a few Swicki titles and creators, however, makes me think that the clientele is a mixture of corporate entities and end users. The Aloha House Recovery Center in Maui has published a Substance Abuse Swicki, *Popular Science* magazine has a Swicki, and the blogging network Lockergnome posted a computing hardware and software Swicki. But the Hannah Montana Lyrics Swicki and Benelli Motorcycles Swicki appear to be the work of enthusiasts. I also noticed some individuals have created multiple Swickis. Here's a quick list of examples: "Chris" is responsible for several searches that deal with bike shops, "Vulcan" created seven Swickis on different models of BMW automobiles, and "Lynsey" has authored multiple searches on various topics as well.

When a user creates a Google CSE, that user can grab code to embed the CSE on a webpage. Google also issues the CSE a unique web address. Until the end of 2010, you could easily retrieve a very long list of Google CSEs that were created by using a search shortcut, but Google recently negated this search. You may still be interested in exploring the CSE Links Directory (www.cselinks. com), which lists hundreds of custom searches. The CSE Links Directory is searchable, so it is possible to identify CSEs on your favorite topics.

When we were able to employ the search shortcut just mentioned, I looked at 50 pages with my preferences set at 100 results per page, and while I cannot make any scientific claim about the Google CSE userbase, it seems that the largest group is software developers. This group is followed by information professionals (including librarians), then individual educators, and then hobbyists. Some examples are listed in Tables 11.2 and 11.3. (Note the especially ambitious Google CSE DRAGNET that appeared in September 2010. Developed by Terry Ballard with colleagues in the Mendik Library at the New York Law School, DRAGNET searches 80 free legal websites and databases).

The diverse interests of many users are represented by the CSEs. In addition to those listed in Tables 11.2 and 11.3, I saw the obligatory Harry Potter CSE, one for "All Greek Universities," another for "Everything Babies," several by hackers looking for "unprotected files," lots of gamers, one called "GRRRL Power" (with search results rendered in Google CSE theme "bubblegum," i.e., pink), and another called simply "Sneaker Search" (see Figure 11.4).

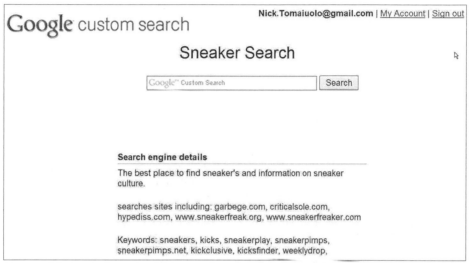

Figure 11.4   A Google CSE searches the web for athletic footwear. [Courtesy of Google]

Implications for End Users and Information Professionals

CSEs are another example of end users' applications of web tools and content to suit their specific needs. CSE creation demonstrates that end users have a wide range of interests that they combine with their preferences for specific websites and their knowledge of search engine behavior. End users have considerable control over CSEs and how those CSEs will appear on their blogs and webpages. One conspicuous social aspect of CSEs is that they may be open to collaboration. Hobbyists, be they viticulturists, opera aficionados, or Trekkies, have a way to organize focused searches; they needn't rely on outdated web directories or a web search that retrieves 100,000 "matches." As my inspection of Google CSE retrieval revealed, CSEs have caught on not only with end users but with professionals from a range of occupations.

   CSE deployment has potential applications in a library or information center. Librarian Meredith Farkas suggested pasting the code from a Google CSE into a LibGuide to help students search a predefined set of appropriate websites.[13] I did exactly that on an Art LibGuide that I write and manage at

Table 11.2   General examples of user-generated Google CSEs

Google CSE	Possible/probable user	Representative websites searched
American Studies Research Engine (tinyurl.com/2amsf2n)	Educator	americanhistory.si.edu, moma.org, www.ibiblio.org, espn.go.com, memory.loc.gov, econlib.org
AvaxHome eBooks Search (tinyurl.com/pcukea)	Content provider	gutenberg.org, manybooks.net, planetpdf.com, rapidshare1.com, ebook3000.com
Beer Search (tinyurl.com/2dtlj4e)	Home brewer	www.cerveza.ch, www.beerpal.com, ohhh.myhead.org, beeradvocate.com, fraterslibertas.com
Blackboard Building Blocks Search (tinyurl.com/2bkno2k)	Online educator	www.blackboard.com, bbug.ca/jforum, bb-opensource.org, edugarage.com, workgroups.clemson.edu
Caribbean Newspaper Search (tinyurl.com/2ef94qx)	Special librarian, travel agent	newsmontserrat.com, svgtoday.com, jamaicaobserver.com, antiguasunonline.com, sunstkittsonline.com
COINSHEET Numismatic Directory (tinyurl.com/2fr4uuq)	Coin collector	4preciousmetals.com, coinsheetlinks.com, 3centnickel.com, colnect.com, londoncoins.co.uk, coinmaven.com
ColdFusion Community Search (tinyurl.com/26pncv3)	Software developer	mxunit.org, rocketunit.riaforge.org, cfunit.sourceforge.net, coldmock.riaforge.org
Expanding Your Horizons (tinyurl.com/2fbhqvw)	Young women's mentor programmer	binarygirl.com, thefutureschannel.com, engineergirl.org, computergirl.us, www2.lv.psu.edu/jkl1/sisters
Free Christmas Music (tinyurl.com/2bgwkun)	Music teacher, musician	freechristmasmusic.blogs, feelslikechristmas.com, rhythmontherock.com, www.archive.org, songsofpraise.org
Genealogy Sleuth Search Engine (tinyurl.com/2fqcddl)	Genealogist	rootsweb.ancestry.com, ukbmd.org.uk, familytreesearcher.com, familyrecords.gov.uk, accessgenealogy.com
Google for Medical Transcriptionists Only (tinyurl.com/2ayyqzc)	Medical transcriptionist	ucomparehealthcare.com, vitals.com, finddoctors.org, healthgrades.com, medicinenet.com

Horse Associations Information (tinyurl.com/24mo35a)	Breeder, horse enthusiast, equestrian	walerhorse.com, horsetalk.co.nz, kwpn.nl, ashs.com.au, wbstallions.com, ponyclub.org, shetlandminiature.com
Toastmasters Websites (tinyurl.com/2am6d98)	Toastmasters club member	freetoasthost.com, freetoasthost.info, freetoasthost.net, freetoasthost.org
My Way, The Entrepreneur Network (tinyurl.com/2apd5no)	Entrepreneur	52reviews.com, www.terrygold.com, herman.org/blogs, galai.typepad.com/blog, startupceo.wordpress.com
Transportation Meta Search: Quality Transportation-Related Websites for Transportation Professionals (tinyurl.com/2dwlzpn)	Agency head, engineer, contractor	wvdot.com, virginiadot.org, dot.state.wy.us, mtc.ca.gov, nysdot.gov, metrocouncil.org, ct.gov/dot, okladot.state.ok.us

Table 11.3 Examples of Google CSEs created by information professionals

Google CSEs created by information professionals	Representative websites searched
AuseSearch (tinyurl.com/2a6naro)	espace.library.curtin.edu.au, adt.caul.edu.au, arada.cdu.edu.au, epress.lib.uts.edu.au/dspace, ro.uow.edu.au/asdpapers/44
Co-op Copyright Search (tinyurl.com/2a4nmbu)	creativecommons.org, sethf.com/infothought/blog, yro.slashdot.org, msl1.mit.edu/furdlog, akira.arts.kuleuven.ac.be
DOAJ English Journal Content (tinyurl.com/23n5w5x)	zeithistorische-forschungen.de, yakushi.pharm.or.jp, yenisymposium.net, zrc-sazu.si, zoosystema.com
DRAGNET: Database Retrieval Access using Google's New Electronic Technology (tinyurl.com/23ucvj5)	www.abanet.org/publiced/practical/books/family_legal_guide, www.plol.org/Pages/Search.aspx, Thomas.gov, jurist.law.pitt.edu, glin.gov/search.action
Fulltext Content Slavistics (tinyurl.com/24rrpqn)	www.diva-portal.org/su, www.ohiolink.edu/etd, dspace.mit.edu/handle, ruthenia.ru/sovlit, www.ruhr-uni-bochum.de
Health-Related Videos & Other Media (tinyurl.com/26t8kcp)	www.researchchannel.org, familydoctor.org/online, www.blinkx.com/video, www.healthvideo.com/video
IRSpace: Search South African & African Research Repositories (tinyurl.com/yfayzrs)	dk.cput.ac.za, repository.up.ac.za, uir.unisa.ac.za, ir.uz.ac.zw, www.aluka.org, pubs.cs.uct.ac.za
Law Research (tinyurl.com/23xcnux)	www.findlaw.com, law-thinker.com, civillaw.com.cn, 87187.com, chinalawinfo.com, lawguru.com, www.law.com

Table 11.3 *(cont.)*

Librarian's E-Library (tinyurl.com/2e82m7f)	www.urbanlibraries.org, www.nedcc.org, www.niso.org, www.nclis.gov, www.loc.gov/index.html, musiclibraryassoc.org
LIS-ITA Search Engine (tinyurl.com/23fbumj)	utenti.lycos.it/diglib, web.uniud.it/libroantico, www.infer.it, w3.uniroma1.it, www.cordis.lu/librarie
Mrs. Gray's Research Sites for Kids (tinyurl.com/y8g2x5g)	smithsonianeducation.org, www.timeforkids.com/TFK, www.dibdabdoo.com, www.kidsclick.org, www.factmonster.com
tabletSearch (tinyurl.com/28osw26)	maemo.nokia.com, garage.maemo.org/forum, www.forum.nokia.com/main/platform, maemo.org
Library Questions and Answers (tinyurl.com/2eghmp6)	msugovdocs.blogspot.com, web.library.uiuc.edu, askasl.blogspot.com, infocenter.stanford.edu, radicalreference.info, eb.library.uiuc.edu/ugl/qb/science.asp
ROAR Search Engine (tinyurl.com/23wv66m)	depot.erudit.org, eprints.ens-lsh.fr, www.arboles.org, calvados.c3sl.ufpr.br, www.zora.unizh.ch/zora
Theological Journals Search (tinyurl.com/nxbpvl)	ifphc.org/pdf, atijournal.org, via.library.depaul.edu, www.tyndale.org/TSJ, www.tyndalehouse.com

Central Connecticut State University (libguides.ccsu.edu/content.php?pid= 59695&sid=438643). Instruction librarian Krista Graham at Central Michigan University suggested a possible information literacy assignment: Have students collaborate to develop an authoritative CSE.[14] To imagine how information professionals can otherwise benefit from the knowledge and use of CSEs, we can look to our peers. (See the interview at the end of this chapter with multibook author Ran Hock.)

Super searcher Greg Notess commented, "If nothing else, it [the ability to work with CSEs] positions the library and information professionals as cutting-edge information technology experts."[15] Well-known information professional Mary Ellen Bates raises the stakes, writing, "There's nothing as compelling as showing clients that not only are we not threatened by search engines, but we are also able to improve upon them."[16] I'll add that search engines don't intimidate us, because we know how they work and we know how to tweak them, and, with no apologies to George Costanza, "We are masters of our domain."

Conversation With Ran Hock

Ran Hock is the author of *Yahoo! to the Max*, *The Traveler's Web: An Extreme Searcher Guide to Travel Resources on the Internet*, *The Extreme Searcher's Guide to Web Search Engines: A Handbook for the Serious Searcher*, and the recent third edition of *The Extreme Searcher's Internet Handbook: A Guide for the Serious Searcher*. He set aside some time to discuss CSEs.

Nick Tomaiuolo: *Would you please share some of your insights and experience with CSEs?*

Ran Hock: A couple years ago I tried three or four of them. The one that I concluded best fit my needs was Google CSE, because of the ease of use, number of sites it handled, and some other features. I found that Microsoft Live Macros was a rather different animal, a "canned searches" approach rather than selective sites. Rollyo just didn't match up to Google CSE in terms of capabilities.

NT: *I find that many of the Google CSEs I have come across are written by software developers. Many are created by librarians. But I've found more "end user" custom searches on Swicki and Rollyo. Have you noticed this? If you agree with this observation, why do you think this is true?*

RH: Generally, I just don't run across CSEs very often. The one exception is the case of the many websites (including some big, high profile sites) that use Google CSE as their "site search" tool. I have done quite a bit of comparing (nothing "scientific") of searches done using a site's own "site search" box (where they didn't use Google) to searches done of that same site using a Google "site search" (with the site: prefix). Much of the time, Google did a better job. Since in effect, the site search is, I think, the same mechanism as Google CSE, I think a lot of sites would be well-advised to switch to Google CSE for their site search. Speaking personally I currently have just one CSE in use at onstrat.com/osint/#terrorism.

NT: *What else about Google CSE impresses you?*

RH: Its ease of use, the number of sites it can handle, its use of tags (that enable limiting in the same way that "traditional" descriptors and identifiers do in commercial services), and the ability for others to collaborate in adding sites. I also like the options for how the CSE is displayed when you place it on a webpage.

NT: *Ran, please comment on Swicki. It's really quite different inasmuch as it brings end user voting, or the "wisdom of the crowds," into the mix. What do you think of Swicki?*

RH: This week I'm not very much of a "populist." In general, relying on votes of others to help me find the most useful information has just not worked for me. I am much more inclined to control my retrieval by means of search strategies and features rather than "votes" of others.

NT: *Do you think end users (people who are not information professionals or developers) are becoming more adept at searching and more savvy about web resources in general? What demonstrates this?*

RH: In general, no. I train people from a variety of backgrounds and even countries, and I see a very small percentage of end users who become quite well-versed in techniques or who use a range of websites, and a few who have picked up two or three useful tricks; but most have not had the time or inclination to become proficient searchers. There are still too many people whose approach is "I know how to search Google perfectly well. I don't need to know any more."

Fortunately, what "saves" many end users is the retrieval technology, particularly the use by search engines of "expert systems" approaches. For example, the technique that many of us feel is the single most useful technique that can be taught in 2 minutes—the use of quotation marks for phrases—isn't as critical as it used to be. Because of the heavy weighting that ranking algorithms place on proximity, even when quotation marks are not used, the items that contain that phrase are often given a rather high ranking. On the other hand, as you and I are very aware, having the skill is even better, especially for something like name searching.

NT: *Why do you think some of the players drop out of the custom search game (e.g., Yahoo! Search Builder, Microsoft Live Macros)?*

RH: Because they didn't see it as contributing significantly to their bottom line. For the world at large, it is a relatively esoteric feature.

NT: *Is there still a lot left to do to position information professionals and librarians as facilitators in the information quest in this end user world?*

RH: I see it as continuing to be an uphill battle. The "I know Google, what more do I need?" problem is pervasive.

NT: *I think of you as an information professional above all, with a special interest in unearthing new resources, but how do you feel about user-generated content? Some say its day has passed (e.g., "Is User-Generated Content Out?" Newsweek.com, www.news week.com/id/119091/page/1), and some say it's going strong (e.g., "Latest Web Trends Begin to Influence Real Estate Websites: Web Trend #1: User-Generated Content," PRNewswire, www.prnewswire.com/news-releases/latest-web-trends-begin-to-influence-real-estate-websites-82585142.html). What do you think?*

RH: I have never fully bought into the user-generated content phenomenon. I myself make almost daily use of that type of content, for getting answers to computer problems, hotel reviews, and so forth. For quality information for other things, though, I first head for "vetted" sources. I make use of blog content, but I go to blogs written not by the great unwashed masses but by "experts"—people who know what they are talking about and have some credentials that attest to that. For news, I go to "real" news sites, not to Digg or Reddit. For the people who spend significant amounts of their time contributing to those sites (Digg, Reddit, etc.), I am happy that they have found some meaning to their lives. (Dare I say, to use an old expression, perhaps "It keeps them off the streets and out of the bars.")

As for predicting where UContent is going, fortunately I will never be so famous that anyone will be likely to remember my predictions, and therefore bad predictions will never come back to bite me. So here goes.

UContent will continue to play a significant role, in large part due to the "Long Tail." One one-thousandth of 1 percent of 7 billion internet users is still a large number. For someone who wants to share his or her daily thoughts about the philosophical aspects of duct tape, the internet is the place to go to find the other three people in the world with the same interest. UContent in combination with the long tail phenomenon serves a significant function.

NT: *Ran, you have a way with words! Thank you for your comments.*

Endnotes

1. Greg R. Notess, "Subset Search Techniques," *Online* 29 (Sept/Oct, 2005): 40–42.

2. Mary Ellen Bates, "The Information Drought," *Econtent* 29 (Sept/Oct. 2005): 29.

3. Phil Bradley, "Custom-Built Search Engines," Ariadne, vol. 55, April 2008, accessed August 3, 2011, www.ariadne.ac.uk/issue55/search-engines.

4. Dave Pell, "Rollyo: Roll Your Own Search Engine," Davenetics, September 28, 2005, accessed August 3, 2011, www.davenetics.com/2005/09/rollyo-roll-your-own-search-engine.

5. Gary Price, "Roll Your Own Search Engine with Rollyo (beta)," SearchEngine Watch, September 25, 2005, accessed August 3, 2011, www.searchenginewatch.com/article/2060937/Roll-Your-Own-Search-Engine-With-Rollyo-Beta.

6. Phil Bradley, "A Swicki is…" Phil Bradley's Blog, November 5, 2005, accessed August 3, 2011, www.philb.com/blog/2005/11/what-is-swicki.htm.

7. Tom Duerig, "Better Search Results [keywords]," Custom Search Blog, September 12, 2007, accessed August 3, 2011, googlecustomsearch.blogspot.com/2007/09/better-search-results.html.

8. Jay Davies, "Star Power," Custom Search Blog, May 17, 2007, accessed August 3, 2011, googlecustomsearch.blogspot.com/2007_05_01_archive.html.

9. Readers interested in a more technical discussion of advanced Google CSE deployment may like to read C. Hennesy and J. Bowman, "Curating the Web: Building a Google Custom Search Engine for the Arts," *Computers in Libraries* 28 (May 2008): 14–21. For the most thorough treatment of the Google CSE API, see Google Custom Search APIs and Tools: Google Code at code.google.com/intl/en/apis/customsearch/docs/dev_guide.html.

10. Ethan Zuckerman, "What Google Coop Search Doesn't Do Well," My Heart's in Accra, October 27, 2006, accessed August 3, 2011, www.ethanzuckerman.com/blog/2006/10/27/what-google-coop-search-doesnt-do-well.

11. Vrishali Wagle, "The Search Engine that Could," Custom Search Blog, November 6, 2006, accessed August 3, 2011, googlecustomsearch.blogspot.com/2006/11/search-engine-that-could.html.

12. Ethan Zuckerman, "Google Fixes My Custom Search Problems," My Heart's in Accra, November 6, 2006, accessed August 3, 2011, www.ethanzuckerman.com/blog/2006/11/06/google-fixes-my-custom-search-problems.

13. Meredith Farkas, "Pathfinder in a Box," *American Libraries* 40 (October 2009): 45.

14. K. Graham, "Search and Search-ability: Google Custom Search & Library Instruction," *LOEX Quarterly* 34 (spring 2007): 6–7, accessed August 3, 2011, www.emich.edu/public/loex/341.pdf.

15. Greg R. Notess, "Building Vertical Search Engines," *Online* 31 (July/Aug. 2007): 37–40.

16. Mary Ellen Bates, "Building a Better Search Engine," *Online* 31 (March/April 2007): 64.

Cybercartography

In Chapter 1, I listed several definitions of UContent. One of them, issued by the Organisation for Economic Development and Cooperation (OECD), specified "content made publicly available over the Internet which reflects a certain amount of creative effort, and is created outside of professional routines and practices." The emphasis in this definition is on the phrase *creative effort.* If you're creative, have an interest in a subject, and are willing to expend some effort, producing maps is a great outlet. Maps don't have to be exclusively about places; they can be about places and "something else." The something else is whatever subject matter you find stimulating. Using free mapping tools on the web, end users have made maps for their businesses, travels, communities, events, and personal interests. These maps can contain photos, audio, video, and other information. Creating maps allows you to add useful content to the web while having fun and learning something, too.

The Cybercartographers

Anyone with an idea for a useful map can become a cybercartographer. The *New York Times* reported that acts of "geo-volunteerism" can be motivated by both self-interest and a desire to help others. For example, Richard Hintz, an engineer from Berkeley, California, has taken the initiative to tweak 200 business listings in a map of his state; he has also created maps of parts of Laos and Cambodia, where he takes motorcycle trips. "Paul" combined craigslist real estate listings with Google Maps to create the popular HousingMaps.com mashup ("Paul" is affiliated with neither Google nor craigslist). Writing about these amateur mapmakers, Miguel Helft observed, "Like contributors to Wikipedia before them, they are democratizing a field that used to be the exclusive domain of professionals and specialists. And the information they gather is becoming increasingly valuable commercially." Recently 200 volunteers with GPS devices, cameras, and paper maps added missing alleys, restaurants, condominium complexes, and hotels to the Free Wiki World Map site, OpenStreetMap (www.openstreetmap.org). Adapting crowdsourcing,

Google is beginning to rely on "in the trenches" volunteers, who include John Kittle, a Georgia engineer who corrects street names in Atlanta.[1]

Naturally, legacy map firms such as NAVTEQ (www.navteq.com) warn that the amateur approach to navigation has downsides. For instance, it has been reported that at Map Maker (www.google.com/mapmaker), volunteer editors from India attempted to make Pakistan part of their country. But geography professor Michael Goodchild at the University of California, Santa Barbara, believes, "As far as we can tell, these new sources are as accurate as the traditional ones. This is putting mapping where it should be, which is the hands of local people who know an area well."[2]

Airline passengers are frequently interested in what their seatmates are reading. Finding out what they are mapping can also be a delicious personal indulgence. End users can choose from many free map-making websites, but Google Maps (maps.google.com) is a great starting point; it's also a prime place to look for maps others have created. Searching Google Maps, you'll notice that many maps are aimed at helping people orient themselves geographically. You'll encounter numerous garden variety maps of roads, places, GPS coordinates, elevation contours, and train routes that tell you where things are or how to get from point A to point B.

While useful, these are often only embellished variations of traditional paper maps. Keep exploring and you will find many extremely imaginative applications of Google Maps. (You may find some maps that will inspire you, as I did.) I'll list a few, but bear in mind that this is merely the tip of a huge iceberg. The Seven New Wonders of the World map (tinyurl.com/yg4zh6d) combines photos with geography with links to Wikipedia. For the sports fan, there is Football Stadiums of the World (tinyurl.com/yjqohc8). Indiana Jones Filming Locations & Attractions (tinyurl.com/y9k7gca) is a fairly unique contribution that uses a world map as an interface to the locations where scenes were shot for all four films in the series. A generic Google web search can also unearth goodies such as Everyblock.org, which geographically displays news from 15 major U.S. cities (and displays recent crime reports for Chicago ZIP codes). Similarly, Track This Now (www.trackthisnow.com) allows you to search for news throughout the world, in a group of countries, or in one specific country. I searched for *Habitat for Humanity* on July 7, 2011, and located news stories from India, Australia, Nigeria, Argentina, and 20 other countries.

Searching for a Destination

Not long ago, Google Maps made it possible to restrict searches to maps submitted by end users. Beginning at maps.google.com, one could simply choose "User-Created Maps" from the search options. Early in 2011, this search option vanished. Dozens of befuddled and dismayed map creators and map users posted messages to the Google Maps Help Forum under the thread "Why doesn't the 'Show Search Options' link appear next to the search button anymore?" (You can find these remarks by going to the Google Maps Help Forum at tinyurl.com/5s9xwza, paging back through the comments to March 2, 2011, and reading the comments up until at least April 25, 2011; you will also see related remarks by going to tinyurl.com/6ed738j and paging back to December 12, 2010.)

Attempting to assuage the group, several individuals identifying themselves as Google employees entered the thread. One wrote, "This is definitely a priority. We need to make sure our best users—those that are the thoughtful creators of excellent content like those chiming in here—are rewarded for their time by giving them an audience for their creations. The product is *not* going away, and in fact we are investing a great deal (in the near-term) in the more invisible but fundamental aspects of the product (like infrastructure), and have several really interesting projects lined up to take advantage of that new infrastructure shortly after it's complete, which will include a focus on making maps more discoverable." (Note: See this comment at tinyurl.com/mapshelp). Nonetheless, the ability to search for user-generated maps had not been reinstated as this book went to press. For now the best search we can perform is accomplished by going to the Advanced Search of plain vanilla Google.com, entering keywords, looking for the line "search within a site or domain," and restricting your search to the URL maps.google.com. It's a crude workaround because it does not ensure that all the retrieval will be user-generated, but it works relatively well. For example, being a bit of a Poe devotee I was delighted to see that when I accessed the advanced Google search and entered the phrase *Edgar Allan Poe* (while restricting the search to the maps.google.com URL), I discovered "Sheryl" had created a map on July 24, 2008, showing pushpins that represented events in the author's life. Sheryl's map had more than 500 views (tinyurl.com/ycrr9zd). But my searches aren't always about literature. I also found the map by "luv2dance40" called "My Favorite Spring Break Vacation Spots" (tinyurl.com/yc3ltsd), which according to the author covered "each hotel that I have stayed at and [I] explained what makes it unique to me."

Google is not the only place you should look if you want to discover what others have mapped. The Programmable Web (www.programmableweb.com) is an outstanding site for locating not only maps that users have created but mashups in general (you can also list your mashups with the site). At the Programmable Web you will find a directory of mashups and a directory of application programmable interfaces (APIs). To locate mashups that utilize maps, search the directory (I retrieved 1,920 maps that were made using Google Maps) or use the Mashup Tag Cloud. Not all the maps are created by end users. For example, the first listed map is "10 Fascinating Googlers" (www.programmableweb.com/mashup/10-fascinating-googlers) and was submitted by *Fortune* magazine. But "NBA From Above" (www.programmable web.com/mashup/nba-from-above) is credited to "robustone," and "marshall" is responsible for "Find Garage Sales by Map" (a map that helps you plan your shopping trip by comparing garage sales by location at www.programmableweb.com/mashup/find-garage-sales-by-map). Note: When you get to these URLs via the Programmable Web, just click the image on the page to access the actual maps.

Calling itself "the world's largest blog focused exclusively on Web 2.0 and Social Media news," Mashable.com is another good place to find lists of user-generated maps (see Maps Lists at www.mashable.com/category/labels/lists/maps-lists and "Google Maps: The 100+ Best Tools and Mashups" at www.mashable.com/2009/01/08/google-maps-mashups-tools). Mashable will link you to sites such as Grüvr (www.gruvr.com), a map that tracks live music throughout the U.S., the World's Most Polluted Cities (www.mibazaar.com/pollutedcities.html), a map with geotagged photos of the most polluted cities), and Wines and Times (www.winesandtimes.com), which maps winery tours and wine tastings in the United States. Mashable covers the serious (e.g., the Gaza Conflict Map at www.mibazaar.com/gazaconflict.html, which shows the latest YouTube videos from that region) and the goofy (e.g., the *Dr. Who* Locations map at www.doctorwholocations.org.uk, which fans of the long-running British science fiction series will enjoy).

If you seek offbeat or unique maps, the only limitation you'll encounter is the amount of time you have to spend in the discovery process. The Unofficial Google Maps Directory (GMdir; www.gmdir.com) and Google Maps Mania (googlemapsmania.blogspot.com), an unofficial blog that tracks websites, mashups, and tools influenced by Google Maps, are two additional places to locate great user-generated maps. In fact, Keir Clarke, who writes for Google Maps Mania, has his own page at homepage.ntlworld.com/keir.clarke/web/directory.htm, where you can find hundreds of (Google) maps, including: a World of Warcraft map (www.mapwow.com) and several *Lord of the Rings* maps. Clarke also has a link to an excellent Bible Map (www.biblemap.org) that allows you to select a book and chapter from the Bible and view a map with markers indicating the geography mentioned in the passages. Table 12.1 is a list of websites where you can create maps for free, and you can use most of the sites to look for other interesting maps as well. For example, ZeeMaps (www.zeemaps.com) features a new map every day. The last time I checked, it was the Teacher Sex Scandal map from www.schoolteachernews.com/map2010.html. You can hover on a marker to see the exact location and then click a link to take you to news content discussing the issue.

Table 12.1   Websites for creating free maps

Website	Register?	Embed and/or link?	Add other links or files to map?
Aardvarkmap (www.aardvarkmap.net)	No	Embed: Yes; Link: Yes	Yes
BatchGeo (www.batchgeo.com)	No	Embed: Yes; Link: Yes	Yes
CommunityWalk (www.communitywalk.com)	Yes	Embed: Yes; Link: Yes	Yes
Donkey Magic Map Maker (mapmaker.donkeymagic.co.uk)	Yes	Embed: Yes; Link: Yes	Yes
Embed Google "My Maps" (www.dr2ooo.com/tools/maps)	No	Embed: Yes; Link: No	Yes
Faneuil Media Atlas (www.fmatlas.com)	Yes	Embed: Yes; Link: Yes	Yes
GeoCommons (www.geocommons.com)	Yes	Embed: Yes; Link: Yes	No
Google Maps (maps.google.com)	Yes	Embed: Yes; Link: Yes	Yes
Google Maps API Family (code.google.com/apis/maps)	Yes	Embed: Yes; Link: Yes	Yes
Map Channels (www.mapchannels.com)	Yes	Embed: Yes; Link: No	No
MapFling (www.mapfling.com)	No	Embed: No; Link: Yes	No
Map-Generator (www.map-generator.net)	No	Embed: Yes; Link: Yes	No
Mapicurious (www.mapicurious.com)	Yes	Embed: Yes; Link: Yes	Yes
MapLib.net (www.maplib.net)	Yes	Embed: Yes; Link: Yes	Yes
OpenStreetMap (www.openstreetmap.org)	Yes	Embed: Yes; Link: Yes	No
Tagzania (www.tagzania.com)	Yes	Embed: Yes; Link: No	Yes
Wayfaring (www.wayfaring.com)	Yes	Embed: Yes; Link: No	No
Wikimapia (www.wikimapia.org)	Yes	Embed: Yes; Link: Yes	Yes
Yahoo Maps Web Services (developer.yahoo.com/maps)	Yes	Embed: Yes; Link: Yes	Yes
ZeeMaps (www.zeemaps.com)	Yes	Embed: Yes; Link: Yes	Yes

What Are Information Professionals Mapping?

The aforementioned maps may have aroused your interest, but information professionals haven't been left behind in the map-content-creation process. Many maps display a marker for an individual library or its branches; they are called "Here We Are" maps. Several maps show all the libraries in the United States. Counting Opinions, a library consultancy firm, has constructed a Find Libraries Near You map (www.libraries411.com) that lists addresses and phone numbers and has several added-value components, including links to library websites and directions. The American Library Association (ALA) has used Google My Places to produce a geographical listing (tinyurl.com/ala gradprogs) of all ALA-accredited library and information science graduate programs in the U.S. and Canada.

Info pros are also going far beyond basic depictions by imaginatively mixing content to bring information seekers some very lively maps. Maps are good tools for keeping track of people and what they have been doing. Law enforcement officials have known this for years, and Suzanne H. Calapestri, director of the Foster Anthropology Library at the University of California, Berkeley, picked up on it as well. At anthromap.lib.berkeley.edu you can see a sophisticated map in which you may search for information about dissertation research performed by Berkeley graduate students. Retrieval comes in the form of markers in various regions and countries around the world. The map, shown in Figure 12.1, is further enhanced with links to the library catalog and University Microfilms International dissertations.[3]

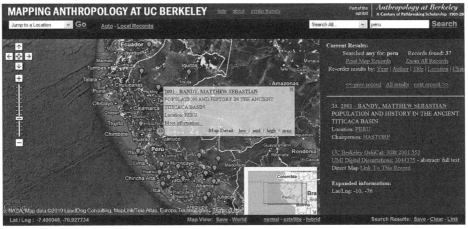

Figure 12.1   The Foster Library tracks UC Berkeley anthropology graduate work throughout the world. [Courtesy of the University of California, Berkeley, Foster Anthropology Library]

Here's another example of using maps to track people: Posting on her LibraryJournal.com blog, Cheryl LaGuardia notes that she and colleagues at Harvard have used Google My Places to create the Harvard College Library Collaborations map at tinyurl.com/ygzzenh. It presents information on work being done among librarians and colleagues, augmented with links to more content.[4]

I was also able to find maps by using the social bookmarking site Delicious (www.delicious.com). I initially searched for items tagged *libraries*, and then I searched within that retrieval for items tagged *maps*. Among the maps the Delicious community had bookmarked was the library catalog at the Florida International University Library. Its OPAC has "map it" functionality: When you identify an item, the catalog will show you where it physically resides in the library (see Figure 12.2).

Michael Vandenburg, a librarian at the Kingston Frontenac Library in Canada, reported that he successfully mashed up bibliographic information with Google Maps to produce a geographical interface to the library catalog. Vandenburg placed 284 markers on a map, one for each country. Each marker was then linked to items in the library catalog that reflected the Boolean search *Name of Country AND history OR (travel AND description)*. If you clicked on the marker for Egypt, you would see two links. One link would take you to items on the history of Egypt; the other link would take you to items on travel and description of Egypt.[5] Librarians at the Harold B. Lee Library at Brigham Young University in Utah made various parts of the library's digital collections available through the Google Maps API in a project called Mappify at lib.byu.edu/DigitalMaps (see Figure 12.3). The materials, including photographs and travel diaries, are "accurately pinpointed on a Google Maps interface and are found by navigating the map, browsing by geographical location, or performing keyword searches based on harvested metadata."[6]

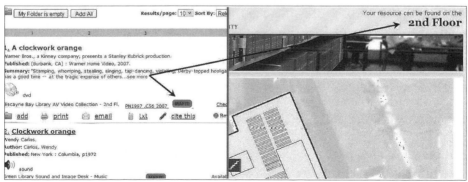

Figure 12.2   A "Map It" functionality within the library catalog helps users find materials at Florida International University libraries. [Courtesy of the Florida International University Libraries]

Figure 12.3   Brigham Young University's map shows geographical access to
its digital collections. [Courtesy of the Lee Library]

A Journal of My Places

Just about the time I was ready to create my first map, I read something
Mikael Jacobsen had written in *Library Journal*: "Librarians use online mapping services such as Google Maps, MapQuest, Yahoo! Maps, and others to
check traffic conditions, find local businesses, and provide directions.
However, few libraries are using one of Google Maps' most outstanding applications, My Maps, for the creation of enhanced and interactive multimedia
maps."[7] I could say that this resonated with me, but it was more like, "Dude!
It's like you're inside my head!" Social software affords us so much leverage
over what we can accomplish that just making a mere "Here We Are" map
seems like heresy! (Incidentally, the My Maps option that appeared on the
maps.google.com page was changed to My Places in mid-2011. The name
change was confirmed on June 15, 2011, at the Google LatLong blog at
google-latlong.blogspot.com/2011/06/my-places-now-helps-you-manage-
your.html.) The functionality of the option remains the same. Go to
maps.google.com, sign in, click My Places, and then Create New Map.

  Jacobsen explained how he and his colleagues at the Franklin Park
Library in Chicago took the user-friendly Google My Places platform and
made three informative, interactive maps of the Franklin Park area of
Illinois. One map pinpoints historical neighborhood places (with markers
that pop up with images and text), another marks Place of Note, and a third
warns about Road Construction. Jacobsen and his colleagues wanted to
devise maps that not only showed where things are, but answered questions
and provided information.[8]

Before experimenting with an actual map, I went to YouTube for guidance. A simple but helpful video from the 5Star Development Network explained how to make a walking tour (see tinyurl.com/y8pxpjt); it included links to images and video, and I decided that a walking tour would be a good first map to work on.

I live in Wethersfield, Connecticut. It's a suburb that the natives like to refer to as "Connecticut's Most Ancient Town," and there are some old buildings and historic sites here. I sent my daughter out with her Nikon D3000, and she took 17 photos of points of interest, including a shot of the "Ancient Burying Ground" (where the oldest headstone dates back to 1637) and one of the Webb House (headquarters for George Washington in 1752). She uploaded them to my Flickr account, and we were ready to commence working on the map.

Before setting to work, I still needed to decide whether the map I wanted to create would need to be done with the Google Maps API or whether I could use the more user-friendly Google My Places format. I had just read Derik A. Badman's chapter in *Library Mashups*, edited by Nicole Engard (Information Today, Inc., 2009), which described how he created campus maps with the Google Maps API. So I contacted him and asked which utility he would consider a better choice given my walking tour map concept. Badman had just moved from Temple University's Libraries to Springshare (originators of LibGuides), and he promptly provided this guidance:

> With the Maps API you can use the existing Google Maps as a canvas for adding anything you want to it. That's how you get some of those well-known map mashups, such as the Chicago crime stats (www.everyblock.org) or the craigslist housing search (www.housing maps.com). That data isn't in Google Maps itself; you can add it to a map with the API in a programmatic way so that you are not adding any markers or shapes individually on the map. Those markers could be changed by the program rather than by hand by a user. It's really all about what you want to do. If the features of My Places work for one's needs, then use it, but if My Places seems to be limiting, then the API is the way to go.[9]

The walking tour map would be a basic but relatively unique map; the information wouldn't change, and manually placing the dozen or so markers wouldn't necessitate automation. I took Badman's advice and chose Google My Places as appropriate given my mapping objective.

To work in Google My Places, sign in to your Google account, go to maps.google.com, click on the My Places link, and then click the Create New Map link. Give your map a title and a description and decide whether you want the map to be public or private. At this point you can also decide whether you want others to collaborate by clicking the Collaboration link and emailing invitations. Save your map frequently.

Next, move the map around until you find your location and then zoom in as close as possible. For me this meant finding Connecticut and zooming into Wethersfield. You can also type an address or ZIP code into the search form, and Google will find the place on the map.

There are three tools in the upper left corner of the map: a hand for moving the map, a marker for marking a location, and a zigzag line for drawing routes. My daughter and I dropped our first marker at a playground called Mikey's Place, which is handicap-accessible, and changed the default marker to a wheelchair icon. We also created some text. To add a photo, we opened our Flickr account. (When you find the right photo in Flickr, click the All Sizes choice above the photo. At the next page, we chose an appropriate size for Google My Places; we picked small, which is 240x161 pixels.) Flickr will then generate code, so grab the photo's URL.

Back in the My Places editor, we chose Rich Text and clicked the Insert Image icon; then we pasted the URL from Flickr into the pop-up. (You can continue adding text by using the Rich Text editor or switching over to the HTML editor.) When we were done, we clicked OK, and we had made our first marker. To continue our walk, we next chose the zigzag (line) tool and traced a path to the next photo stop. Our finished walking tour is viewable at tinyurl.com/walkinweth (see Figure 12.4).

Encouraged by this first attempt, I wanted my second map project to combine more content. I decided to create a map that would show the birthplaces of 10 American authors from the 19th century. I wanted the markers for the

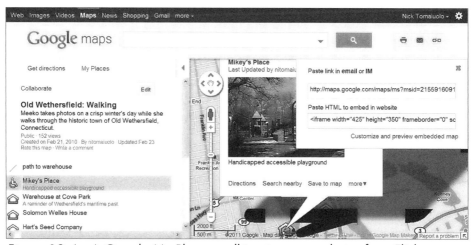

Figure 12.4   A Google My Places walking tour uses photos from Flickr. [Courtesy of Google and Flickr]

birthplaces of each author to be images in the public domain and labeled "for reuse" (discoverable at Wikimedia Commons, commons.wikimedia.org). For each author, I also decided to include a link to a brief biography (most came from LitWeb), a link to one representative full-text work in the public domain (most came from Google Books or Project Gutenberg), and, if possible, a link to a sound file for a representative work (these were a little trickier to find).

To create the map, I essentially recreated the exercise for the walking tour, except I edited the default markers and included small images of each author's head (64x64 pixels). I also exercised my HTML proficiency and added several links to each marker. When you click an author's image on the completed map, a pop-up will provide links to the three files I included. It's pretty good if I say so myself (see Figure 12.5).

Because I was enjoying the mapping aspect of UContent, I looked for other websites (just to get an idea of the available resources) that would permit equivalent or additional functionality. Table 12.1, featured earlier in this chapter, lists 20 websites, and I experimented with the majority of them. Some were better than others or offered different features. For example, I used Map Channels (www.mapchannels.com) to make a nifty "switch map," in which you can toggle among views, including Road Map, Satellite, Hybrid, Physical, Street Map, Bing Map, Open Street Map, and Yahoo! Map. I used BatchGeo (www.batchgeo.com) to construct a government depository map that includes links to the libraries in the pop-ups (see Figure 12.6). Both of these maps are viewable (and usable) at web.ccsu.edu/library/tomaiuolon/

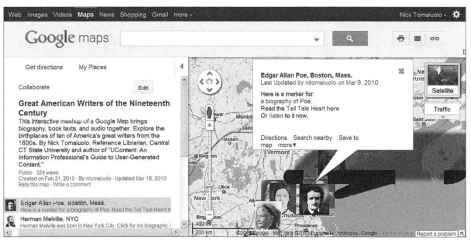

Figure 12.5   This Google My Places mashup with Wikimedia Commons shows images and biographies, links to full text at Google Books and Project Gutenberg, plus links to audio when available. [Courtesy of Google and Wikimedia Commons]

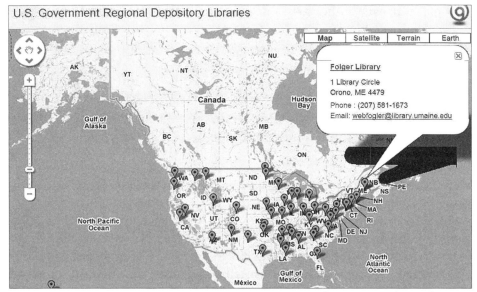

Figure 12.6   This map is another UContent creation featuring markers for U.S. Government Regional Depositories, with links to libraries and other directory information. [Courtesy of BatchGeo]

mapmashup.htm. To see maps made with Aardvarkmap, MapFling, and Map-Generator, please see web.ccsu.edu/library/tomaiuolon/UContent/usermaps.htm. The Wethersfield Walking Tour and American Authors of the Nineteenth Century maps are embedded at web.ccsu.edu/library/tomaiuolon/UContent/GoogleMyMaps.htm.

The Advantages of Using Google's My Places

1. It is free (you must, however, register for a Google account).
2. It permits considerable range of interactivity and customization.
3. You add markers from a nice palette of colors, shapes, and icons (e.g., houses, churches) by simple drag and drop.
4. Once your location is marked, you are given three input functions to describe the marker: plain text, rich text, and HTML. If you know the tiniest smattering of HTML, you are all set to create maps that would dazzle Magellan! Even if you do not know much HTML, you can add links to sound, video, photos, and full text (think Google Books, think Project

Gutenberg). Note that Google won't let you upload images or other files, so they need to be online somewhere (e.g., Flickr, Picasa, and Photobucket).

When your map is done, save it to My Places. Whenever you log in to Google, your maps will be available. Google generates two bits of information to help you share or reuse your maps. It will give you a link, but the link URL will be very long. Make the address more manageable by using a URL shortener (e.g., tinyurl.com, snipurl.com, or bit.ly).

Other Mapping Sites of Interest

Maybe you're thinking "Maps aren't exciting." I originally thought that, too, but maps can be robust, engaging information sources that take on lives of their own. Banned Books Week has its own Google My Places of censored books (www.bannedbooksweek.org/node/2). Clicking on markers throughout the U.S. will reveal titles of challenged books and other relevant information. Stuart Lewis, chair of the DSpace UK & Ireland User Group (leaders in the open source movement), created the Repository66 Maps (maps.repository 66.org). Lewis's maps mash data from the Registry of Open Access Repositories, the Directory of Academic Open Access Depositories, and Google Maps. His map shows markers for repositories worldwide, with directory information and links when available.

The CodexMap (www.codexmap.com/codexmap.php) is the creation of doting Mark Watkins, who exhorts us to "explore the world of books." CodexMap mashes up information from Amazon, LibraryThing, Wikipedia, and Google Book Search. When it's working, it's pretty sweet. For instance, a search for *John Updike* on CodexMap will retrieve a map with markers in various places throughout the world. Click on the Updike marker in Denmark and up pops a link to his novel *Gertrude and Claudius*; click the link and you're whisked to a page with book prices, ISBN, and links to Amazon and LibraryThing. Following is a descriptive list of other maps for bibliophiles:

- Authors' birthplaces (www.microformats.dk/kort/streetview/top250 booksuk.html): Answers the question "Where are the authors of the most borrowed books from U.K. libraries born?"

- Joyce Walks (www.joycewalks.com): "A psychogeographic art project that generates walking maps for any city in the world based on remapping routes from *Ulysses* allowing users to create a mashup of their own walk to be shared with other users both on the Joyce Walks site and as embeddable maps on any site."

- Littourati Blog (littourati.squarespace.com): Maps the journeys laid out in selected books and offers reflections corresponding to the various stops (mostly concerned with Jack Kerouac's work).

- Londonist Sherlock Holmes Map (www.londonist.com/2009/11/the_london_of_sherlock_holmesmapped.php): Traces Holmes's jaunts and favorite haunts.

- Here, There, and Everywhere (www.beatlesbible.com/map): Traces the Beatles' history geographically. Markers provide addresses, history, and photos, and a link to the Beatles in the U.S. is included.

- Patrick O'Brian Novels Mapping Project (www.cannonade.net/map.php?Master_and_Commander): The goal of this site is to accurately map the progress of Jack Aubrey and Stephen Maturin over the course of the 21 novels by Patrick O'Brian.

- Poetry Atlas (www.poetryatlas.com): This site hosts a map with pushpins representing places that have been written about; pins link to the full-text poems when available.

About Geocodes and Geocoding

Geocode can mean a variety of things: It can be the letters and numbers in the index of an atlas of street maps, such as a page number and a square number that pinpoints the location of a place on the street maps. It can be any combination of values that lead to the identification of a geographical place, including ZIP code, street address, altitude, and longitude and latitude. With that in mind, end users such as ourselves can be satisfied with a definition of geocoding as the longitude and latitude of a given geographical place.

You're getting this information second hand, but I've tried it and it works; a tip of the cap to LiquidX's Alastair Tse (www.liquidx.net/blog/2007/04/19/find-latitude-longitude-from-google-maps). Here's a slick way for finding the latitude and longitude of a place:

1. Go to maps.google.com, and in the search box enter as much of the full address (or as much as you know) as possible. Click Search Maps.

2. Zoom in to the retrieved map and get as close as possible to the desired location.

3. Right click on that exact location and select Center Map Here.

4. When the map re-centers itself, put this code into your browser bar: javascript:alert(window.gApplication.getMap().getCenter())

5. A pop-up will magically appear with the location's coordinates! (You can copy the code from one of the UContent webpages at tinyurl.com/latlongformula.)

Here are resources for finding latitude and longitude (which some mapping websites may require):

- Find Longitude and Latitude (www.findlatitudeandlongitude.com)

- Get Lat Lon (www.getlatlon.com)

- Google Maps and Geocode APIs (81nassau.com/demos/geocode)

- Google Maps Longitude, Latitude PopUp
  (www.gorissen.info/Pierre/maps/googleMapLocation.php)

- GPS Data Team (www.gps-data-team.com/map)

- Infoplease Latitude and Longitude Finder (finds places such as Yosemite National Park—not cities, etc.;
  www.infoplease.com/atlas/latitude-longitude.html)

- iTouchMap.com (www.itouchmap.com/latlong.html)

- MyGeoPosition.com (www.mygeoposition.com)

Endnotes

1. Miguel Helft, "Online Maps: Everyman Offers New Directions," NYTimes.com, November 17, 2009, accessed August 3, 2011, www.nytimes.com/2009/11/17/ technology/internet/17maps.html.

2. Ibid.

3. Suzanne H. Calapesti, "On the Google Maps API," Google Librarian Central—Your Stories, accessed August 3, 2011, www.google.com/librariancenter/librarian_tot. html.

4. Cheryl LaGuardia, "Google Maps and Its Uses," E-views, May 29, 2008, accessed August 3, 2011, blog.libraryjournal.com/eviews/2008/05/29/google-maps-and- its-uses.

5. Michael Vandenburg, "Using Google Maps as an Interface for the Library Catalog," *Library Hi Tech* 26 (2008): 33–40.

6. Scott Eldrege and Project Team, *Mappify*, accessed August 3, 2011, www.cni.org/tfms/2009b.fall/Abstracts/Handouts/CNI_Geographic_Eldredge.pdf.

7. Mikael Jacobsen, "Using Google Maps to Bring Out Your Library's Local Collections," LibraryJournal.com, October 15, 2008, accessed August 3, 2011, www.libraryjournal.com/article/CA6602836.html.

8. Ibid.

9. Derik A. Badman, email message to author, March 20, 2010.

Yahoo! Pipes

Some of the properties of social software include user participation, sharing, and trust in the user. The architecture of participation has given rise to easy collaboration via blogs and wikis and attracted contributions to user-driven databases such as Google Knol, Flickr, and YouTube.

Remixable content is another characteristic of social software. Combining the elements of disparate data sources or software applications to produce a new source or application is a concept that everybody "gets" but one that may prove challenging to execute. Remixing information to create mashups often stretches beyond the average end user's skills. I say "average end user" because programmers and developers take mashups for granted. The application programmable interfaces (APIs) permeating cyberspace allow the tech savvy to create a smorgasbord of remarkable content remixes. In addition to distributing APIs, Google and other resources offer even simpler ways for their users to generate content. For example, Google My Places lets us use its interface to link geolocations to Flickr and other websites. Other services, like Matt Well's Gigablast Custom Topic Search, permit the slightly befuddled to cautiously pick their way through code until something usable can be embedded on the end user's site. Luckily for people like me, who know where the remixable information resides and can envision how useful a mashup might be, there is Yahoo! Pipes (pipes.yahoo.com). Because mashups rely on the web as a platform, and end users using Yahoo! Pipes define information sources and limiters, mashups fit into the milieu of UContent. Mashups are also in the spirit of social media in that they can be shared, edited, repurposed, and reused.

Yahoo! Pipes' graphical user interface enables individuals without software development training or experience to take content and combine it with other content; then it enables us to sort and filter that content. Unfortunately, several other services that were poised at the starting block a few years ago, ready to place the means to mash up data in the everyday user's hands, are gone now. One business mashup-maker company called Teqlo ambitiously launched in late 2006, when ZDNet announced, "Teqlo to let users assemble

Web applications."[1] Just 11 months later, Erick Schonfeld of TechCrunch blogged, "Making my point that it is hard to make money from mashups, investors have pulled the plug on Teqlo."[2] Microsoft had included a "mashup creator" in its Popfly product, which was discontinued in August 2009, and Google decommissioned a "mashup editor" in early 2009. But Yahoo! Pipes, which has been around since 2007, is an enduring and robust tool that enables end users to mash up content from around the web. It's a godsend for would-be mashup creators.

A Basic Example of Yahoo! Pipes

You probably have a Yahoo! account that you use for email or Flickr, but if you do not, sign up for one, because you'll need it to use Yahoo! Pipes. Go to pipes.yahoo.com, and you'll see a section that reads, "Create Pipe: How to Build a Pipe in Just a Few Minutes." If you click Browse at the top of the page, you may begin exploring hundreds of Popular Pipes. Take a look at some, such as Jonathan's U.S. Population by State (tinyurl.com/cq8g7x). (Note: When you access any Pipe you may see a "no results" message. You can usually kick-start the Pipe just by clicking Run Pipe, if that option is available, or by refreshing your browser.) After you have looked at a few Pipes, you'll begin to understand how they work. If you inspect Jonathan's U.S. Population by State, you can see that its creator (Jonathan), used one source and eight sub-modules and gave his creation three tags. We all know what the word *tags* refers to, but let's examine the rest of the nomenclature by looking at Figure 13.1.

Begin by looking at the Pipes' editor. Yahoo! defines the editor as "a powerful composition tool that lets us aggregate, manipulate, and mash up content from around the Web in an intuitive visual interface." The editor is divided into three panes: the Library, the Canvas, and the Debugger. In Figure 13.1, the pane at the left, beginning with Sources, is the Library. The large area occupying most of the screen is the Canvas, and the tab about midway down on the page and to the right is called the Debugger. To become acclimated to the editor, I configured a very basic Pipe to search Flickr for images of horses. When I ran the Pipe, the Debugger pane (at the bottom) displayed information about the first image.

The Library

In Figure 13.1, notice on the left that each bullet in the Pipes library points to items called modules. The modules contain sub-modules (such as the items shown indented under the word Sources). Frequently used Source sub-modules include Flickr, Google Base, Fetch Feed (Fetch Feed enables you to "OR" RSS

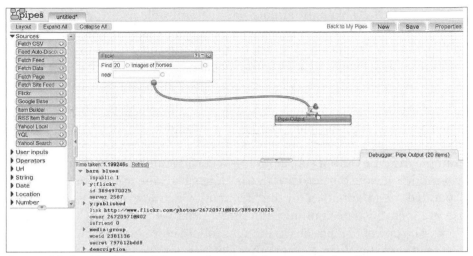

Figure 13.1 The Yahoo! Pipes editor and the author's first Pipe were configured to find images of horses at Flickr. The Flickr sub-module is within the Sources module. [Courtesy of Yahoo!]

feeds together), Yahoo! Local, and Yahoo! Search. Each of the sub-modules listed under Sources performs one specific task, such as retrieving a data source (e.g., Fetch Feed or Fetch Data). Other available modules include User Inputs, Operators, URL, String, Date, and so forth.

The Canvas

The canvas is the work area. Pipes are constructed and edited by dragging sub-modules from the library into the canvas and then connecting them with pipes (which actually look like wires).You do this by clicking on a sub-module, holding the mouse button down, and dragging the sub-module onto the canvas. You connect sub-modules by clicking on one sub-module's output and connecting it to another sub-module's input. Caveat: Trying to connect one sub-module to another sub-module that doesn't accept the connection indicates that the sub-modules are incompatible. In Figure 13.1, I have dragged the Flickr sub-module to the canvas and connected its output to the Pipe Output sub-module's input using a pipe. You can confirm the compatibility of sub-modules by mousing over a sub-module's input or output to see what kind of data that sub-module emits or expects to receive. In this case, the Flickr sub-module expects to emit "Items" and the Pipe Output sub-module expects to receive "Items." You can disconnect sub-modules by clicking on one of the connections; a small scissors will appear, as in Figure 13.1.

Note that the Flickr sub-module has customizable user input fields. You supply the input, but what you enter must be appropriate to the sub-module. In Figure 13.1, I've specified that each time I run this Pipe, I want to find a maximum of 20 images of horses from Flickr.

The Debugger

When you are sure the Pipe Output sub-module will receive appropriate information, you can test the Pipe with the Debugger. (Remember, in our example the Pipe Output sub-module is receiving information from the Flickr sub-module). Note our retrieval in the Debugger pane at the bottom (I have expanded the information for the first item). Of course, this extremely basic use of Pipes illustrates nothing more than what we could do if we searched Flickr. The power of Pipes lies in the subsequent combination and manipulation of information by means of other features of the editor.

A Second Example With More Variables

My next example is only slightly more complex (see Figure 13.2). I began by using the Fetch Site Feed sub-module, preparing to "OR" several news sites' URLs together. Fetch Site Feed uses a website's auto-discovery information to find an RSS or Atom feed. Next I used the Filter sub-module to restrict the content that comes from Fetch Site Feed. I specified that I wanted to see only items that mentioned various computing keywords. In one test run of this Pipe, which is shown in Figure 13.2, the Fetch Site Feed sub-module shows that items from five news sites are running to a Filter sub-module that permits items containing any of the designated keywords from the feeds to be forwarded to the Pipe Output sub-module. The Debugger tab states that seven items met the criteria; the Debugger pane shows the first six (the description of the sixth has been expanded to display a preview). In the upper left of the image, I have named this Pipe *computing_news*. When you're satisfied with a Pipe, you can save it and keep it private or click the Properties tab and publish it. The creator may also add tags and a brief description during this process. If the creator publishes the Pipe, it will show up in search engine retrieval and also be listed with other creations at pipes.yahoo.com.

Figure 13.3 shows the output of another run of the computing_news Pipe. When you view a Pipe in this hosted interface, you can see its tags and the number of sources and sub-modules used. The Pipe shown in Figure 13.3 has been published, but the creator may still edit, delete, or unpublish it. Users that come upon published Pipes can reuse or edit them by clicking Clone.

All Pipes, whether published or private, are hosted at Yahoo! If you want to use your Pipe (or someone else's you found useful) on another webpage, you

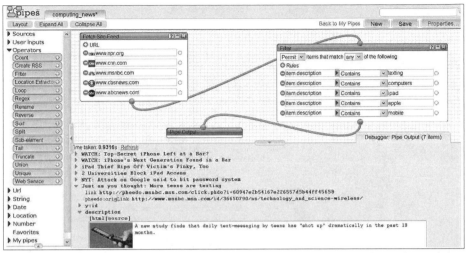

Figure 13.2   This Yahoo! Pipe uses Fetch Site Feed with the Filter sub-module and shows the first six items in the Debugger pane. [Courtesy of Yahoo!]

Figure 13.3   The published computing_news Pipe lists the first three search results. [Courtesy of Yahoo!]

need to get the embed code for it. In Figure 13.3, clicking Get as a Badge (located just above the List tab) will generate code you can customize and copy into another webpage. Figure 13.4 shows a simple placement of this content on a page. Depending on your tastes, the elegance of the presentation will vary.

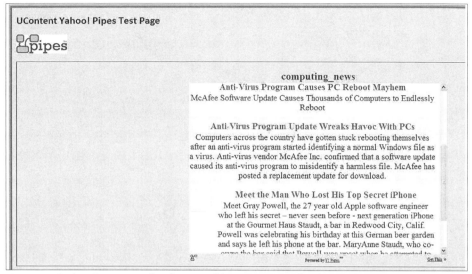

Figure 13.4   Getting a badge enables you to embed a Yahoo! Pipes project on a webpage. Clicking the links displayed by the embedded badge will take you to the site where the information originated. [Courtesy of Yahoo!]

Exemplary Pipes

Pipes let us create mashups from scratch or re-purpose the mashups of others. Although a comprehensive list of Pipes does not exist (there are thousands of them; just check the left column at pipes.yahoo.com/pipes/pipes. popular), Corvida, a blogger at ReadWriteWeb, published a list of ultimate Yahoo! Pipes back in 2008 (www.readwriteweb.com/archives/the_ultimate_ yahoo_pipes_list.php) that included the Content Keyword RSS Pipe (pipes.yahoo.com/prmpipes/contentkeyword), which uses nine sub-modules and seven sources. The sources for this Pipes' keyword search include Digg, Technorati, Yahoo! News, PRWeb, and Google News. After a search is run, the Pipe compares the results, removes duplicates, and sorts them by date. The output is a unique RSS feed full of content related to your keywords.

Another blogger called my attention to the Online Brand Protection Pipe (tinyurl.com/8wb5pf). A simple Pipe that uses only three sub-modules and five sources, it aims to enable user monitoring of "what the world is saying about your brand, company, product or URL." It checks Google Blogs, Technorati, IceRocket, Blog Pulse, Yahoo! News, MSN News, and Google News. I tested this Pipe, which used the User Input sub-module, with Fender Stratocaster, Toyota Prius, Procter & Gamble, and Stanley Hardware and returned 20 relevant items with each search.

But there are thousands of bloggers, and each has an opinion. The HyveUp blog listed its favorite Pipes, including the Add Images to Any RSS Feed Pipe (tinyurl.com/ 67nkm9z). Enter any RSS feed's address, and this Pipe will analyze each item in the feed for keywords. The Pipe then takes the keywords and performs a Yahoo! image search, takes the first result of the image search (in the form of a small thumbnail), and places it within the item's description. It's a popular Pipe: It has been cloned nearly 800 times.

Cloning comes in handy. If you lack programming experience, some of the more attractive and useful applications of Pipes may be too complicated to create. Mixing population data with disease data, for instance, and then plotting the results on a map could be challenging, but if you can clone a similar Pipe and edit it through trial and error, you'll save considerable time and consternation.

In the information professional trade literature, Jody Condit Fagan was the first librarian to report working successfully with Pipes. Although she admitted initial skepticism, she conquered the conundrum by exploring the published Pipes of other librarians. Like many new Pipes users, she began with the Fetch Feed sub-module and created a Pipe that grabbed the output of her library's RSS feed. With the success of that Pipe under her belt, she progressed to a Pipe that used the "RegEx" (regular expression) Operator; roughly speaking, RegEx is a programming term that approximates the Find and Replace function of some word processing software. Fagan reported she quickly created several additional, successful Pipes.[3]

Grabbing, Mixing, Sifting, and Sorting RSS Feeds

Nicole Engard, editor of *Library Mashups* (Information Today, Inc., 2009), also described grabbing news from RSS feeds, which, as I've mentioned, is probably the easiest Pipes mashup to construct. I asked Engard to describe her most basic but practical Pipes project. She replied, "I write for many websites and not everyone knows about all of them, so I decided to combine the RSS feeds from them all to one Yahoo! Pipe. This Pipe pulls in five RSS feeds and filters them based on author (since some of the sites I write for are multi-author sites) and finally it sorts them in descending publication date. This way people can subscribe to all of the content I write in one feed." She took the feeds from five blogs she is involved with (Library Mashups at mashups.web2learning.net, What I Learned Today at www.web2learning.net, Practical Open Source Software for Libraries at opensource.web2learning. net, ByWater Solutions at www.bywatersolutions.com/blog, and the Accidental Systems Librarian at tasl.web2learning.net) and "OR'ed" them together using the Fetch Feed sub-module. Next she connected Fetch Feed to a Filter sub-module and configured it to filter out all authors except "nicole." She then connected the Filter sub-module to a Sort sub-module and configured it to display items from the feeds by date of publication in descending order. Her last step was connecting the Sort sub-module to a Pipe output sub-module. The Pipe output sub-module takes the sorted information that originated at Fetch Feed, and displays it. You can run this working Pipe at pipes.yahoo.com/nengard/blogs.

Combining information from several feeds can be useful, especially if it is customized so that the output displays so that you see only items that are of the greatest interest to you. When I asked Nicole how frequently she uses Pipes, she replied, "I use Pipes on a regular basis for various tasks, both personal and professional. I find that while the Pipes tool can sometimes be a bit unstable (crashing and loading slowly), it is still the best tool out there for many of my mashup tasks. In addition to creating my own mashups with Pipes, I enjoy browsing through others' creations both to get ideas and to learn more about what Pipes could do. Just the other day I learned that Pipes is not limited to using Yahoo! Local for map mashups. You can use Google Maps by using slightly different modules in your pipe."[4]

More Success in the Field

Before I personally tried to use Pipes, I was skeptical when I read middle school media specialist Jeff Hastings's account of his test drive. He found Pipes "interesting" and added they were a "highly addictive tool."[5] I'm leery about anyone who seems overly enamored with technology, and I am always a little suspicious about any of Yahoo!'s resources. I mean, after all, the company takes its name from Jonathan Swift's epithet for a race of uncivilized beings. But Hastings's praise was not unfounded! As I began experimenting with them, I had to admit that I couldn't find anything to pan about these Pipes.

I've created several Pipes. My favorite is an RSS mashup. In my Bloglines RSS reader, I subscribe to the feed from Gary Price's ResourceShelf (www.resourceshelf.com/feed). ResourceShelf posts stories about technology, libraries, scholarly publishing, screencasts, and other assorted topics at such a rapid pace that if I fail to check my RSS reader every day, I fall hopelessly behind in my reading. The information ResourceShelf passes along always provokes thought, yet some of the postings simply don't matter to me. I'm not going to click the link about the Law Library of Congress digitizing Haitian legal resources, nor am I necessarily interested in a collection of games heading to a museum in Canada. But I am very interested in ebooks, databases, copyright, and wireless technology.

Using the experiences of Jody Condit Fagan, Nicole Engard, and a couple of video tutorials at YouTube (for example, see www.youtube.com/watch?v= y_9Rx25d4Fw), I constructed a Pipe that took the feed from ResourceShelf (along with six additional sources) and connected it to a keyword search through a User Input/Text Input sub-module. Taking a page directly from Engard, I removed duplicates with the Unique sub-module. The Searchable Library Technology RSS Feed Combiner (see Figures 13.5 and 13.6) is published at tinyurl.com/searchrss.

Author Bill Dyszel (*Microsoft Outlook for Dummies*) praised Yahoo! Pipes in *PC Magazine* but added, "Truly sophisticated mashups still demand coding and often require a Web server, but anyone can accomplish quite a lot with Yahoo! Pipes."[6] Despite Dyszel's assessment, some complex projects have been rendered with Pipes. The State Cancer Profile originating at Yale University shows how mashups may be used in healthcare (tinyurl.com/ 28ej2kv).[7] It does not rely on RSS, as so many Pipes seem to. Using two sources (www.cancer.gov and statecancerprofiles.cancer.gov) and Google Maps, the team of four researchers constructed a Pipe that employed the User

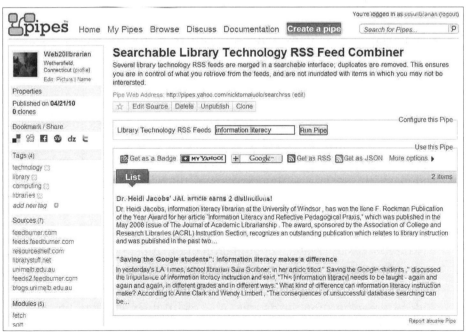

Figure 13.5   This Pipe uses seven sources and five sub-modules, including User Input (note the box for the user to enter keywords, adjacent to the Run Pipe button) and Unique. [Courtesy of Yahoo!]

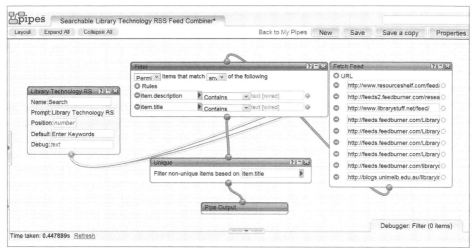

Figure 13.6   The canvas of the Searchable Library Technology RSS Feed
Combiner shows how the Pipe was created. [Courtesy of
Yahoo!]

Input sub-module and the Geotag sub-module to fetch an interactive map of
the U.S. displaying cancer mortality statistics.

Comprehensive documentation for Yahoo! Pipes is available at
pipes.yahoo.com/pipes/docs, but users can pick up some good ideas by
browsing or searching the Pipes website. Here are a few Pipes that may interest you:

- EduComm Twitter Group (tinyurl.com/6zph7e): "EduComm is a
  national conference designed to bring the best business and
  technology solutions to today's higher education leaders. EduComm
  promotes creative collaboration, shared information, and innovative
  ideas, with special attention to dynamic new leadership opportunities
  empowered by new technologies."

- Green Living (tinyurl.com/y522c63): This Pipe uses nine Sources and
  two Modules to create "a compilation of the most popular green living
  blogs" including Treehugger, Inhabitat, Autobloggreen, Greenbean,
  Dwell, and others. "Topics include building green, home improvement
  ideas, green automobile reviews, new technology, gadgets, lifestyles,"
  and more.

- GRIN (tinyurl.com/y3khghl): Prashamik Chatterjee, a technology
  consultant who is responsible for more than 100 Pipes, is the author

of this mashup on Genetics Robotics Information Technology and Nanotechnology.

- Issues in Education (tinyurl.com/y2za92l): This Pipe features news about the No Child Left Behind Act, standardized testing, homeschooling, literacy, and vouchers.

- Library Job Listings (tinyurl.com/y5kje5v): This Pipe retrieves "combined job listings for library careers in the United States and beyond."

- Library Literature Journals (tinyurl.com/445hczd): The tables of contents of many library literature journals can be found here.

- New Books With Cover Images (tinyurl.com/newbookcovers): This mashup is a natural for libraries. It takes the feed for new library books and combines it with book cover images from WorldCat.

- PNAS NEJM JBC JCS MCB AACR Journals Filtered (tinyurl.com/y7sbouq): This Pipe "collects RSS feeds from scientific journals listed in title, and allows you to filter on words included in the title and abstract to generate a feed."

- Quick Online Tips: Technology News, Blogging Tips, Computers and Web 2.0 (tinyurl.com/y53jeab): This Pipe is designed to aggregate the current day's technology news.

- Technology (tinyurl.com/yyqy2gg): This Pipe features "information about technological gadgets: iPods, cell phones, computers, digital cameras and more."

- Technology News (tinyurl.com/y5853mj): "Information Technology News from around the world [combines] feeds from Slashdot, InfoWeek, InfoWorld, CNET, PCMag, MIT, etc."

- WorldCat.org Citations (tinyurl.com/m63jk5): "Search WorldCat for books and get their citations in APA, Chicago, Harvard, MLA, or Turabian format."

Endnotes

1. Dan Farber, "Teqlo to Let Users Assemble Web Applications," ZDNet, October 11, 2006, accessed August 3, 2011, www.zdnet.com/blog/btl/teqlo-to-let-users-assemble-web-applications/3766.

2. Eric Schonfeld, "Deadpool: Teqlo Finds Out that Mashups Don't Make Money," TechCrunch, November 8, 2007, accessed August 3, 2011, www.techcrunch.com/2007/11/08/deadpool-teqlo-finds-out-that-mashups-dont-make-money.

3. Jody Condit Fagan, "Mashing Up Multiple Web Feeds Using Yahoo! Pipes," *Computers in Libraries* 27 (November 2007): 10–17.

4. Nicole Engard, email message to author, April 24, 2010.

5. Jeff Hastings, "Yahoo! Pipes: Interactive Feed Aggregator/Manipulator," *School Library Journal*, June 2007, accessed August 3, 2011, www.schoollibraryjournal.com/article/CA6448203.html.

6. Bill Dyszel, "Create No-Code Mashups with Yahoo! Pipes," *PC Magazine*, October 10, 2007, accessed August 3, 2011, www.pcmag.com/print_article2/0,1217,a=216742,00.asp?hidPrint=true.

7. Kei-Hoi Cheung et al., "HCLS 2.0/3.0: Health Care and Life Sciences Data Mashup Using Web 2.0/3.0," *Journal of Biomedical Informatics* 41(2008): 694–705.

Chapter 14

Flickr

My first exposure to online "photo sharing" in a library environment was early in 2005. The library director sent staff a link to his Picasa web albums account so we could view pictures he had taken of the building's first floor— a floor which would soon be gutted to undergo a major renovation. As the project continued, he periodically photographed the improvements and uploaded them to his account, and each time, he would send an email that included the link to his Picasa account. Time passed, and this online photo journal chronicled the metamorphosis every step of the way. This is one possible use of a web-based photo sharing program, but there are limitless possibilities, and there are dozens of photo sharing websites.

When I determined which UContent resources needed to be covered in this book, I read reviews of multiple sites, combined that information with Alexa traffic rankings, and researched the ways the general public and information professionals were using the resources. But for this chapter I deferred to name recognition and reputation. Flickr is the photo sharing resource of choice not only because of its involvement with the Library of Congress and the establishment of the Commons on Flickr, but because it enjoys such popularity with the general public and librarians (visit www.flickr.com/press_archive.gne to see a concise list of links to the venture's accolades). Google's Picasa software, with numerous advanced editing capabilities, is a great download (for an excellent tutorial on Picasa 3, see Janine Weston's 4-minute video at www.youtube.com/watch?v=ojRQPrfacXw), and Picasa is a great place to upload photos and share them (or limit them to your eyes only), but even with Google branding behind it, Picasa doesn't rival Flickr in terms of popularity. For example, a search of the LISTA database for *(librar* or information pro*)* and *picasa* (including searching within "all text") yields only two documents, but a search for *(librar* or information pro*)* and *flickr* retrieves 143 items (retrieval is higher for both searches in various education databases, but the proportion of articles is roughly the same).

A Love Affair With Photo Sharing

When a web service demonstrates staggering growth, I assume its users have made a strong, durable, positive connection with that service. In February 2005, Flickr had enrolled 270,000 users;[1] by 2008, an unofficial calculation put the number at 8 million, and in mid-summer 2011, the community had swelled to almost 24 million members.[2] People enjoy taking photographs, and with a digital camera you can take an almost limitless number of pictures hoping one of them will be just the right shot. Perhaps we print a few of the photos, but we'll upload, email, and post dozens more. To determine the current number of images hosted at Flickr, just go to the site's Explore page (www.flickr.com/explore) and click Most Recent Uploads. Look at the URL of the most recent photo. For example, in mid-July 2011, this strategy happened to produce the following URL: www.flickr.com/photos/rika76101/5954231605, thus indicating the site was on the verge of hosting 6 billion images (i.e., the group of numbers following the last slash is the number of total photos). To find the number of photos uploaded in the last minute, sign into your Flickr account and go to www.flickr.com/photos. On July 19, 2011, at noon eastern time Flickr stated "there were 6,003 uploads in the last minute." (This number changes constantly but is always between 5,000 and 6,000+.)

Fortune and Fame?

Although the amateur paparazzi snapping photos at ballgames and family reunions comprise a segment of Flickr's users, the site is also a hub for both professional photographers and serious hobbyists. The pros confer and critique one another's work. In 2011, there were nearly 3,000 groups with the words *professional* and *photography* in their description. Flickr's Pro Corner (www.flickr.com/groups/procorner), a group more than 17,000 members and 210,000 uploads (in 2011), is a forum where professional and semiprofessional photographers discuss lenses and equipment, lighting techniques, copyright, editing, and other pertinent topics. Landscape photographers, portrait photographers, wedding photographers, and real estate photographers are all represented by groups within Flickr. The site is a natural for pro photographers and photography firms wanting to showcase their talent.

Professionals also offer amateurs guidance. The groups in which thousands of individuals with a passion for camerawork participate include To Improve Your Photography Skills, Photography Mentor, and Am I Talented? From Amateur to Professional. Do you use a Nikon D3000? There are about 7,000 groups you could join. Or is your "third eye" a Canon PowerShot SX100IS? Sign up with the PowerShot SX100IS Addicts group.

In addition to using Flickr to share photos with family, friends, and the wider user audience, amateur photographers may find that their work has been "discovered." Newspapers, including Liverpool's *Daily Post*, for instance, encourage shutterbugs by publishing photos they find on Flickr with appropriate Creative Commons licensing. Not only does the *Daily Post* regularly run readers' photos, but it also has its own Flickr group, with 1,159 members who had, as of summer 2011, contributed 54,000 photos to its "photostream" (www.flickr.com/groups/liverpooldailypost08/pool). Because publishers are keeping an eye on Flickr, what begins as a hobby may become lucrative. *Time* magazine examined 100,000 Flickr images as it prepared its slideshow of then president-elect Barack Obama (tinyurl.com/64z6dg). An accompanying article stated, "In keeping with the theme of citizen art, we open our Person of the Year package with a dazzling array of images culled from those created by thousands of individuals from around the world and posted on the photo sharing site Flickr. Obama always said his candidacy was not about him, but 'you,' and now, along with Flickr, we're helping give 'you' a voice."[3] Flickr member B. Jefferson Bolender earned $1,500 by selling her images—not a fortune, but enough to pay for a new camera; one of her images appeared as the cover of the *New York Times Magazine* on August 16, 2008. The Flickr Collection on Getty Images (tinyurl.com/23jfopc) is this story's latest chapter. Getty monitors public photostreams for photos, and a new option was added in 2010 that allows Flickr members to enable a "request for license" badge on photos they upload; this license will bring their images to the attention of Getty Images more quickly. If Getty elects to license a photo, it pays the photographer if the image is used. By summer 2011 Getty had selected more than 120,000 Flickr photos; the fee to use one of them begins at $5.

Getting Started With Flickr

If you've used Flickr (or have uploaded any photo to a website or sent one to a friend via email), you know it's so easy a neanderthalensis can do it. You have several choices for uploading:

1. Use the Flickr Desktop Uploadr, a downloadable program for PCs and Macs. It uses a drag-and-drop interface and is ideal for large uploads.

2. Use the upload webpage at www.flickr.com/photos/upload.

3. Use the "basic" uploader at www.flickr.com/photos/upload/basic, which works like attaching files to email.

4. Email the photo to your account.

5. Use third-party plug-ins.

6. Use the Flickr application programmable interface (API) available at www.flickr.com/services/api/upload.api.html for batch uploading.

After you've uploaded your photos, you can add titles and descriptions to the images. Tag them with keywords for easy searching. If you are a librarian adding images to a library photostream, provide at least one tag for each item (you can apply up to 75 tags to each photo). This will help you and others find the images you contribute, and encourages other viewers to add more tags. "While the idea of a patron creating a taxonomy, or even simply the idea of the folksonomy, may sound absurd to some librarians, the fact of the matter is tagging is a hot property on the cyber landscape," says WebJunction's Andrea Mercado. "Librarians, as a rule, should never cease to excel at organizing even using new systems, or evolving their skills to meet the needs and interests of patrons. An excellent way for librarians to get a grip on the homemade metadata movement is to guide patrons on how to effectively tag their photos."[4]

Flickr can connect you seamlessly to its partner Picnik to quickly edit images (remove red eye, crop, sharpen, etc.). After editing your photos, you can use the Batch Organizer to perform common operations over large numbers of photos (e.g., change the permissions for who may view the photos). Most users organize their images into sets that have a common theme (e.g., vacation, holidays).

In your account settings under the Privacy & Permissions tab, you may choose to keep your images private or share your photos with different categories of potential viewers (some examples include everyone using Flickr, groups that you belong to, your contacts, or your family). Other privacy settings that you manage include determining whether others may comment or apply tags to your images. You may also designate a usage license if you want to allow others to reuse your photos or perhaps restrict use (e.g., "all rights reserved").

Flickr is not without its commercial side. It can connect you with one of its partners, Snapfish, for ordering prints, making calendars, creating posters, and more. The more frequently you use Flickr, the more you'll learn about its features. For example, although it's not immediately evident, you'll discover that when you click an image in your photostream and then click Share, you'll be able to copy the unique URL for the photo (so you can link to it) or grab the embed code to place it on a webpage (see Figure 14.1 and the next section for more Flickr tips). This is how I embedded photos in maps I made at Google My Places (see Chapter 12).

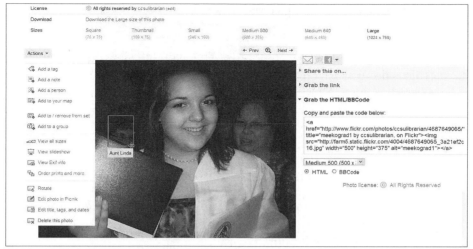

Figure 14.1   Note Actions (on the left), including Add a Note, which draws
the rectangle to which text may be added. Note Share options
(on the right), which give the user HTML to embed the image on
a webpage or the URL to link directly to the photo, and provides
options for emailing, posting to Facebook, or sending to
WordPress. [Courtesy of Flickr]

Things You Can Do With Flickr

Browsing through photographs may be passive, but Flickr is highly interactive. Here are just a few of the things you can do:

- Visitors can designate any images they view as favorites by clicking the Favorite link (appearing above a photo) while viewing an individual picture. To retrieve the picture (i.e., see your Favorites), you need to sign in, access your photostream, and then click Favorites (plural) from the main navigation links.

- When you encounter an interesting pic, consider making the photographer a contact. While viewing an individual image, look over to the right near the user's name and click Add Contact.

- Here's another social element of the site: Post a comment on images that you like (or ask a question of a user you've never met). Your comment links back to you; anyone viewing the comment can use the link to visit your photostream.

- Tags may be applied by the image creator or by people who visit the image (if the image creator has enabled tagging). The tag is added to the photo, and the image creator can see (and contact) the person who contributed the tag.

- You may also add notes to photos. While you are viewing an image, this is done by clicking Actions and then Add a Note. Enter a comment and click Save. When you (or another user) mouse over the area of the photo where you left the note, the note's text will appear.

- You can join a group. There are thousands of them, and they are all easy to locate via search. After joining a group, you may participate in discussions by replying to comments or posting a new topic.

- Members of Flickr groups may add an uploaded photo to a group, by clicking Actions then Add to group. The image will appear in the photostream of the designated group.

- Like a photo? Want to post it on your Facebook wall or blog? Click the Share arrow and select one of the default sharing sites or configure your sharing preferences to send it directly to your blog.

- Flickr includes photo editing. Under Actions click Edit Photo in Picnik. The edit mode will help you sharpen the image, get rid of red eye, crop, resize, and rotate.

- Display Flickr images on your website by creating Flickr badges. Badges may be horizontal or vertical strips of your images (Flickr will generate the code you need to embed the badge on your webpage). Start at www.flickr.com/badge.gne. (See Figure 14.2 for an example of a Flickr badge.)

- Embed a slideshow in a webpage. Begin by opening a set of images from your photostream and clicking the slideshow graphic to the right of the screen. Once the images are in slideshow mode, click Share in the upper right corner of the screen, grab the embed code, and paste it into a webpage.

- At the bottom of most pages, you'll be able to grab the RSS feed code. This will allow you to subscribe to the feed in a feed reader. To display some items from the feed on a webpage, try a feed-to-javascript utility such as Feed2JS (www.feed2js.org).

- Look for the appropriate app at www.flickr.com/tools/mobile and use your Flickr account on your smartphone to send pictures from your phone to your photostream.

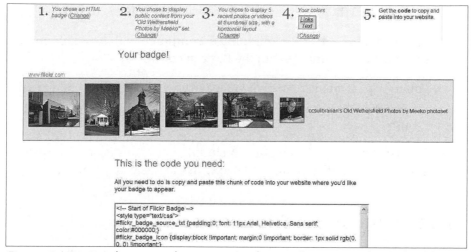

Figure 14.2   Display a random rotation of your photostream by embedding a Flickr badge. [Courtesy of Flickr]

Please visit my page at web.ccsu.edu/library/tomaiuolon/UContent/flickr badges.htm to see examples of Flickr badges, RSS feeds, and slideshows. On the same page, you'll also find links to over a dozen library or librarian Flickr groups with varied foci (web.ccsu.edu/library/tomaiuolon/UContent/flickr badges.htm#smattering).

Free or Pro?

Individuals who are serious about using Flickr as their primary archival and social photo sharing service should consider a Pro account, which in 2011 cost $24.95 per year. A library committing to a Flickr presence would also benefit from a Pro account. A Pro account has several advantages over the Basic account, including the ability to upload an unlimited number of photos. A price of $24.95 a year is all the Library of Congress pays, and its photostream contains 14,000 items. Here's a breakdown of features for both types of accounts:

- Pro accepts unlimited photo uploads (20 megabytes per photo), compared with a 300-megabyte monthly photo limit for Basic.

- Pro allows unlimited video uploads (90 seconds max, 500 megabytes per video), compared with two video uploads per month (150-megabyte maximum per video) for Basic.

- Pro enables HD Video playback (not available to Basic users).

- Pro accounts have unlimited storage, compared with a maximum of 200 most recent images with the Basic account.

- You may post single photos or videos from your collection in up to 60 groups with a Pro account; Basic users may post a photo in up to 10 groups.

- Pro users get statistical reports, including view counts and referrer statistics; no statistics are available with the Basic account.

Libraryland Meets Flickrverse

Librarians have covered Flickr in articles, blog entries, and book chapters. Michael Stephens, blogging at TameTheWeb (www.tametheweb.com), is an ardent Flickr advocate. Many librarians, including Sarah Houghton-Jan[5] (www.librarianinblack.net), were influenced by Stephens's blog posting of December 13, 2005, in which he gives "10 Reasons to Use Flickr at Your Library."[6] They include promoting book signings, showcasing specific programs, posting photostreams for friends of libraries groups, and publicizing book displays. In a 2006 article "Priceless Images: Getting Started With Flickr," Stephens urges librarians to "take advantage of the graphical nature of the web and the interactive nature of many Web 2.0 sites to make a big splash with pictures—images of our libraries, our programs, ourselves."[7]

There are more than 6,000 Flickr Groups with *library, libraries, librarian, librarians*, or *librarianship* in their name or description. The raisons d'être of these groups vary, but several commonalities emerge. The librarians in these groups want to share something about themselves, their libraries, the profession, or their collections. "The simplest way to communicate the library and its spirit was to show it," writes Lichen Rancourt, head of technology at New Hampshire's Manchester City Library. "I opened a Flickr account in the library's name. This allowed us to share photos of the library and capture some of the warmth, diversity, culture, and social benefit as well as give the public some insight into the lives, professional and otherwise, of the staff."[8] The Manchester City Library's photostream (www.flickr.com/photos/manchesterlibrary), which began in October 2007, is updated regularly and contains more than 1,000 photos.

Flickr use is not unique to any particular type of library, nor is it unique to libraries in the U.S. The Massachusetts Institute of Technology Libraries has a Pro account (www.flickr.com/photos/mit-libraries), as does the Irene DuPont Library at St. Andrew's School (a private secondary school) in

Delaware (www.flickr.com/photos/49669925@N05). There are 200 items in the Copenhagen Public Libraries photostream (www.flickr.com/photos/kkb) and 150 in Ontario, Canada's Waterloo Public Library's photostream (www.flickr.com/photos/waterloopubliclibrary). The Glasgow (U.K.) School of Art's Archives and Library (www.flickr.com/people/gsalib), with 1,700 uploads, has a Pro account.

Librarians have demonstrated considerable creativity in what they've uploaded to their photostreams. For example, the Lansing (IL) Public Library posted 30 posters in the style of the American Library Association's (ALA's) celebrity "READ" series (www.flickr.com/photos/lansinglibrary/sets/72057594106946697), but rather than George Clooney or Taylor Swift with books in their hands, its set depicts local celebrities, including the police chief reading *One Fish Two Fish Red Fish Blue Fish* and the mayor reading the *American Heritage Illustrated History of the Presidents*. With more than 2,700 uploads, this library is serious about promoting itself on Flickr (and making an impression on not only patrons but the town's politicians).

The Skokie (IL) Public Library's photostream (www.flickr.com/people/skokiepl) also capitalized on the READ-poster zeitgeist. Before Barack Obama became president, he posed for a READ poster for the library (www.flickr.com/photos/skokiepl/sets/72157594171085212). You can look into the ALA READ Design Studio at www.alastore.ala.org/readdesignstudioinfo/default.aspx.

Library Snapshot Day

Snapshots play a featured role in a promotion designed to increase awareness of the importance of libraries and the activities that go on within them. What culminated in a national campaign aimed at making politicians aware of libraries' usefulness began with Norma Blake, the New Jersey state librarian, in 2008. Her "Libraries Transform Lives Task Force," with 40 members from all types of libraries in New Jersey, held monthly think-tank meetings aimed at creating a program that would provide indisputable evidence of libraries' value: "We wanted to come up with a simple, effective method to capture all the ways that libraries offer vital services every single day. We decided that we would ask library staff to document in statistics, stories and photographs 'a day in the life' of their library. We knew that we could take this data and aggregate it and come up with powerful statistics that would show the positive impact libraries have on community members in every part of our state on a daily basis."[9]

On February 9, 2009, a blog posting on behalf of the New Jersey State Library rhetorically asked, "What would New Jersey be like if there were no libraries? What valuable services do we provide on a daily basis that simply go unrecognized and unappreciated?" Announcing that its first Snapshot Day would follow 10 days later, it continued, "The New Jersey State Library and the New Jersey Library Association need your help. We're taking a snapshot of a typical day in the life of New Jersey's libraries."[10] A total of 250 libraries participated. In addition to the 1,162 photos and 11 videos uploaded to Flickr (www.flickr.com/photos/njla/sets/72157613977204372), thousands of patrons' comments were collected (see snapshot.njlibraries.org/comments.html and snapshot.njlibraries.org/comments.pdf). To educate state policymakers and library patrons about the impact of libraries on society, including improving literacy and reducing unemployment, the New Jersey State Library and the New Jersey Library Association jointly announced the following information about the first Snapshot Day:

In just one day:

- 161,367 people walked through the doors of New Jersey libraries.

- 156,793 books, movies, and more were borrowed from New Jersey libraries.

- 27,742 people used computers at New Jersey libraries.

- 18,537 questions were answered at New Jersey libraries.

- 1,245 people got employment help at New Jersey libraries.

- 1,241 programs were offered at New Jersey libraries.

- 984 people learned computer skills at New Jersey libraries.[11]

Each participating library generated "day in the life" statistics, and Snapshot Day provided concrete proof of the value of libraries, to be passed along to mayors and council members. Moreover, 2010 *Library Journal* Mover and Shaker Peggy Cadigan, associate state librarian for innovation and outreach strategies for the New Jersey State Library (and early advocate of Snapshot Day), took the campaign to another level. She selected 24 pictures from the momentous New Jersey Snapshot Day Flickr photostream. Those images were aggregated into one poster, with copies of the poster delivered to every legislator in New Jersey. (See it at www.ala.org/ala/issuesadvocacy/advleg/advocacyuniversity/librarysnapshotday/posterandtotebag.cfm) A second New Jersey Library Snapshot Day took place on October 9, 2009 (more information is at newsletter.njstatelib.org/blog/2009/10/16/snapshot-day-at-the-nj-state-library).

At the 2010 ALA Midwinter Meeting, New Jersey state librarian Blake presented ideas and results from the first two Snapshot Days to Marci Merola, director of ALA's Office for Library Advocacy. With the help of a primer written by Cadigan, which covered everything a library needs to do to participate in a Snapshot Day, including useful information on why Snapshot Day will help justify funding to libraries, interested librarians had access to the New Jersey Library Association wiki containing forms for collecting statistics and comments, step-by-step instructions on how to upload photos to Flickr, a promotional page featuring templates and graphics for Snapshot Day publications, and a list of "20 Easy Ways to Make Snapshot Day a Success." The ALA Advocacy Coordinating Group, along with the ALA Chapter Relations Committee and the Chief Officers of State Library Agencies, asked libraries across the U.S. to reserve a day in April 2010 for National Snapshot Day. (Cadigan's primer is posted at njla.pbworks.com/f/20+Easy+Ways.doc.) A total of 27 states took part in the spring 2010 National Snapshot Day; some of the libraries are listed at www.ala.org/ala/issuesadvocacy/advleg/state localefforts/snapshotday/states.cfm.

Here are more links to Snapshot Day results. Remember, you don't need to enter these URLs manually—just consult the *UContent* Chapter 14 webpage at web.ccsu.edu/library/tomaiuolon/UContent/photos.htm. Note that although most slideshows, photos, and videos are hosted at Flickr, a few institutions chose other photo and video sharing resources:

- "A Chance to Show Off: Library Snapshot Day," *American Libraries Magazine* (www.americanlibrariesmagazine.org/inside-scoop/ library-snapshot-day)

- Gail Borden Public Library District (Elgin, Illinois) Snapshot Day Video (www.youtube.com/watch?v=_lyNK-pZuYk)

- I Love Libraries, ALA (www.ilovelibraries.org/loveyourlibrary/ librarysnapshotday/librarysnapshotday.cfm)

- Connecticut Snapshot Day (www.flickr.com/photos/ctlibraries snapshot2010)

- Georgia Snapshot Day (www.flickr.com/photos/georgialibrary association/sets/72157623555847346)

- Idaho Snapshot Day (www.idaholibraries.org/node/675)

- Illinois Snapshot Day (www.flickr.com/groups/illinoissnapshotday)

- Iowa Snapshot Day (www.flickr.com/groups/iowasnapshotday/pool)

- Kansas Snapshot Day (snapshotkansas.wordpress.com)

- Maine Snapshot Day (www.maine.gov/msl/snapshot/results.htm)

- New York Snapshot Day (www.protectnylibraries.org/snapshots/index.php)

- North Dakota Snapshot Day (www.flickr.com/groups/ndlibsnapshot2010/pool)

- Ohio Snapshot Day (www.flickr.com/groups/ohiosnapshotday2010)

- Pennsylvania Snapshot Day (www.flickr.com/photos/snapshot_pa/sets/72157622692239937/show)

- South Carolina Snapshot Day (www.flickr.com/groups/nlwsccontest2009/pool)

- Utah Snapshot Day (www.flickr.com/photos/utahstatelibrary/sets/72157624000630128/show)

- Virginia Snapshot Day (www.flickr.com/groups/snapshotvalib)

- West Virginia Snapshot Day (www.flickr.com/photos/wvsnapshotday)

- Western Illinois University Snapshot Day, 2010 (www.wiu.edu/library/events/snapshotday2010)

- Wisconsin Snapshot Day (www.flickr.com/groups/wisconsinlibraries)

- Young Adult Library Services Association Blog on Snapshot Day (yalsa.ala.org/blog/2010/04/27/library-snapshot-day)

Adventures in Crowdsourcing

One startling example of Flickr as a venue for crowdsourcing was reported in 2009 when Sameer Agarwal, then heading up a team of researchers at the University of Washington but now a Google employee, harvested 150,000 Flickr images and constructed a three-dimensional model of Rome, Italy.[12] To accomplish something of this magnitude, consider that several information scientists needed to access a huge database of images licensed for reuse. While a compelling illustration of crowdsourcing, it is not the example most information professionals would recall in the Flickr context.

Picture this: You are a trained cataloger with a backlog of 3,000 items to process. You don't have a clue as to the descriptive details for any of them. Would you have ever thought of inviting the world to do it for you? This is essentially what the Library of Congress did on January 16, 2008, when, after paying $24.95 for a Pro account, it used a Flickr API to upload 3,115 images, becoming the original and still foremost entity at the Commons on Flickr. (See the Library of Congress's Flickr photostream at www.flickr.com/photos/library_of_congress.)

While planning the pilot project, associates at the Library of Congress formulated several research questions: "Could web users contribute useful information, knowledge, and energy for the Library? Could the Library tap the knowledge and energy of the user community to augment its own efforts? As users become increasingly accustomed to tagging online content for their own purposes, would they be interested in contributing information for community benefit? What's the quality of the information gained through crowdsourcing? Would the pay-off justify the Library's investments in such an effort?"[13]

Early in 2007, members of Library of Congress's Office of Strategic Initiatives articulated three objectives for a possible pilot program with Flickr:

- Increase awareness by sharing photographs from the Library's collections with people who enjoy images but might not visit the Library's own website.

- Gain a better understanding of how social tagging and community input could benefit both the Library and users of the collections.

- Gain experience participating in the emergent web communities that would be interested in the kinds of materials in the Library's collections.

Flickr was chosen because of its popularity. The single obstacle was that none of Flickr's available "rights statement options" were appropriate for the Library of Congress's images, which all bear the "no known copyright restrictions" statement. Flickr accommodated this new designation by instituting a separate area of its site for these images, the area now called the Commons. The project was social from the word *go*; only the Library of Congress blog and the Flickr blog announced the birth of the Commons, yet it took off overnight (see blog.flickr.net/en/2008/01/16/many-hands-make-light-work).

Matt Raymond, director of communications for the Library of Congress, is a master of bon mots. On the day the images appeared at the Commons, he explained that the Library of Congress had extensive collections that he wished could be shared with the world; alas, he sighed, "There are only so many hours in the day, so many staff in Library offices and so many dollars in the budget." The initial upload of 3,115 photographs came from two popular Library of Congress collections, the George Grantham Bain Collection, and the Farm Security Administration/Office of War Information collection (photos of rural or farm life and World War II mobilization taken between 1939 and 1944).

Raymond did not call it *crowdsourcing*, but he did tell readers the library hoped the project would "enhance metadata." Nor was he explicit about what Flickr users should do, although he did mention that photos might be missing key information "such as where the photo was taken and who is pictured." He continued, "If such information is collected via Flickr members, it can potentially enhance the quality of the bibliographic records for the images." Raymond stated that each item initially had only one tag: *Library of Congress*.[14]

In addition to the *Library of Congress* tag, each image bore two machine tags correlating the Library of Congress and Flickr photographs through identification numbers. There must be some truth to the "less is more" adage because by the next day, 19,000 tags (4,000 of them unique) and more than 500 comments had been applied to the photostream.[15]

By the fall, the Library of Congress had uploaded 1,500 additional photos. A Library of Congress report published in October 2008 released additional impressive statistics. Comparing the period from January to May 2008 with the same period in 2007, the average monthly traffic coming from Flickr to the Library of Congress website had increased 2,205 percent! Items in the photostream had been viewed more than 10.4 million times; 79 percent of the photos had been made favorites on Flickr; 15,000 Flickr members had made the Library of Congress a contact; 7,166 comments had been left on 2,873 photos by 2,562 unique Flickr accounts; 67,176 tags were added by 2,518 unique Flickr accounts; nine photos had reached the limit of 75 tags (and people commented that they were disappointed they could not add more tags on those photos); and 25 instances of UContent were deemed inappropriate and removed.[16]

Library of Congress associates working on the project learned that their interactions with Flickr members could take on a more casual tone than they were accustomed to at the Library's reference desks. They also noted that the photos elicited comments and participation from experts, stimulated memory and conversations about the past, and were viewed by Flickr members from all over the world who were willing to reflect on related experiences.

Although there was some concern over the control of the images, the report stated that the benefits far outweighed the risks. The Library of Congress had tapped into the community's enthusiasm while providing the public with expanded access to historical materials. "We satisfied a desire for high-quality content without copyright restrictions. Web 2.0 is all about sharing. Providing a rich pool of images that users can easily add to their blogs, download, and reuse in a variety of creative ways satisfied that voracious appetite for unrestricted content." Furthermore, Flickr member input had resulted in the enhancement of more than 500 records in the Library of Congress's Prints and Photographs Online Catalog.[17] The *Boston Globe* got it right with its article "Everyone's a Historian Now," which mentioned the Library of Congress and Flickr.[18] In September 2009, the Library of Congress photostream had 6,700 images; by midsummer 2011, the number of images had nearly reached 14,000. (For more on this topic, check out Library of Congress Photos on Flickr: Frequently Asked Questions, www.loc.gov/rr/print/flickr_pilot_faq.html.)

Although the Library of Congress is the original and foremost institution at the Commons on Flickr, 52 other members had joined as of July 2011. (There had been speculation that Flickr may have been considering divesting itself of the Commons, but the Commons appears to be alive and well and accepting new applicants, with its newest member, the Royal Library of Denmark joining in June 2011.) The members may have had different motivations for deciding to place materials online with Flickr, but according to a 2009 survey of 26 participating institutions, all but one said the primary reason was to "expose collections to a broader audience/facilitate discovery of our materials." The second-most-popular reason listed was to "utilize Web 2.0 features to engage user involvement and discussion."[19]

Differences Between Flickr and the Commons on Flickr

The Commons on Flickr states its two main objectives as 1) to increase access to publicly held photography collections and 2) to provide a way for the general public to contribute information and knowledge (i.e., through tagging, commenting, and other social media activities). This contrasts with the main Flickr site in three ways. First, the main Flickr site is generally used by members to share contemporary photos. The 53 members of the Commons on Flickr are collectively called *cultural heritage institutions*, with photos more historical in nature. Second, while anyone may create a Flickr account, there is an application-and-review process involved when an institution wishes to join the Commons. Finally, the rights statement that accompanies all images in the Commons on Flickr states "no known copyright restrictions." So while individuals who upload photos at the main site may choose to reserve all rights or provide a Creative Commons license, every image uploaded to the Commons bears the "no known copyright restrictions" statement, and every member of the Commons accepts this statement as a condition of membership. In fact, it is the basis for the founding of the Commons.

Because there are no known copyright restrictions, it may be nice to think that all the images in the Commons can be used by anybody for any purpose. This is not necessarily the case; there are quite a few conditions that may warrant the "no known copyright" statement, and it is important to understand what they are. Here is Flickr's elaboration of the rights statement (see www.flickr.com/commons/usage).

Participating institutions may have various reasons for determining that "no known copyright restrictions" exist, such as:

1. The copyright is in the public domain because it has expired;

2. The copyright was injected into the public domain for other reasons, such as failure to adhere to required formalities or conditions;

3. The institution owns the copyright but is not interested in exercising control; or

4. The institution has legal rights sufficient to authorize others to use the work without restrictions.

Under "The Commons," cultural institutions that have reasonably concluded that a photograph is free of copyright restrictions are invited to share such photograph under their new usage guideline called "no known copyright restrictions."

By asserting "no known copyright restrictions," participating institutions are sharing the benefit of their research without providing an expressed or implied warranty to others who would like to use or reproduce the photograph. If you make use of a photo from the Commons, you are reminded to conduct an independent analysis of applicable law before proceeding with a particular new use.[20]

Flickr Groups

Library promotion and archival photographs aside, librarians show off their whimsical predilections in some Flickr groups. (Visit Librarians in Showercaps at www.flickr.com/groups/419254@N21 and Librarians' Desks at www.flickr.com/groups/librariansdesks, and be certain to visit the famous Librarian Trading Cards at www.flickr.com/groups/librariancards.) The groups, however, can also take on a more serious mien. Using Flickr as a documentation resource, more than 500 members of the 365 Days Library Project group (www.flickr.com/groups/365libs) are committed to adding one image per day to the group photostream. The Library Websites—Mobile Interfaces Group (www.flickr.com/photos/users_lib/sets/72157606324688497) is a forum for showcasing different graphical user interface designs for hand-helds. With 166 members, the Archives & Archivists Group (www.flickr.com/groups/archivists) has uploaded nearly 6,000 items. Information profession-als also create groups for specific events. For instance, 29 people joined The Future is Now: Libraries and Museums in Virtual Worlds, 2010 and docu-mented a March 2010 virtual conference on Second Life (www.flickr.com/groups/1401109@N22).

Other information professionals share images of individuals as well as internal and external events. At www.flickr.com/photos/theloneconsultant, you will find—you guessed it—the Lone Consultant. His profile states only that he is "a hired IT gun [who] takes on Toronto." Incite Research, based at the University of Surrey (U.K.), is a group of researchers at www.flickr.com/photos/incite concerned with critical inquiry. Forrester Research Group, in Cambridge, Massachusetts (www.flickr.com/photos/forresterresearchinc), and MMR Research, in Roswell, Georgia (www.flickr.com/photos/127222 32@N04), are both market research firms with Flickr Pro accounts; their pho-tostreams cover meetings, employees, and customers.

Behind these groups are their members, moderators, and administrators. Administrators create the groups and regularly post new items or begin new discussions. These last two activities are essential for holding members' inter-est and, in turn, motivating members to post and comment. Michael Porter, whose sobriquet is *libraryman*, is a Flickr advocate and an expert in all things Flickr. His participation in Flickr photo sharing is stratospheric. Porter belongs to 276 Flickr groups and has more than 1,500 Flickr contacts. He is also the administrator of Libraries and Librarians, a major Flickr group connecting 3,776 information professionals across six continents (www.flickr.com/groups/librariesandlibrarians). Libraries and Librarians has an impressive interactive track record, with a total of 633 comments in 95 discussions going back to the group's 2005 inception. Its photostream, essentially an ongoing Library Snapshot Day for the world, consists of 41,000 uploads. Along with Steve Lawson of the Tutt Library at Colorado College, Porter, who is commu-nications manager at WebJunction, covered the basics of Flickr during Week 4 of Five Weeks to a Social Library, with a webcast called Social Networking, Flickr, and Massively Multiplayer Online Games/Online Worlds. The presenta-tion, accessible at www.sociallibraries.com/course/week4, still wears well.

How to Create and Administer a Flickr Group

Flickr is nothing if not easy to use. If you're a member, you're a potential group creator and group administrator. I created a group called Librarians

Information Professionals Playing Musical Instruments and designated myself as the group "Admin." (I know that sounds weird, but Flickr only permits a certain number of characters in a group's name. I couldn't even squeeze in an ampersand.) From the main navigation menu (at the top of any Flickr page), follow these steps:

1. Click Groups, and then click Create a New Group.

2. Choose the type of group you want to create: Public (anyone can join), Public (by invitation only), and Private (great for families or groups of friends). Click Create.

3. Name your group and give it a description (if your group is public, use words that people might enter in a search). Then click Next.

4. You'll be asked "What would you like to display to *non-members* on your group page? (Members can see everything)." Select Group Discussion (display a list of recent discussions with links to each topic), Group Photo Pool (display the most recent additions to the group pool and a link to all the content in the group pool), or both (sharing your images and comments with others is the main idea, right?). Then click Next.

5. Choose how you will refer to the Administrators, Moderators, and Members. Accept defaults, and then click All Done.

6. Next, assign keywords to your group to aid others in searching for it, upload a group icon, and create an easy-to-remember alias URL (mine is www.flickr.com/groups/musicallibrarians). Click Save.

7. Flickr prompts you to Add Something. It's a good idea to upload a couple of photos and start an initial discussion. Keep adding items regularly so members and potential members will consider it an active group.

8. Promote your new group (if you're a librarian, post a promo comment to the Libraries and Librarians group), and wait for the photostream to grow.

Flickr and Creative Commons

Flickr is a social networking site where we can build communities by posting comments, making contacts, and contributing images and video. It's also a great place to show off our buildings, events, staff, books or anything else we can photograph. Using Flickr to host images of historical maps, which the University of Connecticut Library does, is a logical use (see www.flickr.com/photos/uconnlibrariesmagic/sets). But there are still other ways we can use Flickr. For example, if we want to use the work of others in our classrooms, libraries, or publications, Flickr can help by allowing us to search the site's photostreams by Creative Commons license.

You control the usage rights for the pictures in your photostream. After you upload a photo, you can designate a rights setting by clicking on the individual image and scrolling to the bottom of the screen. On the right, under Owner settings, you may change the default settings by clicking the Edit link which appears to the right of the default rights statement under your photo. After clicking the Edit link, you'll be able to assign a Creative Commons license to the photo, or you may choose "all rights reserved." Figure 14.3 shows the "Set a license for this photo" menu.

Creative Commons, initially funded by Duke University's Center for the Public Domain, released its first copyright licenses in 2002. In 2009, Creative Commons estimated that 350 million works carried a Creative Commons license (see www.creativecommons.org/about/history). The idea behind Creative Commons is to make it easy for content creators to share their work

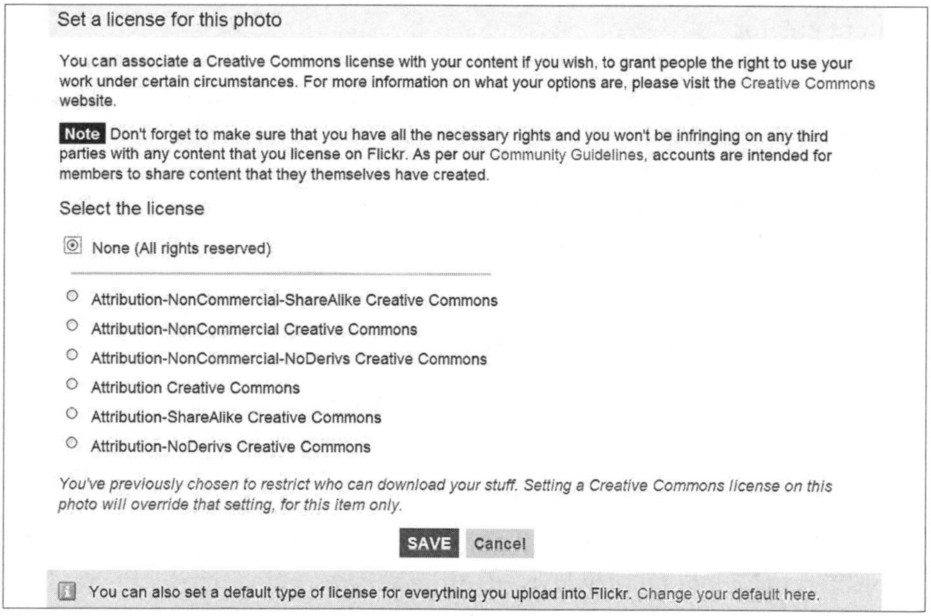

Set a license for this photo

You can associate a Creative Commons license with your content if you wish, to grant people the right to use your work under certain circumstances. For more information on what your options are, please visit the Creative Commons website.

Note Don't forget to make sure that you have all the necessary rights and you won't be infringing on any third parties with any content that you license on Flickr. As per our Community Guidelines, accounts are intended for members to share content that they themselves have created.

Select the license

◉ None (All rights reserved)

○ Attribution-NonCommercial-ShareAlike Creative Commons

○ Attribution-NonCommercial Creative Commons

○ Attribution-NonCommercial-NoDerivs Creative Commons

○ Attribution Creative Commons

○ Attribution-ShareAlike Creative Commons

○ Attribution-NoDerivs Creative Commons

You've previously chosen to restrict who can download your stuff. Setting a Creative Commons license on this photo will override that setting, for this item only.

SAVE Cancel

You can also set a default type of license for everything you upload into Flickr. Change your default here.

Figure 14.3   Flickr members control the rights to the use of their photos by choosing a license from this menu. They may elect to reserve all rights or decide to let others use their images based on the terms of one of the six main Creative Commons licenses. [Courtesy of Flickr]

on their own terms while making it simple and legal for people to reuse the work of others (when creators have granted permission). The Creative Commons website states, "Creative Commons defines the spectrum of possibilities between full copyright and the public domain. From *all rights reserved* to *no rights reserved*. Our licenses help you keep your copyright while allowing certain uses of your work—a 'some rights reserved' copyright."[21] Creative Commons accomplishes this by providing six main licenses. See Table 14.1 for an explanation of the Creative Commons licenses.

Searching by Creative Commons License

Imagine you need an image to reuse commercially by merely giving attribution to the creator, without paying. Flickr can help; it permits searching and browsing for images by the Creative Commons license.

To search by Creative Commons license, go to www.flickr.com/creative commons (shown in Figure 14.4). Beside the item count for the type of license you seek, click See More. On the landing page, you can browse or search through all Flickr items that have the license you've chosen. For example, if you click See More for the Attribution license, you should be able to reuse the items, even for commercial purposes, just by giving credit to the content creator.

There are two ways to search for media licensed via Creative Commons. On the Flickr Advanced Search page, look for "Only search within Creative Commons licensed-content" near the bottom of the page. You can also search Flickr and other services for content licensed under Creative Commons by visiting search.creativecommons.org. (See Figure 14.5. Note the disclaimer on the left side of the webpage.)

Help and Ideas for Using Images From Flickr

The web hosts valuable information that will help individuals use or remix Flickr content. You might consider looking for ideas by searching commercial databases, Delicious tags, blogs, or Google. I learned about Jakesonline.org, an excellent site for discovering Flickr's uses in the classroom, by searching EBSCO's Academic Search Premier and reading one of the retrieved articles published in *School Library Journal*. At www.jakesonline.org/flickrsites.htm, David Jakes, a high school instructional technology coordinator, lists links to his Delicious bookmarks, several presentations on Flickr's uses in education, and specialty webpages, such as Using Flickr in Digital Storytelling Projects (which, coincidentally, gives instructions on how to find and use content from the Creative Commons items in Flickr).

Table 14.1   The six main Creative Commons licenses [Courtesy of www.
             creativecommons.org/licenses]

Name of license	Properties	Commercial/ noncommercial use
Attribution (CC BY)	This license lets others distribute, remix, tweak, and build upon your work, even commercially, as long as they credit you for the original creation. This is the most accommodating of the licenses offered, in terms of what others can do with your works licensed under Attribution.	Commercial use: Yes Noncommercial use: Yes
Attribution Share Alike (CC BY-SA)	This license lets others remix, tweak, and build upon your work even for commercial reasons, as long as they credit you and license their new creations under the identical terms. This license is often compared to open source software licenses. All new works based on yours will carry the same license, so any derivatives will also allow commercial use.	Commercial use: Yes Noncommercial use: Yes
Attribution No Derivatives (CC BY-ND)	This license allows for redistribution, commercial and noncommercial, as long as it is passed along unchanged and in whole, with credit to you.	Commercial use: Yes Noncommercial use: Yes
Attribution Noncommercial (CC BY-NC)	This license lets others remix, tweak, and build upon your work noncommercially, and although their new works must also acknowledge you and be noncommercial, they don't have to license their derivative works on the same terms.	Commercial use: No Noncommercial use: Yes
Attribution Noncommercial Share Alike (CC BY-NC-SA)	This license lets others remix, tweak, and build upon your work noncommercially, as long as they credit you and license their new creations under the identical terms. Others can download and redistribute your work just like the BY-NC-ND license, but they can also translate, make remixes, and produce new work based on your work. All new work based on yours will carry the same license, so any derivatives will also be noncommercial in nature.	Commercial use: No Noncommercial use: Yes
Attribution Noncommercial No Derivatives (CC BY-NC-ND)	This license is the most restrictive of the six main licenses, allowing redistribution. This license is often called the "free advertising" license because it allows others to download your works and share them with others as long as they mention you and link back to you, but they can't change them in any way or use them commercially.	Commercial use: No Noncommercial use: Yes

Caveat Paparazzi

Libraries use Flickr photostreams for virtual library tours, photography competitions, slideshows of book displays, coverage of author book signings, and novelty READ posters featuring local celebrities. The first two or three I have listed may be accomplished without involving any human faces, but it may be impossible to shoot the last two without having people in the photographs.

The legal issue involved centers on the rights of privacy and publicity. "Using a photograph of an identifiable person could be a one-way ticket to a lawsuit," according to Bryan Carson, an attorney and librarian at Western Kentucky University. "If the picture contains identifiable people, you must always ask permission before using it for marketing or promotion. On the other hand, photographs in which the subjects are not identifiable (for example, a crowd shot taken from behind with no faces visible) do not require permission." In a

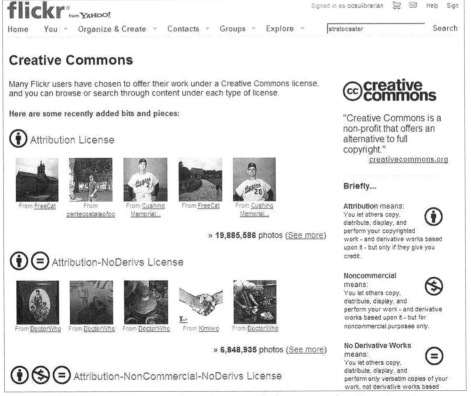

Figure 14.4   Users can search or browse Flickr content by Creative Commons license. Click See More to begin to browse or search images with that license. [Courtesy of Flickr]

2008 article in *Marketing Library Services*, Carson cautions photographers. "It is clearly a violation of the right of privacy to use photographs from library programs in order to market or advertise the library or to call attention to future programming. You should *always* get written consent if you plan to use images for these purposes. If the subject is under 18, the parent or guardian should sign a consent form."[22]

One way around the problem is to take photos from the back of a room (i.e., avoid photographing faces). Carson mentions that freedom of the press, however, applies to library newsletters and blogs; photos could be published in these (without consent) if they were taken in a newsworthy context. Because this news context denotes a recent event, photos should be deleted from blogs after 2 weeks. Legally speaking, the bottom line is that Flickr is not a good place for libraries to archive photographs that have people's faces (unless you have consent). Carson recommends reviewing the University of

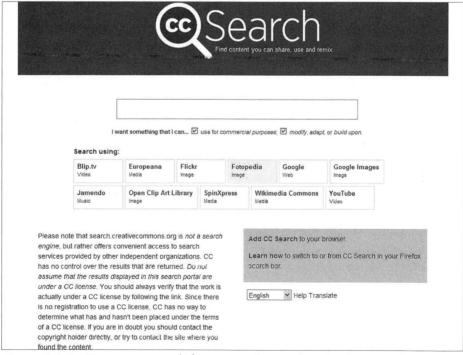

Figure 14.5   Users can search for content licensed under Creative Commons at search.creativecommons.org. Note that, as the language in the left of the body of the webpage states, this utility is offered as a convenience, but Creative Commons has no control over the retrieval, and the user must verify the licensing. [Courtesy of Creative Commons]

Arizona Web Developers Group's Guidelines for Using Photographs of People (uaweb.arizona.edu/people.0.html).

Although laws must be respected, some information professionals think the laws are out of step with social networking. "I certainly believe we should acknowledge and respect people's privacy," blogs Michael Stephens. "But I also think using Flickr (and Facebook, Myspace, blogs, etc.) is part of a new landscape of participation and inclusion. The law needs to catch up with these tools. I would hate to see any libraries stop using Flickr because of fears of a lawsuit—which in libraryland gets bantered around too much as a reason to *not* do a whole lot of things."[23]

The Underexposed (Dark) Side of Flickr

When people freely meander through a huge pool of images, a number of abuses and misuses may occur. Several blogs have mentioned problems, and at least one lawsuit has stemmed from photos uploaded to Flickr and viewable by drive-by browsers.

Jim M. Goldstein, a professional photographer who uses Flickr to share his work with other professionals and to provide exposure for his creations, blogged in February 2007 about sharing his work in online photography forums since 1993:

> The amount of traffic generated by sites like Flickr means that photographers have an opportunity to share their work with a large audience. This is something I've particularly enjoyed as of late, but in the process I've experienced and taken note of an alarming trend of small and large companies looking to take advantage of photographers. Flickr seems to have become a stock photography alternative where companies entice business naive photographers into making their photos available for use for free. What blew my mind this week is the attempt made by Yahoo to do this with my photography. Yes! Yahoo. While flattered with the initial inquiry to use my photo I relayed my basic licensing terms only to be told "unfortunately, we do not have a system or mechanism in place to offer payment for photos."[24]

Goldstein reasoned that Yahoo! pays the Associated Press and Reuters for photos it runs in its news articles—why not him? He continued:

> I'd love to have had my image used by Yahoo and other firms that have previously inquired. Unfortunately if I or others continue to

give away their photos the remainder of the photography business will erode. I am deeply passionate about photography, but how can I continue that passion if I cannot afford to do it? A company such as Yahoo, and all companies for that matter, should be ashamed of this practice. Not just because Yahoo owns/runs Flickr, but because it's an extremely poor business practice. Photographers be warned. Educate yourself and if you truly love photography stand up for your rights and ability to pursue your passion.[25]

A huge database of searchable online photos has implications for one's right to privacy. In 2007, a Dallas District Court considered the arguments revolving around Virgin Mobile, Creative Commons, and a 17-year-old girl. Virgin Mobile had used a photograph of the young woman on a billboard. The company found the photograph on Flickr, where it had been uploaded by a member of the young lady's church. The church member had given it a Creative Commons license allowing commercial use of the photo. In the case of *Chang v. Virgin Mobile*, the plaintiff claimed that the uploading of the photo was not authorized by the person in the picture; however, the case was dismissed because of "lack of jurisdiction."[26] Essentially, Virgin Mobile won the case, which demonstrates that the person uploading content (in this case, an image file) and granting a license may not have had permission to do so from everyone who has an interest in the content. Additionally, the photo was used for commercial purposes, and the young woman in the picture had no recourse.

Another potential problem is that images may be used out of their original context. For example, on his blog The Travelin' Librarian, Michael Sauers has posted the following license: "This work is licensed under a Creative Commons Attribution-Noncommercial-Share Alike 2.5 License." This essentially means that a noncommercial entity may use his work (and pass it on with the same license) if the entity attributes the work to Sauers. Sauers noticed that the noncommercial Public Broadcasting System (PBS) had used one of the Flickr images posted on his blog (the image was of a sign that read "Please turn off cell phones in the library"), giving him credit for it. But the image, Sauers remarks, was used out of context in the article. Although Sauers would advocate banning rude behavior, he is not in favor of banning cell phones in libraries, as PBS suggested. Nonetheless, PBS had followed his licensing stipulations. (See "The Hazards of Letting People Use Your Flickr Images" at travelinlibrarian.info/2006/11/hazards-of-letting-people-use-your. The PBS article, including the cell phone image, may be viewed at www.pbs.org/mediashift/2006/11/the-definitive-guide-to-cell-phone-no-nos310.html.)

In his blog, Sauers wrote, "The point of this post is two-fold. First, to point out to readers of the PBS post that I do not agree with the comments made in association with my photograph. Second, to remind people that do follow my advice to post their photos to Flickr and let others use them, that once you do so, you will lose some control over your work and [you] need to be able to live with that."

That's a Wrap

I saved this topic for the last chapter because taking photos, viewing them, editing them, and sharing them with our friends is simply fun. Even a brief dip into Flickr reveals that its members are enjoying photo sharing and all the activities associated with it. By placing the Flickr chapter here, I hope to leave readers with a lasting impression of the extent of user-generated content, how easy it is to accomplish, and the benefits of participating. Photo sharing sites are quintessential examples of social media resources, and Flickr is the quintessential example of photo sharing: It provides the space and software tools, and we use that space and those tools to create content individually and collaboratively. Flickr validates the maxim "If you build it, they will come."

Endnotes

1. Richard Koman, "Stewart Butterfield on Flickr," O'Reilly, February 4, 2005, accessed August 3, 2011, www.oreillynet.com/pub/a/network/2005/02/04/sb_flckr.html.

2. "Number of Flickr Accounts Is Over 23 Million—Make That 24—Just in Time for the 4 Year Anniversary," Flickr Central/Discuss, February 25, 2008, accessed August 3, 2011, www.flickr.com/groups/central/discuss/72157603987303586.

3. Richard Stengel, "Why We Chose Obama," Time.com, December 17, 2008, accessed August 3, 2011, www.time.com/time/specials/packages/article/0,28804,1861543_1865068_1867014,00.html.

4. Andrea Mercado, "Get Flickr-tastic!" WebJunction, September 2, 2005, accessed August 3, 2011, www.webjunction.org/technology/web-tools/articles/content/438213.

5. Sarah Houghton, "Why Should Librarians Care About Flickr?" Librarian in Black, December 13, 2005, accessed August 3, 2011, librarianinblack.net/librarianinblack/2005/12/why_should_libr.html.

6. Michael Stephens, "10 Reasons to Use Flickr at Your Library," TameTheWeb: Libraries and Technology, December 13, 2005, accessed August 3, 2011, www.tametheweb.com/2005/12/10_reasons_to_use_flickr_at_yo.html.

7. Michael Stephens, "Priceless Images: Getting Started with Flickr," *Computers in Libraries* 26 (November/December 2006): 44.

8. Lichen Rancourt, "Mashing Up the Library Website," in *Library Mashups*, ed. Nicole C. Engard, 77 (Medford, NJ: Information Today, 2009).

9. "Why Host a Snapshot Day in Your State?" American Library Association, accessed August 3, 2011, www.ala.org/ala/issuesadvocacy/advleg/advocacy university/librarysnapshotday/whyhost.cfm.

10. Eric Schwarz, "Snapshot: One Day in the Life of New Jersey Libraries—Feb. 19," NJSLA, February 9, 2009, accessed August 3, 2011, sla-divisions.typepad.com/ njsla/2009/02/snapshot-one-day-in-the-life-of-new-jersey-libraries-feb-19.html.

11. "People Need Libraries. People Need You," New Jersey State Library, accessed August 3, 2011, njla.pbworks.com/f/People%20Need%20Libraries.pdf.

12. "Entire Cities Recreated From Flickr Photos," *New Scientist* 203, no. 2727, 2009, 21.

13. Michelle Springer, et al., "For the Common Good: The Library of Congress Flickr Pilot Project," October 30, 2008, accessed August 3, 2011, www.loc.gov/rr/ print/flickr_report_final.pdf.

14. Matt Raymond, "My Friend Flickr: A Match Made in Photo Heaven," Library of Congress Blog, January 16, 2008, accessed August 30, 2011, blogs.loc.gov/loc/ 2008/01/my-friend-flickr-a-match-made-in-photo-heaven.

15. George Oates, "Wow," flickrBLOG, January 17, 2008, accessed August 3, 2011, blog.flickr.net/en/2008/01/17/wow.

16. Springer, "For the Common Good."

17. Ibid.

18. Stephen Mihm, "Everyone's a Historian Now," *Boston Globe*, May 25, 2008, accessed August 3, 2011, www.boston.com/bostonglobe/ideas/articles/2008/05/ 25/everyones_a_historian_now.

19. Jason Vaughan, "Insights Into the Commons on Flickr," *portal: Libraries and the Academy* 10 (2010): 190.

20. "About the Rights Statement," Flickr: The Commons, accessed August 3, 2011, www.flickr.com/commons/usage.

21. "About," Creative Commons, accessed July 22, 2011, www.creativecommons. org/about.

22. Bryan Carson, "How-To: Laws for Using Photos You Take at Your Library," Marketing Library Services, September/October 2008, accessed August 3, 2011, www.infotoday.com/mls/sep08/Carson.shtml.

23. Michael Stephens, "Legally, Should Libraries NOT Be Using Flickr," TameTheWeb, accessed August 3, 2011, tametheweb.com/2008/09/18/legally-should-libraries-not-be-using-flickr.

24. Jim Goldstein, "The Dark Side of Flickr: Photo Phishing by Corporate America," February 24, 2007, accessed August 3, 2011, www.jmg-galleries.com/blog/2007/02/24/the-dark-side-of-flickr-photo-phishing-by-corporate-america.

25. Ibid.

26. Evan Brown, "No Personal Jurisdiction Over Australian Defendant in Flickr Right of Publicity Case," Internet Cases, January 22, 2009, accessed August 3, 2011, blog.internetcases.com/2009/01/22/no-personal-jurisdiction-over-australian-defendant-in-flickr-right-of-publicity-case.

Conclusion

To determine whether the general public is concerned about the validity of user-generated content, a group of researchers from Singapore's Nanyang Technological University showed 160 study participants eight simulated websites. Four of the sites were carefully crafted and appeared to be authored by experts. The other four appeared to be user-generated. The expert sites included references; the user-generated sites did not. After analyzing the subjects' ratings of the sites for credibility, Poorisat Thanomwong and her colleagues concluded in a paper presented at the 2009 Annual Meeting of the Communication Association, "The results from this study suggest that people are willing to accept the contributions of non-experts to collaborative websites. Even though there is no clear indication of their level of expertise, a website with user-generated content is thought to be as credible as [one] produced by experts. This interpretation is based on the fact that there was no significant difference in perceived credibility between [a] user- and expert-generated content site." They continued, "The results indicate that neither the type of website nor the presence of references have a significant effect on perceived credibility in the context of the study."[1] Think about that last sentence: The presence of references, on which information professionals heavily rely when assessing web content, was found *not* to be connected with perceived credibility.

As Thanomwong's research and the preceding chapters demonstrate, UContent is well established and widely accepted in our information landscape. Were you to require more evidence, consider that the *Encyclopaedia Britannica* opened its Britannica.com website to outside contributors in early 2009. When the world's most esteemed reference encyclopedia bows to take a page from Wikipedia, we must concede a paradigm shift. According to Britannica, "If your submission is accepted, you'll become a Britannica contributor and your name will appear along with the other people who have contributed to [an] article." The Submission Guidelines webpage (corporate. britannica.com/submission.html) invites end users to add to articles or submit entirely new ones; that page also discusses writing standards, tone, objectivity, and sourcing, among other things. Outside contributors may also submit links to external webpages, images, and video. When you find an article at Britannica.com, click the Contributors link on the left of the screen. As you mouse over each contributor's name you'll see various designations including "Expert contributor commissioned by Britannica," "Britannica editor," and "Community contributor of revisions accepted by Britannica." An example of this is the main article on Stonehenge at www.britannica.com/EB checked/topic/567331/Stonehenge. Although Britannica does not name the community contributor in this example, if you mouse over the contributor icon you'll see the latter designation mentioned above. Further investigation is possible by clicking Article History. Stonehenge's Article History shows that the community contributor added media. I performed dozens of on-the-fly searches looking for articles where users had created content. In my unscientific sample, I could count the number of community contributors on one hand.[1]

Critics argue that when we encourage and accept UContent, we sacrifice reliability. Perhaps Britannica's decision to allow user contributions indicates the way many sites will operate in the future. Rather than allowing a "free for all," site administrators may become gatekeepers who determine which end users' content can be published after the submissions have undergone review. Britannica.com has a vetting mechanism, but very few of the websites I explored stated a revision policy, though we should always look for one.

A succession of events at Wikipedia shows that the pendulum still swings away from the close oversight of content imposed by Britannica. Although any Wikipedia user can edit most articles on the site, Wikipedia's lengthy and detailed "deletion policy" (see en.wikipedia.org/wiki/Wikipedia:Deletion_policy) provides *administrators* multiple justifications for removing content. It also guides administrators to less severe actions, such as Incubation (whereby not-ready-for-prime-time articles are filed in the Wikipedia Incubator).

Recently, the online encyclopedia made a more formal attempt to monitor itself. First announced in 2009 and adopted in June 2010, Wikipedia's introduction of Pending Changes was another step toward stricter control of content. Specifically aimed at reducing vandalism to biographies of living persons, Pending Changes put more control in the hands of experienced volunteer editors. Instead of locking articles, users could submit changes but senior editors had to approve the edits before the edits went live. Critics argued that the policy would result in a backlog of edits and hamper Wikipedia's democratic nature. Proponents said the change would enhance accuracy. Wikipedia ultimately removed Pending Changes on May 11, 2011, after a dialogue among editors ended with 127 supporting its removal and 65 opposing it.

The two preceding examples illustrate that some websites (at least the prominent ones) see the need to keep an eye on user contributions. But ensuring reliable content shouldn't necessarily be the responsibility of site administrators. End users must become more actively involved. Consider that individuals may have encountered misinformation at Wikipedia or erroneous place-names in Google My Places but decided not to bother correcting them—even though they could have. Worse still, a user may have submitted a correction, seen it deleted, and may have resubmitted it, only to have it deleted again. It happens.

Recently I was interested in going back to read some of the public domain play I had uploaded to Project Gutenberg called *The Treason and Death of Benedict Arnold*. You may recall from the Project Gutenberg chapter that plays are very difficult to format, but I did post a scanned copy to the Gutenberg Consortia (ebooks.gutenberg.us/AuthorsCommunity/Treason_and_Death_of_Benedict_Arnold.pdf). When I used that address to revisit the book in 2010, I was redirected to www.docstoc.com/docs/10309779/The-Treason-and-Death-of-Benedict-Arnold-A-Play-for-a-Greek-Theatre. I didn't find my PDF there, but instead saw a .txt file of the play. Of course, the text file would have been good enough if I had only wanted to read the play, but I wondered what had happened to the scan I uploaded. I reported the anomaly to Project Gutenberg's founder, Michael Hart. An exchange of seven emails was required to solve the mystery. The final email came from John Guagliardo, executive director of the World Public Library (italics inserted by the author for emphasis):

> Dear Nick,
> Thanks for the email. I really appreciate your pointing out the missing file. *Apparently, we had an error on our server that we were unaware of, and this caused many of the titles to not be accessible. The error has now been fixed and all the titles are now available again.* Your title is once again at ebooks.gutenberg.us/Authors Community/Treason_and_Death_of_Benedict_Arnold.pdf.
>
> Best regards,
> John

Apparently many titles had become lost in the shuffle. Had I not reported my concern, the content would have been lost.

As UContent increases its prevalence, the responsibilities of both content creators and content consumers will also increase. Contributors need to work diligently to promote trust in user-generated content. Yet trust in UContent rests not only in the ethics of content creators but also in the ability and willingness of readers to critique content. In the read/write web world, end users not only have the right to generate content but are also accountable for revising content, adding information, or submitting corrections when necessary. The antidote for the shortcomings of UContent lies in better users generating better content; affirm the proverb "Wise people talk because they have something to say; fools, because they have to say something." That's where this book comes in. Take the information it offers and make user-generated content the best it can be.

Endnote

1. Thanomwong Poorisat, et al., "Perceptions of Credibility: A Comparison of User-Generated and Expert-Generated Websites," Paper presented at the annual meeting of the International Communication Association, May 20, 2009, accessed October 14, 2011, www.allacademic.com/meta/p300996_index.html.

About the Author

Nick Tomaiuolo earned his MLS at Southern Connecticut State University where he was named a Scholar of the School of Library Science and Instructional Technology, inducted into Beta Phi Mu (the International Library and Information Studies Honor Society), and has been designated a Distinguished Alumnus. He teaches online research skills courses for both Central Connecticut State University and the University of Maryland University College. Likes: database searching, literature, marottes, Stratocasters, theater, and travel. Dislikes: hubris, martinets, officiousness, opportunists, and technology for technology's sake. Nick also writes for *Searcher Magazine*. This is his second book for Information Today, Inc. His first book, *The Web Library*, was published in 2004.

Index

More Great Books from Information Today, Inc.

The Librarian's Guide to Micropublishing
Helping Patrons and Communities Use Free and Low-Cost Publishing Tools to Tell Their Stories

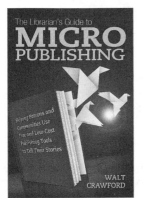

By Walt Crawford

In this timely book, Walt Crawford explains the how, what, and why of libraries and community micropublishing. He details the use of no-cost/low-cost publishing tools Lulu and CreateSpace and equips librarians to guide their patrons in the production of quality print books. He offers step-by-step instructions for using Microsoft Word to design and edit manuscripts that can be printed in flexible quantities via on-demand technology.

No stone goes unturned as Crawford demonstrates how, with a little attention to detail, anyone can produce books that rival the output of professional publishers. His advice is geared to making it easy for librarians to support local publishing without any additional budget, and libraries purchasing the book are granted permission to reproduce and supply key sections to their aspiring authors.

184 pp/softbound/ISBN 978-1-57387-430-4 $49.50

Mob Rule Learning
Camps, Unconferences, and Trashing the Talking Head

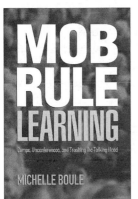

By Michelle Boule

This is the first comprehensive book about the unconference movement. Author, blogger, and *Library Journal* Mover & Shaker Michelle Boule explains why traditional conferences and learning environments increasingly fail to meet the needs of professionals. She looks at the impact of "internet mob rule" on continuing education and training, and shows how an array of new solutions—including camps, unconferences, and peer learning strategies—are putting the power of knowledge back in the hands of those who need it most.

In addition to providing a step-by-step approach to planning a camp or unconference, *Mob Rule Learning* features numerous case studies, interviews, and examples of emerging education and training models for small and large organizations, businesses, and community groups.

248 pp/softbound/ISBN 978-0-910965-92-7 $24.95

The Cybrarian's Web
An A–Z Guide to 101 Free Web 2.0 Tools and Other Resources

By Cheryl Ann Peltier-Davis

Here is a remarkable field guide to the best free Web 2.0 tools and their practical applications in libraries and information centers. Designed for info pros who want to use the latest tech tools to connect, collaborate, and create, you'll find resources to help you

- Launch a local news & events blog
- Build a customized social network
- Create a virtual reference desk
- Start an ebook lending program
- Host virtual art & photo exhibits
- Publicize programs & innovations
- Survey the library community
- Help aspiring authors get published
- Produce & stream live video
- And more!

You'll discover dozens of lesser-known resources and learn exciting new ways to use many of the most popular sites and tools. With all this and a supporting webpage, *The Cybrarian's Web* is a winner!

512 pp/softbound/ISBN 978-1-57387-427-4 $49.50

Blogging and RSS, Second Edition
A Librarian's Guide

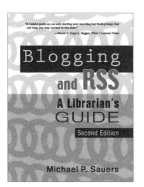

By Michael P. Sauers

In this fully updated second edition of his popular 2006 book, author, internet trainer, and blogger Michael P. Sauers shows how blogging and RSS technology can be easily and successfully used by libraries and librarians. Sauers provides a wealth of useful examples and insights from librarian bloggers and provides easy-to-follow instructions for creating, publishing, and syndicating a blog using free web-based services, software, RSS feeds, and aggregators. The second edition covers new blogging tools and services, introduces numerous useful library blogs and bloggers, and includes a new chapter on microblogging with Twitter. *Blogging & RSS* is a must-read for librarians, library managers, administrators, tech staff, and anyone interested in utilizing blogs and RSS in a library setting.

336 pp/softbound/ISBN 978-1-57387-399-4 $35.00